❧ The Dialogue in Early Modern France, 1547-1630

The Dialogue in Early Modern France, 1547-1630

Art and Argument

Edited, with a Prologue, by

Colette H. Winn

The Catholic University
of America Press

Washington, D.C.

The paper used in this publication meets the minimum requirements of
American National Standards for Information Science—Permanence of
Paper for Printed Library materials, ANSI Z39.48-1984.
∞

Library of Congress Cataloging-in-Publication Data
The dialogue in early modern France, 1547-1630 / edited, with a
    prologue by Colette H. Winn.
        p. cm.
    Includes bibliographical references and index.
    1. French literature—16th century—History and criticism.
    2. French literature—17th century—History and criticism.
    3. Dialogues, French—History and criticism.   I. Winn, Colette H.
    PQ239.D5   1993
    840.9'003—dc20
    92-35530
    ISBN 0-8132-0777-0

The most fruitful and natural exercise of our mind, in my opinion, is discussion. I find it sweeter than any other action of our life; and that is the reason why, if I were right now forced to choose, I believe I would rather consent to lose my sight than my hearing or speech.

—MONTAIGNE, "Of the Art of Discussion"

CONTENTS

ACKNOWLEDGMENTS

I am grateful to the readers of The Catholic University of America Press for their comments and suggestions. I should like also to express my warmest thanks to Professor Kenneth Lloyd-Jones for his close reading of the manuscript and his scholarly advice and criticism.

CONTRIBUTORS

JOAN A. BUHLMANN, associate professor of French at the University of Nebraska, is coeditor (with Donald Gilman) of a critical edition of Louis Le Caron's *Dialogues* (Droz, 1986). She has published on Maurice Scève and emblems, and is currently at work on a critical edition of Barthélémy Aneau's *Imagination poétique*.

DONALD GILMAN, associate professor of French at Ball State, co-edited (with Joan A. Buhlmann) a critical edition of Louis Le Caron's *Dialogues* (Droz, 1986). He is the editor of *Everyman and Company: Essays on the Theme and Structure of the European Moral Play* (AMS Press, 1990). He has also published on Ronsard, Racine, and dialogue theory in sixteenth-century France.

ANN ROSALIND JONES, associate professor of Comparative Literature at Smith College, is the author of *The Currency of Eros: Women's Love Lyric in Europe, 1540-1620* (Indiana UP, 1990). She has contributed articles on Renaissance female writers to various collections including *Rewriting the Renaissance: The Discourses of Sexual Difference in Early Modern Europe*, *The Ideology of Conduct*, and *The Poetics of Gender*.

EVA KUSHNER has taught mostly at Carleton, McGill and Toronto Universities. She has authored books and articles on nineteenth and twentieth-century themes and writers in France and French Canada. She has also published many articles on Pontus de Tyard, Montaigne, the Renaissance dialogue, and theory of literary history. She is the co-editor and co-author of *L'Avènement de l'esprit nouveau (1400-1480)* (1988) and *Théorie littéraire: Problèmes et perspectives* (1989).

PAULA SOMMERS, professor of French at the University of Missouri, has authored *Celestial Ladders: Readings in Marguerite de Navarre's Poetry of Spiritual Ascent* (Droz, 1989) and published on

Jacques Tahureau, Bonaventure Des Périers, Louise Labé, and Marguerite de Navarre.

COLETTE H. WINN, associate professor of French at Washington University, is the author of *La Poétique de l'accoutumance: Les Sonnets de la Mort de Jean de Sponde* (Studia Humanitatis, 1984); *L'Esthétique du jeu dans l'Heptaméron de Marguerite de Navarre* (Montréal: Institut d'Etudes Médiévales, Université de Montréal; Paris: Vrin, 1993); and articles on Marguerite de Navarre, Hélisenne de Crenne, Pernette du Guillet, and Bonaventure des Périers.

CATHY YANDELL, associate professor at Carleton College, has edited a critical edition of Pontus de Tyard's *Solitaire second* (Droz, 1986). She has also written articles on Pontus de Tyard, Montaigne, Tahureau, Catherine des Roches and the *Blasons du corps féminin*.

COLETTE H. WINN

₷₷ Prologue

Joan A. Buhlmann, Colette H. Winn, and Cathy Yandell presented earlier versions of their chapters as papers at the Twenty-first International Congress on Medieval Studies (1986) in a program on "Poetics and Dialogue" chaired by Donald Gilman. The program stimulated an animated discussion and raised fascinating questions, which challenged the participants to pursue their investigations further, and finally led to this project. The audience's lively interest in dialogue matched that of Renaissance man: Why was dialogue so widely employed in the Renaissance? Who were the dominant ancient authorities for mid- and late-sixteenth-century France? How do post classical dialogic forms differ in content and purpose from humanist dialogues? And, at times, the questions posed echoed the concerns of sixteenth-century dialogue practitioners and theorists: How does dialogue relate to fiction and to other arts of discourse such as dialectic (the art of subtle disputation) and rhetoric (the craft of artful communication)? What are the rules and precepts of the genre? Should dialogue even be regarded as a "genre"?

Indeed, the rigidity of generic classifications and nomenclature was called into question. Should works in which thought proceeds monologically be called dialogues at all, simply because they are written in dialogue form? What about those works in which the argumentation does not unfold through a process of contradiction, but which everyone would agree are dialogues? Or those in which dialogue functions as a supporting structure for interpolated narrative such as the novella collections of the mid- and late century; do they really belong to the genre of dialogue?

The present volume addresses these questions. It is divided into two parts: theory and practice (though in the world of sixteenth-century French dialogue, creative work and theorization went hand in hand).

In Part 1, "Theories of Dialogue," Donald Gilman sets the cultural, historical, and theoretical context, reviewing the dialogue's previous history: texts and concepts inherited from classical antiquity and reworked during the Middle Ages. In the light of representative theoretical writings from the second half of the sixteenth century, Le Caron's *Dialogues* (1554–56), Carolus Sigonius's *De dialogo liber* (1562), and Torquato Tasso's *Discorso dell'arte del dialogo* (1586), he examines the early sources that determined the substantive and aesthetic qualities of the genre. One must keep in mind that there was no complete ancient treatise devoted to the genre. Only scattered comments on dialogue had survived from antiquity, and these were later pieced together to support divergent views on the genre. This may explain why Renaissance theorists found it difficult to formulate a theory of dialogue.

In Part 2, five different authors examine "Contemporary Practices" and the many-sidedness of French early modern dialogue. They expand on the theoretical part in several ways.

They do not devote themselves exclusively to examining the expository, didactic, argumentative dialogues that draw more or less freely on the classical models—Platonic, Ciceronian, Lucianic—that Gilman examines, but treat in addition works that borrow from the medieval tradition of the *débat*, *jeu parti*, *tenson*, invective, and *conflictus*, still very much alive throughout the sixteenth century as illustrated in Marguerite de Navarre's "dialoguelike" works and the so-called dialogues of Les Dames des Roches discussed by Ann Rosalind Jones. Indeed, French writers of dialogue imitated ancient authorities but also freely read and appropriated the works of their own immediate predecessors, showing remarkable resourcefulness in adapting various discursive models to their own situations and intentions. They did not always adhere rigorously to a particular discursive model. Obviously, there was no consistent praxis or theory readily available to them. As a result, their freely creative efforts liberated dialogue almost completely from the generic constraints imposed on the more formalized genres.

Therefore, while Joan A. Buhlmann attempts to define genre boundaries in studying Le Caron's *Dialogues*, Paula Sommers and

Colette H. Winn find that early modern practices challenge the very notion of genre. In the light of the "transgressive endeavors" they examine, one comes to realize that, as Gilman argues, genres, far from being fixed in structure and style, actually "adapt to the exigencies of substance and as modes blend with other literary kinds to convey individual thoughts and perceptions" (74). Dialogue does not function solely as a genre but also as a mode, a technique, a strategy by which the writer conveys his or her own vision of man and his world.

Finally, in her essay on Tahureau's *Dialogues*, Cathy Yandell ventures far beyond genre definitions, challenging the very nature of dialogue, and disputing previous claims about its "dialogicity."

Thus, Part 2 offers a fair sampling of the wide variety of texts written in dialogue form between 1547 and 1630. Obviously, we are not undertaking a complete history of dialogical writing in early modern France. The selection is representative rather than comprehensive. By limiting the breadth of our investigation, we are able to attend more closely to the detail of texts which, except for the *Heptameron*, have not yet received the critical attention they deserve. The succession of the chapters is chronological by date of publication; it is not intended to imply a progressive development of dialogical forms.

The essays are close readings of individual texts. Diverse approaches to the notion of dialogue meet here, sometimes overlapping within the same essay: rhetorical, textual and comparative, thematic and intertextual, feminist, historical and perspectival. Although the essays vary in methodology, each focuses on content and technique, examining setting, characterization, decorum and verisimilitude, the dialogue's internal organization, the process of contradiction, and the uses a particular author makes of dialogue, thus further highlighting the rich potential of the genre and its possibilities of combining with other genres.

The volume closes with Eva Kushner's reflections on what she calls "the dialogue of dialogues," the affinities that exist between the texts studied here and other texts by major dialogists of mid-century: Guy de Brués, Bonaventure Des Périers, Etienne Pasquier, and Pontus de Tyard.

PART I

✿ Theories of Dialogue

DONALD GILMAN

❧ In Search of Definition

In his *Apology for Poetry* (1595) Sir Philip Sidney alludes to the nature and function of dialogue. Plato, he asserts, incorporates into this genre philosophical topics that, recalling the subject matter of earlier thinkers,[1] become the substance of his work. But if metaphysics, ethics, aesthetics, epistemology, and political theory are the "inside and strength" (Shepherd 1973, 97) of Plato's dialogues, the exterior and shape of these discussions reflect a sort of poetic creation. Sidney's assessment of Plato's writings is hardly original: Quintilian (*Institutio oratoria* 5.11.39; 10.1.81) had reached a similar conclusion, and Daniello (1536/1968, 22–23), Minturno (1559/1970, 16–17), Scaliger (1561/1964, 13–14), and Le Caron (1555, 19–20) repeated the idea in sixteenth-century Italy and France. Although the didacticism of Platonic dialogue justifies the utility and respectability of fiction and thereby fits nicely into Sidney's defense of poetry, Sidney describes dialogue as a sort of via media that links the substance of philosophy to the craft of poetry. The poet is both a seer into the nature of things and a "maker" of fictitious form. And if Plato, like other philosopher-poets, selects aspects of nature as appropriate objects of imitation, he conveys this vision of reality through the medium of an imagined conversation enhanced by fable, myth, and rhetorical expression.

1. According to Sidney in his *Apology for Poetry* (Shepherd 1973, 96–97), such pre-Socratic philosophers as Thales, Empedocles, Parmenides, Pythagoras, Phocylides, and Tyrtaeus conveyed their thoughts in verse; and the legislator Solon describes in poetry the mythical continent of Atlantis which Plato appropriates to his *Timaeus* (25A). Minturno (1559/1970, 15) and Scaliger (1561/1964, 11) repeat the idea.

In spite of Sidney's elegant discussion of the genre, French humanist dialogue defies precise definition. As Barbara C. Bowen (1972) writes, "it is very difficult to treat the genre because many examples we have are so different in subject matter and technique" (24). A cursory reading of dialogues published in sixteenth-century France presents a diversity of topics that staggers the imagination: we find dialogues about language, music theory, calendrical calculations, astrology, rhetoric, orthography, poetic creativity, love, ethics, epistemology, religion, statesmanship, education, law, justice, and more.[2] Further, writers of dialogue developed their subjects by means of a variety of strategies that included demonstrative presentation, theoretical explanation, positive and negative argumentation, vituperative attack, satiric invective, and comic exposition. Like all Renaissance genres, moreover, dialogue displays an amazing array of techniques—including, enigma, paradox, irony, ambiguity, analogy, example, parody, antithesis, understatement, and amplification—that contributes to its aesthetic depth and complexity. These resources of topics and external forms enabled the dialogist to convey knowledge and opinions that inform or undermine, affirm or deny, and applaud or attack. Dialogue shares these considerations of creativity with other Renaissance literary kinds, but, as Sidney's statement implies, it also has a special identity as a "hybrid" or "mixed" genre. As a sort of philosophical discourse, dialogue can be categorized as an expression of dialectics, and may therefore incorporate every type of argumentation defined in the manuals and practiced in disputation. As a poetic presentation of discussion, the genre puts forward a portrayal of interlocutors, whose development requires adherence to rhetorical precepts and a creative use of established motifs, topics, techniques, and structures.

The elusiveness of exact definition for dialogue reflects the tension between the search for poetic innovation and the uses of established forms that defines any genre. Any rule or prescription that decides categorization obviously exerts an influence on form but, at the same time, invites violation of that prescription. If, for example, prosody defines the external form of ancient Greek elegy,

---

2. For a chronological listing of humanist dialogues, see Mustapha Bénouis, *Le Dialogue philosophique dans la littérature française du seizième siècle* (Paris: Mouton, 1976), 211–21.

subject matter offers guidelines for the classification of Renaissance elegy. Admittedly, some genres conform to established extrinsic types: by definition, the sonnet contains fourteen lines. But even as the critic is pleased in identifying this fixed form, he must eventually encounter variations in the treatment of this pattern. Petrarch and his Italian, French, Spanish, and German imitators divided the form into an octave and a sestet, but Shakespeare and most fellow Englishmen preferred three quatrains and a concluding couplet. And Edmund Spenser, by reworking the rhyme scheme of his countrymen (from *abab cdcd efef gg* to *abab bcbc cdcd ee*), sought a compromise between continental and British models, and in the process obliterated any notion of fixed form. In many respects the delineation of generic boundaries becomes more confused and complicated through the application of thematic criteria to the definition of types. The encyclopedia or allegorical narrative, such as the *Roman de la Rose* (1229–80), differs in theme and tone from the historical romance, such as the *Orlando Furioso* (1516). But if Jean de Meung and Guillaume de Lorris and Ariosto convey their tales and thoughts in verse, Nathaniel Hawthorne selects prose for his Gothic novel, *The House of the Seven Gables: A Romance* (1851).

Generic classifications, then, present many more questions than answers. But if shifts in generic conceptions and the transformation of literary kinds produce a welter of terms and schematic tables, a "genre idea," according to E. D. Hirsch (1967) has a "vague heuristic function" (81). Several principles emerge. First, according to Claudio Guillén (1971), "the concept of genre looks forward and backward at the same time" (109). Literary kinds do reflect the prejudices and predilections of a cultural matrix determined by time and place. Each particular genre exhibits certain characteristics detailed in handbooks or associated with the practice of their respective literary kinds. In adapting history, myth, or fable to tragic action, Shakespeare and Racine both enacted the fall of a good or noble man. If they did not respect every aspect of hamartia, or if they overlooked other prescriptions of Aristotelian tragedy, the concept of this genre, as practiced and theorized by their predecessors and contemporaries, assisted them nevertheless in shaping the matter of their narrative and thematic visions to the restrictions required by tragic representation and staging. Poetic individuality calls for a reworking of the established generic mode and thereby enables the artist "to proceed from one order of life to another by virtue of his modeling, reshaping, informing skills" (Guillén 1971, 111). As Heather Dubrow (1982) has observed, each poetic form possesses attributes that are associated with, or more readily adapted to, particular prosodic patterns, narrative shapes, modal tones, or rhetorical conventions (7). Thus genre becomes a sort of technique, structure, or strategy by which the poet employs a suitable vessel to convey his vision and thought. His use of these conventions indicates the resources of forms that account for the thematic dimensions and aesthetic varieties of poetic creativity.

Literary representation is therefore a poiesis that explains the role of genres in the process of fitting content to form. Guarini's *Pastor fido* (1590), for instance, marks the invention of a new genre, but the identification of this work as a tragicomedy necessitates an understanding of established sixteenth-century conceptions of both tragedy and comedy. Genres, then, become signals; each generic form exists, in the words of Renato Poggioli, as a "traditional model or conventional pattern" (1959, 1: 194; Guillén 1971, 73) for poet and reader-listener-spectator alike. These assumptions may derive from critical commentaries or from the practice of the imitation of models. Thus genres become sorts of techniques integral to poetic creation, and literary kinds represent essential signs for the effective communication and subsequent appreciation of a text.

As signs, generic forms become part and parcel of the discourse employed by the poet in conveying his respective thought and vision, which is concurrently required by the reader in the act of interpretation. Like words, motifs, and images, genres convey meaning, and in order to assure accurate reception they must be related to a cultural context determined by period and locality. Historicity, then, must be taken into any account of the uses of genre in the dynamics of poetic creativity or in the reception of the literary work. In describing the stages of generic evolution, Alastair Fowler (1982) acknowledges the existence and acceptance of generic forms that critics have defined and systematized, and that poets have employed and reworked. The rules that emerge from commentaries and practice become, in the terminology of Saussure (1916), the *langue* by which the artist communicates and the reader understands. Although a specific literary work may manifest characteristics of the genre, individual speech forces a departure from the accepted extrinsic form, so that the particular poetic expression becomes the *parole* that derives from, but remains related to, its respective generic system. As individual words accrue, *paroles* become *langue* for new *paroles* (Fowler 1982, 20); in this third stage that reflects a generic or modal transformation, both poet and interpreter must revise their conceptions of the form. As texts generate texts, and as the definitions of literary kinds are refined and corrected, schematic classifications underscore simplistic and restrictive approaches to an understanding of genres. Absolute norms do not exist. But even if extrinsic types are continually undergoing change and revision, both the theory and practice of a literary kind combine to establish its general characteristics. And through an identification of the formal motifs, accepted structures, and rhetorical properties associated with the conception and creation of a genre produced at a particular time, the critic can attempt to fix, through the formulation of a general definition, the extrinsic contours and intrinsic functions of the respective genre.

Guillén's (1971) theory of genre as a sort of "literary system" supports the evolutionary nature of poetic kinds, and suggests the powers and possibilities of generic transformations which, as Rosalie Colie (1973) argues, provide the means of expression during the Renaissance. The elaborate charts and explanations of generic forms that sixteenth-century Italian critics compiled recall the rhetorical handbooks. In spite of the incomplete and restrictive nature of their definitions, such descriptions furnished the practicing poet with a storehouse of generic structures and strategies. The Renaissance writer respected the individuality of theme and technique. Situated between a Scylla of tradition and a Charybdis of originality, poets employed the standard definitions and, through the diachronic variations of generic conventions, discovered, in the words of Colie, the "resources of kind." Polonius's statement in *Hamlet* (1601) (2.2.392–98) confirms the astonishing assortment of literary kinds available to the practicing poet. Du Bellay experiments at first with Petrarchan love poetry, in *L'Olive* (1550); later, in his sonnet sequence *Les Regrets* (1558), he combines satiric, elegiac, and pastoral modes and, unlike the other Pléiade poets, abandons the theme of unrequited love often associated with such cycles. The imitation of models and an adherence to prescriptive norms preserved respect for tradition and assured an intelligible expression of themes and topics. But new forms constantly emerged. The epic and heroic romance were thriving genres during the Renaissance but coexisted, and were even amalgamated, with other literary kinds. For example, a picaresque novel, such as *Lazarillo de Tormes* (1554) or *Simplicissimus* (1669), records the wanderings of a hero who recalls Odysseus or Chrétien de Troyes's Yvain, but who is portrayed as an *ingénu* contending with, and learning from, social, economic, and psychological realities. By culling the generic conventions from treatises and compendia, Renaissance writers adapted and reworked standard generic forms that were used as techniques to express their particular theme and vision.

Genre as a "literary system" proposes two principles that seem especially relevant to the study of Renaissance poetic forms. Both critics and practitioners set forth, through prescriptions and imitations, characteristics identified with respective forms which, in turn, become codes and instruments of communication. Genres become established and thereafter their expectations exist in the consciousnesses of theorist, writer, and interpreter. The pressures of creativity, however, promote revisions in the generic norms; in order to accommodate content to form, poets assimilate into one single work several literary kinds that surpass the initial model. As Alastair Fowler (1982) has pointed out the mock-epic did not suffer extinction (107–11). In writing *The Rape of the Lock* (1712), Pope benefited from the satires of Juvenal and the epigrams of Martial, and his work served to complement Swift's *Gulliver's Travels* (1726) and survives, in theme and structure, in Joseph Heller's *Catch 22* (1961). Thus "modal transformation," as Fowler terms the phenomenon (108, 111, 167–69), may serve to explain the apparent contradictions in sixteenth-century French dialogue: as inheritors of the writings of Plato, Xenophon, Lucian, and Cicero, French humanists revived and reworked a meaningful and viable literary form.

The resources of genres as "the craftsman's tools" (Colie 1973, 127) did not pass unnoticed by sixteenth-century critics. In fact, the Italian critic Julius Caesar Scaliger applied similar principles to dialogue.[3] In his *Poetices* (1561) he defines dialogue as a mode of imitation that evolves as a defined genre, and that at the same time, affords to the practitioner a technique integral to other literary kinds. In its most general sense, dialogue is a mimetic mode that provides the poet with the means to record the words of fictitious personages. Such a definition restricts the practitioner from describing events or impressions through his own voice; dialogue in particular requires the recording of imagined speeches through the statements of two or more interlocutors (bk. 1., chap. 3). Such a theorization of imitation enables Scaliger to relate this concept of dialogue to a specific sort of genre, and then to demonstrate the uses of this mimetic mode in other poetic forms. The substance of dialogue, he asserts, is a disputation that, invented by Alexamenos of Teos, became a genre identified by "illuminating arguments and divine discourse" (6).[4] Clearly, Scaliger is referring to a genre defined and established in the poetic canons; however, he stops short of describing the sorts of disputation to be employed or of tracing the history of this literary kind. Rather, he elaborates upon its function as a technique that influences the shapes of other forms. For example, dialogue as a means to represent speech is essential to drama. But if genres share the technique of dialogue, themes often distinguish the generic forms: drama, unlike dialogue as a genre, sets forth deeds and actions, and it also relies upon a mixed mode in which the poet narrates in his own voice and at the same time introduces conversation. As a mode of imitation, then, dialogue is limited neither to disputation nor to drama. In fact, it is even associated with the technique of characterization: Scaliger notes that the artistic representation of the speech of others should reflect the character of the personage being portrayed (bk. 3, chap. 48, p. 126). Such a definition recalls an earlier thought proposed, and perhaps more clearly elucidated, by Erasmus. In his *De copia* (1512), Erasmus sees dialogue as a means through which the poet endows "each person with utterances appropriate to his type, country, way of life, cast of mind, and character" (Knott and Thompson 1978, 586). For Erasmus, dialogue

3. For a discussion of the theoretical premises of Scaliger's definition of genre, see Bernard Weinberg, *A History of Literary Criticism in the Italian Renaissance* (Chicago: University of Chicago Press, 1961), 2: 743–50, and "Scaliger versus Aristotle on Poetics," *Modern Philology* 39 (1942): 337–60.

4. "argumentis illustribus et divina oratione" (*Poetices libri septem* 1561, 6).

is a technique to enhance vividness (*evidentia*) in writing, and is therefore to be employed in historical writings, letters, and personal records. Similarly, Scaliger defines the same word (*dialogismos*) as a technique that, as used by Cicero in his orations and by Virgil in epic verse, depicts and animates characterization. Dialogue is indeed a genre, but it is also a technique.

Scaliger's statement on dialogue is significant. As he sees the form, it functions both as genre and mode. His allusion to its ancient origins and thematic substance indicates his awareness, and certainly suggests a sixteenth-century critical consciousness, of dialogue as a discrete literary kind. But if the precepts of dialogue are determined by thematics and form, he cannot deny the application of these rules to fiction making and to their uses in the enhancement and evolution of other poetic forms. *Genre* and *mode* seem therefore to be distinctions useful for examining the confusing theorizations and numerous varieties of humanist dialogue. The themes associated with this literary kind in ancient, medieval, and Renaissance writings define the form and function of dialogue as a generic model. Technique, however, also informs generic models; the blending and altering of other poetic forms within the recognized framework of dialogue may lead to an understanding of the theory of this genre that defined and encouraged creative practice. Consequently, an elaboration of Scaliger's references both to the historical evolution of a distinct genre and to the fluidity and flexibility of a technique seems relevant to a description of a form which, as *paragone*, enabled humanists to mold conceptual ideal to individual vision.

Modern critics have only recently turned their attention to the thematics and aesthetics of sixteenth-century French dialogue, and they have barely begun to chart the theoretical principles that delineate the prescriptions and admit the poetic license accounting for the development of the genre. Texts have not been readily accessible: some of the works of Bonaventure Des Périers, Pontus de Tyard, Louis Le Caron, Guy de Brués, and Jacques Tahureau have only lately become available in modern editions.[5] Other sig-

5. Bonaventure Des Périers, *Cymbalum mundi*, ed. Peter H. Nurse (Manchester, England: Manchester University Press, 1958); Pontus de Tyard, *Solitaire premier*, ed. Silvio F. Baridon (Geneva: Droz, 1950); Pontus de Tyard, *Solitaire second*, ed. Cathy M. Yandell (Geneva: Droz, 1980); Pontus de Tyard, *Mantice*, ed. Sylviane Bokdam (Geneva: Droz, 1990); Pontus de Tyard, *L'Univers*, ed. John C. Lapp (Ithaca: Cornell

nificant sources must be consulted in nineteenth-century editions. Quite frequently, one must seek out original printings. In spite of the difficulties of obtaining these works, critics have offered surveys of the range of subject matter and some comments on the dimensions of form. Barbara Bowen (1972) has made a number of incisive observations, and Mustapha Bénouis (1976) has summarized the writings of the major dialogists. More recently, Eva Kushner (1972, 1977, 1978, 1981, 1982, 1984, 1986) and John McClelland (1985) have presented some of the principal attributes of the genre and suggested directions for future analysis. A review of the secondary literature reveals examinations of the thought conveyed in individual works; the *Cymbalum mundi* (1537) of Bonaventure Des Périers has provoked considerable discussion,[6] and the works of Des Périers, Tyard, and Tahureau have generated recent book-length studies.[7] But an emphasis upon thematic content has obscured the aesthetics of dialogue as a genre. And even when critics have attempted to describe the form and functions of this literary kind, they have employed the more recent approaches of Bakhtin, Derrida, Paul de Man,[8] and others. Such methods of inquiry have produced some interesting insights that have enhanced our appreciation of the genre, but the results of these investigations plead, even more forcefully, for an examination of dialogue within its cultural context.

Although Rudolf Hirzel (1895/1963) traced the history of the genre, and although Bénouis (1976) and David Marsh (1980) have outlined some of the characteristics of humanist dialogue, their remarks do not take into account Renaissance critical writings. K. J. Wilson (1981, 1985) and Jon R. Snyder (1989) have recog-

---

University Press, 1950); Louis Le Caron, *Dialogues*, ed. Joan A. Buhlmann and Donald Gilman (Geneva: Droz, 1986); Guy de Brués, *The Dialogues of Guy de Brués: A Critical Edition*, ed. Panos P. Morphos (Baltimore: Johns Hopkins University Press, 1953); Jacques Tahureau, *Les Dialogues*, ed. Max Gauna (Geneva: Droz, 1981).

6. See, in particular, studies by Febvre (1942), Kushner (1972, 1977, 1978, 1981, 1982, 1984, 1986), Neidhart (1959), Saulnier (1951a, 1952b), and Screech (1956, 1959, 1969).

7. Especially relevant studies are: Kathleen Hall, *Pontus de Tyard and his "Discours philosophiques"* (1961); Silvio F. Baridon, *Pontus de Tyard (1521–1605)* (1953); and studies on Bonaventure Des Périers by Febvre (1942) and Neidhart (1959).

8. Bakhtin's *The Dialogic Imagination* (1981) has, in many ways, become the *point de repère* for any discussion on dialogue. Jacques Derrida (1981) relates the phenomenon of dialogue to the relativity of discourse; and Paul de Man (1983) demonstrates the undermining of meaning inherent in dialogic discourse.

nized this deficiency and, in a series of very valuable studies, have placed the genre within its critical and cultural contexts. Many of my remarks are indebted to their findings. But through a more detailed analysis of the observations of ancient and postclassical critics and their subsequent interpretations by humanist theorists, I will endeavor to record more fully the prescriptions and parameters that formed the thematic and aesthetic dimensions of the French problems that humanist critics confronted: (1) the defense of dialogue as poetic kind; (2) the definition of a philosophical (or nonfictional) genre as a poetic (or fictional) form; and (3) a description of a structure that accommodates the seriousness and validity of argumentative discourse and the pleasure and variety of imaginative writing. C. J. R. Armstrong (1976) has correctly noted that dialogue was linked with dialectics.[9] But if dialogue is, according to Sidney, a poetic form encasing philosophical argument, epistemology influences expression: the dialogue writer's vision of an individual concept informs the substance and determines the shape of his poetic creation. An exploration into the uses of this literary kind as developed by individual writers will undoubtedly heighten our appreciation of the substantive and aesthetic qualities of dialogue, and will also indicate its possibilities of combining with, and stimulating the formation of, other literary types. However, an examination of the precepts and assumptions that constitute the prescriptions, or *langue*, of dialogue is preliminary to, and necessary for, descriptions of individual expressions, or *paroles*, of the genre. Thus, through a review of the representative writings on dialogue by Louis Le Caron, Carolus Sigonius, and Torquato Tasso, I will survey attempts to defend, define, and develop the limits of poetic structures consistent with epistemological functions and didactic expressions. Ultimately, a literary work conforms to a writer's perception, thereby explaining creative individual forms collected into, and conve-

9. In offering this interpretation of dialogue, C. J. R. Armstrong (1976, 36) notes that Quirinus Breen (1957) and Brian Vickers (1968) have advanced similar ideas in their respective studies on Calvin and Francis Bacon. K. J. Wilson (1985, 47–74) has demonstrated the relationship between dialectics and dialogue in the educational process; and Lisa Jardine (1974, 1–75) and Seth Lerer (1985, 32–93) have studied the interrelation of logic and rhetoric in classical and postclassical traditions which, in turn, inform the respective methods of writing in Francis Bacon and Boethius.

niently designated by, respective exception. But in delineating more fully the substantive and formal boundaries by which theorists defined dialogue, I will attempt to denote some of the limits that enabled practitioners to reconcile creative aspirations with the expectations of effective communication.

✹ A Defense and Classification of Dialogue

Louis Le Caron

The sixteenth-century French humanist Louis Le Caron[10] opens his dialogue *La Claire* (1554) conventionally and unobtrusively. In his preface he attributes the source of his insight to a semidivine lady who, through her knowledge, virtue, grace, and kindness, commends and directs the writer's hand. As a young lawyer-poet in mid-sixteenth-century Paris, he must have been aware of this commonplace which both Dante and Petrarch had used so effectively, and which subsequent poets had employed so routinely. Indeed, writers of dialogue had replaced one of the Muses with an ethereal, half-human, half-heavenly guide. But if Claire resembles Leone Ebreo's Sophie or Pontus de Tyard's Pasithée, Le Caron moves decisively and quickly away from a recapitulation of the Neoplatonic concept of inspiration to a defense and classification of dialogue as a form of poetry. According to Le Caron, these creative efforts should not be exercises in amorous thoughts. Rather, disregarding the authority of the Italian Petrarchists, he has selected law as the subject to be treated and dialogue as the suitable genre. Attacks against his choices of content and form, he asserts,

10. For a survey of the life and works of Louis Le Caron, see the studies of L. Pinvert, "Louis Le Caron, dit Charondas (1536–1613)," *Revue de la Renaissance* 1 (1901): 1–9, 69–76, 181–88; F. Gohin *De Lud. Charondae (1534–1613): Vita et Versibus* (Thèse, Université de Paris, 1902); Donald R. Kelley, "Louis Le Caron Philosophie," *Philosophy and Humanism: Essays in Honor of Paul Oskar Kristeller*, ed. Edward P. Mahoney (New York: Columbia University Press, 1976), 30–49; and Joan A. Buhlmann and Donald Gilman in Le Caron, *Dialogues* 1–24.

will ensue. But by placing himself in the company of the ancients, he steels himself for the vituperation and defamation which, previously endured and overcome by Plato, will certainly result from his rehandling of an ancient but renascent literary form.

Le Caron's defense is necessarily based upon definition. However, such a polemical position seems inconsistent with the accepted practice of a genre that had been so extensively employed by classical and medieval writers, and that had already appeared in various humanist forms. Le Caron may have deliberately assumed such a posture in order to draw attention to his contribution to the literary development of the French language. In fact, later in the preface he affirms the suitability of the French language to express philosophic thought in dialogic form. But beyond this widening of the scope of intention of Du Bellay's *Deffence et Illustration de la langue françoyse* (1549), Le Caron's assertions take the form of a defense that is based upon an implied definition.

Recently, Margaret W. Ferguson (1983), in her study of Renaissance defenses of poetry, examined the relationship between literary defenses and poetic definitions. In applying J. L. Austin's thoughts on the dynamics of excuses to apologetic discourse (1979), she notes (1) that defenses point out an "abnormality," "failure," or "deviation," and (2) that these departures from established thinking may illuminate the accepted notion of a particular theory or literary form. This backdoor approach to the definition of discourse may appear circuitous and complicated. But with the absence of any complete ancient treatise on dialogue from which humanists could have shaped their ideas, the reading of defenses offers a sensible avenue of inquiry into the eventual classification of dialogue as a poetic form and into Le Caron's definition of this genre.

In his preface to *La Claire* (1554), a dialogue completed by a series of poems, Le Caron foresees attacks against his structure and style. The seriousness of his subject matter, he writes, is normally expressed through concise and direct language, without poetic embellishment and sophisticated syntax. Although he is deviating from the stylistic expectations of poetic writing, he finds protection in the writings of Plato. Since Plato combined philosophic disputation with poetic form, he incurred slanderous criticism. But, according to Le Caron, Plato's most strident and persistent maligners could not deny the validity of his ideas. Such themes should be soberly treated, but Plato, he notes, also injects into his discourse humorous, familiar, everyday, and fabricated narratives. Within these dialogues, then, a cloak of fiction coexists with, and even blends into, the substance of truth; Plato is therefore a poet-philosopher associated with poetry. Le Caron anticipates another attack: dialogues are written in prose. Again, ancient writers provide the authority to justify his practice; for the eloquent oratory of Demosthenes, Theophrastus, and Cicero, he contends, recalls the grace and elegance of lyric expression. And, of course, Plato employed prose to convey intellectual inquiries, placed in an imaginary setting and presented through fictitious speech.

At first, this justification of dialogue as a poetic form may appear unnecessary. Earlier, the dialogues of Plato and Cicero provided the models for fifteenth-century humanist works. And, certainly, Erasmus, in his *Colloquies* (1516), Castiglione, in his *Courtier* (1528), and St. Thomas More, in his *Utopia* (1516), had successfully and artistically employed fictitious characterization, conversation, setting, and story in a discussion of ideas. Nevertheless, Le Caron as theorist was standing at a crossroads between dialogue as dialectical disputation and dialogue as imaginative literature. In imitating ancient examples, humanists may have recognized the fictitious elements that characterize the genre. But, in theory, postclassical dialogue was perceived almost exclusively as a form of dialectical disputation.

From Poetics to Dialectics

As K. J. Wilson (1981) has demonstrated in his survey of medieval dialogue, postclassical writers of the genre stress dialectical argumentation and didactic explanation, and seem to overlook the importance of the fictitious elements that enliven Platonic debates and Ciceronian discussions. Defined simply as an exchange of questions and answers, the earliest example of postclassical dialogue is perhaps the *altercatio*. Evolving from Roman legal practice, it examines a controversial topic which, taking the form of statement and retort, evaluates and challenges the facts of an issue. Medieval practitioners, however, expanded the uses of the genre, and Church Fathers applied this type of inquiry not only to debate or persuasion but to demonstration or instruction. In form, the *altercatio* resembled *aporia* ("difficulties") which, originally used in

Homeric exegesis, assumed the label of *quaestiones*. Whereas the question-and-answer structure of the *altercatio* stresses debate, the *quaestio* that subsequently emerges assumes the form of a demonstrative treatise that sets forth information, and that employs questions to alleviate tedium and to facilitate instruction. Thus, dialogue is both a debate and, in its later form, a catechism that, serving as a textbook, instructs the young primarily in grammar and affirms the uses of the form as a didactic instrument.

The *altercatio*, then, seems to be the progenitor of two medieval dialogic forms: the debate and the colloquy. Although differences of purpose distinguish these two sorts of dialogue, both forms affirm the seriousness of subject matter and imply the classification of the genre as a sort of dialectical disputation. In his study on the dialogues of Solomon and Saturn, Robert J. Menner (1941) identifies three characteristics of the debate. First, these dialogues were eristic, or "match-winning"; for practitioners, in taking a stance, employ debate to validate a Christian idea and to disprove a pagan position. Second, through their attempts to persuade, writers used a variety of styles that include diatribe, conversation, and logical analyses. Fictitious elements, moreover, enriched the pleasure of reading the genre, and the use of different styles may account for subsequent developments. For example, twelfth-century allegorical debates between Church and Synagogue present exchanges between universal but fictive characters. Other writers, though, adapt historical incidents to unreal situations and use actual characters as interlocutors, thereby establishing a dialogic model that Reformationists later employed for polemical purposes. Third, this form becomes associated with the poetic dialogues of *débat* and *pastourelle* which, like theological debates, are verbal disputes employing both conversation and dialectics and expressing opposing views on a particular issue.

Similarly, colloquies share the characteristics of didactic intention and fictitious form. As catechisms on grammar, colloquies were initially question-and-answer schoolbooks that explained the rules for effective and appropriate communication. The appearance of *elucidaria*, however, marks a reaction against the seriousness of instruction. Like colloquies, they present interlocutors who exchange knowledge through inquiry and response. But unlike its more sober ancestor, the elucidary includes all sorts of information in both Latin and the vernacular languages. Verbal contests and riddles often characterize this type of colloquy. Humor, especially the biting attacks associated with the *demandes joyeuses*, becomes integral to the genre, and is eventually assimilated into the colloquies of Aelfric and Erasmus. This lightness of tone may have alleviated the ponderousness of instruction in grammar; Erasmus's use of daily situations in his *Colloquies* (1516), for example, certainly facilitates the acquisition of essential vocabulary and fundamental structures. In each case, however, the colloquy is a form of dialogue that, as a sort of disputation, underscores the didactic intent of the form, but that also facilitates instruction through the pleasure of fiction.

The subsequent emergence of Scholastic disputation, however, obscures the role of the colloquy and enhances the significance of dialectics. In form, disputation recalls the contentions that the speakers in debate advanced and defended. But unlike debate, so often polemical in intention and tone, disputation reflects the use of questions and objections which, informed and animated by dialectical argumentation, lead to a plausible conclusion. As K. J. Wilson (1981) explains the progressive interconnections of debate and colloquy with Scholastic disputation (29), dialogue was the mode of instruction for the trivium (grammar, logic, rhetoric). The colloquy, as we have already seen, presents the essentials of correct communication. Words are meaningless without thought, and dialectics, or logic, which defines techniques of debate, inquiry, defense, and disputation, complements the effective use of grammar. Rhetoric provides the means to embellish, through forceful expression and appropriate arrangement, the thesis that has been intelligibly and intelligently proposed. According to Gordon Leff (1968, 120: also see Wilson 1981, 31), two reasons account for the increasing importance of dialectics in the twelfth and thirteenth centuries: (1) Arabic translations of, and commentaries on, the works of Aristotle and Greek science, which provided methods of disputation and reasoning, and (2) the application of these dialectical procedures to the apprehension of philosophy and theology. The recovery and subsequent evaluation of dialectics resulted in the formulation of a Scholastic method that gave structure and substance to disputation. The grammar presented in colloquies emphasized composition, and was increasingly restricted to the curriculum of schools. At the university level, though, grammar became a science to be studied and debated in its own right. Thus, in the twelfth and thirteenth centuries dialectics became the method to penetrate into the workings of semantics and syntax, and it emerged both as a procedure for debate and as a means to analyze the properties and processes of the other sciences.

Dialectics, then, provided a system of inquiry, and dialogue became its modus operandi. In assuming the form and function of the colloquy, dialectics furnished the procedure for instruction: students were expected to respond to specific questions, and legal training required competence in argumentation. Pedagogy molds practice. Accordingly, common and civil deliberations proceeded by disputation which, similar to Christian debates, set forth a question calling for a response. Dialectics no longer denoted logic. Rather, as G. Wallerand (1913, 21n3; see also Wilson 1981, 33) informs us, a thirteenth-century thinker identifies dialectics as disputation, or as an "ars opponendi et respondendi."

As a jurist, Le Caron was trained in the complexities of debate, and was probably acquainted with the association of dialectics and dialogue. At the same time, though, he must have been aware of the elements of fiction that characterize the genre's classical predecessors: Socrates's use of myth and irony, Lucian's employment of comic and satiric modes, Cicero's transcription of imaginary but verisimilar speeches. C. J. R. Armstrong (1976), moreover, demonstrates the identification of dialectics and dialogue in the theorizations of Rudolph Agricola, Johannes Sturm, and Philip Melanchthon. Admittedly, Agricola,[11] in his *De inventione dialectica libri tres* (1515), defines dialectics in terms of disputation: "the art of arguing convincingly on any subject" (*De inventione dialectica* 1534, 2.2; McNally, 1967, 401).[12] However, instead of viewing dialectics solely as a procedure for disputation, he designates its aim as one of instruction. Teaching, he contends, proceeds

11. The transition of the place of dialectics from a discrete art to one intrinsically related to grammar and rhetoric has been traced by Jardine (1974, chap. 1) and Wilson (1985, chap. 3). For general studies on Rudolph Agricola, see W. Woodward, *Studies in Education during the Age of the Renaissance, 1400–1600* (Cambridge: Cambridge University Press, 1906); and M. Gilmore, *The World of Humanism 1453–1517* (New York: Harper Torchbook, 1962). C. Vasoli (1957) and especially J. R. McNally (1966, 1969) have explored Agricola's views on the interrelation between dialectics and rhetoric.

12. "ars probabiliter de qualibet re proposita disserendi" (*De inventione dialectica* 1534, 155).

through speech, which expresses thoughts in language, and which relies upon dialectics to carry out its purpose. But although "discourse can teach without moving or delighting . . . , it cannot move or delight without teaching" (1534, 1.1; McNally 1967, 395). [13] By shifting the focus and purpose of dialectics from argumentation to instruction, Agricola integrated dialectics with grammar and rhetoric. Dialectics enables the teacher to discover the truth. Like the *grammaticus*, though, the dialectician must speak correctly and clearly. And, by striving to argue "convincingly" and "to move and delight," the dialectician assimilates the requirements of the orator.

Although Agricola's association of dialectics and disputation conformed to Scholastic doctrine and established practice, his theorization concerning the interrelation of all the arts of the trivium enlarged the scope and applications of dialogue. Dialectics, he asserts, affords a discussion of "things dubious and uncertain" (1534, 2.4; McNally 1967, 410). [14] However, if the writer aspires to "argue convincingly," then his discourse must stir the affections and seize the mind. Persuasion, pleasure, and the arrangement of topics all play their part; in reviewing representative tricks of the trade the writer demonstrates the interdependence of dialectics and rhetoric in the writing of dialogue. Syllogism and induction are essential tools in argumentation. But through allusion to the dialogues of Plato and Lucian, Agricola notes the effectiveness of digression, vividness, and characterization in the practice of a genre that informs and instructs. Similarly, Johannes Sturm, [15] in his *Partitionum dialecticarum libri* (1539; completed in four books, 1561), continued the reforms initiated by Agricola. According to Sturm, as a mode of examination, dialogue depends upon dialectics in the advancement of argumentation. But the *ratio* of disputation is conveyed by the *oratio* of dialogue which, as practiced by Plato and Cicero, displays the tripartite structure of speeches (introduction, presentation, conclusion). The rhetorical principle

13. "Hoc in praesentia dixisse sufficiat posse docere orationem, ut non moveat, non delectet: movere aut delectare, ut non doceat, non posse" (4).

14. "quo dubia incertaque colligimus" (160).

15. Schmidt's (1855) nineteenth-century study on J. Sturm remains the only comprehensive study on this significant humanist. C. J. R. Armstrong (1976, 38–39) notes the importance of Sturm's contribution to the relationship between dialectics and dialogue. See also studies by Kückelhahn (1872), Sohm (1912), and comments by Ong (1978, 231–36, 247, 307).

of decorum, moreover, enlivens the writing and defines characterization. Finally, Philip Melanchthon extracted dialogue from the
classification of Scholastic disputation. In a reply to a fifteenth-
century controversy (1484) between the Scholastic stance of Giovanni Pico della Mirandola and the humanist position of Ermolao
Barbaro, Melanchthon designates, in 1558, dialectics as the instrument of philosophers who seek wisdom. But "there is no use
for wisdom unless we can communicate to others the things we
have with wisdom deliberated and thought upon" (Breen 1952,
414). Rhetoric, then, is not an "adventitious adornment" (Breen
1952, 416). Rather, eloquence is the aim of the rhetorician who
aspires "to represent the mind's thoughts themselves in appropriate and clear language" (Breen 1952, 416). By extension, the
writings of Aristotle and Cicero "can be truly said to have been
sprinkled with ambrosia" (Breen 1952, 421).

By 1550, then, dialogue could be viewed as a form that draws
upon the resources of the trivium. If I may use Zeno's metaphor,
it combined aspects both of the "literature of the fist," or the philosophical argument, and of the "literature of the palm," or rhetorical composition.[16] Intelligibility required correct grammatical
expression. But dialectical disputation dependent upon grammar
and enhanced by rhetoric does not place dialogue within the poetic
canons. In fact, Agricola's assertion may have encouraged the
amalgamation of the arts of the trivium; but, in describing the
primacy of dialectics, he indirectly confirms Armstrong's (1976)
contention that humanist dialogue was essentially viewed as a
form of dialectical disputation.

From Dialectics to Poetics

According to Bernard Weinberg (1961), the sixteenth-century
theorist confronted at least two dilemmas when defining an aesthetic topic. First, he had to situate a subject into a particular science that established its limits, an act that, by extension, enabled
the critic to determine the aims, means, and possibilities of the
topic (1961, 1:1). Such a classification determined methodology.
Next, in describing a poetic precept, genre, or practice, the Re-

16. W. S. Howell (1956, 14–15; 1975, 76–77) traces this metaphor in the
theoretical works of the English rhetoricians.

naissance critic had to reconcile contemporary concepts and tastes with texts and traditions inherited from Greece and Rome and reworked by medieval thinkers and practitioners (1961, 1:38). Le Caron meets these expectations. Through his description of dialogue as a form of "poetic disputation," and through his definition of the genre in terms of ancient texts, he integrates this philosophical-literary kind into Renaissance poetic canons.

In arguing for the classification of dialogue as a poetic genre, Le Caron draws upon the Platonic notion of poetic inspiration. He confesses in the "avant-propos" that, unlike Ronsard, Du Bellay, and Tyard, he is uncomfortable composing verse. But form is accidental or incidental to the essential of substance. Although dialogue differs in structure and style from sonnet sequences, this literary kind nevertheless sets forth an idea that describes a truth. Resembling Ronsard's Cassandre or Du Bellay's Olive, Claire commands the interlocutor Le Caron to undertake a philosophic voyage that, in turn, will be transcribed in dialogic form. Le Caron does not reject precedent. By assuming the name of the Athenian legislator Solon, he employs the principle of verisimilitude that characterizes Ciceronian dialogue. And by proposing an examination of law, he seems to have kept in mind Diogenes Laertius's observation ("Life of Plato," 3:49; Hicks 1966, 321) that the thematic limits of dialogue rarely extend beyond demonstratable knowledge (for example, music, astronomy, mathematics) or beyond political or ethical questions. The medium of poetry, he earlier acknowledges, assures immortality and admits its practitioners into the company of "divins espritz" (*La Claire* 1554, Biii verso). Plato, though, was also divine, and he recorded his thoughts in dialogue. The road to truth, moreover, is single and certain, and the inspiration that guides the hand of the "divin Pindare François Pierre de Ronsard" (4v) moves the thoughts and chooses the words of the dialogue writer Louis Le Caron.

Inspiration is equally applicable to poets and philosophers; and, according to Scholastic traditions and to conventional sixteenth-century thinking, dialogue writers were dialecticians. But in attaining and describing his vision of truth, Le Caron relies upon the process of inspiration that assures the immortality of ancient and contemporary poet-seers. As a philosopher-poet, the interlocutor Le Caron rids his mind of physical and external distractions. The *vacatio* prepares his soul to be enraptured by the vision and thoughts of Claire. During his ascent to truth the philosopher-poet is not a passive agent of the deity. Rather, reflections of truth that are discovered in nature and are recorded in books provide touchstones which, preserved by the faculty of memory, recall and identify a single and clear idea. Like Ramus's reworking of Platonic and Ficinian dialectics, Le Caron's quest for truth requires a method of inquiry or an inspired use of natural reasoning that eventually supports the integration of humanly perceived phenomena and divinely ordained reality. Dialectics, or the art of subtle disputation, passes beyond rhetoric, or the craft of artful communication, and the system of correspondences between earthly perceptions and heavenly visions is clarified and demonstrated through human or natural reasoning. Claire enables the interlocutor to penetrate the meaning of law which, divinely ordained, explains the harmony of nature. Thus Claire personifies an Augustinian *claritas*; and, like the *discipulus* at the feet of the *magister*, the interlocutor Le Caron falls silent before the vision of truth. Dialogue and dialectics fuse into a vision of truth. But if the personage of Le Caron recalls the Boethius who ultimately submits himself to the goddess Fortuna in the dialogue *Consolation of Philosophy*, Le Caron also resembles Dante the poet-seer who becomes speechless at the vision of the Empyrean. At the end of *La Claire* the prose of dialogue becomes the verse of *La Clairté amoureuse*. But as Le Caron describes himself later in *La Philosophie* (1555), he is a philosopher-seer who, like his inspired contemporaries, employs dialectics to perceive the secrets of the world. Both the poet-versifier and the dialogue-*prosateur*, then, are inspired to discover and convey the "choses cachées au vulgaire" (69r). Differences in form assist in the identification of genres. However, if the fables of Boccaccio and Marguerite de Navarre merit the label of poetry, like the sonnets of Petrarch or Ronsard, then the criterion of form becomes irrelevant in Le Caron's classification of dialogue as a literary kind.

Through his efforts to defend dialogue as a poetic form, Le Caron carries off a tour de force. Like Agricola, Sturm, and Melanchthon, he never denies the significance of dialectics in the thematic structure of the genre. As a humanist, though, he implies a necessary interrelationship among the arts of the trivium. Dialogue is no longer associated exclusively with dialectics; in complying with the reforms proposed by his humanist predecessors, he situates dialogue within a broader literary context. Le Caron is a modernist. In attempting to perceive and express a single truth, he rejects the cut-and-thrust of Scholastic disputation and employs Platonic dialectics as interpreted in Ficino's commentaries and as reworked by Ramus. Ancient, medieval, and humanist examples establish dialogue as the appropriate medium for such an epistemological journey. But Le Caron reconciles conventional practice with theoretical reform. As we have seen, Agricola defines dialectics as "the leader and the directness of the arts" (1534, 2.1; McNally 1967, 405)[17] which encompasses grammar and rhetoric. Accordingly, dialogue remains categorized as a form of dialectics. Although Le Caron demonstrates the goals and methods shared by philosophers and poets, he adheres to the aims of the Pléiade to enhance the French language through poetry. For Le Caron, dialogue enables the practitioner to develop the language and, as a genre, deserves a place in the poetic canons. Form, moreover, follows function. If dialogue belongs, at least thematically, to the classification of poetry, then its structures, strategies, and techniques should reflect the precepts of this philosophic-poetic genre. Aside from several adhesions to Plato and Cicero, though, Le Caron does not consider the question of form. Rather, a few years later in Italy, Carolus Sigonius addresses this unanswered question; and, after defining dialogue as a type of poetry, he attempts to reconstruct the ancient prescriptions of dialogue and to delineate the characteristics of a Renaissance genre.

17. "dux illa directrixque . . . artium" (144).

✌ Definitions and Prescriptions

Carolus Sigonius

Carolus Sigonius (ca. 1524–84) was a historian and literary theorist. As professor of Greek at Venice (1552–60) and as professor of rhetoric at Padua (1560–84), he directed his attention primarily to historiography. But in gathering, editing, and interpreting fragments of ancient writings, he attempted to present the precepts of dialogue formulated by the classical critics and employed by humanists. In the absence of any ancient treatise on dialogue, then, Sigonius's *De dialogo liber* (1561) presents a significant reconstruction of the classical concepts of the genre.[18] Sigonius's recovery of these tenets, though, is neither a compilation nor a thematic grouping of scattered writings. Rather, in synthesizing ancient rules from brief passages and oblique allusions, he describes the genre within a sixteenth-century critical context that enables him and his followers to view dialogue as a poetic expression of dialectical discourse. And, equally important, this humanist recon-

---

18. For an analysis of this treatise, see Jon R. Snyder, *Writing the Scene for Speaking: Theories of Dialogue in the Late Italian Renaissance* (Stanford: Stanford University Press, 1989), chap. 2; see also the studies by G. Raffaele, "'Elegans imitatio et erudita': Sigonio e la teoria del dialogo," *Giornale storico della letteratura italiana* 103 (1986): 321–54; and Donald Gilman, "The Reconstruction of a Genre: Carolus Sigonius and the Theorization of Renaissance Dialogue," in *Acta Conventus Neo-Latini Torontonensis: Proceedings of the Sixth Triennial Conference on Neo-Latin Studies*, eds. A. L. Dalzell, C. Fantazzi, and R. Schoeck (Binghamton, New York: Medieval and Renaissance Texts and Studies, 1991). In his *Carlo Sigonio: The Changing World of the Late Italian Renaissance* (Princeton: Princeton University Press, 1989), W. McGuaig examines the humanistic currents that inform Sigonius's historiography.

struction of the theory of ancient dialogue provided the prescriptions by which practitioners shaped themes to expected structures and strategies.

Defense and Definition of a Poetic Genre

At the beginning of his treatise Sigonius recognizes that dialogue was invented and promoted by philosophers. In their commentaries on Aristotle's works, Ammonius and Simplicius, he notes, employ dialogue (1) in the presentation of knowledge and (2) in an inquiry into problems that are examined through the resources of dialectics.[19] But dialogue is not a treatise through which the author speaks solely from his own perspective. Rather, through the alternation of speeches expressed by two or more interlocutors, dialogue goes beyond an exposition of knowledge or a summary of perspectives on political or moral questions. In short, dialogue is, according to Sigonius, a literary kind which requires a defense as a poetic form, and which, by extension, calls for a refined and expanded definition.

Like Le Caron, Sigonius attempts to place dialogue into a specific science which, in turn, would lead to a distinguishing of its aims and characteristics. But whereas Le Caron only refers to Plato and Cicero, Sigonius appears to elaborate on the thoughts of Diogenes Laertius who, in his "Life of Plato" (3:47–65; Hicks 1966, 1:319–35), provides perhaps the most complete account of dialogue surviving from ancient criticism. According to Laertius, "dialogue is a discourse consisting of question and answer on some

19. The commentaries on Aristotle's *Categories* by Simplicius and Ammonius were circulated widely throughout sixteenth-century Europe. Both of these commentators designate serious thought to be the subject matter of dialogue. But form cannot be divorced from substance. Simplicius, for example, ascribes to dialogue an exchange of ideas voiced by the respective interlocutors. Plato, he notes, obfuscated thought through his use of metaphors, narratives, riddles, and conjectures, whereas Aristotle practiced a more direct style. Since the strength of dialogues resides in the exposition of thought, Aristotle's clarity of expression in his dialogic writing (and epistolary forms) enhances the usefulness of this literary kind.

Similarly, Ammonius concurs on the essential question-and-answer form that identifies the genre. Ammonius, however, is more sensitive to the reader-listener. Aristotle, he contends, employed the form to present subject matter to a readership less capable of appreciating demonstrative knowledge. In respecting these "simpler arguments" ("simpliciora argumenta" in *Praedicamenta Aristotelis commentarii* 1544, 5 verso), dialogue writers explicate ideas which, though ultimately inconclusive, instruct and therefore serve the common needs.

philosophical or political subject" (3:48; Hicks 1966, 1:319). Through a survey of Plato's writings, Laertius sees dialogue (1) as a genre of fiction and (2) as a form of dialectics that examines philosophical and moral topics. The use of direct discourse in dialogue, he contends, requires interlocutors. As a means to represent the speech of others, dialogue is a mimetic mode employed in works that are dramatic, narrative, or a combination of both. Substantively, dialogue may be used for the demonstration of knowledge or for the inquiry into an issue. As an instrument of instruction, dialogue may present theoretical (that is, ethical or political) issues. As a tool of inquiry, dialogue may be used for the training of the mind or for the winning of verbal contests. In spite of these variations of form and purpose, dialectics is the method that, in expanding knowledge or in examining opinion, characterizes the genre.

For Sigonius, dialogue is a poetic form; like his ancient predecessors, he denotes the object of imitation as the means to distinguish dialogue from other genres. Since dialogue was invented and developed by philosophers, and since it was later used for demonstration and disputation (1596, 1–2), Sigonius deduces its differences from history that chronicles events. But just as the epic poets Silicus Italicus and Lucan incorporate actual happenings into fictive representation, the dialogue writer injects historical personages, places, and events into his imaginary exchanges. In dialogue, interlocutors propose and analyze perspectives of an idea. The representation of thought, then, becomes the object of imitation as reflected by the speech of others. Thus the dialogue writer presents the premises to be affirmed, rejected, or examined, and employs the rhetorical-poetical techniques that identify the character, appearance, and language of the respective speakers. In describing the genre as a poetic form, Sigonius reflects Aristotle's practice, for his representation of human character is secondary to his delineation of "precepts of the most serious matters [that] are presented in prose."[20] Dialogue, as a poetic form that establishes and elucidates philosophical topics, is more inclusive. Argumentation, he contends, requires the artful copying of the exchange of viewpoints; the representation of these speeches defines dialogue

20. "praecepta rerum gravissimarum pedestri oratione complexi sunt" (*De dialogo liber* 1596, 5).

as a poetic genre that explains and examines philosophical or political content.

Through this attempt to define dialogue as poetry, Sigonius recognizes the need to reconcile philosophic themes with imaginative discourse. The identification of the object of imitation and the means and manners of representation become crucial to his classification of the form as a genus of poetry. Accordingly, he applies Aristotle's methodology of defining and categorizing literary discourses: "With regard to types of subject matter which poets represent through imitation, the poet invents actions of men of serious or light character or a mixture of the two; the instruments which contribute to the imitation are speech, harmony, and rhythm; the manners of undertaking the imitation include narration or action or a combination of both."[21] In drawing upon Aristotle's criteria of things, means, and manners, Sigonius employs an accepted approach to the definition of a genre. But if his methodology is Aristotelian, his definition and categorization of dialogue as a poetic form recall Plato's notions of artistic representation.

As Richard McKeon (1952) has observed in his analysis of Plato's ideas on poetic representation, "All discourse is imitation" (161), and narration is the means to convey discourse (see also Wilson 1985, 7). In his *Republic* (392d–394c) Plato distinguishes the types of discourse which, according to McKeon (1952) include (1) "pure narrative, in which the poet speaks in his own person without imitation, as in the dithyramb; (2) narrative by characters, as in comedy and tragedy; and (3) mixed narrative, in which the poet speaks now in his person and now by means of imitation" (161; see also Wilson 1985, 7). Like Plato, Sigonius designates discourse as the distinguishing characteristic of poetic representation. Indeed, the invention and subsequent re-creation of the "actions of men" that are reflected in speech conform to two of Plato's three modes of poetic mimesis: narrative and mixed narrative. Thus speech, the essential form of dialogue, is the means to depict human actions. By insisting on the imitation of the "actions of

---

21. "Res, quas poetae imitando simularent, aut graviorum, aut leviorum hominum, aut qui his interiecti essent, actiones esse invenit; instrumenta, quae ad imitandum afferrent, orationem esse, concentum, et rhythmum; modos ineundae imitationis, cum iidem aut perpetua uterentur narratione, aut quasi agentes inducerent, aut utrunque" (30).

men" as revealed through direct discourse, Sigonius excludes from the dialogue genre history, lyric poetry, and expository treatises through which the writer speaks in his own voice. Rather, by selecting and copying qualities that portray "men of serious or light character," the dialogue writer is a poet who does not simply see and record an image. It is through the image or idea expressed by the speech of others that the dialogue writer as poet perceives and imitates the distinguishing features of the respective interlocutors.

If both dialogue and drama depend upon the same mimetic mode through which the characters articulate the writer's thoughts, dialogue manifests additional characteristics associated with poetry. But is dialogue a form of drama? Although the narratives of comedy and tragedy transcribe the actions of men, Plato's concept of discourse does not exclude the representation of ideas as appropriate subjects, and would therefore classify dialogue and drama as similar literary kinds. In fact, according to Wilson (1985, 8), Plato's understanding of poetry expands to an inclusiveness of themes and thereby accommodates philosophical topics to forms associated with dramatic representation. Aristotle, in contrast, takes an equivocal stance on the classification of dialogue. In his *Poetics* he groups the mimes of Sophron and Xenarchus and Socratic Conversations in a nameless "art which employs words" (1447a; Fyfe 1965, 7). Both Homer and Empedocles, he notes, wrote in meter; and, according to a critical consensus that identifies form as the criterion for poetic classification, the epics of Homer and the philosophical writings of Empedocles are labeled as poetry. But the fictionality of narratives and the demonstrability of physics present more differences than similarities. By itself, the representation of discourse is not a suitable standard for evaluation and, for Aristotle, becomes secondary to the object of imitation selected and verbally presented. Accordingly, he states in the following chapter that, "since living persons are the objects of representation, these must necessarily be either good men or inferior" (1448a; Fyfe 1965, 9). Dramatic actions expressed through direct discourse would obviously conform to this concept of poetry. And epic, in spite of its mixture of speeches and fables, depicts the actions of men which may be dramatized (1459b). On the basis of its object of imitation, the discussion of ideas, Aristotle cannot classify dialogue as a form of drama, and he even appears to exclude it from the poetic canons. But Aristotle's view of imitation (mimesis) that dialogue and drama share in common begs the question (1447b), and invites later classifications of dialogue as a poetic form.

As we have already seen, K. J. Wilson (1985) terms this ambivalent view as an "incomplete fiction" (9). Dialogues trace the course of discussions, but the use of characters, setting, and circumstances justifies the imaginary nature of the genre. Practitioners, moreover, develop these fictional elements. As Michel Ruch (1958, 45–55) has noted, such Peripatetics as Theophrastus, Praxiphanes, Heraclides of Pontus, Dichaerarchus, and Ariston of Ceos retain, in their works, the exposition of ideas as the object of imitation but, at the same time, expand the use of the imaginary. In a letter to Atticus (6.2.3), for example, Cicero doubts Dichaerarchus's knowledge of geography in his "Descent into the Trophian Cave," and suggests his fabrication of Peloponnesian ports. Such fictionality violates historical accuracy, but Cicero sees the use of the fantastic as appropriate to the writing of dialogue. In fact, Cicero acknowledges his debt to Dichaerarchus's thoughts on the practical life (*Atticus* 2.16), and later (*Atticus* 3.30–33), expresses his intention to imitate this style and structure in his own works. Cicero abandoned the project. But on the basis of these seminal statements, and on the basis of the artistic evolution of the Peripatetics' and Cicero's dialogues, Ruch has correctly proposed, I think, the importance of fictional elements that inform the genre, and that designate its classification as a poetic form.

Clearly, the characteristics of dialogue established by practice and set forth in subsequent descriptions present problems of categorization. As Ruch (1958) has demonstrated in a brilliant reconstruction of ancient dialogue theory (23–30), Cicero indirectly confronts the peculiarities of this genre that eludes classification but required theorization and, by extension, justification and formalization. In his *De inventione* (1.19.27; Hubbell 1960, 55), he defines narrative as "an exposition of events that have occurred and are supposed to have occurred." Narrative, as he views it, assumes one of three forms: (1) *fabula*, "in which the events are not true and do not have verisimilitude" (1.19.27); (2) *historia*, "an account of actual occurrences remote from the recollection of our own age" (1.19.27); (3) *argumentum*, "a fictitious narrative (*ficta res*) which nevertheless could have occurred" (1.19.27). *Argumentum*, in turn, is manifested by one of two sorts: (1) the transcription of events, or (2) a narrative of fictitious happenings integrally related to character portrayal. Dialogue, as we have seen, is not history. Nor can it be categorized as *fabula*, for that form is distinguished by its totally imaginary nature. Thus dialogue, which does incorporate into its narrative historical events and personages, would seem to meet the expectations of *argumentum*. Finally, the use of interlocutors and, as we shall see, the importance of verisimilitude enable critics to define dialogue as a sort of fictitious narrative that derives from, but reinforces, character representation.

Through his definition of dialogue as "a representation of dialectical disputation" (45),[22] Sigonius identifies the "actions of men" as a discussion of ideas. But if dialogue is distinguished from drama by its object of imitation, Sigonius employs Plato's thoughts on imitation to justify the classification of dialogue as a poetic form. Aristotle's references to dialogue in his *Poetics* do not deny the poetic nature of the form. Indeed, according to Sigonius (32–34), Athenaeus (*Deipnosophists* 1.2), Proclus (*Commentary on the "Republic"* 1.3; see also Snyder 1989, 230 no. 59; 1.163), and Plutarch (*Table-Talk* 8.8., 711c) confirm the designation of Plato's dialogues as a sort of poetry. For Sigonius, the object of imitation is the "actions of men" that take the form of disputation. *Disputatio* is not necessarily *argumentum*; and, as dialogue excludes storytelling as its principal theme, it omits the detailing of a series of events. But the discussions presented in dialogue nevertheless approach Cicero's concept of *argumentum*. In several places, moreover, Sigonius uses almost interchangeably the words *disputatio* and *argumentum* (35, 38). And in complying with Laertius's definition of dialogue ("Life of Plato" 3.48), Sigonius does not overlook the significance of character portrayal and their respective representation in speech. Dialogue, then, may draw on the speech of others, it is a form of poetry, and, in many respects, it reflects Cicero's concept of *argumentum*.

In relying upon Plato's theory of mimesis, Sigonius places dialogue into the poetic canons and thereby designates the nature of this literary type. The rationalization of dialogue as a poetic form, though, asks the critic to describe the characteristics of the genre.

---

22. "est dialecticae diputationis imago" (45).

Aristotle's approach to the definition of epic and tragedy appears applicable to the delineation of the substance, style, and structure of dialogue. Sigonius sees Aristotle's categories of things, means, and manners as the representation, in dialogue, of men, words, and modes, respectively. Men are both the subjects and actors in dialogue, for, in speaking, they produce the words that form dialectical disputation. Words express the speech of the interlocutors which, in turn, conveys thought and perspective. The modes of dialogue are reflected through disputation which, enunciated by the speakers, is produced through the denotation and connotation of language. Thus three constitutive arts define dialogue: poetics, rhetoric, and dialectics. Dialogue, then, goes beyond poetic imitation; if the genre deviates from history or expository treatise, it is also distinct from drama, epic, and lyric verse. As theorist, Sigonius proceeds to outline and elucidate the resources of rhetoric and dialectics which may satisfy the Aristotelian demands of defining the "means" and "modes" of dialogue, and which may convert the abstract precept of dialogue as poetry into a description of the concrete techniques essential in the representation of the actions (or words) of men.

The Resources of Rhetoric

Like his ancient predecessors, Sigonius assumes an ambivalent stance toward the nature and function of dialogue. But if the genre mediates between the nonfiction of a discussion of philosophical and political topics and the fiction of the representation of imaginary speeches, Sigonius reminds the reader of the definition borrowed from Laertius: a disputation in the form of questions and responses. Within this broad definition, the roles of poetics, rhetoric, and dialectics that contribute to the distinctive individuality of dialogue enable Sigonius to delineate the characteristics that relate and differentiate the form from other literary kinds. As we have seen, the mimesis employed in the creation of dialogue identifies the genre as a poetic form. But Sigonius notes that dialogue is not lyric poetry. In lyric verse the poet speaks singly and personally, whereas in dialogue multiple interlocutors examine a didactic topic. Further, unlike lyric poetry composed in meter, dialogues are written in prose that reflects the ordinary and daily speech of men. Dialogue, then, may be poetic in its process of imitation but rhetorical in its representation of form; the genre resembles oratory which, delivered in prose, argues for or against a philosophical or political issue.

Although dialectics establishes the validity of the argument, the dialogue writer, like the rhetor, employs tropes and techniques to enhance the subject matter. According to Sigonius, "among these [dialogues], [a disputation] is waged with naked arguments; among them arguments are dressed with the copiousness and elegance of words" (45).[23] Eloquence unites the substance elucidated by dialectics with the possibilities afforded by rhetoric.

Lucidity, concision, and subtlety, Sigonius observes, characterize Plato's use of language, which Aristotle criticizes as excessively elaborate and overly erudite. Sigonius counters these objections, however. Dialogue is no longer an *altercatio* that is solely informed by the cut-and-thrust of Scholastic logic. Rather, by defending Plato's refined usage of vocabulary and creative coinage of phrases, Sigonius adapts ancient practice to the humanist taste for eloquence.

In spite of Sigonius's praise of Plato's style, he offers Ciceronian dialogue as the model to be imitated. Long allegories in Plato's dialogues detract from the smoothness of language, and an inattention to copiousness results in a sparseness and coarseness of expression. Cicero overcomes these deficiencies through the use of a fuller, more florid style, building upon Plato's dialogues through his use of higher, more florid style, building upon Plato's dialogues through his use of higher, more exalted modes of expression. Rhetorical formulae that contribute to this more elegant, abundant style do not compromise lucidity. On the contrary, the rhetorical techniques and devices used by Cicero assist the dialogue writer in practicing the principle of decorum that becomes the means to denote the individuality of the respective speaker. Literature imitates life; just as the orator depends upon the doctrine of appropriateness, or decorum, in speaking, the poet (and dialogue writer) cannot deny its significance in literary creativity.

Dialogue, then, simulates reality and, through the rhetorical precept of decorum, sets before the reader's eyes a verisimilitude or an illusion of truth. Sigonius defines verisimilitude explicitly

23. "Nam apud eos nudis pugnatur argumentis, apud eos argumenta verborum copia, et elegantia vestiuntur" (45).

and traditionally as "such power and such a nature that when it is present it causes the thing which is invented not to seem so" (Weinberg 1961, 1: 484).[24] Such a credible illusion, he contends, must be established at the outset of any dialogue, and he advises the dialogue writer to represent, in the introduction to his work, a probable and plausible reality that includes (1) the identity and description of characters; (2) the time, place, and circumstances of the debate; and (3) the relationship between the individuality of the respective speakers and the situation of the imagined dialogue.

Sigonius's concept of decorum (60–61) recalls Aristotle's thoughts on *prepon*, or *appropriateness*, discussed in his *Rhetoric* (3.7). Employed primarily by orators, the principle of decorum prescribes the use of a style consistent with the character, emotion, and thought of the respective speaker. In dialogue, speech or oration in its etymological sense (*oratio*) is the subject matter perceived in reality and represented in writing. If poetry is the imitation of an action, then dialogue, as one of its types, must convey its "action" of speech. And if the precepts of decorum result in a plausible representation of the thoughts and words of the respective interlocutor, adherence to its expectations therefore becomes the means to present a persuasive argument. According to Sigonius (and Aristotle) (63–64), man acts in words and deeds that conform to his character and situation: Homer's Achilles, for example, is easily angered and, if provoked, emits language and commits actions expected of a man with his thoughts and temperament. Like Homeric epic, dialogue is a fictive creation, but the dialogue writer can attain a more vivid illusion of the credible through reference to historical personages. By portraying living and dead figures, the writer relates to the reader fictive discourses that evoke recognizable associations between historical characters and verifiable events. Cicero, Sigonius observes, introduces into his dialogues such actual personages as Cato, P. Africanus, and C. Laelius. The imaginary of fiction fuses with the authenticity of reality; by portraying the respective interlocutor through allusion to the commonly held perceptions of a historical personage, the practitioner utilizes the potentialities of decorum to create a verisimilar illusion.

---

24. "hoc autem poeticum eius est potestatis, atque naturae, ut cum adest, efficiat, ne res, ut est ficta, sic videatur" (58).

The doctrine of decorum that Sigonius borrows from Aristotle is incorporated by Cicero (*Orator* 21.71) into his rhetorical theory, and is integrated by Horace (*Ars poetica* 338–40) into his poetic art. In the first half of the sixteenth century, moreover, such critics as Daniello (Hall 1945, 49), Minturno (Hall 1945, 58), and Cinthio (Hall 1945, 63) continued to apply the precept of decorum to both oratorical compositions and poetic forms, and they argued for a characterization consistent with narrative exposition. In his *Poetices* (1561) Scaliger, for example, states unequivocally that, in depicting "res excellentes," the poet must employ "personas graves" (Weinberg 1961, 2: 745n47). According to Joel Spingarn (1899) and Vernon Hall (1945), factual happenings, persons, conditions, and circumstances provide the material to produce impressions of the plausible: noble deeds and aristocratic, dignified personages form the substance and style of epic and tragedy, whereas middle-class characters and concerns enhance the verisimilitude of the daily, mundane occurrences depicted in comedy. Baxter Hathaway (1962) explains the further importance of decorum in poetic creation; as he sees it (131), the role of decorum is integral to the elucidation of *enargeia*, or vividness, that is useful in particularizing the universal or concretizing the abstract (115).

Within the context of his argument, then, Sigonius stresses the significance of a principle which, originating in rhetorical doctrine, becomes fused with prescriptions of poetic forms. Consequently, dialogic structures incorporate rhetorical precepts and, at the same time, remain within the poetic canons. But as a theorist who aspires to present motifs and techniques employed in dialogue, Sigonius expands the function of decorum to the expectations of verisimilitude. Time and place, he notes, complement characterization. In his *Tusculan Disputations* Cicero situates the dialogue at a specific time (October 16) and in a recognizable place. As questions appropriate for the Senate or the Forum, moreover, would rarely include theoretical discussions of poetry, philosophy, or ethics on holidays, such debates should take place in a *locus amoenus*, or on a rustic estate away from the distractions of political controversies and commercial negotiations.

Besides advocating these applications of decorum to the portrayal of characters and to the description of the setting, Sigonius implies the importance of relating character representation and ideological stance. Plato, he remarks (75), presents Socrates as human and knowledgeable, and he conveys the arrogance and shallowness of such interlocutors as Hippias, Prodicus, and Gorgias. Such character portrayal facilitates Plato's depiction of Socrates's justified triumph in debate. But in spite of this use of characterization, Sigonius, as Snyder (1989, 59–60) points out, does not see Plato's characters as especially decorus. If the subject matter of dialogue touches upon philosophical and political topics, the speakers should include senators, statesmen, and other honorable men of the Republic (84).[25] Cicero, however, selects speakers who, as philosophers and statesmen, occupy a social rank congruent with their background, thoughts, and demeanor. If, however, Cicero's representation of Cato conforms more closely to Renaissance thoughts on decorum, Sigonius (79–80) affirms the essential need to assign arguments to speakers who, through actions and attitudes, reflect a particular thought. Interlocutors are to teach, confirm, refute, and listen, and the description of setting and the topics and circumstances of the discussion determine the respective parts to be expressed. Characters should be associated with their individual views, just as Cicero's interlocutors in De finibus reflect philosophies consistent with their perceived social traits and identified with their thoughts set forth in the dialogue.

Clearly, Sigonius commends the Ciceronian practice of decorum. Plato, according to Sigonius, does not elaborate on the time and place, and occasionally even violates the principle of verisimilitude, but he does appropriate suitable characteristics to the respective speakers. Like Cicero, he employs historical personages and situates them in identifiable locations: in the Republic Socrates goes to Piraeus on a holiday (73); in the Phaedrus Socrates argues with the rhetor Phaedrus along the banks of the Ilissus just outside Athens (90). Interlocutors, moreover, represent particular views; as Sigonius remarks (80), Glaucus, in the Republic, opposes justice in thought and reflects this stance in the dialogue. But as Sigonius implies, Cicero's attention to details conforms to historical and geographical accuracy, thereby affirming the relevance of decorum. And Plato's use of parody contrasts with Cicero's more dignified wit which, enjoyed through anecdotes, ironies, and jokes, corresponds to the serious subjects of philosophy and politics.

25. "Itaque noster ille, qui neminem fere, nisi senatorem, et summis in rep. perfunctum honoribus in dialogos coniecit suos" (ibid).

This shift of emphasis in the creation of verisimilar characters and settings marks a difference in style from the dry disputation of Scholastic debates and the didacticism of medieval colloquies. But decorum also supports and enhances the validity of argumentation, and the representation of respective characters varies according to the sort of debate or discussion presented in the dialogue. As Snyder (1989, 59–60) has demonstrated, Sigonius argues for a dignity of style which Cicero incorporates into his character portrayal and dialectical argumentation. Humanist practitioners may have viewed the expression of Ciceronian dialogue as more consistent with Renaissance tastes. But, as we have seen, Sigonius does not deny the artistic attributes of Platonic dialogue. In fact, since Sigonius stresses the interrelation between the delineation of character and the directions of debate, the sort of discussion and its subsequent structure should be congruent with the thoughts and words of the respective speakers. According to Sigonius (92–93), the levity of Platonic dialogue serves a purpose that touches upon substance. Socratic didacticism results in match-winning, and exaggerated characterization, irony, and language all contribute to the demonstration of a position proposed by Socrates. In brief, Socrates's reasoned restraint in the *Symposium* contrasts with Aristophanes's humorous hiccuping, and therefore establishes a context consistent with the acceptance of his argument. Similarly, Cicero's dignity and seriousness of style complement the structure of analysis recorded in his dialogues.

Whereas Platonic dialogue leads to assertion and affirmation of a single thought, Cicero's examination-arguments dissect and evaluate the issues under discussion. Each interlocutor is correct in his analysis, but, through the limitation of perspective and the controvertible nature of a complex topic, he provokes dissension and discussion. In spite of the inaccuracy that derives from the narrowness of a particular stance, each speaker aspires to argue convincingly for his case. Thus the interlocutor draws upon the rhetor's tricks of the trade; and the poet who portrays these speakers becomes an orator who records the multiple perspectives of an issue. The sort of argument therefore influences the delineation of character. And just as the doctrines of decorum and verisimilitude enable the dialogue writer to create a plausible character consistent with setting and circumstances, the substance of discussion influences the structure of argumentation and, as we shall see, becomes interrelated with the importance of credible characterization.

The notion of decorum thus implies the importance of consistency. Although Sigonius indicates the relevance of historical and geographical accuracy in character delineation, discourse actualizes and enlivens the representation of the respective interlocutor, conveys thought, and thereby reflects the "actions of men" conveyed in dialogue. However, argumentation, or *contentio*, provides the subject matter, and, in spite of characteristics shared by all examples of the genre, disputation determines the structure and strategy for demonstration, debate, or discussion.

Dialectics and the Structures and Strategies of Dialogue

According to Sigonius (55), dialogues are bipartite, consisting of (1) an introduction or *praeparatio*, and (2) a debate or *contentio*. Like the prologue in tragedy and comedy, the *praeparatio* in dialogue introduces the speakers, scene, and the subject to be examined. Besides observing the principle of decorum in the elucidation of character and in the description of time, setting, and circumstances, the dialogue writer attempts to capture the listener's attention and to direct it to the issue to be discussed. Through an examination of Cicero's dialogues, Sigonius distinguishes three approaches: (1) the asking of a direct question in a restrained way ("modeste"); (2) an indirect broaching of a topic, by which the speakers in the *Brutus*, for example, talk initially about literary debts and move naturally into a discussion on rhetoric; and (3) a combination of the direct and indirect introductions, where, for instance, the interlocutors in the *De natura deorum* gather socially on a religious holiday to engage in a discussion about the existence of the gods. This introduction of speakers and topic leads into the discussion, and at the same time forms the basis of the conclusion that summarizes the proofs or arguments.

A debate, or *contentio*, on a philosophical or political topic comprises the second, and central, structural segment of the dialogue. The question raised in the introduction (*propositio*) becomes now the topic to be analyzed and tested (*probatio*). Like the story in a fictional work, the *contentio* is a disputation that becomes the soul of dialogue. But if the *contentio* recalls the narratives recounted in epic and drama, the relationship between rhetoric and dialectics cannot be dismissed. Like Aristotle who defines rhetoric as the counterpart of dialectics (*Rhetoric* 1.1), Sigonius sets forth the significance of rhetorical techniques and dialectical disputation. In practicing the rhetorical precept of decorum, the dialogue writer enhances the plausibility of character and setting and thereby induces the credibility of an argument. But according to both Sigonius and Aristotle, the aim of rhetoric goes beyond an appeal to the emotions. For Aristotle, argumentation provides the substance of rhetorical expression that results in the affirmation or refutation of a thesis or the demonstration or elaboration of an idea. Similarly, Sigonius sees the *contentio* as a disputation "to be confirmed or refuted" (56).[26] The syllogism of the logician and the *enthymeme* of the orator become for Aristotle (*Rhetoric* 2.1) the dialectical ploys to persuade and, for Sigonius (119), the tools and techniques to debate.

A consistent application of thematics determines the structure and style of dialogue. In establishing a taxonomy of the genre, Sigonius seems to be borrowing from Diogenes Laertius's earlier classifications. Dialogue, according to Laertius, may be used for the demonstration of knowledge or for an inquiry into an issue. As an instrument of instruction, dialogue may present theoretical (for example, scientific or logical) information, or it may examine (for example, ethical or political) questions. As a tool of inquiry, the genre assumes two forms. The first type of inquiry aims at the training of the mind and, divided into two subgenres, recalls the Platonic discourses of the "midwife's art" (*maieutic*) or the "merely tentative" (*peirastic*) (Diogenes Laertius, "Life of Plato," 3:49; Hicks 1966, 1:321). The second sort of investigatory dialogue is employed in debates and controversies; intended to win verbal contests, it raises objections to, or undermines the validity of, the primary proposition. In spite of these variations of form and purpose, dialectics is the method that, whether expounding knowledge or examining opinion, decides the strategy and subsequent shape of argumentation.

A reading of Plato's dialogues leads Diogenes Laertius to his categorization of dialogue into two types of discourse that, in turn, recalls Aristotle's definition of arguments. In his *Sophistical*

---

26. "Contentio, qui *agōn* graece dicitur, est quidquid verborum de re ad disputandum proposita vel confirmandi vel refellandi gratia fit" (56).

Refutations (165a–165b) Aristotle distinguishes didactic argument from dialectical disputation. Didactic argument presents the existence, causes, and consequences of an incontrovertible topic and thereby parallels Laertius's description of the substance and style of dialogues of instruction. A thesis or principle emerges from the initial proposition, and then through analysis of the subject the interlocutors demonstrate to the reader or listener the validity of the opening statement. Dialectical disputations, which call to mind Laertius's dialogues of inquiry, assume three forms. The first sort, which Aristotle terms *eristic*, is composed of questions that, requiring affirmative or negative responses, proceed to refute and eventually deny the validity of a generally accepted thesis. As we shall see, eristic debate was often associated with "match-winning" dialogues, and it parallels Plato's concept of the *maieutic*, or "midwife's art," dialogue. Examination-arguments, which exemplify the second type of dialogue of inquiry, assume the label of *peirastic* discussions. Like eristic debates, such arguments drive the respondent to an *elenchus* or yes-and-no replies, and thus often duplicate the structure of eristic debates. But the nature of the topic being discussed does not permit the validation of a particular premise. Like didactic or demonstrative dialogues, examination-arguments analyze aspects and explore the facets of a topic. But since the subjects of these arguments deal with speculative questions (for example, political and ethical issues), such inquiries probe into areas of human experience but cannot demonstrate, or instruct in, irrefutable information (such as, mathematics, astronomy, or music). Sophistical debates comprise Aristotle's third type of dialectical argument. Practitioners of this sort of disputation, though, misuse dialectics. Unlike eristic arguments, in which interlocutors deny the soundness of an accepted but false premise, speakers in sophistical debates argue for, and conclude in the validity of, the untrue opening proposition.

Laertius recognizes the poetic or fictional qualities of dialogue ("Life of Plato" 3:50 and 56). The grouping of Plato's works, he notes, brings to mind the dramatic plan of three tragedies followed by a satiric play; indeed, Plato has been classified as a tragic poet. The exploration of philosophical topics, moreover, does not preclude concerns for character portrayal and diction: in fact, the relevance of character representation to both dramatist and dialogist implicitly classifies the craft of dialogue writing as a poetic art. But in stressing the philosophical and political themes that characterize the genre, Laertius does not expand upon its fictional attributes. Later, both Cicero (*De partitione oratoria* 67) and Seneca (*Epistolae* 95.1) affirm the didacticism inherent in dialogue, and see it as a *praeceptiva philosophica* which, as a method of instruction, denotes the pedagogical intention of Plato's Socratic and Cicero's philosophical dialogues (Ruch 1958, 71; Wilson 1985, 34). Pedagogy, however, encompasses a comprehensive range of subjects, and Laertius's compilation of Plato's works attest to the encyclopedic scope of the subject matter appropriate to the genre ("Life of Plato" 3.49–62). A demonstrative, treatiselike presentation of physics, logic, mathematics, and music, for example, is as suitable to dialogue as refutative, occasionally comic undercutting of moral concepts and beliefs. Thus the thematics of dialogue accommodates both complex, ponderous explanations of the nature of things (for example, Plato's *Timaeus* or Tyard's *Solitaire second*) and analytical discourses on government (such as, Plato's *Laws* or Brués's *Dialogues*). Form complements function; according to Laertius, certain structures seem more suitable to various topics ("Life of Plato" 3:49). Within these structures, however, practitioners exercise flexibility that assures an appropriate expression of individual concept. Consequently, the genre excludes neither the comic scenes in Plato's analysis of love in the *Symposium* nor sharp, polemical attacks in the philosophical and political discussions in Cicero's *Brutus* (218) (Diogenes Laertius, "Ariston" 7.163; Ruch 1958, 53–54).

Sigonius's observations on the stylistic differences in the dialogues of Plato, Xenophon, and Cicero indicate his awareness of the license and latitude that writers enjoyed in order to shape individual vision to expected form. But for Sigonius too the interrelation of form and theme enables the dialogue writer to select and employ effective argumentative structures. The practitioner, he observes, employs dialogue to distinguish knowledge from opinion. Knowledge, though, is based upon demonstration, or true and primary premises. In explaining these scientifically verifiable truths, philosophers profess their learning through *expositio*, or demonstrative dialogue. Initially, a subject is proposed, and the philosopher-interlocutor elaborates upon the topic through elucidation of its complexities and refutation of possible misunderstandings. Analysis leads to a synthesis that establishes, through the prior explanation, the validity of the premise. Normally, topics such as mathematics, music, natural science, dialectics, and astronomy lend themselves to this type of argument. Colloquies that employ the brief questions posed by a pupil and the lengthier explanations provided by the teacher would certainly provide an appropriate structure for this sort of dialogue.

Sigonius, however, encounters the epistemological difficulty of excluding from demonstrative dialogue topics that cannot be fully verified but that inform human understanding based upon faith. In other words, the discussions of nature in Plato's *Timaeus*, beauty in his *Phaedrus*, immortality of soul in his *Phaedo*, and justice in his *Laws* may seem to present arguments on controvertible topics. But since they reflect premises predicated on faith, they are for Sigonius examples of instructive or didactic arguments. *Expositio*, then, shares characteristics with, but goes beyond the thematic dimensions of, colloquies that recapitulate knowledge. Form, moreover, reflects subject matter.

Demonstrative dialogue opens with a proposition and, through the instruments of logic, investigates and discloses the consequences of the premise. Although the sort of proposed question may require the use of demonstrative dialogue, approach to the question and the validity of arguments proceeding from such certain instruments of reason as syllogism, definition, causes, and effects characterize this sort of didactic discourse. Thus, the precepts are not necessarily true. But the ramifications of an argument can result in the discovery of a principle that explains, and supports faith in the validity of, the opening premise. For example, beauty in the world induces belief that the world is beautiful; beauty is eternal; therefore, the world reflects and thereby becomes an example ("simulachrum") of beauty and eternity. Approach and method, then, determine the limits of demonstrative dialogue or didactic argument. And through his tools of investigation, or logic, the philosopher can instruct in, and explain, both verifiable fact and probable belief. *Inquisitio* differs from demonstrative dialogue in topics, aims, techniques, and structure. Whereas *expositio* presents the analysis of a philosophical principle premised on knowledge or belief, *inquisitio* is an investigation into generally accepted opinions on such questions as ethics, rhetoric, and politics. This examination into probable or even possible premises results in disputation rather than demonstration, and offers two intentions: match-winning and truth-hunting. The dialogue writer who creates *inquisitio* does not assume the stance of a philosopher who explains the nature and ramifications of a proposition. Rather, he becomes a dialectician who employs oratorical arguments and rhetorical techniques that enable him to prove a point or to investigate conflicting thoughts regarding an issue. Besides the tools of logic employed by the philosopher in demonstrative dialogue, the *enthymeme* becomes essential in convincing the reader of the validity of a thought. In spite of the impossibility of determining the certainty and consequences of a proposition, *inquisitio* does advance understanding, for dialectics provides the argumentative means to substantiate or refute a premise and to elucidate varying aspects of the subject being discussed. Sigonius's two sorts of *inquisitio* correspond to Aristotle's definitions of dialectical disputations and examination-arguments. Dialectical arguments are "match-winning," or eristic, in nature; Sigonius terms this type of debate *obstetricus*, or *maieutic*, or art-of-the-midwife dialogue. Socratic method characterizes the approach which, as described in Plato's *Theaetetus* (150b–151a), argues against an accepted premise through a series of sharp questions. Socrates, acting as antagonist, confesses ignorance and abstains from the position of any opening proposition. Through his contradiction of the other interlocutors' assertions, he compels the respondents to deny their statements and to admit their ignorance. Their recognition of confused conceptions is, in fact, a realization of "many fair things" within themselves. According to Sigonius, Plutarch in his *Platonic Questions* attributes two consequences of this approach: refutation of sophistic learning, and training of minds in effective disputation. Sigonius, though, sees this argumentative strategy as another vehicle for the advancement of human understanding. The elenchus that characterizes eristic dialogue leads to the refutation of a belief, reflects a negative approach to learning, and thereby contrasts with the matter-of-fact presentation and description of knowledge in demonstrative dialogue. In spite of the differences of method, both sorts of dialogue guide the interlocutors and readers to a deeper, more accurate understanding of the respective topic. But whereas demonstrative dialogue sets forth information, Socrates, in his dialectical disputations, employs questions to indicate and affirm the inaccuracy of the initial accepted premise and the confused reasoning of his interlocutors.

The second sort of *inquisitio*, which Sigonius labels *tentativa*, recalls Aristotle's description of examination-arguments, and corresponds to a type of dialogic discourse defined in Plato's *Protagoras* (337e–338a). As inquiries into accepted premises, examination-arguments take the form of peirastic or "truth-hunting" dialogues that intend to revoke the complexities of a topic based upon general knowledge. Although differing in aim and structure from "match-winning," or eristic, disputations, examination-arguments share stylistic characteristics of demonstrative dialogue and maieutic method. Like didactic dialogues, they present a discussion of insights into a particular topic through dignified language and serious attitude. Examination-arguments, though, are investigatory, and the initial questions elude complete explanations. Extensive speeches posit perspectives. But since the topics are not predicated upon logically verifiable premises, insights may appear contradictory, and the pointed questions that distinguish eristic debate also deflate the respective positions. Besides the rhetorical techniques and dialectical strategies associated with *inquisitio*, induction provides, in both "match-winning" debates and "truth-hunting" dialogues, an elenchus which Socrates uses to entrap his opponent, and which results in the delineation of a position. In driving his respondent to a confession of ignorance in such peirastic dialogues as Plato's *Gorgias* and *Republic* 1, Socrates combats sophistry and, through an analysis of conflicting views, directs the reader to a clearer understanding of the topic. Thus, like Xenophon's *De re familiari* that combines both the didactic techniques of explanation and the incisive reasoning of eristic debates, peirastic dialogues reveal the complexities of a speculative issue through extended speeches ("perpetua oratione") and elucidating questions ("luculentis interrogationibus") (161).

Although Aristotle's classification of arguments informs the thematic and formal structures of Sigonius's categorization of dialogues, sixteenth-century theorizations of the genre require a study of extant texts. In his description of the sorts of possible arguments, Sigonius relies upon Plato's dialogues to exemplify Aristotle's types of disputation. Ultimately, for Sigonius, the validity of the premise determines the shape of expression. Propositions that are logically verifiable or rationally assumed recall, respectively, Plato's higher epistemological certainties of truth and belief, and they correspond to the ascertainable topics defined in

Aristotle's *Posterior Analytics*. Such subjects call for explanation; since contention of the validity of the premise is irrelevant, the philosopher-dialogist draws upon the resources of demonstrative dialogue (*expositio*) to delineate the intricacies and consequences of the initial statement. As we have seen, the refutability of topics in dialectical dialogues and examination-arguments (*inquisitio*) derives from propositions predicated upon Plato's lower epistemological levels of opinion and sense perception, and these subjects suggest the sorts of topics presented in Aristotle's *Prior Analytics*. In both of these types of dialogue the writer assumes the tasks of dialectician-dialogist who, through persuasive argumentation, attempts to disprove a premise or to present varying views of an issue.

Cicero, according to Sigonius, imitates Platonic and Aristotelian modes of argumentation. But instead of elaborating upon demonstrative, dialectical, and peirastic types of discourse, Cicero denotes only two patterns: "open" and "obscure," which seem to correspond respectively to Sigonius's classifications of *expositio* and *inquisitio*. Unlike his predecessors, moreover, Cicero does not distinguish degrees of certainty that determine the argumentative approaches and structural designs. Rather, as K. J. Wilson (1985) has remarked, "the former [Platonic method] is perhaps better suited to the *discovery* of the truth, while the latter [Ciceronian method] is concerned with the disposition or *presentation* of knowledge" (34).

Explanation characterizes the "open" sort of dialogue. Resembling colloquies, this type of discourse takes the form of a *magister-discipulus* exchange, where the authority of the teacher's voice is maintained, and where all information is expressed fully and clearly. Further, if thematic substance determines the argumentative discourse and structural shape of Platonic dialogue, style defines the forms of Ciceronian discourse. In his *De partitione oratoria*, for example, the master instructs his pupil in the aims, approaches, functions, and techniques of rhetoric. Such a topic could incite questions and discussions. But whereas Plato has Socrates debate these issues in an eristic dialogue, such as the *Gorgias*, Cicero presents information inherent in the topic. Conjecture cannot be avoided; in the *Brutus*, for example, another "open" dialogue that examines rhetorical issues, the questions ensuing from doubts are answered. Through explanations and relevant examples, then, the teacher resolves conflicting thoughts, and by elaborating upon the issue he illustrates the meaning of the topic and expands his pupil's knowledge. Sigonius, though, continues to stress the idea that dialogue is not a treatise. In the *De amicitia*, for instance, characters may be restricted in participation, but the teacher sustains the conflict of ideas and the verisimilitude of a fictitious setting through the use of similarities, oppositions, contradictions, and collateral circumstances.

If the style of Cicero's "open" dialogue parallels the structure required by Aristotle's demonstrative argumentation, Sigonius's notion of the "obscure" dialogue recalls characteristics of peirastic discourse. Like examination-arguments, "obscure" dialogues present various insights into a particular issue and, according to Sigonius, resemble the aims and functions of *inquisitio*. But if explanation typifies "open" dialogue, disputation forms the structure of "obscure" dialogue. A question is proposed, and is analyzed *in utramque partem* (166).

In arguing his case, each respective interlocutor contends most vigorously ("acerrime") (167), employing every possible dialectical and rhetorical technique. Style and structure distinguish Platonic peirastic discourse from Ciceronian "obscure" dialogues. Whereas Plato blends short statements with longer explanations, Cicero has each speaker defend his position through extended discussions. The subject being examined eludes resolution; in such dialogues as *De finibus*, *De natura deorum*, *De fato*, and *De oratore*, refutation disproves the validity of the other arguments. According to Sigonius, this sort of dialogue teaches less forthrightly ("obscurius") than the other type that presents explanations (161). Further, as each presentation argues for a particular position, validity of the discourse depends upon the probability of, or the credibility in, the respective statement. Besides the tools of the logician, the tricks of the rhetorician assist each interlocutor. And the doctrine of decorum plays a significant role in the representation of character, speech, and setting, and thereby reinforces the substantiability of both corroborating and conflicting arguments.

In his distinctions between "open" and "obscure" dialogues, Sigonius summarizes Ciceronian thoughts. The "open" sort of dialogue, according to Cicero, was practiced by Gorgias and other Sophists, and it resembles a formal lecture on a topic which, prompted by an "invited question" ("poscere questionem"), is discussed and dissected by a single interlocutor (*De finibus* 2.1–3). But if Plato's later dialogues seem to conform to this model, Socrates, as Cicero notes, ridicules this form and prefers a method of cross-examination that elicits from others opinions to be debated, refuted, and eventually replaced by Socrates's own views. This type of dialogue recalls Laertius's description of dialogues of inquiry and Aristotle's delineation of the three sorts of dialectical arguments (eristic, peirastic, and sophistical refutation). Dialogues of instruction and inquiry conclude with an assenting thesis. Cicero, though, offers a third pattern: *disputatio in utramque partem*. In his *Tusculan Disputations* (2.1.1–3) he sees the elusiveness of truth and affirms the need to examine all sides of an issue. Like the speakers in peirastic dialogues, or examination-arguments, the philosopher-interlocutors in Cicero's dialogues seek a probable truth. But unlike Socrates's use of such a strategy that drives his opponent to an elenchus, Cicero rejects the possibility of assigning a conclusive answer to ethical or political questions. Thus his interlocutors resemble orators who, through use of their acquired skills in argumentation, attempt to explore all aspects of the assumptions and pronouncements of a topic defying resolution.

For Cicero, dialogue is a vehicle to express philosophy, "the content of which has few judges" (*Tusculan Disputations* 2.1.4; King 1950, 149). Accordingly, he discards the aims and methods of inquiry in Plato's works, and defines this third sort of dialogue as a form "in whose books nothing is stated positively and there is much arguing both *pro* and *contra*, all things are inquired into and no certain statement is made" (*Academica* 1.12.46; Rackham 1967, 455). By positing probable beliefs, this peirastic type of dialogue, which Cicero attributes to Aristotle (*De finibus* 5.4.10), seeks to examine opinions. Truth remains elusive; and, as Cicero states toward the end of the *Academica* (2.3.7–8; Rackham 1967, 475), "the sole object of our discussion is by arguing on both sides, to draw out and give shape to some result that may either be true or to the nearest approximation of the truth." Like Plato, Cicero employs dialectics. But he replaces Plato's absolute determinations with relative conclusions. After a prologue each interlocutor, including the author, presents and maintains a particular opinion (*De oratore* 3.80). Subsequent speakers argue for and against the statement, accepting the valid and disputing the controvertible.

By analyzing both sides of an issue the dialogue writer offers a thesis and antithesis which calls for a summary presented by the moderator.

In alluding to the Ciceronian disputation *in utramque partem*, Sigonius stresses the importance of the interrelation between rhetoric and dialectics in sixteenth-century dialogue. As we have seen, the nature of the topic that is debated or discussed determines the sort of argumentation to be employed. Premises may be controvertible or incontrovertible. For Sigonius, the resources of rhetoric strengthen style and enhance credibility in all dialogic discourse. But *inquisitio*, or the sort of dialogue that examines controvertible issues, presents problems of definition. Plato employs eristic and peirastic forms to debate such subjects; his dialogues, in relying upon adept uses of reasoning and irony, record the dynamics of a discussion intended to discover truth and to posit an absolute. Such an approach affirms the significance of dialectics in dialogue. And, like Aristotle's depiction of the rhetor who draws upon the technique of dialectics, Plato's Socrates employs in both "match-winning" debates and "truth-hunting" discussions the definitions, syllogisms, enthymemes, examples, and other tools of the orator-cum-dialectician.

Cicero assumes a more cautious stance. The controvertible nature of such arguments eludes resolution, and dialogues that analyze issues *in utramque partem* recall the Peripatetic method of presenting all sides of a question (*Tusculan Disputations* 2.9). The reserved skepticism inherent in such discussions contrasts with the closures in Platonic debates. Like Plato, Cicero sees the dialogue writer as both dialectician and rhetorician. But the controvertible conclusions of dialogues *in utramque partem* seem to present problems of persuasion that go beyond Socrates's agile argumentation and linguistic manipulations. For Cicero, credibility appears a more realistic end than the conviction that results in Platonic discourse. Thus the conventions of verisimilitude, tried and tested in other poetic forms, become essential in the dialogue writer's arsenal of tricks; by creating an illusion of truth, they induce belief and prompt persuasion.

In his *De oratore* (3.21.80) Cicero identifies the ideal orator as the ideal philosopher, and he observes that the presentation of opposing views of an issue is the duty of "the one and only true and perfect orator" (8.21.80; Sutton and Rackham 1960, 2:65). Si-

gonius would certainly agree. Through his analysis of the structures and strategies of Platonic and Ciceronian discourse, he too
elevates the dialogue writer to the stature of philosopher-orator.
Eloquence distinguishes dialogue from disputation. And through
his insistence on the complementary functions of rhetoric and dialectics, dialogue writers become practitioners of a form that conveys the certainties and controversies of a subject through the
plays and ploys of oratorical craft.

Summary

Bernard Weinberg (1961) has observed that Sigonius's "total
theory of dialogue is really a theory of decorum" (1:484). Renaissance critics would have concurred with this assessment; if the
principle of decorum requires practitioners to satisfy expectations
of consistency and appropriateness, Sigonius denotes the relationship between style and substance. Admittedly, Sigonius treats individually and separately the *verba* that are expressed through the
demonstrative explanations or dialectical disputations of philosophical or political topics. But the exclusion of overly abstract
elements or inappropriate description calls attention to the need
to match concrete character delineation and accurate geographical,
historical settings with the arguments recounted in dialogue. As
we have seen, moreover, substance influences the strategy and
structure of the debate. In borrowing, via Diogenes Laertius, Aristotle's taxonomy of arguments, Sigonius sees that incontrovertible
evidence should be presented through *expositio*, or demonstrative
dialogue. Controvertible evidence, on the other hand, calls for *inquisitio*, or an investigation into opinions that evolve from probable or possible premises. Such disputations may take the form of
"match-winning" (eristic) debates or "truth-hunting" (peirastic)
explorations employed by Plato and reworked by Cicero. In every
case, though, dialogue is a didactic genre which, inducing a credible illusion, explains knowledge or reveals divergent but connected aspects of an issue. Toward the end of the treatise Sigonius
alludes again to the poetic nature of dialogue. As comedy results
from ridiculous and amorous characters, and as tragedy evolves
from unfortunate and noble personages, dialogue presents,
through the speech of others, a harmonious blending of contentions that reveals an insight into divine happenings, and leads to

an understanding of daily existence and to a training of intellectual faculties. Lucian, in ridiculing his subjects, corrupts this intention, whereas practitioners who employ wit and humor as defined by Hermogenes contribute to the creation of the verisimilar and to the elucidation of argumentation. Decorum, then, provides the precept that shapes Sigonius's theorization. Consistency of words and thoughts prevails, for, through their reflection of perceived reality and expressed ideas, characters enunciate a discourse that links the demands of poetic invention with the coherence of logical argumentation.

In this reconstruction of the notion of ancient dialogue, Sigonius goes beyond a defense and definition of the genre as a poetic art. His reading of the works of Plato, Xenophon, and Cicero enables him to propose characteristics that reflect critical expectations and set forth practical prescriptions. Within the limits of appropriate themes, styles, and structure, however, the practitioner works creatively and freely. For Sigonius, dialogue is a poetic genre that expresses philosophical content. But if characters become associated with their respective ideas, they become representatives of, and tools for, argumentation. Decorum and verisimilitude enhance credibility; Sigonius, like his humanist contemporaries, sees the importance of plausible characterization in the confirmation or refutation of a premise. Dialogue, then, shares this quality with oratory, but Sigonius seems to emphasize the significance of verisimilitude that enables both the dialogue writer and the dramatist to create a logical and necessary action. Oratory persuades, and dialogue, according to Sigonius (12–13), declares. But if Sigonius's description of the rhetorical techniques and argumentative approaches employed in Platonic and Ciceronian dialogues denote the characteristics of a humanist genre defended and defined, individual examples do not necessarily conform to these theoretical assertions. Thus, Sigonius proposes a doctrine that sets forth a framework but calls for the elaboration of a theory adapting precept to practice.

✿ Enlarging the Form

Torquato Tasso

In his *Discorso dell'arte del dialogo* (1586) Torquato Tasso reinforces the thoughts on dialogue previously proposed by Le Caron and Sigonius. In fact, this brief description of dialogue recalls, in organization and argumentation, the more expansive and detailed treatise of his teacher of rhetoric at Padua, Carolus Sigonius. Tasso's statement, though, is not a slavish recapitulation of earlier ideas. First, he does not explicitly defend dialogue as a poetic kind. Ancient practice, medieval disputation, and humanist imitation of classical models have established the validity and vitality of the genre, and Sigonius's examination of poetic imitation and its application to dialogue justifies its placement in the poetic canons. Further, in 1574 Sperone Speroni had defended his dialogues before a papal court and, in his subsequently published *Apologia dei dialoghi*, had argued for the moral and social usefulness of the genre.[27] Sigonius's theorizations and Speroni's defense inform Tasso's thoughts on dialogue. But instead of writing an apologetic discourse or an aesthetic analysis, Tasso elaborates on the stylistic characteristics of the genre which, through an enlargement of the form, enable the accommodation of individual expression to theoretical expectations.

27. For an analysis of Speroni's defense of dialogue, *Apologia dei dialoghi*, which was originally presented orally in Rome in 1574, see Snyder (1989, chap. 3).

Imitation and a Blending of Genres

By organizing his treatise into the tripartite structure of imitation, types of argumentation, and style, Tasso examines the topics treated by Sigonius. Although Tasso does not deviate from previously proposed tenets, his observations on imitation and style indicate a broadening of Sigonius's prescriptions that shape conceptions to expressions.[28] Through a reading of numerous dialogues, Tasso defines the genre as "an imitation of a discussion, made in prose for the benefit of civil and speculative men, and . . . it needs no stage or theater" (Lord and Trafton 1982, 41).[29] Dialogue is a distinct and established literary kind that differs from drama. Whereas drama enacts "deeds [proper] to active men," dialogue records "discourses proper to speculative men" (19).[30] In spite of these distinguishing features, dialogue, like drama, is a sort of poetic imitation; and, as Tasso's readings confirm, it shares characteristics with comedy and tragedy. For example, through the characterization of Hippias, Prodicus, Protagoras, Gorgias, Agathon, and others, Plato injects comedy into his dialogues. Conversely, the tragic is perceived in his *Laws*. A blurring of genres results. Drama may include debates and discussions. In adhering to Aristotelian thought, Tasso insists that "tragedies and comedies . . . imitate actions" (21).[31] And the dialogue writer, in recording discussions, incorporates action into his works. Such a view of poetic representation implies the converging and intermingling of genres. But, ultimately, the object of imitation distinguishes drama from dialogue; for in drama, speculative discourse is subordinate to action,

28. Snyder (1989, chap. 4), Lord and Trafton (1982), and Baldassari (1971) discuss the major themes of Tasso's treatise and the ideas that inform his writing of dialogues. Although Snyder sees the work as a response to Castelvetro's remarks on dialogue, none of the critics sees Tasso's theory as an expansion of form designed to accommodate poetic innovation to the restrictions of structure as prescribed in Sigonius's reconstruction of the theory of ancient dialogue.

29. "imitazione di ragionamento fatto in prosa per giovamento degli uomini civili e speculativi, per la qual cagione egli non ha bisogno di scena o di palco" (*Discorso dell'arte del dialogo*, 1586, 40).

30. "Due saran dunque i primi generi dell'imitazione; l'un dell'azione, nel qual son rassomigliati gli operanti; l'altro delle parole, nel quale sono introdotti i ragionanti" (18).

31. "le tragedie e le comedie propriamente sono l'imitazioni dell'azioni" (20).

and "in a dialogue the action is more or less adjunct to the discussion" (21).[32]

Tasso, then, retains Sigonius's boundaries dividing dialogue from drama, and like his teacher he states that "what the plot is to a poem, . . . the subject of debate is to a dialogue: its form and, as it were, its soul" (25).[33] But if the object of imitation determines generic classification, creativity requires the blending of forms. Plato and Lucian, according to Tasso, transcribe a reasoning that is dramatically expressed. Cicero "speaks in his own voice and, like a historian, narrates what this character says and what that one replies" (19).[34] In presenting discussions that touch upon moral and civic or upon speculative issues, dialogues examine topics associated with historical, political, philosophical, and scientific writings. And although dialogue is not enacted on stage, it is poetic in its mimetic art and thereby admits the use of imaginary scenes, characters, images, and speech.

Through this description of dialogue both as a distinct literary kind and as a poetic form employed secondarily in drama and history, Tasso expands Sigonius's more rigid definitions. Prescriptions denote characteristics, but individual vision and creativity lead to an effective use of dialogue. Such a flexibility and expansion of the form recall earlier definitions advanced by Julius Caesar Scaliger. As we have seen, Scaliger sees dialogue as a genre with fixed and accepted attributes. Dialogue, though, is not confined to the structures of disputation. As a mode of imitation, dialogue is the means whereby the poet conveys the words of portrayed personages. For both Tasso and Scaliger, the poet molds vision to form. The imitation of discussion results in the writing of debate and disputation which identifies the literary kind of dialogue. The representation of deeds and actions, on the other hand, characterizes drama. But in both forms the speech of others is integral to appropriate expression. In brief, it is the object of imitation that determines the form of expression, and that decides the use of dialogue as a poetic form or as a mimetic mode in other genres.

32. "ma ne' dialogi l'azione è quasi per giunta de' ragionamenti" (ibid).
33. "e quale è la favola nel poema, tale è nel dialogo la quisitione; e dico la sua forma e quasi l'anima" (24).
34. "conservando l'autore la sua persona, come istorico narra qual che disse il tale e 'l cotale; e questi ragionamenti si possono domandare istorici o narrativi; e tali son per lo più quelli di Cicerone" (18).

The process of imitation is central to Scaliger's thoughts on dialogue as a generic form and mimetic technique. Poetic imitation, he asserts (*Poetices libri septem* 1561, 80; Weinberg 1961, 2:744–45), does not adhere necessarily to the prescriptions of structure and style compiled in the handbooks. Form proceeds from vision, and words represent things that reflect the higher Ideal. Images of the Idea are found in nature and are perceived by the poet; and words employed by the poet become the material which, through appropriate styles, are conveyed to the reader. Scaliger recognizes the need to shape perception to intelligible form, and he stresses the significance of verisimilitude and decorum for effective expression. Gods and heroes, for example, are personages associated with tragedy and epic, and elevated speech is consistent with their social roles. Within these general constrictions, however, the poet in general and the dialogue writer in particular convey the *res* of reality through the *verba* of expression. As Scaliger states, "These things, which are thus constituted by nature, must be discovered in the bosom of nature and, selected and plucked out therefrom, must be exposed before the eyes of men" ("sub oculis hominum") (1561, 83; Weinberg 1961, 2:746).[35]

For Scaliger, genres are *verba* that in theory express the respective *res* or object of imitation (1561, 6–12; Weinberg 1961, 2:745–46). Individual characteristics, he contends, distinguish one literary kind from another; like his contemporaries who link the doctrine of decorum with the uses of genres, Scaliger defines a relationship between the object of representation and the appropriate form of expression. For example, a grand style conveys nobility of character which, in turn, the reader-spectator expects in tragedy or epic. But the poet, in keeping his prospective audience in mind, does not diverge from the prescriptions associated with rhetorical principles. Rather, in representing an object of imitation drawn from nature, the poet attempts to attain qualities of logic, utility, and pleasure. Four principles assure the intelligible ordering, moral effectiveness, and stylistic suitability of the material: (1) "prudentia," or a plausible disposition of the subject matter; (2) "varietas," or a creative blending of accepted forms; (3) "suavitas," or an appropriate or decorous use of style; and (4) "efficacia," or an effec-

---

35. "Haec quae natura ita constant, in Naturae sinu inuestiganda, atque inde eruta sub oculis hominum subiicienda erunt."

tive representation of the object of imitation (1561, 113–20; Weinberg 1961, 2:747). Form, then, evolves from these principles, and genres, like tropes, techniques, and words, are tools or modes that afford adequate expression of the mimetic object. According to Scaliger, (1561, Bk. 3, especially p. 83; Weinberg 1961, 2:746), the Idea conceived and subsequently conveyed by the poet takes precedence over defined and established structures. Through a selection of a genre or several genres, the poet expresses an individual vision in an intelligible aesthetic form. As Weinberg (1961, 2:743–50), Guillén (1971, 132, 383, 404), and Colie (1973, 27–29) have told us, genres reflect both prescribed forms classified and canonized by theorists and conventional modes combined and used by practitioners to express selected material. In both cases genres provide a literary system that results in effective communication. Some literary kinds exist as discrete, distinguishable structures that denote fixed forms (for example, tragedy, comedy, epigram, sonnet); individually, they may serve to convey the poet's perception. Other genres (for example, pastoral, paradox, satire) defy such rigid arrangements and, in rendering a particular vision, combine with other structures that demonstrate the predominance of theme over form. Genres therefore become modes of expression that produce a mixed form (for example, the sonnet in Shakespeare's *Romeo and Juliet* 1.5.96–110). S. K. Heninger (1989, 200–222) notes numerous inconsistencies in Scaliger's theory of mimesis that question Weinberg's description of this critic as an "orderly thinker" (1961, 2:744). In spite of the difficulties in describing his process of imitation or in designating and defining the *res*, the critic must still note Scaliger's conclusion: "Poets shape all things when they shape their vision" (347; Heninger 1989, 218).[36] And, as Heninger himself points out, Scaliger's poet "uses language to paint word pictures" (218). Poetic forms afford the representation of such a discourse which, individually employed or creatively blended, reflects a respective vision, and which explains and justifies the uniqueness of specific works.

Tasso stops short of defining genre as a poetic mode, and in his *Discorsi dell'arte poetica* (1587) affirms the presence of fixed and invariable characteristics of literary kinds. As Weinberg indicates, the poet, according to Tasso, discovers the object of imitation in

36. "Haec igitur omnia quum poetae opera effingantur."

nature. The epic poet, in particular, does not imagine a fictitious image; rather, he selects from historical records certain events that furnish the subject matter. In sum, "the poet chooses a 'materia' which by its 'natura' contains the 'dispositio' to receive the 'qualitas' of the 'forma'" (Weinberg 1961, 2:649). Thus the object of imitation provides the poetic vision and, through its individual characteristics, determines the structure and style of expression.

Like Scaliger, Tasso sees poetic invention as a process of selection. But if the object of imitation guides the poet in the effective employment of generic structure and stylistic expression, Tasso does not overlook the significance of poetic artistry. As he states at the beginning of the treatise, the poet is "to select such matter as will be capable of receiving in itself that most excellent form which the artistry of the poet will seek to introduce into it" (Weinberg 1961, 2:649).[37] Poetry, then, is not a photographic re-presentation of an event, and Tasso assigns to the poet the duties of instructing, and moving the passions of, the reader. In his expanded *Discorsi del poema eroico* (1594/1959), he defines the ends of poetry as those of profit and delight (498–503). Poetic creation, he asserts, is a philosophy that instructs in morals and in the truths of life. But pleasure enhances the worth of instruction and induces the reader to pursue the activity. Tasso's interpretation of this Horatian dictum, though, goes beyond an insistence on the didacticism of poetry. The poet, in affording pleasure, affects the reader's emotions. And through an artistic presentation of the respective object of imitation, he injects a vividness of "marvelous things" that results in a pleasurable appreciation of thought and in a constructive stimulation of the passions (*Poema eroico* 502–3, 537–42).

Adherence to the doctrine of verisimilitude and the representation of extraordinary actions and marvelous images enable the poet to fulfill the didactic aim of poetry through delight. The poet is "a maker of images"; and, like Scaliger's description of verse, the poet's creation becomes a "speaking picture."[38] But the fantastic must be restrained by the credible. By basing his work on some true action, the poet creates a probable situation that assures the

37. "à sceglier materia tale, che sia atta à receuer' in se quella più eccellente forma, che l'artificio del Poeta cercarà d'introdurui." (*Arte poetica* 1).

38. "Laonde quantunque il poeta sia facitor de gl'idoli, ciò non si dee intendere ne l'istesso significato nel qual si dice che il sofista è fabro de gl'idoli; ma dobbiam dir più tosto che sia facitore de l'imagini a guisa d'un parlante pittore" (*Poema eroico* 528).

reader's acceptance. Poetry shares characteristics of both dialectics and rhetoric (*Poema eroico* 528–33). Unlike the Sophist, Tasso's poet does not create images that lack aspects of accepted reality. And unlike the Scholastic, he does not instruct solely through demonstrations. The marvelous therefore distinguishes poetry from historical or scientific writing and, along with the constraints of verisimilitude, results in profit and pleasure. The epic poet, in particular, exercises a necessary license; in respecting the Aristotelian demands of completeness, proper magnitude, and unity, he injects incidents and images of the marvelous that delight and more effectively instruct.

Tasso's comments on the characteristics of epic complement and elucidate his observations on the form and uses of dialogue. In defining dialogue as the imitation of discussions, Tasso sets forth a framework for this genre. As we have seen, he includes in his theorization many of the prescriptions that Sigonius had previously defined: the use of prose; the didactic intent; the utility of certain argumentative approaches; the importance of decorum and verisimilitude. Dialogue, then, is a poetic genre and, like epic, is identified by distinguishing characteristics. Within these constraints, though, Tasso permits the dialogue writer to employ a freedom that may explain the variety and vibrancy of certain examples. Toward the end of the treatise, Tasso turns his attention to matters of style. "Purity and simplicity," he writes, "is fitting, for excessive ornamentation impedes arguments and blunts, so to speak, insight and subtlety" (37).[39] But just as the marvelous in epic poetry enhances the telling of a probable action, ornamentation in dialogue is a necessary complement to argumentation. Again, Tasso places the writer between a Scylla of restraint and a Charybdis of innovation. Moderation must guide the writer in his elaborations. In the words of Tasso, "the other parts should be diligently ornamented; in them the writer of dialogues ought to resemble the poets in his expression and in his effort to make us see the things he describes" (37).[40]

39. "perch'in lei si conviene la purità e la simplicità dell'elocuzione, e 'l soverichio ornamento per ch'impedisca gli argomenti, e che rintuzzi, per così dire, l'acume e la sottilità" (36).

40. "Ma l'altre parti debbono esser ornate con maggiore diligenza; e dovendo lo scrittor del dialogo assomigliare i poeti nell'espressione e nel por le cose inanzi a gli occhi" (36).

Tasso also stresses the significance of *enargeia* or *evidentia* in his theorizations on

Enargeia and the Style of a Poetic-Philosophic Genre

By attempting to express things as if they were "before our eyes" (37),[41] the dialogue writer, according to Tasso, employs the principle of clarity. The use of vivid images identifies an effective use of *chiarezza* which, as Tasso reminds us, was termed *evidentia* by Roman writers. Plato, moreover, drew upon this device, and Tasso provides numerous examples of vivid images that induce delight and stir the passions. In the *Protagoras*, for example, "we read with marvelous delight about the eunuch at the door, who had slammed it with both hands on Socrates and his companion and would hardly open it even when he learned that they were no friend of the Sophists" (39).[42] Similarly, in the *Charmides*, Plato "sets . . . effectively before our eyes . . . the youth sitting on one end of the bench [who] falls off while the fellow at the other end is constrained to rise" (39).[43] Besides instilling pleasure, lifelike images produce empathic effects, and Tasso draws such examples from the *Crito* and *Phaedo*:

> Nothing could fill us with more compassion and wonder than to see Crito come to the prison before daybreak to wait for the condemned Socrates to wake up, then to see Socrates himself draw up his leg, which had been bound, and while scratching it discourse on pain and pleasure, whose extreme manifestations are closely connected, and finally to see him stretch himself, sit up in bed, and begin to speak about great and elevated contemplative matters.[44]   (39)

the narration and representation in epic poetry; for, in his *Discorso del poema eroico*, he writes: "E dunque la poesia investigatrice e quasi vagheggiatrice de la bellezza, e in duo modi cerca di mostrarla e di porcela davanti a gli occhi: l'uno è la narrazione, l'altro la rappresentazione" (*Poema eroico* 503).

41. "inanzi a gli occhi" (36).

42. "leggiamo con maraviglioso diletto che l'Eunuco portinaio, perchè i Sofisti gli erano venuti a noia, serra con ambe le mani la porta a Socrate ed al compagno, ed a pena l'apre, udendo che non erano di loro" (38).

43. "e quasi veggiamo gli estremi, che se devano da questa parte e da quella, l'uno cadere, e l'altro esser costretto a levarsi" (38).

44. "Ma sopra tutte le cose c'empie di compassione e di maraviglia il venir di Critone alla prigione inanzi al giorno, e l'aspettar che si destasse Socrate condannato alla morte. E poi ch'il medesimo raccoglia la gamba, la quale era stata legata, e grattandosi discorra del dolore e del piacere, l'estremità de' quali son congiunte insieme; e distendendosi, e postosi a sedere sovra la lettiera, dia principio a maggiore e più alta contemplazione" (38).

Thus, through the application of *chiarezza*, the dialogue writer does not merely describe. Rather, he presents impressions of the marvelous that enable the reader "to see and hear" (41)[45] the text and to engage more directly with the discussions and debates. Like Scaliger, who advises the writer "to select, pluck out, and expose before the eyes of men" the object of imitation, Tasso sees, in his *Arte poetica*, verbal representation as a process of selection and, in his *Discorso dell'arte del dialogo*, as the expression of vivid images that imprint upon the reader pleasurable and marvelous impressions. Scaliger's reference to *efficacia* and Tasso's description of *chiarezza* recall the ancient rhetorical technique of *energeia* or *evidentia*. As Neil Rudenstine (1967, 149–71), Forrest Robinson (1972, 131–35), Kathy Eden (1986, 71–75, 88–94), and S. K. Heninger (1989, 96–97, 261–62) have amply demonstrated, Aristotle applies to rhetoric the metaphysical notion of *energeia* that denotes the exercise of power, the dynamics of operation, and the actualization of an idea. In his *Rhetoric* (1411b21–1413b1) he insists on the importance of vivid images that make readers see things (1411b21), and that give metaphorical life to lifeless things (1411b31). A sense of activity produces a vigor that is especially evident in Homer's *Illiad*: (1) "the arrow flew" (13.587); (2) "flying on eagerly" (4.126); (3) the spears, "buried in the ground, longing to take in their fill of flesh" (9.574) (*Rhetoric* 1411b32–35; Freese 1947, 407). Movement reflects activity and endows the inanimate with vigor and vibrance. Metaphors, riddles, proverbs, and hyperboles are techniques that enable the orator to present lifelike images and to become more persuasive in his argumentation.

Quintilian elaborates upon Aristotle's notion and distinguishes *energeia* from *enargeia*. In particular, he sees *enargeia* as a means to stir the reader's passions. *Energeia*, Quintilian seems to believe, reflects a forcefulness that assists the orator in presenting a persuasive position. *Enargeia* enables the rhetor to detail the facts "clearly and vividly" (*Institutio oratoria* 8.3.62; H. E. Butler 1963, 3:245). Such clarity (*evidentia*) "thrusts itself upon our notice," and conveys facts "in their living truth to the eyes of the mind" (*Institutio oratoria* 8.3.61–62; H. E. Butler 1963, 3:245). This visualization created by the orator affects the mind's eye of the reader. And

45. "ci par di vedere ed ascoltare quel che leggiamo" (40).

like Cicero, who refers to the power of speech activating the mind or the reader's *mentis oculis* (*De oratore* 3.41.163; H. Rackham 1960, 2:129), Quintilian views *enargeia* as a means to induce credibility and to stimulate the thought and emotions of the reader-listener.

In spite of Quintilian's distinction between *energeia* and *enargeia*, Erasmus and subsequent sixteenth-century critics confuse the terms. Erasmus in his *De copia* (bk. 2, method 5) translates *enargeia* as *evidentia*, or "vividness" (Knott 1978, 577). Amplification produces such an effect which, in turn, affords pleasure to the reader. The process of creating this clarity is likened to the painting of a scene, and its effect goes beyond description. Just as colors enhance the substance of the design, appropriate words and figures of speech enable the writer to convey an impression "as vivid and clear to the reader as possible" (577). Such a vivid verbal picture moves the reader; for, as Erasmus advises the writer, "Instead of presenting it in bare and insubstantial outline, bring it before the eyes with all the colors filled in, so that our hearer or reader is carried away and seems to be in the audience at a theatre" (577).

Erasmus, like Aristotle, details the means to vivify the descriptions of things, persons, places, and times. Similes, metaphors, allegory, and epithets enrich the delineation of things, persons, and times. Dialogue and *prosopopeia*, he notes, are especially useful in endowing fictional or historical characters with vitality. Erasmus does not define dialogue as a discrete genre. Rather, dialogic form is a mode to elaborate character portrayal; in animating the personage, the writer records "utterances appropriate to his age, type, country, way of life, cast of mind, and character" (586). Erasmus leaves to Sigonius and his followers the linking of character portrayal in dialogues with the principles of verisimilitude and decorum. But dialogue as a rhetorical technique enlivens discourse. In its visualization of characters, it is a mode that transcends generic boundaries; employed in historical records, letters, and even soliloquies, dialogue enables writers to create a vividness that results in pleasure and stimulates the emotions.

Erasmus's discussion of *enargeia* recapitulates ancient views on poetry as painting, on the capacity of words to exercise effects on the mind's eye, and on the power of this technique to stir the passions. Scaliger, Richard Sherry, George Puttenham, Henry

Peacham, Sir Philip Sidney,[46] and, of course, Tasso allude to, and summarize, these thoughts. A review of the rhetorical theory and accompanying techniques of *enargeia*, however, leads to two ideas that may elucidate Tasso's expansion of the concept of dialogue. First, *enargeia* is a poetic technique that enables the orator to capture the attention of his listener and therefore to argue more persuasively. In describing *energeia* in his *Rhetoric*, Aristotle draws examples from the poets Homer, Euripides, and Simonides, from the philosophers Archytas and Thrasymachus, and from the rhetor Isocrates. Further, as Kathy Eden (1986, 71–75) has demonstrated, Aristotle's definition of the "*energeia* of the rhetorical-poetic image corresponds to the *enargeia* of tragic fiction" (71). Likewise, Erasmus denotes examples of the device employed by historians, philosophers, epic writers, poets, dramatists, and such dialogue writers as Plato, Lucian, and Boethius. Verisimilitude too is a rhetorical principle utilized by poets. According to Snyder (1989, 48–49), Sigonius's insistence on the use of different voices derives from principles of decorum that serve to enhance credibility. But *enargeia* is not simply a mimetic mode that identifies poetic works, and which induces the validity of a particular argument. For Tasso, the uses of *enargeia* are integral to the creative expression of dialogue as poetic-rhetorical genre. The pain of tragedy in the *Phaedo* is reinforced by the "marvelous" images of Socrates's "toying with the beautiful locks of Phaedo" (39).[47] And the comic personage of Hippias is animated through the vivid image of his "sitting on his throne" (39).[48] Plato's concept of narrative mimetic mode, through which characters verbalize the writer's thoughts, may identify drama and reflect the use of *enargeia*. But such a technique which characterizes comedy and tragedy extends to dialogue and, through its resources, enables the dialogue writer to

46. For a discussion of *enargeia* as presented by Scaliger, Puttenham, and Peacham, see S. K. Heninger, *Sidney and Spenser: The Poet as Maker* (University Park: Pennsylvania State University Press, 1989) 200, 255, 529n146, 530nn148 and 150. See also the comments by F. G. Robinson, *The Shape of Things Known: Sidney's "Apology" in Its Philosophical Tradition* (Cambridge: Harvard University Press, 1972), 131–35; and N. L. Rudenstine, *Sidney's Poetic Development* (Cambridge: Harvard University Press, 1967), 149–71.

47. "quando scherza con le belle chiome di Fedone" (38).

48. "ci par di vedere Ippia seder nel trono" (38).

heighten the credibility of argumentation with "marvelous delight" (39).[49]

Besides enhancing the possibilities of creative expression, *enargeia* is essentially a rhetorical technique and, effectively employed in dialogue, affirms the definition of the genre as one of "artful argumentation." In his *Institutio oratoria* (8.3.61; H. E. Butler 1963, 3:245), Quintilian describes *enargeia* as a device that "thrusts images upon our notice," and that enables oratory to attain "its full effect." Such a view confirms Kathy Eden's (1986) contention that *enargeia* evolved from forensic oratory and afforded rhetors a technique to demonstrate evidence and to plead a point more persuasively and forcefully. According to Snyder, Tasso's description of *enargeia* has "no specific utility" (173). Admittedly, Tasso restricts his statements to a description of style. But the purposes of rhetoric in general and the aim of *enargeia* in particular conflict with this assertion. Further, as we have seen, Tasso argues for the didacticism of dialogue and, in his discussion of *enargeia* in his *Discorsi del poema eroico*, sees the creation of marvelous images as a means to instruct and delight. Possible parallels between Longinus's thoughts on *phantasia* and Tasso's description of *enargeia* also support the utility of this rhetorical device to debate a case and to move the reader-listener to the acceptance of a respective argument. In *On the Sublime*[50] Longinus depicts the visual effects that, exerted by words, move the imagination and contribute to the enunciation of an effective oration: "For the term imagination is applied in general to an idea which enters the mind from any other source and engenders speech, but the word has now come to be used predominantly of personages where, inspired by strong emotion, you seem to see what you describe and bring it vividly before the eyes of your audience" (15.1; Fyfe 1965, 171). The aim of poetry, Longinus continues, is "to enthral," and that of prose is "to present things vividly" (*enargeia*) (15.1). But ultimately this technique enhances both poetry and prose, and enables writers to "enthral" (15.1). In exerting the same effect, *enargeia* empowers both the poet and the rhetor to move the mind and to advance the didactic purpose of their respective discourse.

---

49. "maraviglioso diletto" (38).

50. For a listing of the editions of Longinus's *On The Sublime* available to Tasso, see Bernard Weinberg, "Translations and Commentaries on Longinus, *On the Sublime*, to 1600: A Bibliography," *Modern Philology* 47 (1950): 145–51.

Similarly, for Tasso, *enargeia* moves the reader; as a technique in epic to evoke the marvelous or as a device in dialogue to induce pleasure and delight, it seizes the reader's attention, stirs his passions, and moves him to the acceptance of an argument cogently reasoned and vigorously presented. As Snyder (1989, 197–213) has pointed out, Pietro Sforza Pallavicino, in his *Trattato dello stile e del dialogo* (1646), relates more fully and explicitly the concept of *enargeia* to the aim of argumentation that informs the substance and structure of dialogue. But Pallavicino's theorization was the expression of an idea that Tasso had earlier suggested, for, in his *Discorso dell'arte del dialogo* and in his *Arte poetica* and *Discorsi del poema eroico*, Tasso clearly indicates the resources of this rhetorical device that strengthen argumentation and embellish expression. The tricks of the orator, then, have become the techniques of the poet; and, as Tasso succinctly concludes, the dialogue writer "occupies a kind of middle ground between the poet and the dialectician" (41).[51]

Summary

Contextually, Tasso's concept of dialogue implies an expansion of form. Through a borrowing of Sigonius's precepts and prescriptions, he sets forth characteristics that identify the genre. But his comments on artistic representation in his *Arte poetica* and on *enargeia* suggest a poetic license that may explain, and admit into the canons, the varied forms of dialogic writing. Jon Snyder (1989, 48) has argued that Tasso's treatise on dialogue serves as a response to Castelvetro's attack on the form. This may have indeed sparked Tasso's defense of a genre which, as he admits in the opening paragraph, he practiced and aspired to establish through the compilation of rules. Tasso's essay, though, complements his other critical writings, for, just as the marvelous affords pleasure for the readers of epic, *enargeia* provides a "marvelous delight" in ancient and humanist dialogues. In his *Discorso* Tasso stresses the mimetic nature of dialogue. But if he does not describe the process of imitation in this work, he does detail in his *Arte poetica* the poet's selection of material that is shaped to a structure embellished and enhanced

---

51. "lo scrittor del dialogo non sia imitatore o quasi mezzo fra 'l poeta e 'l dialettico" (40).

by rhetorical tropes and techniques. As the substance and style of epic unite to attain the ends of instruction and pleasure, the dialectical and poetic nature of dialogue presents "truly marvelous perfections . . . for the benefit of civil and speculative men" (41).[52]

In his introduction to the *Discorso*, Tasso confesses to the difficulties of collecting rules for writing. The dialogue writer, in particular, must chart a course between convention and innovation. The imitation of other voices and the recording of disputation in the form of questions and answers define the genre and result in fixed characteristics: (1) its didactic purpose; (2) its incapacity to be enacted on stage; (3) the use of prose; (4) the employment of established argumentative approaches appropriate to the topic of discussion. Within this framework, however, Tasso admits a freedom of expression that enlarges upon Sigonius's rigid form, and that approaches Scaliger's views on genre as concrete structures and abstract modes. Plato's blending of comedy and tragedy in the *Menexenus* does not undermine the dialogic nature of the work. And if Plato's *Crito* is essentially tragic in tone (21), the presentation of the vivid image of Crito's visit to the condemned Socrates (39) draws upon the resources of *evidentia* which, as a poetic-rhetorical principle, transcends genres and affords profitable appreciation through pleasurable reading. Tasso avoids specific allusion to *genera mista*; and, if Polonius's description of the blending of genres (*Hamlet* 2.2.392–98) reflects Renaissance poetic practice, Tasso suggests, and resists explicit definition of, any flexible and creative use of genres as modes. Nevertheless, in recognizing the significance of supporting generic modes in dialogue, and in insisting on the resources of *enargeia*, he expands the structures of dialogic form and defends, defines, and develops a poetic-dialectical genre, emotionally pleasing and didactically useful.

52. "Queste son le perfezioni di Platone, veramente maravigliose . . . per giovamento degli uomini civili e speculativi" (40).

꧁ The Dialogue as Artful Argumentation

The theorization of dialogue presented the sixteenth-century critic with complex issues to be understood and resolved. As Bernard Weinberg (1961) portrays the critical climate, the theorist had to reconcile contemporary concepts and practice with texts and traditions inherited from Greece and Rome and reworked by medieval thinkers and practitioners (1:38). Any genre defies a complete, correct, all-encompassing definition, and the transmission of relatively full, ancient statements on tragedy and epic did not assure agreement of interpretation among the Renaissance critics. But the defense and description of dialogue were complicated by the absence of classical treatises devoted solely or even partially to this literary kind. Thus the humanist critic had to assume the role of philological detective, seeking clues in literary examples and in allusions collected in epistles, biographies, and philosophical and critical treatises. Unlike the critics of genres formulated and developed during the Renaissance (for example, romance), and unlike readers endeavoring to determine the genre of accepted texts (such as Dante's *Divina Commedia*), the theorists of dialogue did not assume controversial positions. Dialogue had flourished in postclassical forms; written in Latin and the vernacular languages, it was firmly established in literary, educational, and rhetorical expressions. Humanist interpretations and subsequent imitations of Plato, Xenophon, Lucian, and Cicero, moreover, affirmed the place of this widely employed genre that revealed to critics a philosophical depth and poetic diversity. Theorists responded to tradition and taste and, through an appreciation of ancient and modern texts, set forth a doctrine that attempted to integrate classical precepts with Renaissance practice.

Sixteenth-century criticism of dialogue, then, reflects a generalization and systemization of works spontaneously conceived and constructed. Certainly, the creative impulse that stimulated the writing of so many varied examples required a poetic license that challenged rigid definitions and authoritarian postulations. Intelligibility, however, calls for a structure which, in the case of humanist dialogue, emerges as "artful argumentation." Tasso's view of the form as a poetic "imitazione di ragionamento" provided a framework that acknowledged the freedom of creativity but afforded a code to classify, and to delineate the limits of, a viable and valuable genre. As we have seen in this examination of three representative critics, the attainment of this consensus evolved from defense to prescription and, finally, to the expansion of a definition that attenuates the oppositions between creative innovation and critical conceptualization.

Through his efforts to enrich the poetic canons of the Pléiade, Louis Le Caron extols Platonic and Ciceronian dialogues and thereby integrates medieval disputation with the more stylized humanist forms of Castiglione, Speroni, Leone Ebreo, and Pontus de Tyard. As a preface to *La Claire*, Le Caron's statement justifies and explains his practice; and his promotion of the genre as a poetic kind determines classification. Agricola's rethinking of the trivium informs his concept of a "hybrid" form that combines medieval dialectics with rhetorical embellishment. But although the transfer of this literary kind from Scholastic argumentation to poetic imitation leads to an understanding of the nature, aim, and function of dialogic discourse, Le Caron's reading of ancient models results in a description more implicit than explicit. Carolus Sigonius, though, defines a genre that Le Caron had defended. By reconstituting numerous premises advanced by ancient critics, he adds authority to Le Caron's suggestions. And through an application of Plato's theory of mimesis, an analysis of the rhetorical principles of verisimilitude and decorum, and a categorization of argumentative approaches, he inscribes the limits and identifies the features of this literary kind. In spite of Sigonius's careful culling and coherent combining of classical tenets, he neglects a stylistic examination of certain texts. Torquato Tasso, though, does not discount Lucianic satire; moreover, although recognizing dialogue as a discrete form with undeniable characteristics, he acknowledges the use of other genres and techniques that enhance the possibilities of this literary kind. Sigonius's prescriptions become proscriptions. But Tasso's hinting of genre as mode and his insights into the effects of *enargeia* extend the boundaries of a form that invites the accommodation of creative utterance with generic convention.

In spite of the elusiveness of a complete and consistent definition, two patterns emerge in the critical reception of humanist dialogue. For the theorist and practitioner, subject matter influences argumentative approach and structural design. In borrowing Diogenes Laertius's analysis of disputations used in Plato's works, Sigonius and Tasso link Aristotle's taxonomy of arguments to the forms of dialogue. As we have seen, demonstrative dialogue becomes a means for instruction and may explain the extensive use of dialogue in medieval elucidaries and Renaissance colloquies. The incontrovertible topics of the trivium, quadrivium, and theology could be conveyed through this form which, heightened by rhetorical techniques and ornaments, induced pleasure and facilitated learning. Most issues, though, resist certification, and the two forms of dialectic discourse (eristic debate and peirastic discussion) furnished suitable structures in setting forth dissensions of opinion and in investigating the validity of ideas. As Marion Trousdale (1982) has perceptively and brilliantly described the practice of Renaissance epistemology, things (*res*) and words (*verba*) were necessarily separated. Phenomena exist, but the words that denote the perception are incomplete and imperfect representations. Plato, she observes, designates two Cratyluses: name and person. Richard Rainolde, in *A Booke Called the Foundacion of Rhetorike* (1563), asserts that, through an alteration of the point or frame of reference, the disputant reworks the approach and mode of argument (5). Thus the events of the Trojan War render different and opposing views (15). And the complexities of theme and expression in Shakespeare's *Hamlet* derive from the generality of presented topics that result in multiple perspectives and discourse (10).

As forms of dialectical dialogue, both eristic debate and peirastic discussion proceed, in substance and form, from this epistemology. According to Aristotle, things (*res*) are described by words indicating particularizing qualities, such as substance, quantity, place, time, and action. Although these attributes, or places of invention and definition, identify characteristics of the object, they reflect, individually, partial aspects of the subject; and only in their totality do they present ways to discover the nature of the topic. As Erasmus suggests in his *De copia* (Trousdale 1982, 41), words differ from things; and, because language is an imprecise, artificial mode of denotation, words ultimately fail to capture the essence of truth. In his *Institutio oratoria* (10.5.7; Butler 1963, 4:117), Quintilian writes that "many roads lead us to the same goal." Thus, rhetoric, the art of persuasion, becomes, as Aristotle had earlier defined it, "the counterpart of dialectic" (*Rhetoric* 1.1; Freese 1947, 3). The places of invention result in a clarification of the understanding of a topic. Whereas truth conveyed by demonstrative dialogue is certain, the subjects studied through dialectics, or place-logic, are topics continually controversial in nature. Agricola's refurbishing of Scholastic dialectics provides a mode of investigation, but such topics elude a full and accurate definition, and its accompanying discourse is destined to fail in its attempt to represent absolute certainty.

Credibility, then, becomes the aim of a discourse that inquires into relative topics. Consequently, the techniques and devices of rhetoric afford the means to present a plausible argument in dialogic form. Both eristic and peirastic dialogues incorporate these topics or themes, and the similarity of subjects treated by Plato and Cicero support the notion of dialogue as a form of dialectical discourse. Approach, however, distinguishes the two forms. The subtlety of argumentation ends in a victory in eristic debate and, as Lisa Jardine (1974) notes, culminates with an insight or discovery into the nature of the discussed topic. On the other hand, examination-arguments, frequently associated with Ciceronian discourse, center attention on different aspects of the topic, and emerge perhaps as the prevalent form of humanist dialogue. Varying views may appear conflicting and obfuscating; but, after synthesizing and interrelating the opposing opinions, the dialogue writer presents a more comprehensive picture of a topic which, in its way, results in a discovery of the range and complexities of a subject elusive of truth.

Rhetoric becomes the mode of argumentative expression. Dialectics, the "counterpart of rhetoric," provides the structure of argument. But the writer, in utilizing the devices of rhetoric, seeks to persuade and move his reader-listener. Sigonius designates the doctrines of verisimilitude and decorum as the means to produce a credible illusion and thereby to advance the cogency of the respective argument. Tasso, however, builds upon Sigonius's seminal words on the pleasure provided by dialogue (*De dialogo liber* 1561, 170–79). But instead of recapitulating the role of decorum in the amplification of argument, Tasso turns attention to the uses of *enargeia* which, through the creation of vivid impressions, engenders delight and wonder. Thus *ratio* is integrated with *oratio*; the resources of rhetoric shared by orator and poet expand the boundaries of dialectical discourse and extend to the representation of convincing portrayals and engaging images.

Tasso's treatise suggests the second theoretical strain: dialogue as both genre and mode. By incorporating into his definition Sigonius's fundamental tenets, Tasso sees dialogue as a discrete and established genre. But in his reading of ancient examples, he observes that practice does not necessarily conform to prescriptions. Accordingly, dialogue as a genre reflects distinctive characteristics. However, in defining the form as an "imitation of an argument," he proposes a mimetic process which, outlined later in his *Arte poetica* and *Discorsi del poema eroico*, recalls Scaliger's thoughts on poetic representation. For Scaliger, dialogue is a distinctive genre, but it is also a mode which, along with other forms employed as sorts of discourses, serves as a technique to shape vision to the strictures of structure and style. Dialogue can therefore function as a subgenre, and its essential form of questions and answers and of statements and retorts explains its role in the writing of comedy, tragedy, lyric poetry, and epistle. Such a concept implies reciprocity. Although Tasso does not demonstrate the uses of dialogue as an ancillary or auxiliary mode, he does recognize and respect the practice of Plato, Xenophon, Lucian, and Cicero who employ in their works satire, myth, history, comic anecdote, and tragic situation. In fitting philosophical and political arguments to the restrictions of a distinctive poetic form, dialogue is a defined and accepted genre. But through its assimilation with other forms, its structure expands and contracts according to argument and perspective. Thus, practice becomes reconciled with theory; such diverse examples as Tyard's "demonstrative" explanations of music in his *Solitaire second* (1555) and Des Périers's "satiric-dialectical" inquiry into human nature in his *Cymbalum mundi* (1537) appear more comparative than contrastive.

Conviction in the distinctiveness and use of defined genres seems to have restrained Tasso from designating dialogue as a mode. Toward the end of the century, though, Girolamo Zoppio took the additional step that introduces into theory the practice of mixing and altering generic structures. In his *Poetica sopra Dante* (1589) he draws attention to the various modes of the *Divina Commedia*: it is epic in its narrative structure and comic in its character portrayal and closure.[53] Dialogue, though, cannot be overlooked in a poem that records "arguments and disputes relating to human affairs" (Weinberg 1961, 2:896).[54] Like his predecessors, he argues for the poetic or feigned or invented nature of dialogue. Poetry, as he sees it, is defined as fiction which, as representation uncorroborated by fact, cannot be classified as history. Dante's imaginary voyage is a dream vision that deviates from the actual, and dialogue, he contends, plays a significant role in the poetic imitation of personal salvation. Drama, moreover, shares characteristics with dialogue, for comedy and tragedy present scenes of "discoursings and dialogues among persons arguing and disputing about things and affairs, using propositions and responses in a dialectical form" (Weinberg 1961, 2:896).[55] Genres, then, are not precisely fixed in structure and style. Rather, through their generality of definition and flexibility of use, they adapt to the exigencies of substance, and as modes blend with other literary kinds to convey individual thoughts and perceptions. For Zoppio, Plato's dialogues are fictitious in speech and setting. Consequently, Plato's *Protagoras*, as a poetic form, and Dante's *Divina Commedia*, as a philosophical argument, interact in substance and structure. Each reflects "a poetic imitation of a philosophic action" (Wein-

53. For a discussion of Zoppio's ideas on the mixed genres that define dialogue, see Weinberg, (1961, 2: 883–85, 895–99).

54. "le Poesie pure sono tutte imitationi per via di Dialogi, contrasti e dispute intorno à gli affari humani" (*Poetica sopra Dante* 1589, 11).

55. "Ragionamenti e Dialogi tra persone argomentanti e disputanti di cose, e negocij con proposte, e risposte in forma Dialecttica" (14).

berg 1961, 2:896),[56] thereby recalling and supporting Tasso's view of dialogue as an "imitazione di ragionamento."

As we have seen, theory defines and authorizes practice. But if established structures delineate the framework of humanist dialogue, such definitions derive from models and ultimately become more inclusionary than exclusionary. Argument as the object of imitation and rhetoric as the means of expression remain constant and consistent during the course of critical revaluations. In practice, though, formal structures were combined and reformed: approaches associated with didactic dialogue could be applied to dialectical discourse. The satiric tone of Erasmus, Des Périers, and Tahureau is as appropriate to the form as are the serious investigations of Speroni, Brués, Tyard, and Le Caron. Thus, dialogue does not collapse into an insubstantial, nonsensical generic category. Rather, it emerges as a defined mode of discourse that retains reasoning as its object of imitation, but that assimilates other genres to describe man and his world.

In a seminal and very significant article on the emergence of eloquence in Renaissance Italy, Hanna H. Gray (1963) sees dialogue as "the flexible form of discussing issues of all sorts" (512). Certainly, this study of the theories proposed by Le Caron, Sigonius, and Tasso confirms Gray's assessment and demonstrates the depth and breadth of a defined and developed Renaissance genre. Argumentation was central to its thematic framework, and the accompanying structures could be constricted to the didacticism of demonstrative discourse or expanded to the debates of dialectical discussion. For the sixteenth-century thinker, though, certainty was frequently elusive. In searching for knowledge and understanding, dialogic form affords the presentation of conflicting views that seem to contradict but, in their totality, offer insight into the *discordia concors* of a topic. Michel de Montaigne in his *De l'art de conférer* (1588) recognizes human incapacity to penetrate truth (3.8). But through discussions one confronts contradictions that stimulate thinking, attack pretensions, expand learning, and correct fixed misconceptions. The validities denoted by Scholastic disputation become, through the discussion reworked in humanist dialogues, the relativities of perspective arranged by place-logic and expressed by the fluidity of generic modes. Form reinforces

56. "Imitatione poetica d'attione philosophica" (14).

theme, and the resources of rhetoric and the varieties of generic modes become the means and manners of shaping substance to structure. Poetic creativity defies theoretical definition. However, through their understanding of dialogue as "artful argumentation," sixteenth-century theorists formulated a genre that offered an approach and structure ancient in origins but Renaissance in application and adaptation.

PART 2

✺ Contemporary Practices

COLETTE H. WINN

Toward a Dialectic of Reconciliation

The *Navire* and the *Heptameron* of Marguerite de Navarre

Are not thought and speech the same, with this exception, that what is called thought is the unuttered conversation of the soul with itself?

—PLATO, *The Sophist* (1986, 131)

Marguerite de Navarre displayed her imaginative talents in a variety of literary genres, but she seems most at home in the dialogue. In his introduction (1978) to the *Théâtre profane*, V.-L. Saulnier observes: "Le colloque mondain ou mystique, c'est la structure de pensée de la reine" [xxv: dialogue, worldly or mystical, structures the queen's thought]. Whenever she writes of worldly or divine love, it is almost exclusively in dialogue form. According to Robert Cottrell (1986), "A dialogic impulse animates all of Marguerite's poetry, which is designed to establish or confirm a communicative circuit between the 'I' and the 'Thou,' 'the self and Christ'" (131). Certainly, her collection of novellas, notable for the addition of lively debates concerning the stories, and her important corpus of plays in which, needless to say, the author relies essentially on alternating speeches for the development and transmission of her ideas, establish Marguerite's predilection for the dialogical style of writing. Note that *La Comédie à dix personnages* (1542) and *La Comédie du parfaict amant* (1549) resemble the medieval debate both in substance (both plays concern love casuistry) and in structure (they make a similar use of the traditional strophic retorts).

Marguerite composed three dialogues, of which two indicate by their title their dialogical substance: the *Dialogue en forme de vision nocturne* and the *Discord estant en l'homme par la contrarieté de l'Esprit et de la Chair, et paix par vie spirituelle*. The *Dialogue* (1524) is one of the first productions in France to bear the name of dialogue. According to Mustapha Bénouis (1976, 23), it occupies a pivotal position in the evolution of dialogical writing in France, effecting a shift from medieval discursive forms such as *tensons*, *jeux partis*, *pastourelles*, and *sirventès* to an autonomous genre that develops during the Renaissance in a multiplicity of forms and styles.

Owing much to medieval tradition, the *Navire* and the *Discord* recall the so-called *conflictus*, a dialectical mise-en-scène of the soul and the body. The *Navire*, written on the occasion of the death of Francis I, relates a dream vision (a *visio*) during which the deceased brother appears to the grieving Marguerite to console her and guide her on the path of salvation. The double-voiced dialogue reproduces the interior struggle: the questions, doubts, resistances of the "I" when confronted by the "Thou."

Thus, as a tool of inquiry, dialogue suits the queen's epistemological needs. In a setting congenial to her own mode of thought, she is able to pursue her unrelenting search for truth by way of question and answer, give and take, colloquy, or confrontation among invented characters or diverse aspects of her inner self. Furthermore, dialogical writing is Marguerite's most successful attempt at entertaining while instructing; it serves to expose timely debates and enlivens the most intimate of dialogues, thus sensitizing the reader to the conflict of the spiritual self and, more specifically, to the gradual and painstaking process of inner persuasion. Although critics have previously commented on her predilection for dialogical forms,[1] they have, to my surprise, deemed it unnecessary to explore further the important development of a complex literary genre.

I cannot, in the space available here, offer an exhaustive study of Marguerite's use of dialogical forms. I hope, however, to make the reader more aware of the active part the queen took in what

---

1. In his *Marguerite de Navarre's Heptameron: Themes, Language, and Structure* (Durham, NC: Duke University Press, 1973), Marcel Tetel maintains that "without a doubt . . . dialogue is a mode of expression proper and essential to Marguerite; it is a primary tool in the exchange of ideas and opinions following the tradition of the medieval debate and the Platonic symposium" (144).

has come to be known as one of the great moments in the history
of dialogue,[2] on the one hand, by developing and renewing the
medieval tradition of the *débat*, and on the other, by adapting
Platonic dialogue to her own purposes. This study of two of Marguerite de Navarre's major works, the *Navire* and the *Heptameron*,
chosen for their diversity in form, content, and intent, will demonstrate her remarkable expertise in developing the aesthetic and
philosophical qualities of the genre. Its orientation owes much to
Eva Kushner's well-known studies of dialogue in which she delineates successful avenues for exploring the question of gender
boundaries.[3]

The Dialogue: Its Medieval and Classical Heritage

Marguerite's debt to medieval traditions that use colloquy as a
form of writing should not be underestimated.[4] In the *sirventès* and
jeux-partis, two poets develop their points of view on a question,
raised in a brief introduction, in homage to some illustrious personages of the time who in turn serve as referees.[5] Likewise, in the
Heptameron, the discussants engage in storytelling in homage to the
royal family, who will in turn evaluate the quality of their work:
"et, si Dieu faict que notre labeur soit trouvé digne des oeilz des
seigneurs et dames dessus nommez, nous leur en ferons present au
retour de ce voiage, en lieu d'ymaiges ou de patenostres" [10: And

2. According to Rudolf Hirzel (1895/1963), three major historical moments (all
characterized by political, social, and cultural changes)—the Age of Sophistry, the
Renaissance, and the French Revolution—have been particularly favorable to the
flourishing of dialogue. See Ph. Lacoue-Labarthe and J.-L. Nancy, "Le Dialogue des
genres," *Poétique* 21 (1975): 150.

3. See, for example, Eva Kushner, "Réflexions sur le dialogue en France au
seizième siècle," *Revue des Sciences Humaines* 148 (1972): 485–501; "The Dialogue of
the French Renaissance: Work of Art or Instrument of Inquiry?," *Zagadnienia Rodzajow Literackich* 20 (1977): 23–35; "Le Dialogue en France au XVIe siècle: Quelques
critères génologiques," *Canadian Review of Comparative Literature* (Spring 1978): 142–
53; "Le Dialogue en France de 1550 à 1560," *Le Dialogue au temps de la Renaissance*,
ed. M.-T. Jones-Davies (Paris: Touzot, 1984), 151–69.

4. On the medieval tradition of the *débat*, see Alfred Jeanroy, *Les Origines de la
poésie lyrique en France au moyen âge* (Paris: Champion, 1904), 45–60, and his *La Poésie
lyrique des troubadours* (Toulouse, France: E. Privat, 1934), 175–200, 247–81; and
John G. Cummins, "Methods and Conventions in the Fifteenth-Century Poetic
Debate," *Hispanic Review* 31 (1963): 307–23. On *jeux-partis*, see Arthur Langfors,
Recueil général des jeux-partis français (Paris: Champion, 1926); Mirela Saim, "La Parole
médiévale en dialogue: Les jeux-partis," *Littérature* 6 (1991): 127–38.

5. Etymologically, *sirventès* means the song a *sirven* composed for his master.

if, God willing, the lords and ladies I've mentioned find our endeavors worthy of their attention, we shall make them a present of
them when we get back, instead of the usual statuettes and beads].[6]

For the good of body, mind, and soul alike, Parlamente suggests a pastime, telling stories about ideal and courtly love, in
which everyone will participate on equal grounds. This worldly
pastime is reminiscent of a courtly practice that enjoyed great popularity in France by the end of the eleventh century. It can be
traced from south to north in the *cours d'amour* or *tribunaux fémi-
nins*. It was revived during the Renaissance under the influence
of sophisticated Italian circles in intellectually inclined salons, in
"cenacles," and at court. In the *Heptameron*, the men's courtesy toward women recalls the atmosphere of the courtly societies of
Provence, of the *puys* and *jeux floraux* as well as that of sophisticated
circles of the Italian Renaissance. Indeed, all debates open on a
note of courtesy, "vous voyez, Mes dames . . ." [you see, my
ladies . . .], and the woman is the first to speak. With this revival of courtesy in sixteenth-century France came a new etiquette
that called for refinement in both manners and language.[7] In the
Heptameron daily utterances are mixed with more sophisticated,
scintillating conversation. And at times, as Nicole Cazauran
(1976, 97) argues, this refined language, studded with metaphors, antitheses, and personifications—all reminders of worldly
dialogues—may appear to be inconsistent with the conversational
tone Marguerite had announced in the prologue:

> Mais si le langage des devisants se veut si différent de "l'art" des
> gens de lettres appliqués à écrire, s'il s'inspire si évidemment de la
> liberté du langage parlé, il apparaît aussi comme celui de mon-
> dains, très maîtres de leurs mots et de leurs phrases, accoutumés à
> la rhétorique de la poésie amoureuse, rompus à tous les jeux pré-
> cieux, et soucieux aussi de formuler avec justesse et force la vérité
> que leur expérience leur découvre.   (97)

> [If indeed the discussants' language claims to be so different from
> the "art" of men of letters well versed in writing techniques, if in-

6. All quotations from the *Heptameron* are taken from Michel François's critical
edition (Paris: Garnier, 1967). All subsequent references to this work will be incorporated in the text. Translations are by P. A. Chilton, *The Heptameron* (Aylesbury,
Bucks, England: Hazell Watson and Viney, 1984).

7. See Edouard Bourciez, *Les Moeurs polies et la littérature sous Henri II* (Paris:
Hachette, 1886), 322–54, 388–421.

deed it is modelled so obviously after the freedom of the spoken word, it still appears to be that of worldly society, in total control of its words and sentences, experienced in love rhetoric and preciosity, while also concerned with formulating accurately and effectively the truth disclosed by its experience.]

Renaissance man's thirst for knowledge and his growing interest in Neoplatonism were to transform considerably the status of dialogue from a form primarily valued as entertainment to an essential instrument of inquiry. If the sophisticated circles of medieval times had previously lifted conversation to the level of a minor art, those of the Renaissance would, while continuing to value literary elegance, accuracy, wit, humor, and conciseness, lift it to a level far more complex, that of searching for truth.[8]

The subjects of the debates in the *Heptameron* vary greatly in content and depth. They range from the metaphysics of love; moral, ethical or philosophical questions; timely topics (contemporary mores [see debate 50] or current events); and praise or blame of eminent people of the time (see debates 17 and 12), to more trivial topics which had likewise animated medieval debates: complaints against husbands; arguments in favor of, or against, women; and gossip about acquaintances. The latter often recall the more aggressive tone of the *tensons* and the so-called personal *sirventès*.

The atmosphere and tone of the dialogues also vary greatly. A trivial discussion or an exchange of wry remarks between two speakers may follow a novella in the exemplum tradition to which all have paid devout attention. And again, a frivolous story may elicit the most serious comments, the most constructive reflections. It may lead the participants, as in debate 34, to develop their own theories of laughter, a topic that at the time stirred much passion, or to explore further, as in debate 8, the metaphysics of love.

On the one hand, one may say that the dialogues of the *Heptameron* are polyphonic since they bring into play a variety of solutions to a complex problem, each represented by an individual or group of individuals sharing the same opinions and opposing the solutions proposed by another individual or group. In the end, how-

8. Among medieval dialogical forms, the *partimen* most resembles the worldly dialogues of the Renaissance. See Jeanroy, *Les Origines de la poésie lyrique*, 45.

ever, they often become essentially diphonic. It does not take long for the reader to distinguish two adverse groups of speakers, the "idealists," firm believers in moral values and courtly love, and the "materialists" or "hedonists" who tend to keep their feet on the ground and remain primarily concerned with immediate goals. Dagoucin, an idealist, is constantly ridiculed, while Hircan, the hedonist, is often chastised by his wife and the other women who join in with her to defend their rights. In each case the extremist view provokes ridicule.

The framing dialogues of the *Heptameron* consist of a series of questions and answers. Either the storyteller questions the audience or vice versa, or the story itself elicits questions among the listeners. The dialogues often bring out conflicting commentaries, divergent interpretations of the story just told. In this respect they recall the medieval debate as well as the Renaissance dialogue. Sometimes they proceed as a kind of "offensive-defensive game." One speaker addresses another who in turn addresses a third, and so forth. This procedure brings into play the vivacity, wit, and resourcefulness of the interlocutors. Even though dialogue is not primarily conducted in a spirit of competition, it often turns out to be, in these cases, little more than a verbal argument or, as K. J. Wilson (1985) puts it, "match winning" (49). Take, for example, debate 16 in which Hircan's and Nomerfide's argumentation seems primarily intended to drive Geburon into self-contradiction, the so-called *elenchus*:

> Comment, Geburon? dist Hircan: depuis quel temps estes-vous devenu prescheur? J'ay bien veu que vous ne teniez pas ces propos. . . . Nous vous mercions, Geburon, dist Nomerfide, de quoy vous nous advertissez de nostre proffict; mais si ne nous en sentons pas trop tenues à vous, car vous n'avez poinct tenu pareil propos à celle que vous avez bien aymée: c'est doncques signe que vous ne nous aymez gueres, ny ne voullez encores souffrir que nous soyons aymées.   (133)

> ["What's all this about, Geburon?" said Hircan. "Since when have you turned preacher? I remember a time when you weren't in the habit of saying that sort of thing." . . . "Thank you very much, Geburon, for informing us of our interests," said Nomerfide, "though I don't think we need be too grateful, because that isn't the way you've talked in the past to women when you were in love with them. It just goes to show that you don't really love us, and don't want anyone else to love us either!"]

But, in other cases, as in debate 8, for example, several speakers openly state their views on a specific problem, here Platonic love, with the intent of examining the multiple facets of the question (constancy versus inconstancy, pleasure and profit versus true, disinterested love, and so forth), and thus letting truth prevail.

Among these dialogical techniques, we discern various discursive forms that mark different stages in both the development of dialogue forms and Plato's dialogues.[9] The former type of argumentation resembles *eristic dialectic*, whose primary aim was the mastery of disputation, "how to argue effectively for and against." It is reminiscent of Scholastic practice which evolved from Plato's earlier dialogues, often referred to as *elenctic* dialogues. Eva Kushner (1984) notes that these so-called dialogues are often no more than "exercises in monologism" (154). Rigidly oriented, the argumentation divulges the outcome. The latter type of dialogue, which engages the participants in a more tentative (experimental) philosophical discussion, and which yields to the edification of judgment, seems more directly connected with *peirastic dialectic*, Plato's later dialogues, or what is known as humanist dialogues.[10] André Chastel (1954) notes the importance given to free discussion and the judgment of others in Renaissance dialogue.[11] In the *Heptameron*, the high frequency of interjections, interrogative turns, and incidental clauses—for example, "le reprint, luy respondit, luy dist, s'il estoit tel que vous dictes"—demonstrates this openness to the others. Besides, since the opposition *magister-discipulus* does not exist, the debate never appears to be controlled.[12] Hircan announces in the prologue that all participants

---

9. In the Renaissance, Plato, even more than Cicero and Lucian, continued to be the most renowned and imitated of ancient dialogists. On Plato's dialogues, see Victor Goldschmidt, *Les Dialogues de Platon: Structure et méthode dialectique* (Paris: PUF, 1947), and Jean Laborderie, *Le Dialogue platonicien de la maturité* (Paris: Les Belles Lettres, 1978).

10. The end results ("match-winning" versus "truth-hunting"), rather than the structures, differentiate eristic exchanges from examination-arguments. See K. J. Wilson, *Incomplete Fictions: The Formation of the English Renaissance Dialogue* (Washington, D.C.: The Catholic University of America Press, 1985) 47–51.

11. See André Chastel, "L'Humanisme italien," *Bibliothèque d'Humanisme et Renaissance* 16 (1954): 381.

12. Yet the narrator's presence in the text as the voice reporting the conversation cannot be denied. This is the single most important feature of diegetic dialogue. In his *Apologia dei dialoghi* (1574), Sperone Speroni discusses Plato's distinction between mimesis and diegesis (*Republic* 3: 392–94). He argues that mimetic dialogues, as opposed to diegetic dialogues, gain in naturalness and verisimilitude by silencing

will enjoy equal rights: "au jeu nous sommes tous esgaulx" [10: Where games are concerned everyone is equal]. Thus, even if adverse parties occasionally surface, one never wins over the other. Each discussant expresses his or her own viewpoint in the hope that the others will reach their own conclusions, find their own truth, draw their own lessons. However, we must not be fooled by the open-endedness of these dialogues and conclude that they are devoid of viewpoint. The fiction of authorial neutrality enables the dialogist to provide philosophical support for herself, as we shall see later on.

We turn now to the *Navire*. Note that the *Navire* and the *Dialogue en forme de vision nocturne* were composed under similar circumstances. The latter was written in 1524, shortly after Marguerite's eight-year-old niece, Charlotte, died of rubella, whereas the former dates from 1547 and was occasioned by the death of her brother, Francis I. Critics agree that in the *Dialogue* Marguerite draws quite heavily upon Briçonnet's letter of August 31, 1524, in which he consoles her after the death of Charlotte's mother, and upon a letter dated September 15, published in 1970 for the first time by Christine Martineau and Christian Grouselle. Thus some might find the *Navire* to be more personal and overall a better example of Marguerite's increasing expertise in handling the rhetoric of dialogue.

In this 1464-line poem Marguerite borrows, as in the *Dialogue*, from the *conflictus*, a poetic tradition that enjoyed great popularity in medieval times. Varying in tone from grave to light, the *conflictus* stages two abstract entities at war with one another, for example, wine and water, didactic and love poetry, or body and soul. The *Navire* evokes a dream vision (a *visio*) in which the departed Francis appears to his sister, Marguerite, while she is asleep to comfort her and try to lead her soul along the path to salvation. We soon realize that the speakers are a projection of the author's mental state, that is, that this verbal communication is actually taking place in Marguerite's mind. Thus the setting and the characters both contribute to giving the *Navire* an allegorical dimension and an interiorized quality, which recalls the so-called discord

---

the voice of authority in the dialogical scene. See Jon R. Snyder, *Writing the Scene of Speaking: Theories of Dialogue in the Late Italian Renaissance* (Stanford: Stanford University Press, 1989), 106–10.

between flesh and spirit. The interlocutors' attitudes, their closed-mindedness and obstinate determination to pursue nothing but their own points of view, lead to an ever-renewed conflict. An earthbound perception, represented by Marguerite's persona (to simplify, I shall refer to this voice as Marguerite), sharply contrasts with one of transcendence, voiced by Francis. A lack of nuance in the views expressed gives the individual voices, at times, an abstract and artificial quality again reminiscent of the rigid antagonism of medieval debates between flesh and spirit. When the curtain rises the characters and standpoints are not clearly defined, so the abstract quality of the voices is felt even more strongly. Indeed, at the outset, Francis's voice remains unidentified. The anonymity of the voice that shatters the silence of night, the authoritative tone in which it addresses the sleeping soul (we later learn that it embodies Marguerite),[13] and the biblical overtones of the language at first surprise, and tend to give a dogmatic turn to the dialogue.

The *Navire* is a diptych in the pro-and-contra scholastic tradition, the medieval *disputatio*. We have seen that the interlocutors represent two sides of the author's temperament, two antithetical states of being. Marguerite embodies the terrestrial or corporeal, and therefore man's immoderate love of earthly matters. Francis represents the heavenly or spiritual, and thus man's awareness of the necessity of renouncing the terrestrial world. For Marguerite, death is associated with pain, sorrow, and loss, whereas for Francis, the death of the body is the beginning of everlasting joy. While the methods of controversy appear to derive from eristic dialectic, the dialogue is conducted in the spirit of peirastic dialectic. The pro-and-contra argumentation and the spirit of "competition" are fully present in this ruthless battle between flesh and spirit, but the dialectical process goes well beyond clever argumentation. Inquiries, objections, doubts, clarification requests, and so forth, portray the striving of a divided mind toward resolution, the laborious process by which the author searches for truth—a truth from within. The dialogue evolves along two main lines that are never clearly defined in the text: the self's search for a rational position in the face of death, and the self's effort to silence reason altogether, to annihilate the mind, which will enable

13. This sense of authority is rendered by the high frequency of imperative forms.

it to approach God. The dialogue describes the self's struggling to reach the first step, and when this first endeavor has failed, its effort to move along to the second. It therefore delineates the slow and complex process of enlightenment. Through its forward but at the same time backsliding motion, the dialogue mirrors the confusion and reluctance of the self to consent to the annihilation of the mind, and thus to its own annihilation. The self's gradual progress toward illumination culminates in its acknowledgment that truth is and ever will be beyond the mind's reach. In this sense, the *Navire* is a lesson in humility, as it demonstrates the mind's limitations, and forces the self to renounce its illusion of independence. The rhetoric of dialogue proves to be quite suitable for rendering the mind's search for truth. As soon as the mind acknowledges its failure, however, the dialogue is brought to a close. Logically, only silence, as we shall later see, can possibly translate the final silencing of reason.

Characters and Decor

Seeking to achieve some sense of verisimilitude, medieval poets introduced their debates with narrative. In *pastourelles* and *tensons* the dialogue proper is presented within the context of an account, one stanza or two at the most, of the speakers' encounter, chance meeting, banquet, colloquy, or dream vision. The mimesis of verisimilitude is a major concern of Renaissance dialogists, for verisimilitude induces credibility and enhances the persuasive effect.[14] Setting, time, and circumstances (where, when, and why the conversation takes place) complement characterization.

The pretext or the prologue—which is, in fact, the very introduction to the logos—and the context are of no minor importance in the *Heptameron*. Marguerite's concern with decorum and verisimilitude shows in her careful attention to detail concerning the circumstances of the stories and debates, and in her depiction of characters. First she explains the occasion for the discussants' gath-

14. Taking Cicero as their model, Renaissance theorists of dialogue argue for adherence to the ancient principles of decorum and verisimilitude that enable the dialogist to achieve the "illusion of mimetic probability." See, for instance, Carlo Sigonio's discussion of the *vestibule* in his *De dialogo liber* (1561) or Torquato Tasso's *Discorso dell'arte del dialogo* (1585) and his treatment of the figural language of dialogue through the use of the figure of *enargeia*.

ering (the unexpected floods that prevent them from returning home) and why they chose their pastime. She claims that important contemporary events, the peace treaty between Francis I and the king of England, the confinement of Madame the Dauphine, and so forth, have prevented the royal family from pursuing their storytelling project. She situates stories and debates in a historical context through references to living figures and verifiable events, blurring the boundaries between fiction and nonfiction. Consequently, the discussants' endeavor to complete the court's interrupted project appears to be an authentic event of importance. The fact that they know about the royal family's project suggests their inclusion in the royal circle of acquaintances. Marguerite also specifies the place, time, and atmosphere of her characters' daily gatherings. After having listened to the lesson of Madame Oisille and following a devoutly heard mass, the discussants meet in a lovely meadow. There, sitting on the green and soft grass, they share personal experiences by recounting gallant stories and amusing anecdotes, which are overheard by eavesdropping monks hidden behind the hedge.[15]

Marguerite adopts the garden setting from classical dialogue but, in contrast to Boccaccio, she does not indulge in luxuriant descriptions of the *locus amoenus*.[16] Her concise style, reminiscent of the medieval poets, indicates the primordial function assigned to the dialogical scene in the *Heptameron*. I may add that Marguerite neglects what she considers to be superfluous detail, and a dangerous distraction from her major concern, her search for truth. However, to accredit this search and satisfy the demands of decorum she attempts to convey psychological truth.

She provides us with a portrait of each discussant that, though brief, suffices to distinguish various personalities from the outset. In an effort to individualize her characters and to give credibility to the spoken word, Marguerite fully utilizes the expressive poten-

15. On the triple relationship between time, place, and subject, see Kushner, "Le Rôle structurel du *locus amoenus* dans les dialogues de la Renaissance," *Cahiers de l'Association Internationale des Etudes Françaises* 34 (1982): 39–57; and Henri Mitterand, "Dialogue et littéralité romanesque," in *Le Dialogue*, ed. Pierre L. Léon and Paul Perron (Ottawa, Canada: Didier, 1985), 144–45.

16. I tend to agree with M. Tetel (1973) when, commenting upon the scant description of the *locus amoenus*, he observes: "Marguerite does not create a setting for her characters to move in, but pits them directly one against another to explore their motivations and helplessness in the face of their condition" (159).

tial of dialogue. Much like medieval poets, she develops the dramatic qualities of the genre[17] and captures the discussants' facial and bodily expressions. Tones, gestures, and other emotional signs such as redness of the face,[18] bursts of laughter, and so forth, take on a value of their own. Together they become a language capable of translating the lightness or seriousness of an argument and the speakers' degree of involvement, or, more importantly, capable of exposing the truth often obscured by words, and thus the more private sides of the self. We learn, for example, of Hircan's intimate relationship with Nomerfide through the quarreling tone of their discussion after the seventieth novella. I will digress here to underline another aspect of theatricality. Much like actors, the discussants show complete awareness of the presence of their public, the other discussants, and the monks whose presence behind the hedge is strongly felt (even though they do not participate in the discussions). Their sobriety in eating and drinking, and the care they take in getting ready before their "performances" by retiring to their rooms at a reasonable hour to study their roles thoroughly, show that they, like the author, have a real sense of theatricality.

Characterization, as achieved through the debates, confers an obvious sense of continuity on the work. From one discussion to the next the discussants' individual traits surface and inform their viewpoints. For example, we soon learn that they will all turn to Nomerfide, the practical joker of the group, to cheer them up after a pitiful tale. We also expect Dagoucin to defend idealistic love theories and Hircan, Saffredent, and Simontault fiercely to oppose Oisille's or Parlamente's arguments. In a sense, this continuity eliminates the climate of unpredictability necessary to maintain the reader's interest. Knowing a particular speaker's viewpoint beforehand may indeed cause our interest to slacken, yet we should not misjudge the meaning that is enforced through repetition. In

17. Both Sigonio and Tasso discuss the dramatic qualities of dialogue. For a discussion of the particular gap that dialogue came to fill in the spectrum of literary genres, see E. Kushner, "Dialogue of French Renaissance," 31–32.

18. On the importance given to gestures and emotional signs in the stories, see Gaël Milin, "Coeur/contenance/regard: Du Geste à l'analyse psychologique dans l'*Heptaméron* de Marguerite de Navarre," in *Mélanges de langue et littérature françaises du Moyen Age et de la Renaissance offerts à Monsieur Charles Foulon* (Rennes, France: Institut de français, Université de Haute Bretagne, 1980), 259–65.

fact, the consistency of representation points, as we shall later see, to a lack of "character development" in the discussants, and thus to the failure of dialectic.

In contrast to the novellas, which present hastily sketched characters[19]—characters whom the reader knows only indirectly—the dialogues project carefully defined individuals and a "slice of their life." In lively dramatic exchanges, and through the author's interpolations which constitute in themselves another dialogue (author with reader), the truth of the heart is revealed.[20] Viewed from this angle, the debates play a more primary role than the novellas. Put another way, the debates seem to constitute the "real" story, which the discussants' stories (the novellas) serve to enlighten. But where the novellas aim to reproduce an outside reality from which the narrators are excluded, the debates bring the fictionalized reality to life. In the debates the discussants relate fictionalized situations to their own, creating a hypothetical present that actualizes what would otherwise remain abstract.

This attempt to confer reality on the world of fiction, another aspect of Marguerite's concern with verisimilitude, is evident in the course of the dialogues. The following comment is typical: "Si à quelqu'une de *vous* advenoit pareil cas, le remede y est ja donné" [34, my emphasis: So if anything like this should ever happen to any of *you*, you now know what the remedy is!]. The usage of the pronoun *vous* applies to storytellers and readers alike, and thus effects a shift from a remote past to a vivid present, from the abstract to the actual, from a discourse in the exemplum tradition to one more subjective. The rhetorical tool in fact mirrors our instinctive gesture when we read and, more generally, when we engage in any process of rationalization, showing that man acquires knowledge only through his own concrete, immediate experience. Central to the text's openness, this stylistic device imparts vitality to the dia-

19. In the novella tradition the characters' individuation is minimized to enhance the stories' universality. Marguerite briefly sketches the characters' situation and interrelationships.

20. Contrary to Nicole Cazauran's assertion in *L'Heptaméron de Marguerite de Navarre* (Paris: CDU/ SEDES, 1976), 88, the author intervenes in the dialogues to reveal the truth of the heart, so often obscured in the interlocutors' words. See p. 22: "Saffredent . . . eut bien desiré pouvoir dire quelque chose qui bien eut esté agreable à la compaignye, et sur toutes à une" [Saffredent . . . would be only too happy if he could tell his companions, and a certain lady in particular, something to please them].

logues, for it stimulates hypothetical stories that are in fact recon-
structions, rewritings, of the story just told, and in which the discussants now become the protagonists. Thus, the dialogues can be
considered as rewritings or expansions of the novellas. Note what
happens when the discussants move away from the fictionalized,
impersonal situation to one that engages them directly. The shift
from third-person to first-person narration is responsible for per-
sonalizing the *récit*: "Il me semble, ce dist Hircan, que le grand
gentil homme, dont vous avez parlé, estoit si despourveu de
cueur, qu'il n'estoit digne d'être ramentu" [34: "In my opinion,"
said Hircan, "the tall lord of your story lacked nerve, and didn't
deserve to have his memory preserved"].

Contrast this with: "Si j'en estois jusques là, dist Hircan, je me
tiendrois pour deshonoré si je ne venois à fin de mon intention."
[34: "If I'd gone that far," Hircan replied, "I'd consider my honor
ruined if I didn't go through with it!"]. When simple commentary[21] evolves into self-identification,[22] we see that both the
"truth" of the story (the finished text) and the "truth" of the frame
story are challenged. In the afore-mentioned example, the reader
is invited to "rewrite" the story he has just heard and imagine the
proud Hircan in a role quite different from the one he usually
plays. When more than one of the discussants identify with the
fictionalized characters, the "mascarade," or assumption of roles in
the fictionalized plot, is complete. From this "rewriting process,"
which takes place in the course of the dialogue, results a series of
new stories. The latter are both autonomous and parallel.

In her attempt to imitate the real Marguerite reproduces what
usually occurs in the course of a conversation. Incoherent remarks,
pointless reflections, and unfounded criticisms surface here and
there, mirroring the spontaneity of the discussants' exchanges but
also, one could say, the futility and irrationality of human speech.
Aware of the purely polemic turn the discussion takes after the
account of the queen of Castille's love affair, and thus of its point-
lessness, Oisille refuses to pursue it further:

21. For other commentaries of this sort, see debates 18 and 53.

22. Self-identification occurs in more dramatic passages. Dialogue is no longer a
means of exchanging viewpoints about human behavior but rather of presenting the
interlocutors in a different light. See Nomerfide's reply in debate 5, debate 8 (which
functions as a "mise en abyme" of the novella), and debate 10.

Madame Oisille, voyant que soubz couleur de blasmer et reprendre
en la Royne de Castille ce qu'à la verité n'est à louer ni en elle ni
en autre, les hommes se debordoient si fort à medire des femmes et
que les plus saiges et honnestes estoient aussi peu espargnées que
les plus folles et impudiques, ne peut en durer que l'on passat plus
outre.   (202)

[Although what the Queen of Castille had done was certainly not
something to be praised either in her or anybody else, Oisille could
see that on the pretext of criticizing her behavior the men would
go so far in speaking ill of women in general that they would no
more spare women who were modest and chaste than they would
those who were wanton and lewd. She could not bear the men to
proceed further.]

In a parallel way, when Saffredent's conversation goes beyond the
limits of good taste, Nomerfide puts an end to it: "[Nomerfide
. . . dit:] Qui vous vouldroit escouter, la Journée se passeroit en
querelles. Mais il me tarde tant d'oyr encores une histoire, que je
prie Longarine de donner sa voix à quelcun," [128: "If we listened
to you all day," said Nomerfide, "we'd never stop arguing. But
I'm waiting to hear another story, so I'll ask Longarine if she'll
pick the next person to speak"]. The frequent interjections not
only enliven the debates, they also reflect the impatience we experience when, listening to another, we are eager to express our own
viewpoint—precisely what happens in both debates 18 and 48.

In this imitation of life the endings of a great many dialogues
are most disturbing. The pretext of time often brings about a conclusion which, taking into consideration the plurality of viewpoints expressed by the discussants, appears totally arbitrary.
Take for example the conflict of opinions following the story of
Floride and Amadour, which is miraculously put to rest as soon as
Oisille reminds her audience of the late hour: "Mais voyez où est
le soleil, et oyez la cloche de l'abbaye, qui, long temps a, nous
appelle à vespres, dont je ne vous ay point advertiz . . ." [84: See
how low the sun is already. And listen to the Abbey bell calling
us to vespers! It started ringing a while ago, but I didn't draw
your attention to it . . .]. Marguerite may have been aware of the
artificiality of these endings. And this may be the reason she so
frequently mentions the fact that the discussions, which had remained unfinished in the meadow, were to continue until each
discussant finally retired: "Vespres oyes, allerent souper, qui ne

fut tout le soir sans parler des comptes qu'ils avoient oyz . . ."
[85: After hearing vespers, they had their supper, and spent the
evening discussing the stories they had heard . . .].

The language itself also occasionally sounds artificial. Now and
again the syntax leads one to suspect that these so-called conversation pieces, these "daily utterances," which are supposed to be
"seized on the moment," have in fact been carefully thought out.
In these passages the familiar tone, the proverbialisms, and the
colloquialisms give way to a more sophisticated, more purpose-
fully organized discourse. Composed of declarative clauses, or
highly structured through a variety of explicative, causal conjunc-
tions (*toutefois*, *car*, *d'autant que*, *mais*, *parquoy*, *de sorte que*), this
emphatic syntax departs from everyday conversation to express
well articulated thoughts and close-textured arguments:

> Vous en parlez bien à voz aises, dist Simontault; mais nous, qui
> sçavons que la chose vault, en debvons dire nostre oppinion. Quant
> est de moy, je l'estime . . . car je croy que. . . . Dagoucin le re-
> print, disant qu'il estoit de contraire opinion.   (141)

> ["It is easy for you to talk," said Simontault, "but those of us who
> know the truth in such matters ought to say what we think. As far
> as I'm concerned, I consider that . . . because I believe that. . . ."
> Dagoucin objected to this, saying that his opinion was exactly the
> opposite.]

Skillfully constructed, these passages may appear to be more didactically oriented. Their presence in a discourse that claims to be
based primarily upon daily usage may surprise. But the rhetorical
stance and the solid grammatical armature mirror the dialectical
process of understanding, the mental operation by means of which
man tries to apprehend the truth.[23] Note here that the speakers'
individuality rests not on their rhetoric, but on the content of the
stories they recount, the points of view they represent (thus the
type of argumentation they use), or on some traits of character
(sense of humor or seriousness of manner). In this sense, we may
say that psychological truth is achieved through content rather
than style. Yet, where rhetoric may not distinguish one voice from

---

23. Philosophical dialogue, as Cicero argues in his *De oratore* (19.63–64), differs
from public oratory in purpose and power. The dialogist who intends to instruct
(*docere*) adopts a style that appeals to the intellect. The orator employs an eloquence
that seeks to captivate (*delectare*), stir the emotions (*movere*), and ultimately persuade
(*flectere*).

the next, it points to another presence, that of an author who art-
fully manipulates her mouthpieces.

Although the concern with verisimilitude does not take the
same form in the *Navire*, it is most certainly present. It is worth
noting that Marguerite once again situates her dialogue within a
contemporary context. She brings into play, albeit later in the
text, the great Francis I and the entire royal family, including the
young Henri II who is soon to become king. Nevertheless, in introducing her dialogue Marguerite does not even establish a setting. The poem starts *in mediis rebus* and we know only that the
conversation between Francis and Marguerite takes place at night,
between the *visio*, which arouses Marguerite from her sleep, and
daylight, when Francis reascends to God. The temporal references
(night and dawn), the sleep and awakening motif, and the pretext
for the interruption of the dialogue (daylight dispelling darkness)
take on a symbolic dimension, suggesting the mystical nature of
this dialogue. Yet Marguerite refuses to turn her dialogue into a
barren and abstract allegory. Her inner struggle is real and so will
be the characters whom she chooses as her mouthpieces. By naming them and indicating their reactions in the course of the discussion, she dramatizes the psychic conflict and enlivens the tragic
truth of the self. We see, for example, that Marguerite (the dramatic persona) becomes infuriated when Francis refuses to see her
point of view. At times she will not even allow her brother to pursue his attacks. Francis too shows signs of impatience with the
obstinate Marguerite and reasserts his authority when she persists
in her blindness. The characters' strong emotions reflect the ruth-
lessness of the battle within Marguerite (the dialogist), and therefore the depth of the self's scission.

Dialogue: Instrument of Inquiry and Exposition

In the *Heptameron* dialogues satisfy the need to communicate
that the characters experience when they find themselves trapped
in the Abbaye of Serrances, shut off from the outside world. Dialogues focus on the privileged moment when the self opens up and
gives free rein to thoughts and emotions, speaking the truth of
both heart and mind. They relate the moment of truth, or rather
the moment when each individual shares with others his or her
own private truth. Unlike medieval disputes, polyphonic dia-

logues such as those found in the *Heptameron* seem to be conducted in an effort to exchange ideas and reach a final synthesis. John McClelland (1985) maintains that dispute and inequality are foreign to this type of dialogue. Instead, mutual respect and openness prevail.[24] But is this really the case in the *Heptameron*?

On the one hand, each individual seems eager to hear the opinions of the *others*. Each shows respect by not forcing his or her own views on the *others*. But on the other hand, none of them moves from his or her original position, as the total lack of "character development" I noted earlier demonstrates. From beginning to end, the debaters obstinately persist in their views. The high frequency of incidental phrases such as "says, thus says," shows that, thrown in pell-mell, many comments remain unechoed.[25] These discussions *in utramque partem* are reminiscent of Cicero's dialogues, as C. J. R. Armstrong (1976) explains: "In Cicero's philosophical dialogues . . . *all* the speakers are clearly using dialectic, but every man's dialectic has equal rights with every other man's. None is represented as 'victorious'; none is privileged *eo ipso* like the dialectic of Socrates in *Phaedrus*. Likewise, each interlocutor remains at the end, as at the beginning, in secure possession of his original opinion, again so unlike the young men reduced to a state of *aporia* by Socrates."[26] Thus, as the days pass, the discussions repeat themselves monotonously, and the same conflicts continually return.[27] The narrative devices I mentioned earlier—the fact that it is getting late, or that men would go on forever denigrating women, or the discussants' acknowledgment of their inability to come to an agreement—become more and more obvious, exposing the futility of the speakers' intellectual activities. We note the failure of dialectic in their quest for truth.

24. John McClelland, "Dialogue et rhétorique à la Renaissance," in *Le Dialogue*, 159.

25. Yet the discussions reveal that each one is very much aware of the opinions of the others. For example, arguments are often developed so as to forestall the others' objections.

26. C. J. R. Armstrong,"The Dialectical Road to Truth: The Dialogue," in *French Renaissance Studies 1540–70: Humanism and the Encyclopedia*, ed. Peter Sharratt (Edinburgh, Scotland: Edinburgh University Press, 1976) 43.

27. Individual points of view occasionally vary. For example, Geburon acts surprised to hear about the friars' hypocrisy, even though he himself has denounced their corruption over and over again, which Hircan notices and points out to him (347). Variants, though, attest to Marguerite's attempt to convey psychological truth and expose the fluidity of human truth and the inconsistencies of human speech.

Indeed the truth that soon becomes evident is the fundamental inadequacy of words. But, where the discussants frequently illustrate the limitations inherent in language, and therefore man's limited ability to communicate,[28] they fail to recognize their own inability to communicate with each other.[29] Still, this failure to communicate is sometimes deliberate. Take the case when two speakers engage in a private conversation, exchanging subtle comments that hide a discourse from the others and thus preclude their participation. While adding a human touch, the quarreling or teasing often turn the discussions into one-sided dialogues as in debates 1, 6, 26, 45, 70. In these cases dialogue is no longer associated with discovery and truth but with concealment and deceit.[30] Thus it turns into a parody of the Platonic symposium.

As the novellas gradually disclose the wide spectrum of human behavior and the confusing variety of phenomena, the debaters' continued trust in reason to attain truth seems more and more unfounded and unreasonable. In the eighteenth debate, however, Saffredent admits that they do not possess all of the facts of the situation being examined, and notes that they are therefore unlikely to reach an objective judgment about the protagonist's conduct:

Et que sçavons-nous, dist Saffredent, s'il estoit de ceulx que ung chappitre nomme *de frigidis et maleficiatis?* Mais si Hircan eust voulu parfaire sa louange, il nous debvoit compter comme il fut gentil compaignon, quant il eut ce qu'il demandoit; et à l'heure pourrions juger si ses vertuz ou impuissance le feit estre si saige.   (141)

["And how do we know," said Saffredent, "that he wasn't one of those referred to in a certain chapter headed *De frigidis et maledificiatis?* If Hircan had really wanted to sing this man's praises, he should have gone on to tell us how he acquitted himself once he got what he wanted. Then we could judge whether it was his virtue or his impotence that made him so well-behaved!"]

28. Take, for instance, the stories based upon a misunderstanding such as novellas 11 and 46. In the former, La Mothe interprets incorrectly Mme de Roncex's cry for help, and thus brings shame to her mistress. In the latter, after a mother fails to "read" correctly the intent of a Franciscan friar, paradoxically named Mr. De Valé ("rush down" although he is the one who runs up to girls' rooms to fulfill his evil desires), her daughter is raped.

29. As we have seen earlier, the author then intervenes.

30. In his study of the dialogues in the stories, Tetel (1973) arrives at a similar conclusion: "If an extreme concision of dialogue momentarily fixes a truth, an interpretation, a more dynamic, extended form of dialogue becomes a vehicle for deception, for veiling the truth" (146). See particularly pp. 127–49.

Note that Saffredent's observation is reinforced by the insistent recurrence of hypothetical turns that point to the elusiveness of language and to man's incapacity to "pin down" external phenomena. Besides, as Marcel Tetel (1973) argues, "the more a character attempts to substantiate a viewpoint or a state of mind, the more he or she will reveal, in the eyes of the debaters and of Marguerite, flaws and uncertainties in motivation and attitude toward human conduct" (139).

Taking into consideration the complexity of the discussion topics and the many-sidedness of human truth, the conflicts of opinions are no surprise. They maintain the continual flow of ideas, nurturing doubt in the form of the "que sçavons-nous" [what do we know], which, in turn, keeps generating new efforts to understand and new commentaries. But while this diversity of interpretation, this proliferation of meaning, is crucial to the dynamism of the debates, it also precludes any possibility of reaching an ultimate truth.[31] This diversity demonstrates, on the one hand, the sterility of human speech and, on the other, man's presumptuousness when, inquiring after truth, he claims to solve the unsolvable and pronounce the last word.

Confusion and inconclusiveness may very well be the only outcomes of the debates,[32] yet one must not ignore their intrinsic significance. Indeed, one should remain alert to what is *not* said. The polyphonic dialogues of the *Heptameron*, appropriately named by one of the interlocutors "propos d'impossibilité" [115: talking about impossibilities], are for the author not so much a means by which she inquires after truth but rather a means by which she exposes a particular truth about the unsaid.

The dialogues may appear to be nondidactic. We have seen that all views are equally represented and evenly challenged. As a result, no one view predominates. Yet, as Kushner (1977) argues, "The will to teach is built into every dialogue and not only into those which give the impression of being didactically oriented"

31. This notion of plurality reveals the insufficiency of human intellect, anticipating Montaigne's skepticism (see *Essais* 2: 12) and the humanistic crisis soon to come.

32. Armstrong (1976) argues that this inconclusiveness is a recurrent feature in Renaissance dialogues: "If there is one thing many Renaissance dialogues are characteristically short of . . . it is truth: not that they tend to deliver falsehood—they just don't say anything at all" (41).

(34). It would be incorrect, though, to identify the author with one character (group) or another. Marguerite's message is conveyed through an interplay of viewpoints, through a network of oppositions. Truth is sought through a collaborative process whose very nature leads to a truth blurred, broken, and incomplete, trapped in the limitations inherent in human speech. The fragmentation effect and the open-endedness of the dialogue form seem to suit Marguerite's intent perfectly. Her message is clearly one of Pauline inspiration. The repetitive nature of the debates and their inconclusiveness expose with increasing persistence the discussants' and man's vanity in depending on his own efforts and on the human instrument of language to attain spiritual truth. For characters and readers alike the failure of reason (and dialogue as an epistemological tool) is a lesson in humility.[33] When, on the eighth day, Oisille's spiritual fervor spreads to the rest of the group, they all recognize their inability to speak the language of rational discourse. Consequently, they turn to a language that departs from language's usual meaning-producing function and aims essentially at producing pleasure:

> Parlamente commencea ainsy: "Mes dames, nos Journées passées ont esté plaines de tant de saiges comptes, que je vous vouldrois prier que ceste-cy le soit de toutes les plus grandes follyes, et les plus veritables, que nous nous pourrions adviser." (422)

> [Parlamente began to speak: "Ladies, every day so far has been taken up with so many wise tales that I would like to propose that today should be taken up with stories which are the most foolish and the most true we can think of."]

As the discussants choose to free themselves from the "prison of knowledge" and indulge in "foolishness," and soon after free themselves from "the prison of language," the reader is urged to

33. Marguerite cautions her reader over and over again: "Qui se cuyde saige est fol devant Dieu" [272: He who would be wise is a fool before God]. At the end of story 56, she condemns the pride of those who do not place their trust in God's grace, and "cuydent, par leur bon sens ou celluy d'autruy, povoir trouver en ce monde quelque felicité qui n'est donnée ny ne peut venir que de Dieu" [352: imagine that their common sense or someone else's will serve to achieve happiness in this world, whereas true happiness is given by, and can come from, God alone"]. See also novella 30. On the themes of pride and folly, see B. Jane Wells Romer, "Folly in the *Heptameron* of Marguerite de Navarre," *Bibliothèque d'Humanisme et Renaissance* 46, no. 1 (1984): 71–82.

follow their steps, in the hope that, like them, he or she will reach the desirable state of the *raptus mysticus*.[34]

The *Navire* has been frequently dismissed on aesthetic grounds for its lack of consistency or structural rigor.[35] Most readers deplore the "organizational weaknesses" of the poem and, as a result, the blurring of its main divisions which obscures the step-by-step development of thought. While such judgments carry some truth, they fail to account for Marguerite's tour de force in reproducing both the complexity of the divided mind and the obliqueness of the mental process. The puzzling features can be partly resolved if the text is viewed as an intricate interplay of variations on a set of binary oppositions. I have noted that the dialogue starts out with a confrontation between two entities, embodying two irreconcilable positions (a transcendent versus an earthbound perspective; God versus the sleeping soul; Francis's soul versus Marguerite's). At the outset, then, the dialogue is diphonic, but as the argument unfolds these binary oppositions are enriched by several others, and therefore echoed, in terms of their properties (living versus dead) or interrelationships (Creator versus creature; brother versus sister; lover versus beloved; *magister* versus *discipula*; Spirit versus Flesh; Reason versus Passion; king versus subject). Since most of these polarities are based upon a power relationship, we may say that the *Navire* is basically a disphonic dialogue. At the outset, the schema stands as in Figure 1.

Transcendence	Earthbound Perspective
God	the sleeping soul
Creator	creature
Francis's soul	Marguerite's soul
dead	living
brother	sister

As the argument develops, the schema evolves as in figure 2. Essential to the theme of this dialogue, the relationships between interlocutors are describable in the following terms: lover/be-

34. Significantly, *Les Prisons* and *La Comédie jouée au Mont-de-Marsan* were composed near the end of Marguerite's life, after the death of Francis I (in 1547), when Marguerite was still composing the *Heptameron*. Chronology certainly invites comparisons among the three works.

35. See Pierre Jourda, *Marguerite d'Angoulême, Duchesse d'Alençon, Reine de Navarre (1492–1549)* (Paris: Champion, 1930), 1: 582–591.

Lover		Beloved	
	Spirit	Flesh	
	Reason	Passion	
Magister			*Discipula*
	Spirit	Flesh	
King			Subject
	God	creature	

loved, *magister/discipula*, king/subject.[36] Each rapport is brought to light in the course of a verbal exchange which stands as a dialogue in itself, with a dynamic and a rhetoric of its own. The "erotic" rapport is antagonistic and competitive. It reproduces both the conflict between Flesh and Spirit and the interferences between Passion and Reason. What characterizes this exchange is its aggressiveness. The lover (Spirit/Reason) sees the object of his desire (Beloved/Flesh/Passion) as the declared enemy whom he wishes to conquer. The lover's aggressiveness increases as the beloved continues to resist his assaults. Each new defeat triggers the lover's desire to possess the beloved and thus renews desire perpetually. The battle against the Flesh is, in fact, a "physical" version of a "spiritual possession," which could be called persuasion by force.

The *magister/discipula* relation begins where the lover/beloved relation ends. A level of "spiritual possession" has been achieved but is now being threatened by the separation of lover and beloved. The master once provided his disciple with guidance and counseling while she, in return, expressed her respect and admiration for him. This rapport developed into a mode of dependency that tragically impaired the disciple when separation occurred. Although the dependency was purely spiritual, it is now experienced on an essentially physical level. Marguerite experiences the sense of "being left alone" as bereavement. Deprived of the spiritual guidance her master once offered her, she now misses their frequent "tête à tête." The loss of the master's "presence" brings with it the deprivation of both her sight and her hearing, that is, the impairment of both body and mind. Indeed, the body's

36. Marguerite often uses Briçonnet's motif of family ties as a symbol of the hold of the world on the soul. See Henri Heller, "Marguerite de Navarre and the Reformers of Meaux," *Bibliothèque d'Humanisme et Renaissance* 33 (1971): 288.

dysfunction, the loss of sight and hearing, caused by the disappearance of Light (embodied in the master), results in the mind's dysfunction, a loss of insight and understanding. To put an end to the self's impairment, the master does not aim at its cause, as he should, but at the manifestation of the disease. That is, he once again confronts the Flesh. But this time the battle does not take the shape of an assault against the Flesh. Instead, the Master (Spirit) confronts the enemy in a more "civil" manner, by appealing to its desires. To do so, he resorts to the Word of Seduction, to the "language of pleasure" that governs the Flesh's needs and passions, in the hope of silencing them both, thus allowing the Spirit to revive what was once a rich and fruitful exchange.

The king/subject relation is an intensification of the master/disciple relation. The notion of dependency develops along similar lines, operating at both the physical and the spiritual level. The whole nation, and the royal family in particular, appear to be "physically impaired" by the loss of their king. But this time the Spirit and not the Flesh is solicited. For the Spirit alone is capable of uncovering the Truth, and will, if it wishes, make the appropriate substitution of God for king. In other words, the Spirit will "make the leap" from an earthbound perspective to one of transcendence. The schema can now be rewritten as in figure 3. I shall now focus on the dynamics of the argumentation by examining the three dialogues.

Lover/beloved	*Magister/discipula*	King/subject
subcategory		
Spirit/Flesh	Spirit/Flesh-Spirit	
characteristics		
aggessiveness	admiration/respect	admiration/respect
drive to conquer	dependency	dependency
dynamics/argumentation		
assault on the Flesh	appeal to the Flesh	solicitation of Spirit
forceful convincing	seduction	subtle persuasion
rhetoric/language		
depreciative &	laudatory	hyperbolical
offensive		encomiastic
		grandiloquent

The Dialogue between Lover and Beloved, Spirit and Flesh, Reason and Passion

Gender distinctions, dictated by the gender of *Chair* (feminine) and *Esprit* (masculine), coincide with those of the old Christian tradition. The condition of woman (Flesh) with regard to man (Spirit)—beloved to lover, weak and dependent—mirrors the relationship of the Catholic Church to Christ, and humanity to God. Whereas sinfulness in the dialogue, following tradition, is conveyed by the generic feminine, Marguerite's assimilation of the Christian experience with the feminine experience elevates the feminine condition. More important, the interchangeability of roles, as will appear later (that is, the ambiguity of the voices in the dialogue), and throughout her works, suggests her intention to emphasize the equality of the sexes before God.[37]

In order to defeat the Flesh, the Spirit tries to mortify her by exposing her most base and vile side. He resorts to the well-known beast, decay, and prison metaphors, in language both deprecatory and offensive: "vaine chair" [71: vain Flesh]; "charongne" [332: carrion]; "coffre vieulx, cage, estuy ou panier" [190: old safe, cage, case or basket]; "corps faict pour pourrir" [194: body made to rot]; "L'homme est faict semblable a la beste" [294: man is made similar to beasts]; "senblable a l'elefant / Rendre te veux" [305–6: similar to the elephant / I wish to make you].[38] But the Flesh in turn cleverly responds in the language of the Spirit. She challenges his argument by affirming her "difference" in regard to his representation of her. She claims that, contrary to his allegations, she can rise above her mortal condition. Indeed, she can transcend death: "J'ay faict mon cueur ung pappier d'inventaire"

---

37. Whereas in the *Navire* Francis assumes the role of celestial mentor, in the *Dialogue en forme de vision nocturne* it is Marguerite's niece, Charlotte, who transmits spiritual truth. The narrator of *Les Prisons* may well be, in the cornice, the mentor of Amye, but in the allegorical narrative his role is that of the Christian sinner, much like the Sinful Soul in Marguerite's earlier poetry. For a more complete discussion of the interchangeability of roles and Marguerite's portrayal of a feminine/feminist spirituality, see Paula Sommers, *Celestial Ladders: Readings in Marguerite de Navarre's Poetry of Spiritual Ascent* (Geneva: Droz, 1989), 105–109, and her article, "The *Miroir* and Its Reflections: Marguerite de Navarre's Biblical Feminism," *Tulsa Studies in Women's Literature* 5 (Spring 1986): 29–39.

38. All quotations are from Robert Marichal's critical edition (Paris: Champion, 1956) and are identified by verse number. Translations are my own.

[169: I made my heart an inventory sheet]. Consequently, the Spirit's attempt to humble the Flesh fails disastrously, giving his enemy the opportunity to boast once more of her superiority: "Plus a l'oster raison en moy s'esforce / Et plus avant au fondz elle se mect" [364: The harder reason tries to conquer love / The deeper she falls]. Flesh goes on to claim, "Raison ne fut oncques d'amour maistresse" [376: Reason was never the mistress of love].

The Dialogue between Magister and Discipula, Spirit and Flesh

The mood of this dialogue is dominated by the disciple's grief over the death of the master who once gave her wise counsel: "Je l'ay perdu le plus saige entretien / Qui oncques fut! et le plus profitable!" [118–19: I lost the wisest converse / Which ever was, and the most beneficial]. Or again, "Quant tu vivois, j'oyois ton sainct devis / Ton bon propos, tant vertueux et saige" [226–28: When you were living, I could hear your holy converse / Your good counsel, so virtuous and wise]. As I said earlier, this spiritual dependency now assumes a physical dimension. The Flesh expresses her loss in a language accessible to her, effecting an incarnation of the Spirit: "Cinquante deux ans, j'ay de sa presence / Tousjours jouy, sans estre separée" [72–73: For fifty-two years his presence / I have enjoyed without ever being apart]. Flesh longs for what she misses: "Mais je n'*ois* plus en terre ung tel langaige / Je ne *voys* plus tel maistre et instructeur" [229–30, my italics: But I can no longer hear such language on earth / Nor see such a guide and teacher].

As a result of the master's absence, both Flesh and Spirit are diminished. The disciple's sight and insight, hearing and understanding, are impaired: "Privee suis de l'ouyr et du veoir" [256: Deprived of the sound and the sight]. In a first attempt to end this dependency, the master urges his disciple to stop mourning for him so that she may "faire le sault," rise above her condition. In other words, the Spirit urges the Flesh to embark on her own annihilation: "Laisse ton pleur, laisse ton soupirer / Laisse le deuil qui tant d'ennuy te donne" [607–8: Stop the weeping, stop the sighing / Stop the mourning which such trouble causes you]. The Spirit declares: "Si a moy veulx venir, faictz donc ung sault / Hors de ta chair et toy mesmes renonce / Car nulle chair ne peult sallir si hault" [460–62: If to me you wish to come, then make a leap /

Come out of your flesh, and renounce yourself / For no flesh can rise so high].

Resisting the idea of her own death, the Flesh again resorts to the language of proof, the language of reason, and thus confronts the Spirit on his own ground. She argues that to attempt to overcome despair is a sign of presumptuousness: "C'est ung effect d'un mondain glorieux / Qui dict si fort son cueur estre invincible" [685: It is the deed of the glorious mundane / Who so loudly claims his heart to be invincible]. And again: "O les geans, qui estiment possible / Santir de Dieu, sans les santir les coups" [688–89: O the giants who think it possible / To suffer God's blows without feeling them]. Any effort to ignore her pain would only serve to reinforce her pride. She would give in to her affective self, to nature, while endeavoring to silence it.

Defeated once again by the logic of the Flesh, the Spirit now turns to the language of pleasure, a language that quiets reason while acceding to the senses. He proceeds to evoke the virtues of the world beyond, "la haulte sapience," "la science," "la vraye clarté" [high wisdom, science, true light], and intones a hymn of praise to the World of Light and Knowledge. This world, the Spirit argues, will end the Flesh's present misfortune. It will strike down her fears, terminate her spiritual wanderings, dispel her blindness and ignorance. In heaven, her needs will be once again fulfilled by "ceste celeste et doulce discipline" [this celestial and sweet intruction]. She will recover the happiness she once knew with the Spirit:

Soyons par foy au grand Superieur
Toy et moy joinctz, ainsi que uniz estions.
Vivans ensemble au monde inferieur;

[487–89: Let us through faith be in the Almighty / You and I united as we were / When living together in the lower world].

Though dissociated from the reality it is intended to transmit (the upper world), the language of seduction fails. Indeed, the language of seduction is a language of pleasure, a language that speaks passion. It does communicate with the Flesh, but only to revive in her the desire of what once was, the "terrestre memoire" [terrestrial memories]. These memories prevent the Flesh from reaching the intended goal, and thus from ever attaining "divin sçavoir" [divine knowledge]. The master's argument twice arrives at a dead end. When he recalls to his disciple's memory the very thing he implored her earlier to put out of her mind, he is caught in a web of self-contradiction. When he compares what is in fact incomparable—spiritual union (*unio*) with physical union, earthliness with transcendence—his argumentation loses its persuasive power. His failure to avoid merging the terms that he had intended to distinguish is evident when the Flesh claims with renewed energy her ardent desire to see: "de mes yeulx j'espere *veoir* mon frere" [384, my italics: With my own eyes I hope to *see* my brother]. She proceeds to wish for her own death in order to retrieve her lost sight: "en enfer *voirray mes ennemys*" [388: in hell I shall see my enemies]; "*Voirray* jouir du loier que la foy / Promect" [392: I shall see others enjoy the prize that faith promises]. Later, after expressing joy at the anticipated recovery of her sight, she once again mourns her tragic loss: "ainsi je ne te voy" [396: thus, I cannot see you].

The Dialogue between King and Subject

This dialogue is superimposed on the previous one; the relation king-subject is nothing more than the hyperbolic expression of the relation master-disciple. Marguerite's guide now becomes the French people's guide. Moreover, the death of her guide may well have serious consequences for the entire nation. As the master acquires status, the disciple acquires power (from one disciple to the entire nation) and so does the Flesh. Her protest becomes a hyperbolic eulogy for the departed king,[39] and a powerful incantation that urges the nation to weep ("Pleurez, pleurez," [Weep, weep]). While unexpectedly enhancing the past by evoking the king's exceptional beauty and remarkable deeds,[40] this panegyric piece reestablishes the physical aspect of Marguerite's attachment ("Las!

---

39. The *Navire* presents all the distinctive features of the *planctus* or *planh*, which is generally described as a specialized variety of *sirventès*. The *planctus* recounts the despair and sorrow one experiences along with loss. It also includes a eulogy of the departed as well as a description of public mourning and an address to a ruthless death.

40. "Ta personne tant belle," 757; "ton visage et beau taint," 767; "ton oeil joieulx," 767; "ton assuré maintien," 769 [your face and fine coloring, your joyful eyes, your confident air]. As Robert Cottrell explains, "physical beauty was particularly important, for it was interpreted as a sign of Nature's favor"; see *The Grammar of Silence: A Reading of Marguerite de Navarre's Poetry* (Washington, DC: The Catholic University of America Press, 1986), 214.

Je le sens, mon frere, je le sens" [665: Alas, I feel it, my brother,
I feel it] and, more specifically, a rejuvenated sense of sight: "Devant mes yeulx tousjours je la voy telle," [759: Before my eyes I
still see you as in person]; "on te veoit" [778: one can see you]; "je
te voy" [781, 790, 799, 807: I can see you].[41]

The Spirit once again urges the Flesh to stop her mourning:

> Laisse de moy tous ces charnelz recordz,
> Recorde toy de Celluy qui l'ouvrage
> Faisoit en moy par ses divins accordz.   (814–16)

[Keep from me all these carnal testimonies / Bear testimony of Him
who the work completed in me through His divine decrees.]

In fact, it is not the Flesh he is now addressing but himself. The
Spirit alone can restore the proper order of things by acknowledging the merely instrumental status of the Flesh: "Ce n'estoit riens
de moy qu'un instrument / Ou le savoir du maistre se descueuvre"
[824–25: I was no more than an instrument / In which the master's knowledge may be discovered].

The inner battle takes on a different aspect as it evolves from
that of Flesh against Spirit to that of Spirit against Spirit, evoking
in a tonality of existential pathos the drama of the divided self. On
the linguistic level, the conflict takes the form of a true "competition," a rivalry between third- and first-person pronouns, *Luy* vs.
moy, and a confrontation of similar stylistic pieces. For example,
the incantation to the departed king finds its counterpart in the
chant addressed to God ("Luy seul . . . Luy seul"). In a parallel
way, the early encomium to the King is matched by a later one,
this time to Christ. Furthermore, the revered king is referred to
in terms more adequate to God. Consider, for example, "vostre
humain pardonneur" [980: your human forgiver], or "le non pareil" [1075: the unequalled], or the use of capitals as in "Monsei-

---

41. The physical dependency finds a variety of expressions including father / son,
the two halves of the whole, and of course the Spirit and Flesh metaphors: "O pere
et filz qui par dillection / Furent uniz: comme peurent porter / Voz tristes ceurs la
separation" [1135–37: Alas, father and son who out of love were united / How could
your grieving souls bear their separation]; "La forte amour, qui lyoit fortement / Voz
ceurs en ung, a penne se rompit / A ce cruel et dur esloignement" [1144–46: The
powerful love, which firmly joined / Your souls in one hardly broke / When the cruel
and painful separation occurred]; "Bien que l'esprit, au ciel, joieulx prospere / Le
corps perdons" [1079–80: Joyful, the Spirit in Heavens may prosper / But the Flesh
for us is lost].

gneur" (750) which, in this case, designates the king, thus challenging previous usage.[42] Similarly, God is portrayed in terms used earlier to describe the king: "Luy seul, luy seul doibz nommer frere et pere" [922: Him alone, Him alone, must you name brother and father]. Personal pronouns at times lose their referentiality, leaving the reader totally puzzled:

> Je pleureray toutesfois en *t*'aimant
> Et *t*'aimeray au millieu de mes pleurs,
> Dont *Luy* seul est fin et conmancemant.   (724–26, my italics)

[Yet I shall weep while loving *you* / And I shall love *you* while weeping, / Of which *He*, alone, is the end and the beginning].

Note here that (as is often the case) God's status is merely instrumental. Just as the king will live on in Henri II,[43] love for the king will survive through God. The doubling (the substitution of king for God) explains in part the failure of arguments designed to overcome the Spirit's resistance.

We further note that the Spirit's demand of himself parallels his demand to the Flesh in the first dialogue. Indeed, the Spirit urges himself, as he had urged the Flesh, to humble himself in order to achieve self-annihilation. To yield means to acknowledge that the Spirit is "rien" before the "tout" [Nothing before the All]:[44] "Luy seul mectoit vertu en audiance / Par moy, son *riens*" [821–22, my italics: He alone had virtue listened to / By me, his *nothing*]. When the language of proof (Reason) is found wanting, the Spirit must acknowledge his limitations. This acknowledgment in itself constitutes a first step toward self-annihilation. Logic having failed, only the will remains. The Spirit comes to realize that will alone can guide him to the Superior Spirit who will complete the transformation: "Qui peut tourner mon ceur et mon penser / Fors luy qui est de mon ceur formateur" [943–44:

42. Where "parfaicte amour" has first been contrasted with "forte amour" to oppose love of God with love of the king, "parfaict et vertueux amour" (verse 344) clearly designates the latter, defying the previous distinction.

43. "De son doux ceur amoureux et humain / Es heritier" [1199–1200: You are the inheritor / Of his sweet and loving heart].

44. On the paradox of "All" and "Nothing," and the influence of Lefèvre d'Etaples and Briçonnet, see H. Heller's article cited above and A. Winandy, "Piety and Humanistic Symbolism in the Works of Marguerite de Navarre," *Yale French Studies* 47 (1972): 145–69. Both Lefèvre d'Etaples and Briçonnet condemn intellectual endeavor as a sign of human pride, which prevents the soul from reaching communion with God.

Who can turn my heart and my thought / Save him who is my heart's maker].

Because these three dialogues are superimposed one upon the other, the *Navire* projects a confused mixture of voices which, many readers will agree, turn into a profoundly disturbing chant. Such cacophony (if I may call it that) stems from three factors, the first two of which are interrelated: (1) the fundamental ambiguity of the voices, (2) the discrepancies between addressee and respondent, and (3) the inconsistencies which surface from one dialogue to the next.

When the Flesh speaks the language of reason, and the Spirit speaks the language of the senses—in other words, when each opponent realizes that victory can be more easily achieved by meeting the other on his or her own ground—words become ambivalent. Ambiguity, however, is present from the outset. When Francis addresses the soul stricken with sorrow ("tire toy hors de ton corps non sçavant, / Monte a l'espoir, laisse ta vielle masse, viens avant" [5–6: free yourself of your unlearned body, rise to hope, leave your old mass behind, come forward], it would seem that he addresses the Spirit who alone can silence the Flesh. Yet, it is the Flesh, the senses, that are "d'estonnement fouys" [uttermost surprised] by the "voix douce et tres agreable / Qui des vivans sembloit" [26–27: sweet and most pleasant voice / Which sounded like that of the living souls]. The senses' response implies that the language Francis speaks is in fact accessible to the Flesh.

As the result of these ambiguities and discrepancies, the interlocutors may appear inconsistent and their viewpoints incoherent. Contradictions indeed surface from one dialogue to the next, reflecting the confusion of the divided self, the unpredictable paths taken by chaotic thought. For example, one may wonder why Francis persists in his argumentation, first in the language of reason, then in the language of pleasure, when he knows very well that neither the Flesh nor the Spirit could ever grasp what is beyond its reach:

La bas n'y a felicité pareille,
Ny dont l'on sceust trouver comparaison
A ceste cy que ton Dieu t'appareille.   (616–18)

[Yonder there is no similar bliss / No bliss one could ever compare / To that which your God is preparing for you].

Or again, "Nul ceur mortel ne le peult concevoir / L'eul regarder, ne bien oyr l'oreille" [613–14: No human heart could ever conceive him / Neither his eye see, nor his ear hear]. In dialogue one we saw how, in an effort to humble Marguerite, Francis reminded her of the low status man occupies in the chain of being: "L'homme est faict semblable a la beste" (294). In dialogue two, however, he urges her to "make the leap," and become "spiritually inclined." In other words, he urges Marguerite to be the opposite of what she is, to be contrary to her very nature. By asking her to pursue a goal she cannot possibly achieve, he exposes the fallacy of his own argument. Furthermore, he uses his rational skills to demonstrate man's inability to rise above the beast, ironically relying on reason to prove the insufficiency of reason.

In dialogue one Marguerite claims that she can indeed "faire le sault" [make the leap], whereas in dialogue two she acknowledges her inability to do so. Early on she maintains that her love is "vraye" [true] and that in spite of her separation from Francis it continues to grow, nourished by both her tears and her "ramentevoir" [memories]. She continues to affirm that her love can transcend absence, that death can only fortify her love: "par mort prandre accroissance" [263: by death it grows greater]. Yet in dialogue three Marguerite deplores the limitations of memory, and therefore man's inability to reach transcendence: "Memoire est trop chiche en ceste despence" [639: memory is too frugal for such spending]. As she denounces the limitations of the intellect she gives a remarkable panegyric of the king's deeds, which demonstrates the incredible power of the intellect to recapture the past. In dialogue two Marguerite admits to missing her master's wise counsel. At the same time, however, she refuses to follow the counsel that Francis is now offering her. Totally neglecting the fact that he came specifically to enlighten her, to make her "mieulx par [sa] parolle apprise" [402: better by his wise word], she ignores his advice.

Nonetheless, from these inconsistencies subtle transformations emerge that indicate a slow but constant change in perspective. When, in dialogue one, the Flesh boasts of her ability to transcend death, the idea of sorrow conveyed through tears and memories continues to reflect the Flesh's resistance to death as the ultimate means of self-defense. In dialogues two and three, on the other hand, sorrow means that one is willing to accept, to submit to, the will of God. In dialogue one death is associated with ugliness, decay, disintegration, and separation. In dialogue two death represents a lesson in humility. In dialogue three death represents the way man will recover his lost sight, signifying the restoration of his insight.

Considered in the light of its linearity, the *Navire* will appear to lack not only consistency but the "openness" required in the course of a *real* exchange. Viewed from this perspective, the pro-and-contra argumentation will indeed negate itself. While it maintains the flow of dialogue, the sequence of arguments and refutations (offensives and defensives) precludes any possibility of a final synthesis. In fact, the Flesh's protest grows louder and louder as we approach the end: "ma main te retiendra!" [1413: my hand will hold you back!]. On the other hand, the variations among the three dialogues, or among three levels of discourse, testify to the soul's progress toward enlightenment. When the Spirit acknowledges his fallibility and proclaims his willingness to abide—"A son vouloir mon esprit est soubmis" [955: To His will my mind is submissive]—we know that a significant step forward has been taken. We are not surprised, then, that the dialogue comes to a close. As Reason is defeated the art of reasoning comes to a halt, as does the representation of the reasoning process. The temporal "pretext" ("Voicy le jour . . ." [1399: Here comes daylight . . .]) therefore coincides with the Spirit's defeat or with the achievement of self-annihilation.[45] While giving the dialogue an element of mysticism, the light imagery points to the culmination of the search, to the actual process of illumination that ultimately takes place.

The *Navire* is a scenic illustration of the soul's journey toward God. It traces the various battles in which the Christian soul must engage before achieving communion with the divine (*unio*). The battle against the Flesh comes first and continues until the end. The Spirit discovers in the Flesh a formidable opponent, who has many of the most effective battle skills: cleverness, persuasiveness, endurance. While the Spirit fails to conquer the Flesh, he also fails to recognize his other equally threatening enemy, Himself.

---

45. Earlier, Marguerite had come close to a "degree zero of language": "je me debvrois comme inutille taire" [649: I should keep silent, like a useless person], but her inability to achieve silence means that the Spirit was not yet silenced.

Against this enemy more subtle skills are required, for it is no small thing to persuade the Spirit to acquiesce in his own death. The experience of *mortificatio* is the first step toward the *unio*.

The dramatization of the Spirit and the Flesh represents Marguerite's own experience as a Christian and the complex emotions she feels when the death of her beloved brother forces her to confront her own mortality. As the dialogue evolves from a crisis to its resolution, we may talk of its healing value. Indeed, as the curtain falls Marguerite is not far from the spirit of Christ or from recovering peace. The interiorized quality and the personal resonances of the dialogue convey a sense of genuineness that combines the power both to move and to persuade. Yet the didactic intent is more strongly felt in the authoritative voice of Francis who tends to moralize while instructing Marguerite in the principles of Evangelical doctrine. In a striking reversal of roles the "real convincer," Marguerite, becomes "convinced" or rather guided, soothed. This skillful technique for avoiding explicitly dogmatic discourse suggests to us the curative purpose of the *Navire*. In the course of her lament Marguerite formulates a therapy for the soul in danger. The text serves to introduce the reader to the author's religious beliefs, and more particularly to her personal views on humility, faith, and grace.

Through the representation of the Flesh's repeated assaults, the Christian is reminded of the necessity to keep the faith, especially at those moments when temptation seems the strongest. The various deprecations of human language and reason urge one to suppress one's arrogance and to put will above intelligence. Finally, the sudden change that occurs in the soul at the end of the dialogue teaches the primacy of grace and the necessity of turning to God, for God alone can inspire in man the desire for God.

Dialogue: The Art of Reconciliation

Dialogue, *dia-logos*, may be defined as a confrontation of two speakers of opposite camps or of two conflicting aspects of a temperament. In any case, dialogue implies a scission, but also the will to overcome this scission, to reunite the scattered fragments of the whole.[46] In short, dialogue grows out of the desire to recon-

---

46. It is true, though, that reconciliation will occur at the expense of one of them.

cile opposites. The closing of the *Navire* leaves one with the notion that such reconciliation is about to take place. In the *Heptameron* most arguments remain suspended and debates seldom produce agreement or harmony. Yet it is in this very work that Marguerite carries farthest the notion of reconciliation that is implied in "dialogue."

Critics have often drawn attention to the composite nature of the *Heptameron*. On the one hand, Philippe de Lajarte (1981, 402–3) notes its dialogical orientation:

> Au niveau de la fiction . . . l'oeuvre se donne . . . comme le produit d'une interaction discursive, d'un procès social de communication et d'échange . . . au niveau de l'Histoire, l'oeuvre à naître se présente comme une réponse à une requête, et s'inscrit dans un circuit d'échange social.

> [At the level of fiction . . . the work presents itself . . . as the product of a discursive interaction, of a social process of communication and exchange . . . at the level of History . . . the work to be born presents itself as a response to a request; it inscribes itself in a circuit of social exchange.]

Commenting on the regard for truth that dominates the dialogues, Michel Le Guern (1981) concludes that the *Heptameron* itself belongs—at least partially—to the "dialogue genre."[47] M. Bénouis (1976), on the other hand, contends that narrative prevails, pointing to the large number of characters, peripeteia, frequent descriptive and narrative passages, and chronological concerns.

While such judgments tend to overemphasize one aspect of the work at the expense of the other, others such as this by Henri Coulet (1967) seem more accurate, as they do justice to the underlying dialectical structure—which forms the essential originality of the *Heptameron*—and the author's carefully thought-out plan:

> Si Marguerite avait voulu faire confiance à la vie pour dépasser et résoudre tous les problèmes, elle se serait contentée du récit . . . si elle avait voulu développer des idées, s'exercer au discours et à la dialectique . . . elle eût noyé l'anecdote dans le dialogue.   (126)

> [If Marguerite had wished to entrust life to overcome, and solve all problems, she would have contented herself with narrative . . . if

---

47. Michel Le Guern, "Sur le genre du dialogue, in *"L'Automne de la Renaissance, 1580–1630*, ed. Jean Lafond and André Stegmann (Paris: Vrin, 1981), 143.

she had wished to explore ideas, to engage in oratory and dialectic
. . . she would have drowned the stories in the dialogues.]

Indeed, even at first reading, one is struck by the harmonious
blending of themes, tones, rhythms, styles, genres, and purposes,
in short, by the true sense of decorum as due proportion and balance among the various components of the literary work. For example, as we have seen earlier, the stories and debates range from
light, humorous, and even coarse to grave, solemn, and tragic. A
story may involve quite frivolous matters and yet be followed by
a discussion of the utmost importance. In spite of the deep resonances of her work, Marguerite never loses sight of its recreational
nature, thus satisfying the standard Renaissance prescription of
profit and delight. She does not wish to elaborate spiritual reflections that would soon take a dogmatic turn. Through her characters' words and actions she reveals the doctrines that she values,
but declines further comment, leaving the reader to think for himself or herself. Thus the light tone and effervescence of the debates,
and the vivaciousness of the repartee, engage author and reader
alike to forget the serious for a while, and enjoy the pure diversion
of the game. These changes in mood are part of the narrators-de-
baters' efforts to achieve harmony.[48] Wishing to maintain equa-
nimity, they balance their own lives between their devotion to
God and the more futile storytelling, between the care of soul,
body, and mind. Further, as rigorously constructed narrative passages alternate with more spontaneous conversation pieces, a carefully thought-out discourse gives way to one with a natural flow,
each having its own rhetoric.[49] The rigid, static three-beat rhythm
of the novellas (the narrator's statement of purpose/the narration/
the morality that may or may not differ from the previously
avowed purpose)[50] is counterbalanced by the dynamic and often
erratic pace of the debates, with their continual changes of speaker
or subject matter.[51]

Marguerite formulates her own definition of a novella, which

48. In this sense they bring to mind Rabelais's Thelemites.

49. Yet I have noted earlier that one may occasionally filter into the other.

50. This technique often promotes ambiguity as it underlines the gap between
the truth that is initially claimed and the truth that is finally reached.

51. On twenty-seven occasions the discussants take the floor without asking
permission, a technique, Cazauran (1972) notes, used over and over again beginning
with the Fifth Day; see pp. 70–78.

challenges traditional narrative (and generic) conventions.[52] The novella includes a story that is supplemented by a debate. While two generic modes are being confronted—one narrative and one related to philosophy, dialectic, rhetoric, fiction, and drama[53]—this confrontation never turns to conflict. Instead, as Tzvetan Todorov (1969) explains, it reveals affinities between discursive modes that at first might seem to be in opposition:

> Une histoire ne peut . . . commencer que par une question et ne peut se clore que par une réponse (sinon elle devrait continuer). En même temps, le couple question-réponse forme le noyau même du dialogue, c'est un micro-dialogue; par conséquent la nouvelle est, elle aussi, profondément dialogique. Et inversement, tout couple de répliques dans un dialogue est une nouvelle en puissance.[54]

> [A story can only . . . begin with a question and end with an answer (otherwise the story would have to continue). In a parallel way, the coupling question-answer constitutes the core of the dialogue, it is a microdialogue; consequently the novella is also essentially dialogical. And on the other hand, every question-answer pair in a dialogue is potentially a novella.]

In fact, this harmonious blending of generic modes takes several forms in the *Heptameron*. A story may contain a dialogue of some

52. The relation between narrative fiction and dialectical discourse is a constant concern of sixteenth-century storytellers. In the 1560s we note an increasing tendency to subordinate narrative to dialogue (see, for instance, Des Périers's *Contes et Discours d'Eutrapel* or Jacques Yver's *Printemps*)—a tendency that is at the origin of the so-called discours bigarré. But toward the end of the century, under the influence of Bandello, narrative will regain its primacy and the frame story and accompanying debates will be altogether eliminated. On the development of narrative forms in the sixteenth century, see Gabriel A. Pérouse, "De Montaigne à Boccace et de Boccace à Montaigne—Contribution à l'étude de la naissance de l'essai," in *La Nouvelle française à la Renaissance*, edited by L. Sozzi, with an introduction by V. -L. Saulnier (Paris: Slatkine, 1981), 13–40.

53. "Dialogue is simultaneously an instrument of cognitive inquiry as that used by ancient philosophers and, in terms of its structure and style, a work of fiction. Therefore, to paraphrase Wilson, dialogue is an 'incomplete fiction.' As an art of argumentation, dialectic is its essential tool. In its use of tricks and devices to please, instruct, and persuade, dialogue is related to rhetoric. Like drama, dialogue records the speeches of men, etc. Its indeterminacy makes dialogue not a genre as such but a 'mixture of genres,' including the genre of mixture itself, satire. This is why dialogue is sometimes viewed as a monstrosity, a 'genre dégénéré'" (Lacoue-Labarthe and Nancy 1975, 150). While the synthetic, hybrid nature of dialogue accounts for its unparalleled popularity among writers, it posed a tremendous challenge to Renaissance theorists in their attempts to elaborate a poetics of dialogue.

54. Tzvetan Todorov, *Grammaire du Décaméron* (The Hague-Paris: Mouton, 1969), 77.

sort—usually rather brief—which often occurs at a climactic moment.[55] Likewise, the dialogue may enclose a story, thus eliminating much interaction between the speakers. Moreover, story and debate are born out of each other in an endless succession of rebounds.[56] Their interdependency is brought to light in a variety of ways in the course of the dialogues.

In many a case the debate's primary function is instrumental, transitional. As it brings one story to a close, it merges into another. Part of the paratext, it serves as a preface (prologue) to the ensuing novella, as a kind of foreword allowing the narrator to obtain authority and ensure reader involvement.[57] The discussion may lead someone to request a certain type of story, a particular theme, or a change of tone. Saffredent picks Ennasuite to tell the twenty-seventh tale "la priant qu'elle n'oublye poinct à (les) faire rire" [221: requesting that she take good care to make (them) laugh]. Therefore, the debates participate in the overall balance of tones and registers. The discussants may also request that one of them illustrate what has been said in the course of the dialogue:

> Gardez-vous, dist Nomerfide (à Ennasuite), de l'aymer tant (vostre mary): trop d'amour trompe et luy et vous, car partout il y a le moien: et, par faulte d'estre bien entendu, souvent engendre hayne par amour.—Il me semble, dist Simontault, que vous n'avez poinct mené ce propos si avant, sans le confirmer de quelque exemple.   (395)

55. Tetel (1973) comments on the scant use Marguerite makes of direct discourse or dialogue in the novellas (104–49). In "The Representation of Discourse in the Renaissance *Nouvelle*: Bonaventure Des Périers and Marguerite de Navarre" (*Poetics Today* 3 [1985]: 585–95), Deborah N. Losse challenges this point of view.

56. The interdependency between story and debate gains in interest when it is enhanced and enriched by repetition and reflection. By virtue of its mirroring effect, debate 8 invites the reader to establish correlations between the discussants and the characters of the story just told, thus allowing him or her to join in the general euphoria produced as each character/discussant believes he or she knows more than the other. See Colette H. Winn, "Le Clin d'oeil de l'onomaturge: Les nouvelles VIII, XI et XXXVII de *L'Heptaméron*," *Romance Notes* 26, no. 2 (1986): 149–54.

57. To achieve mastery the sixteenth-century storyteller resorts to various strategies. Among the most common are the following. The narrator lays claim to a "secondary" authority, evoking the name of the most renowned ancient author. In other words, he relies on the intertext as a model or an antimodel (like Marguerite herself). Or he may claim to be in possession of important information and willing to divulge it. And again he may make no other claim than the desire to entertain his audience. On authority and seduction, see Ross Chambers, *Story and Situation—Narrative Seduction and the Power of Fiction* (Minneapolis: University of Minnesota Press, 1984).

["You should be careful not to love him too much," said Nomer-fide. "Too much love could lead you both astray. There's a happy medium for everything. If there's a failure of understanding, love may engender hatred." "I don't think you would have made that point," said Simontault, "if you weren't intending to confirm it with some example."]

The interrelationship between narrative and debate underlines the exemplary nature of the novellas. As Philippe de Lajarte (1975) explains, the dialogue initially posits ideals (universals) and the novella then attests and objectifies their existence.[58] But the novella may also provide an alternate truth. In debate 3, for example, Ennasuitte claims that she has a story to tell "affin que Saffredent et toute la compaignye congnoisse que toutes dames ne sont pas semblables à la Royne de laquelle il a parlé" [27: which will show Saffredent and everyone else here that not *all* women are like the queen he has told us about]. The novellas often reinforce the momentary syntheses, but they may also have a disintegrating effect. In a parallel way the debates reinforce but undermine as well the "truth," and therefore the didactic intent of the novellas.[59] By juxtaposing the narrators' claims to objective truth (the stories) to their widely varying subjective views (the discussions), Marguerite underscores the illusionary nature of truth. When each discussant draws his or her own conclusion about the story just told, the latter loses its power to convince. In debate 9 Parlamente expresses her desire to tell a story to demonstrate the virtue of women:

> Et si je vous en nommois une, bien aymante, bien requise, pressée et importunée, et toutesfois femme de bien, victorieuse de son cueur, de son corps, d'amour et de son amy, advoueriez-vous que la chose veritable seroit possible?   (54)

> ["And just suppose," said Parlamente, "that I were able to name a lady who had been truly in love, who had been desired, pursued and wooed, and yet had remained an honest woman, victorious

---

58. Philippe de Lajarte, "L'*Heptaméron* et la naissance du récit moderne: Essai de lecture épistémologique d'un discours narratif," *Littérature* 17 (1975): 41.

59. M. J. Baker (1971), A. J. Krailsheimer (1966), and Donald Stone (1973) have drawn attention to the notion of didacticism in the *Heptameron*. For an interesting discussion of the way in which the *Heptameron* challenges the didactic possibilities of both dialogue and exemplary narrative, see John Lyons, "The *Heptameron* and Unlearning from Example," *Exemplum—The Rhetoric of Example in Early Modern France* (Princeton: Princeton University Press, 1989), 72–117.

over the feelings of her heart, victorious over her body, victorious
over her love and victorious over her suitor? Would you admit that
such a thing were possible?"]

Determined to praise the virtuous woman, Parlamente nevertheless admits that she is retelling the story once told by "ung de [ses]
plus grands et entiers amys, à la louange de l'homme du monde
qu'il avoit le plus aymé" [54: by a very close friend of hers, a man
who was devoted to the hero of the story and wished to sing his
praises].

The dialogue starts with the moral lesson Parlamente draws,
which is the opposite of that which her friend had drawn: "ne
croire poinct tant de bien aux hommes" [83: not to have so much
faith in men]. It closes with Geburon's moral lesson which echoes
that of Parlamente's friend: "il me semble qu'Amadour estoit ung
aussy honneste et vertueulx chevalier qu'il en soit poinct" [84: in
my opinion Amador was the most noble and valiant knight that
ever lived]. Between the two, the other discussants express their
conflicting views. The exemplary tale demonstrates the impossibility for the discussants to convince, and thus reach final consensus. As a result, stories and debates both contribute to the notion
of ambivalent and relativistic truth. And yet the repeated failure
of exemplary narrative and argumentation is challenged again and
again by the discussants' continued effort to demonstrate and speculate in search of an elusive truth. Finally, the debate may form,
in Lucien Dällenbach's (1977) terms, a "mise en abyme de l'énonciation"[60] as it engages the narrators (and the reader) to reflect on
the rules that govern the art of narrative fiction. Longarine chooses
Saffredent to speak but, aware of his partiality toward men, she
insists that he tell the "truth" (then a common rhetorical device)
which they all swore to tell:

> Je la donne, dist-elle, à Saffredent. Mais je le prie qu'il nous fasse
> le plus beau compte qu'il se pourra adviser, et qu'il ne regarde
> poinct tant à dire mal des femmes, que, là où il y aura du bien, il
> en veulle monstrer la verité.   (207)

> ["I choose Saffredent," she said, "but I would request him to tell
> us the best story he can think of and not to concentrate so much on

60. Embedding, Dällenbach points out, may function as a statement model ("mise
en abyme de l'énoncé"), an utterance model ("mise en abyme de l'énonciation"), or
a code model ("mise en abyme du code"); see *Le Récit spéculaire—Essai sur la mise en
abyme* (Paris: Seuil, 1977), 61–75.

speaking ill of women that in cases where there is something good to say he does not tell the whole truth."]

To engage in storytelling implies the narrator's willingness to satisfy the public's expectations. Saffredent consents to Longarine's request "to tell the best story he can think of": "Vrayement, je l'accorde, car j'ay en main l'histoire d'une folle et d'une saige: vous prendrez l'exemple qu'il vous plaira le mieulx" [207: "Willingly," began Saffredent. "I'll do just as you ask, because the story I have in mind is in fact about a woman who was wanton and a woman who was wise. You may please yourselves which example you follow!"].[61]

In the sense that it anticipates what is about to come, the dialogue is—to paraphrase Henri Mitterand—"un dialogue de programmation, de prévision, de décision [qui permet] au lecteur un contrôle a posteriori de la validité du récit" [a dialogue of programmation, expectation, decision which permits the reader to control a posteriori the validity of the story].[62] But again, the dialogue may refer to the preceding tale and authenticate its coherence. The debaters then turn into "referees," recalling the commentator in medieval debates who likewise pronounced the verdict after the debaters' performance: "il me semble [dist Parlamente] que Dagoucin est sailly dehors de nostre deliberation, qui estoit de ne dire compte que pour rire, car le sien est trop piteux" [427: "it occurs to me (said Parlamente) that Dagoucin has departed from the decision we made only to tell stories that are amusing. The one he's just told us was too sad"].

Debates and novellas follow a three-step procedure: the debate provides the narrators with directions, the ensuing story shows how they put them to use and, in the debate following, their performance is evaluated by the others. This triple operation mirrors

61. A narrator may simply refuse to comply with the audience's requests and embark self-assuredly on a tale of his own choice. In yielding the floor to Oisille, Geburon seeks one who will save the friars' reputation which he has significantly tarnished in the preceding tale. But determined to observe the rule upon which they agreed and maintain her authority, Oisille illustrates once more their hypocrisy: "Ce sera, dist-il, à madame Oisille, afin qu'elle dye quelque chose en faveur de saincte religion.—Nous avons tant juré, dist Oisille, de dire la verité, que je ne sçaurois soustenir ceste partye" [186: "I ask Madame Oisille to speak next, in order that she may tell us something in favour of the religious life."—"We have all so firmly sworn to speak the truth," replied Oisille, "that I could not undertake to plead that case"].

62. Henri Mitterand, "Dialogue et littérarité romanesque," 145.

the production-transmission-reception process, and the continual interlacing that produces the text. Moreover, it reveals the complementarity of storytelling and argumentation, fiction producing and truth hunting, writing and reading. Dialogues and the dialectical format add considerably to the overall design of the *Heptameron*. They impart dynamism and cohesion to apparently irreconcilable elements. The dialogues provide a sense of continuity through the character-portrait technique and allow the development of a plot in which the debaters are the protagonists, and consequently a strong narrative presence. These crucial elements attest to Marguerite's careful planning and her awareness of the aesthetic weaknesses that had plagued earlier novella collections. Finally, the dialogue established between stories on the one hand, and stories[63] and discussions on the other, creates fluidity, thus promoting the dominant theme, the impossibility for man to fix—except momentarily—any kind of truth.

This constant back-and-forth movement was the occasion for a confrontation between various generic modes and literary activities. In fact, it was the occasion for a "dialogue des genres," a dialogue (which echoes the then ongoing dialogue on dialogue) between the discourse of fiction and the discourse of cognition, between narrative and dialectic, profit and pleasure,[64] a dialogue that called into question two traditions, the spoken and the written word, forcing the reader to confront simultaneously his past and his present.[65]

63. Through various devices: repetition, reflection, mirroring.
64. And, of course, the profane and the sacred.
65. A modified version of the study on the *Heptameron* appeared in French in my *L'Esthétique du jeu dans l'Heptaméron de Marguerite de Navarre* (Paris: Vrin; Montréal: Institut d'Etudes médiévales, Université de Montréal, 1993). I am most grateful to Professors Susan Rava and Harriet Stone for their assistance in the final editing of the English version, and to Professor Robert McDowell who gave willingly of his time and expertise as I worked on the various drafts.

✿ The Dialogues of Louis Le Caron, 1554–1556

Louis Le Caron published works in dialogic form between 1554 and 1556, at the beginning of his legal career: *La Claire ou de la prudence de droit* (1554, 318 pp.), *Le Philosophe* (1555, 28 pp. at the end of *La Philosophie*, 156 pp.), and *Dialogues* (1556, 176 fols. or 350 pp). Throughout his writings the concept of law predominates, providing a framework for the individual to develop his potential as an active, contributing member in a social context. The ultimate goal espoused is self-knowledge, the Renaissance ideal of wisdom, inspired by the dialogues of Plato, the *Ethics* of Aristotle, and the dialogues of Cicero. As in the works of François Rabelais that seem to have made a deep impression on Le Caron, action replaces contemplation, and the individual develops, functions, and contributes in and to a whole social system rather than as an isolated creature. Within the system one adheres firmly to faith and trust in the Almighty Creator, to belief in Nature's positive gifts and guidance, and to optimism for potential fulfillment that includes personal tranquillity. Consonant not only with the thoughts of Rabelais, the ideas of Le Caron also reflect those of earlier humanists, notably Erasmus and Budé.

La Claire

While the theory of dialogue had not yet been set forth formally as it would be a few years later by Sigonio, Tasso, and others, Le Caron does reveal an understanding of Ciceronian dialogue that influences his choice of the genre for his own early writings. His model for eloquence in *La Claire* is Cicero's use of digression to apply general principles in specific situations:

Doi je taire Ciceron lequel je me suis principalement proposé? . . .
Ne veon nous ses Dialogues remplis d'infinis discours, lesquelz les
personnes induites egarent de la principale matiere pour descendre
aus propos qui touchent plus leur estat?   (*La Claire* a ii verso)

[Must I be silent about Cicero whom I expressly chose for myself?
. . . Don't we see his dialogues filled with many discourses which
lead away the speakers from the main topic to come down to discussions which concern their own affairs?]

The quotation aptly describes Le Caron's own approach to considerations of serious topics that pertain for the most part to politics,
education, law, ethics, theories of knowledge, poetics, and aesthetics.[1]

A second model is Plato, for like the Quattrocento writers of
dialogue, Le Caron admires Socrates, who in the Platonic texts
identifies philosophy with virtuous living.

Ainsi Platon fait disputer Socrate des choses naturelles, desquelles
toutefois il meprisoit la science, et aus choses seullement s'exerçoit
qui appartenoient aus meurs de la vie humaine, jugeant la vraie
filosofie estre toute en l'action de vertu.   (7r)

[Thus Plato has Socrates discuss natural science which, however,
he scorned knowledge of, and only about the things he perceived
that belonged to the situations of human life, judging true philosophy to be completely in the action of virtue.]

If Le Caron's first dialogue, the lengthy *La Claire*, lacks mastery
of the form, it at least embodies a number of the themes that will
recur in his subsequent attempts at the genre. The main speaker,
Solon, represents Le Caron and acts as a master or adviser to Claire,
the second participant. *La Claire* uses dialogue for a twofold purpose: to demonstrate that law is a part of moral philosophy and to
argue that the lawyer-orator exemplifies both eloquence and virtue, thereby embodying the Ciceronian ideal of orator-philosopher
engaged in *active*, civic virtues. Le Caron cites Cicero frequently
in *La Claire* and defines the four cardinal virtues in terms of neces-
sities for right living, of moderation in actions, of will rather than
habit, of the understanding of the useful and the virtuous.

The two speakers in *La Claire* do not engage in a natural discussion about the material or offer divergent viewpoints or present
two different sides. Rather, Claire's function is to prompt the

1. All translations from Le Caron's works are mine.

main speaker, Solon, to outline for her his ideas on the role and function of law in society. In the early pages Le Caron also dwells upon a subsidiary theme, the intellectual equality of women and men—though he admits that law has not been an area of study open to women. Le Caron will return to the topic of the intellectual equality of the sexes in the fifth of the *Dialogues*. Clearly, Le Caron's close relationship with the young woman Claire, who died at age eighteen of the plague, and to whom he dedicated *La Claire*, influenced his decision to champion the ability of women to discuss on an equal footing with men the highest, most significant intellectual matters.

La Claire introduces a number of other concerns that reappear in the *Dialogues*. First, Le Caron argues that true philosophy is active rather than merely theoretical:

> Je dirai que la vraie filosofie est comprinse dans les livres de droit, et non dans les inutiles et muettes bibliotheques des filosophes, hommes (à dire vrai) de grand etude et erudition, mais ineptes à l'administration publique.   (23r,v)

> [I will say that true philosophy is contained in law books and not in the useless and mute libraries of philosophers, men (to tell the truth) of great study and erudition, but unsuited for public administration.]

Thus Solon responds to Claire's question of why law is *prudence* rather than *knowledge*:

> Car prudence gist es choses particulieres qui consistent en action et lesquelles vienent en deliberation et conseil. Aussi un droit conseillant met son principal etude en ce qui appartient à la science humaine, et ne s'arreste tant aus generales propositions qu'aus singulieres actions qui touchent particulierement les affaires qui s'offrent specialement à sa response.   (24v)

> [For prudence lies in particular things which consist in action and which come into deliberation and counsel. Thus a man of law puts his principal study in what pertains to human society and which doesn't stop merely with general ideas but with individual actions which touch mainly upon matters that present themselves primarily to his reaction.]

Second, Solon cites the importance of Nature for impressing upon men certain firm and unchanging laws of universal society. These laws are manifested in the corpus of jurisprudence. He recognizes flexibility, rather than rigidity, however, in that the law of the leaders or "gents" adapts itself to the laws of the people in order to maintain the republic. This in turn is natural law, right reason that sustains the good and forbids the unjust.

The role of the republic is a third major concern of *La Claire* that reappears in the *Dialogues*. Le Caron emphasizes, as did Plutarch, Cicero, and others, that the king must act in order to preserve peace and tranquillity in his kingdom. As with Plato, the highest form of the republic is that which is joined with a common will to citizens aspiring to common good. Similarly, the good monarch is not solitary and contemplative but instead a just administrator who strives to ensure a peaceful society and to uphold civil law. This ideal monarch has the wisdom to grant the lawyer-orator a major position in both policy and governance. The good monarch also forms the manners and customs of society. In Roman law, one of the first edicts in fact, validates marriage. In marriage, law recognizes, dignifies, and legalizes the place of women in society. For this reason it cannot be lenient to offenders.

While Le Caron tries to duplicate the conversational tone that he so admires in Cicero, his *La Claire* is still somewhat ponderous and didactic. It has little structure, but rambles from point to point; in form, it is really more a conversational discussion of law than a true dialogue. One wishes that Claire might say more than a line or two at a time, for she appears to be reasonable and articulate. As Le Caron's initial attempt at the genre, which will realize its potential in the *Dialogues*, it resembles Plato's early dialogues in which Socrates seeks to make a point or achieve a triumph in argument rather than the later *Phaedrus* and *Republic* in which Plato strives for the truth by means of a more complex, speculative development involving the use of myth and exemplum.

On the other hand, *La Claire* permits Le Caron to substitute his own persona in the figure of Solon and to affirm the importance of law for the good of society. It is Le Caron's personal statement of his own life plan. Henceforth he will devote his life—the next sixty years—to the Parliament of Paris and to a compilation of Roman and French law that can only be described as monumental in such titles as *Coustume de la ville, prevosté et vicomté de Paris, ou droict civil Parisien* (1582), *Memorables, ou observations du droict françois rapporté au romain, civil et canonic* (1601, 1603, 1614), *Nouveau commentaire . . . sur la coustume de la ville, prevosté, et vicomté de Paris*

(1613), *Pandectes, ou digestes du droit françois* (1587), and *Resolutions de plusieurs notables, celebres et illustres questions de droict, tant romain que françois, coustumes et practique jugées par arrests des cours de Parlement de France* (1613).

As a lawyer-orator-writer he will exemplify in his career the precepts he has outlined. For that reason, if for no other, *La Claire* has amply served as an expression of what may have been for Le Caron an interior dialogue that redirected his life's work.

Le Philosophe

In contrast to the substantive and lengthy discussion that informs *La Claire*, *Le Philosophe*, a short dialogue between a philosopher and a Parisian, is appended to the end of Le Caron's extensive treatise *La Philosophie*. This dialogue on philosophy as a royal quality distinguishes the goodness of the earliest philosophers from the corruption and deceit of their successors. When governance ultimately becomes necessary, the prince and philosopher both share the characteristics of true nobility. By showing that the origin of kingship lies in philosophy, that is, in prudence and wisdom, the philosopher argues for a similarity between the lover of wisdom and the prince. Le Caron draws the distinction between those who fall captive to the passion of false, painted beauty, and the philosopher, a different sort of lover who knows true beauty, and thus enjoys both friendship and freedom. This beauty is none other than that of the perfect Idea, the truth of all things. Much of this dialogue sheds light on dialogue 5 concerning beauty, which reflects a dynamic encounter as opposed to the stylized discussion of *Le Philosophe*: the antitheses of false and true beauty; deceptive passion and abiding friendship; the physical, exterior, and outward appearance of beauty experienced only by the senses and the spiritual, interiorized, intrinsic manifestation of the essence of beauty apprehended by the understanding.

Le Philosophe insists that philosophy serves as a guide not only for kings, but for noblemen as well who derive nobility not from birth, but from the force of virtue that raises them above the vulgar. Self-knowledge and self-mastery characterize the prince and the noble in mind and in spirit. Le Caron's philosopher-king would not withdraw into a hermitage to contemplate the universe. Rather, he would engage actively in civic life as a strong, skillful helmsman who guides the ship of state. Like Rabelais's philosopher-prince, Le Caron's leader loves wisdom and seeks truth not as a speculative venture, but within the context of social utility. He promotes justice and demonstrates to others acceptable from nonacceptable behavior. Just as for Barthélémy Aneau in *Imagination poétique,* published three years earlier in 1552, the term "sophist" designates one who threatens the delicate moral balance of society by giving in to pleasures and to vice (57–58). Le Caron's sophist dons a robe that does not belong to him; he is a pirate of philosophy, a thief wearing a mask of pretense. Aneau's sophists, the theologians, appear as savage, quarreling beasts, arguing about frivolous topics such as mythical animals. For Le Caron the arts of the trivium—grammar, rhetoric, and logic—do not lead one to the realm of truth, as does philosophy, a central point that he demonstrates throughout the *Dialogues.* As valid as the long arguments of the courtiers in *Dialogues* 1 and 2 appear, Le Caron reminds us here as in the three following dialogues that the clever orator with his subtle arguments is no match for the virtue that accompanies truth. Erasmus had defined the sophist in *De copia* (1512) as more talkative than wise (1978, p. 583).

Le Caron concludes *Le Philosophe* by observing the powerful attraction of the force of philosophy on those endowed with goodness. This, then, is the true nature of man: to aspire to ethical conduct during this life. Nature, which spurs us to follow virtue, leads not to pleasure, but to study. The five *Dialogues* will serve as an exercise to compare the rhetoric of persuasion to the simplicity of truth; circuitous meanderings to the directness of the path of right living; and laziness, indolence, and self-satisfaction, all static in nature, to civic virtue, which is dynamic, active, productive, and above all useful.

Les Dialogues

The two initial dialogues thus introduce Le Caron's mode of inquiry into ethical and epistemological issues both personal and societal that he treats more extensively in the *Dialogues.* Although the framework of dialogue as form differs greatly in *La Claire* and *Le Philosophe* from the five examples in the 1556 *Dialogues*, the process of dialectic is nevertheless similar. While *La Claire* and *Le Philosophe* permitted exposition of Le Caron's thoughts on law and ethics in which the secondary speaker had the minor role of posing questions to the spokesman for the author's views in the manner of Plato's early dialogues, the *Dialogues* give all speakers the opportunity to speak at length. If dialectic is indeed the search for truth, it shares a common ground with rhetoric, politics, and ethics, as André Stegmann (1976) suggests in his seminal article on the poet and orator (219). Stegmann has shown the evolution in France between 1540 and 1550 from the consideration of the relationship between rhetoric and statesmanship to that joined with the practical, to history and law, particularly with Baudouin and Jean Bodin (223). The author who comes to the forefront in this period is Cicero, philosopher and dialectician, orator and citizen. Like Budé, Rabelais, and others, Le Caron highlights one of Cicero's focal points, prudence—the knowledge of temporal things— and its importance to those who regulate human life, a point that Eugene Rice makes in *The Renaissance Idea of Wisdom* (1958, 150 ff.). Consider the final pages of Budé's *L'Institution du Prince*:

> Aristotle said that Anaxagoras and Thales who were called wise in Greece were not prudent. . . . They didn't understand the things concerning political or economic government nor things that were useful to live well. The knowledge of living well consists in virtue and prudence . . . which is acquired by experience, by examples, by the teachings of wise people of the past, and by reading the histories with good sense and natural judgment.   (139; my translation)

The five dialogues present a program of preparation for the active life, for participation in the life of the city-state, an enterprise that includes education, practical experience, personal sacrifice, and dedication, while taking into account examples, both positive and negative, of the past.

Dialogue 1

While Dialogue 1, "The Courtisan, that the Prince Must Philosophize or Concerning True Wisdom and Royal Philosophy," appears to be a discussion between the literary character Le Caron and Philarete (lover of truth), the Le Caron of the dialogue actually monopolizes more than sixty of its sixty-six pages. A strong supporter of monarchy, Le Caron opens the dialogue with praise of exemplary kings, notably Minos who conversed with Jupiter, thereby learning from him laws useful for maintaining happiness in earthly life. According to his concept of kingship, the prince seeks only that nobility arising from virtue. He governs by his own laws and constitutions which must reflect justice and humanity. His own life follows the teachings of philosophy and so serves as a model to others.

Like Rabelais's prince, Le Caron's ruler would be nobly born, raised in a temperate manner according to ethical principles, and a student of the sciences, and would recognize that royal authority is a divine gift. Le Caron, like Plutarch, emphasizes the resemblance between God and the ruler, particularly in the wielding of divine power by the prince.

Self-governance or self-mastery is the major character trait that enables the prince to put aside his own desires and passions, follow the cardinal virtues, and undertake what is best for the welfare of the kingdom. As Cicero argued in his dialogues, Le Caron indicates that the prince in a modern state should manifest prudence as well as eloquence, thus concretizing the objectives of ethics for the state in the form of laws. Erasmus in the *Education of a Christian Prince* (1516) and Rabelais had previously joined the qualities of prudence in governance with true eloquence to exemplify the public demonstration of positive kingly qualities.[2]

For Le Caron, law bestows human dignity on us, raising us above the animal level by endowing our lives with organization. The corpus of law, of course, originating from the divine gift of reason, permits the enlightened prince to govern according to the highest eternal law, that of Nature. As always, Le Caron's spokesman points out the relativity of laws for a certain time and place. We must adhere to those laws that are appropriate to our own present times, a principle that Le Caron later followed in his compilation of and commentary on French laws.

The ideal prince should also serve as a doctor for the behavior

2. Many of these ideas appear in Cicero's works, for example, *De oratore*, 3.60, where philosophy and eloquence are closely linked. In his *De officiis*, 1.45, however, justice takes precedence over temperance. For a recent discussion of political philosophy and moral philosophy in the Renaissance, see *The Cambridge History of Renaissance Philosophy*, edited by Charles B. Schmitt, Quentin Skinner, and Eckhard Kessler (Cambridge: Cambridge University Press, 1988), 303–452. See also Aristotle's *Nicomachean Ethics* and his *Politics*. As examples of Northern European handbooks for the prince, see Erasmus, *The Education of a Christian Prince*; G. Budé, *De l'Institution du Prince*; and Jacopo Sadoleto, *De pueris recte instituendis*.

of his people, a metaphor esteemed by Erasmus in the *Education of a Christian Prince* (1936, p. 236), and ultimately inspired, no doubt, by Aristotle's *Ethics* (8.10). Rabelais alludes to the moral value of the metaphor of good health in the prologue to the *Quart Livre* (1548, 1552). In another common classical and Renaissance topos, Le Caron notes that the king is a father to his subjects, an idea common to Budé (1965, p. 138), Erasmus (1936, p. 152, 170), Rabelais, and Aristotle (*Ethics* 8.10).

Le Caron approaches the much-discussed question of war and peace by agreeing with his fellow humanists about the damaging effects of war and the *utility* of peace, a key concept in Le Caron's vision of government. Yet, like Rabelais in his depiction of the Picrocholine and Dipsodian wars, he would prefer a just and honorable war to a damaging peace, considering a necessary conflict as an efficacious restorer of order.[3] He distinguishes the just prince from the tyrant in that the former is guided by reason and persuades his people to live by the same criterion.

Two major points that dominate the last fifteen pages of Dialogue 1 serve as a closing. First, the prince undertakes an agenda based solely on public usefulness. The contrary motivation for action, personal ambition and desire for world fame, was exemplified in literature by Rabelais's Picrochole and in contemporary world politics by Charles Quint. In the 1550s under Henri II the opposing worldviews and rivalry of the Valois and the Hapsburgs were still of paramount concern.[4]

The dual concepts of the *vita activa* and public usefulness reflect the ideals of civic humanism in effect in sixteenth-century France in Erasmus, Rabelais, and Budé, among others. Given the relationship between monarchy and law, and thus between the prince and his legal representatives, the *procureurs* or lawyers, the *Dialogues* draw attention to the changing nature of the courtly and legal milieu, taking into account the criteria for individual merit of civic leaders. The remaining dialogues will seek to define merit in terms of epistemology (Dialogue 3), poetics (Dialogue 4), and aesthetics (Dialogue 5).

3. Erasmus, on the other hand, would avoid war at any cost because it is against Christ's teachings; see the final pages of the *Education of a Christian Prince*.

4. See Frederic J. Baumgartner, *Henry II King of France 1547–1559* (Durham: Duke Univeristy Press, 1988); see also *The Entry of Henry II into Paris 16 June 1549*, edited by I. D. McFarlane (Binghamton, NY; CEMERS, 1982).

Dialogue 2

While each of the five dialogues of 1556 illustrates an application of Le Caron's dialectic, Dialogue 2 best concretizes the process. At first glance, "The Courtier or Concerning True Wisdom and the Praise of Philosophy" appears to be totally derived from Jacopo Sadoleto's *Phaedrus, or Attack and Defense of Philosophy*, a 1538 Latin dialogue. But first impressions are deceiving. Le Caron actually gives both sides of the issue equal value. While attacking the deleterious unproductive aspects of contemplative philosophy, he does not allow the Courtier to hang himself with sophistic subtleties. Rather, the reader is won over by his pointed observations and clear reasoning. The narrator wishes above all to keep tranquillity in the republic, a reasonable stance given the unstable religious situation in the France of the 1550s in the midst of the Tridentine and Julian period, and given the era's continuous military encounters, particularly on France's northern and eastern borders.

The Courtier begins with an overview of the earliest philosophers, criticizing their lack of usefulness and real knowledge. Instead, he sees their teachings as nothing but a combination of superstitions and arrogance. He questions how they know and judge human life when they are so far apart from it. According to the Courtier, "Elle est donc le vrai theatre, auquel se doit exercer celui, qui desire le tiltre d'homme noble et vertueux: en elle faut chercher le nom de sagesse: et accommoder touts ses estudes à l'utilité d'elle" [137: The life of man is the true theater in which the noble and virtuous person acts. In life we must seek the name of wisdom and direct all study to its usefulness]. He argues that unlike the early philosophers who lived in solitude, the wise person must live in the company and assembly of others, and his highest end must be to govern the city from a position of authority. Each of the four cardinal virtues is understood as contributing to the knowledge of things useful for the public good, a major topic first raised in *La Claire*. Instead of retreating into solitude, one must show civic pride, "amour de la patrie" and "civisme," in Le Caron's terms. True wisdom is reflected in honorable actions.

The Courtier ends his speech by condemning sophism, vain disputes, and empty arguments. He invokes the notion of dialectic, but merely as a classification of the trivium, not as the philosophical term that ultimately for Le Caron, as for Rabelais, signifies a seeking of truth and self-knowledge, that becomes a way of life— that of becoming a productive member of society.

At Philarete's urging, Le Caron responds to the Courtier that eloquence cannot be separated from wisdom. In fact, their separation is the cause of society's problems, an idea that echos a major theme in Cicero's *De oratore* (3.19. 71–73). He affirms that all art, sciences, and virtues come from Nature which spurs us to the knowledge of God, the source of all happiness. That same Nature endowed all things with a purpose and thus every created being undertakes to accomplish the task suitable to it. If appetite motivates animals, surely the rational soul directs humans and leads them to Nature, thus reaping God's gifts. Le Caron admits that art imitates Nature and that philosophy, one of the arts, is proper to man. Only through philosophy can man aspire to what is most important to him: self-knowledge. Like Rabelais's ideal participants, Le Caron's well-born and properly instructed citizen will use reason to judge what is presented to him and will choose the noble and the excellent. Near the end of Dialogue 1, Le Caron had echoed Rabelais's description of true nobility in the Abbey of Theleme (Gargantua 57), itself similar to Plato's description of virtue in the *Republic* (4.431 c), that is, nobility is the excellence of the well-born enriched with virtue. Dialogue 1, in effect, enlarges upon the criteria for entry into Rabelais's ideal society. Virtue and prudence characterize the truly wise. The narrator finds the best example of this combination of virtue and prudence in the lives of Demosthenes and Cicero, both of whom dedicated their labors and speeches to the public welfare. Again, the orator-statesman-lawyer illustrates merit based on the sum of his public actions and serves as prototype and justification for Le Caron's own chosen career.

Le Caron further distinguishes between mortals unworthy of consideration, who succumb to passions, excess pleasures, and vices, and the wise, who are governed by the order and reason of an eternal law. The focus is on the here and now, as Le Caron, the dialogic participant, paraphrases Budé's definition of prudence: "La prudence s'exerce en la bien-avisée conduite de celles qui sont toutes en action et exposées à divers changements" [172: Prudence is put into practice in the carefully considered conduct of those things that are active and exposed to diverse changes]. Philosophy gives us judgment *to know* and *to choose* what is closest to truth. This, says Le Caron, is what he means by dialectic (175).

Le Caron concludes his response to the Courtier by emphasizing philosophy's utility as a guide in human actions. In it shines prudence accompanied by the other virtues that should rule our lives. Thus the philosopher is not a man hostile to the republic but one who serves a common good.

Le Caron's "Le Courtisan 2" is distinguished from Sadoleto's *Phaedrus* first, by the manner in which Le Caron uses both speakers as a means to express two aspects of his own ideas on philosophy, many of which are nontraditional. Second, his tone and treatment of the two speakers is fair and equitable, unlike those of Sadoleto who sets up the first speaker to be destroyed by the second one. Perhaps the differing points of view of Sadoleto and Le Caron reveal the theologian as opposed to the lawyer and dedicated Ciceronian.

In Dialogue 2 as in his other dialogues Le Caron is ultimately a civic humanist concerned with the active, practical virtues of prudence and temperance in harmony with justice and moral courage, an identity that he shares with Rabelais and Budé. He is probably closest to Cicero in his extreme objectivity in presenting differing points of view and in his syncretic tendency to extract the best from several different philosophies to form his own personal conclusions.

Dialogue 3

In the third dialogue, "Valton, Concerning Tranquillity of the Mind, or the Highest Good," Le Caron shapes a theory of ethics that is closely joined to his epistemological system. That is, tranquillity in one's life depends on self-knowledge and on following the precepts of Nature and seeking the path of virtue. Le Caron had already affirmed in the *Philosophie* that all philosophy consists of two things: knowledge of the secrets of Nature and the maintenance of a companionable tranquillity in life (20).

Le Caron introduces the speakers by means of a double dialogue within a dialogue form. The frame or initial dialogue takes place in a park at the home of Le Caron's uncle, Philippe Valton, in St. Denis. Le Caron, a lawyer in the Parisian Parlement, visits his uncle's home when he can to enjoy its repose, and to escape from the heavy labors of business and study. At his idyllic country estate, Valton recounts to Le Caron an earlier discussion between himself and L'Escorché, who in turn had reported a previous discourse regarding tranquillity of mind and the highest good in which L'Escorché, Cotereau, and Rabelais had participated. Now Le Caron presents the speeches in dialogue form, reserving for his uncle, Valton, an appropriate role as synthesizer which Le Caron, the author, explains thus: "Depuis repensant à ces discours il m'a semblé de les traitter plus amplement, faisant parler ceux, desquelz les sentences estoient propres, et exprimant sous le nom de mon oncle nostre commune pensée" [182–83: Since then, thinking about those speeches, I had the idea to treat them more amply, having those protagonists speak, whose words were so appropriate, and expressing under the name of my uncle our common thought]. This revelation is of great interest to those studying the genre of the dialogue for it allows us to reflect on the creative transformation brought about by the author who is, after all, writing to teach and to persuade. The speeches have the appearance of verisimilitude, but they are in fact the vehicle of the author's carefully planned agenda.

By way of introduction to the main topic, Valton and L'Escorché attempt to define man's nature. Valton identifies two parts of the human soul, the celestial part formed in the image of God, that is, understanding or reason, and the other part conjoined with the body. L'Escorché agrees that the understanding is the governor of the soul and of all human life. Like Aristotle, he believes that the body and soul are joined and not mixed together. The soul, retaining its essence, mediates between celestial force and mortal state. God gives each person a daimon as described in Plato's *Timaeus, Symposium, Phaedo*, and *Apology*. Valton points out that philosophers seem dead in the corporeal prison but that wonder draws their thoughts to God to enable them to distinguish true from false. The philosopher needs contemplation or search for truth, choice or judgment, and use of knowledge.

Defined at length by L'Escorché, the sensitive soul is that power used to guide the senses. He numbers memory among the interior senses and links fantasy to memory, variables in mortals.

Reverting to his initial discussion, Valton recognizes no other soul of the universe but God—eternal, immeasurable, infinite. Valton affirms that only one soul, both affective and rational, exists in the self, and he points to the superiority of understanding to opinion in judging knowledge. God is an idea, not matter, the creator of all, the origin of all virtues and arts, a God living in the individual.

Introducing the topic discussed by Cotereau, Rabelais, and himself, L'Escorché presents first the Stoic's part through Cotereau. At this point Le Caron seems to be inspired by Cicero's *De finibus* where Cicero, like Le Caron, had presented three spokesmen for Epicurean, Stoic, and Peripatetic viewpoints. These, then, comprise the major interior sections of Dialogue 3, but Le Caron does not follow Cicero slavishly, nor does his conclusion resemble in any way that of Cicero. Instead, Le Caron attempts to discover a common thread, a similarity of concepts, in the ends and intrinsic values expressed differently in the three major philosophies. His own spokesman, Valton, in the final twenty pages, provides a truly humanistic conclusion, as original and as inspired as that of Lorenzo Valla's *De voluptate* of 1431 and 1433.

Cotereau, following the Stoic position, cites the instinct for self-preservation that Nature engendered in each living creature. But reason alone must govern humans and control their appetites. In addition, the understanding maintains human life in a society of speech and communication. Reason has by its nature the instincts and roots of all things useful and necessary to maintain life. In fact, Nature forgot nothing for men, an idea that echoes Aristotle's *De anima* (3.9.432b).

For Cotereau, the way of living well lies in two things: action and contemplation. One must seek knowledge of good and evil and then seek truth. Love of the virtues is innate in the individual who is born for nobler things than the body. If one's understanding, inspired by heaven, is not corrupted, it will advance to grandeur and become a fulfilled reason, none other than virtue or wisdom. Goodness can only be found by living according to Nature.

Stoics hold, according to both Cotereau and Cicero's Cato, that the universe is like a city governed by divine will. Cotereau adds that citizens are there to contemplate and interpret the works of God. All things were created for the utility of the individual but also for the glory of God who gave man reason so that humanity might have an alliance with divine nature; here Le Caron transforms the Ciceronian text in *De finibus* (3.20.66).

One has reason in order to judge and discern what is appropriate to do according to Nature. The mind, of course, must dominate the body. But the imagination misleads some. Disorder envelops the person who is enslaved to things. Above all, one must exercise thought and moderation in one's choice of things belonging to freedom of the mind. As a check, Nature accompanies us and warns us of our duty to maintain the mind in accordance with Nature.

Our nobility, grandeur, and strength permit us to endure changes of fortune and to push back attracting pleasures. The good is also the virtuous, perfections of Nature, while evil is in vices, corruptions of Nature. There exists also a neutral category of indifferent considerations such as health, beauty, pleasure, glory, nobility, as well as their opposites. The mind should propose those that are good, so that it will receive contentment in the form of repose and tranquillity.

According to Cotereau, our will should rule itself and use imagination well so as to accommodate the instincts of Nature to individual things. Reason must govern if one is to achieve the height of repose. The passions dominate, according to the Peripatetics, not because they were inborn, but because they were stimulated by an imprudent notion.

Cotereau advises us to imitate the wise Chrysante in Xenophon's *Cyropaedia*. Indeed, a truly noble mind gives to each thing the strength that it has. Human misery, on the other hand, comes from ignorance of self and of the true use of things, taught by Nature. Thus we must obey reason because it agrees with Nature.

In his closing arguments the Stoic spokesman equates the good with virtue and with that which is perfect according to Nature. Virtue is sufficient to live well and happily. Cicero ended the Stoic section of *De finibus* similarly, declaring that none but the good are happy and asking what could be more divine than virtue (*De finibus* 4.19.54)? Unlike Valla in *De voluptate*, and Cicero in *De finibus*, Le Caron does not condemn his Stoic speaker.

Taking a Peripatetic stance, L'Escorché replies that he is unable to respond to all of Cotereau's arguments at the present time but that he does wish to demonstrate that beyond virtue there are other benefits of Nature. Following Aristotle's *De anima*, he outlines the three natures of the soul: vegetative, nutritive or sensitive, and rational. That which is useful lies in the nutritive force, seat of imagination and memory, whose end is pleasure.

On the other hand, the function of the rational part of the soul is to command others and to raise us to contemplation and knowledge of truth, a higher end than the virtue or right living of the Stoics. According to L'Escorché, virtue is the noblest good but not the only one.

The individual is composed of both soul and body, each part having its strength in us and maintaining itself according to its nature. Since no person is entirely spiritual and therefore no one is able to live totally in contemplation, this life exerts itself in action; this concept has its origin in the *Nicomachean Ethics* (1.8.3).

L'Escorché defends the good as praiseworthy and just. Nature maintains life and the senses by the guidance of reason. Happiness, however, is variable, must be an activity, and excludes misery. Contrary to the Stoics, L'Escorché sees an accord of the three benefits in conjunction with the parts of man. Each part seems to have some alliance and natural society with the others.

On the question of riches, he notes that although the Stoics reject them, Plato justifies them, for all products of Nature are created for use and none exists without some cause and purpose. Riches enable us to arrive at love, virtue, and knowledge of truth. L'Escorché points to the fact that Aristotle justifies wealth in his discussion of liberality (*Ethics* 4.1) and that Plato had championed wealth in the *Republic* (9).

To conclude his defense of Aristotle, L'Escorché quotes from Plato's *Laws* and cites two kinds of goods: human and divine. Wisdom or prudence, the first of the divine benefits (*Ethics* 6.5), is joined by the three other moral virtues. Since we participate in two natures, human and divine, and enjoy two sorts of good, human benefits must agree with divine ones, and the divine ones with wisdom, their leader, as Plato affirms in the *Laws* (1:631). Closing his argument, L'Escorché affirms that the passions are sometimes needed to excite virtue. Moderate pleasures should be benefits. In fact, those who attempt to remove the passions from Nature are trying to cut away the best part of the instincts and seem to pervert the mean where virtue lies (*Nicomachean Ethics* 2.6, 1.13). Reason, then, has as its function to moderate and restore order in the movements of the soul.

At this point Cotereau and L'Escorché briefly discuss the nature of virtue, agreeing that it is desired only for itself, and in it lies the highest good; it seems to make individuals better; it is what we desire; it provides one means to lead us to happiness. Cotereau defines virtue as living according to Nature. For L'Escorché, virtue comes from the pursuit and habit of living well. Such a life causes us to acquire virtuous actions.

Then the final speaker, Rabelais, playing the role of the Epicurean although he denies belonging to that sect or any other, begins his argument. If our thoughts and actions have no goal, he asserts, then nothing is certain, happy, nor assured in this life, a Pyrrhonist point of view. Citing the same Pyrrhonist metaphor used in his *Tiers Livre*, of drawing truth out of the dark Cimmerian well where Heraclitus (an error for Democritus in both Rabelais and Le Caron) said it was hidden, Rabelais wishes to reveal the clear truth that could not be seen on the surface (chap. 36). According to Henri Busson (1971), this metaphor is frequent among the Pyrrhonists (234). In *La Philosophie* (6r), Le Caron had written, "God (whom the ancients called best Nature), perfecting man in soul and body, endowed him with a divine excellence. . . ."

Like Epicurus, Rabelais, echoing Cicero's *De finibus* (1:9), feels that everything aspires to its last and highest pleasure. He then asks what can make man happy and affirms that only the mind can judge happiness. Indeed, the pleasures of the mind are much greater than those of the body. In order for the mind to be happy, it must know Nature. For the body, on the other hand, its greatest good is to enjoy a moderate pleasure. Without it, the parts are discordant.

Rejecting the notion of seeking pleasure as the highest good and of fleeing pain as the worst evil as too vulgar, Rabelais turns instead to his own definition of pleasure: the enjoyment of what is desired. Yet, he qualifies this conception: "Nothing can bring us any pleasure if it is not good by its nature," paraphrasing Diogenes Laertius's statement in *Lives of the Philosophers* that Epicurus describes virtue as the sine qua non of pleasure (10.138). Rabelais does not mean to compare the pleasures of the body to those of the spirit, for those of the mind are higher. Our instinctive desire for pleasure is caused by Nature and nothing can bring us this pleasure if Nature is not good. Going a step further, he affirms that the virtues of the mind are the principal benefits that lead us to beatitude—what Cicero calls "beate vivendi" in *De finibus* (1.18.57). Like Cicero in *De finibus*, Le Caron's Epicurean treats

the four cardinal virtues that tend to maintain happiness, and concludes that one cannot live joyously if not also wisely, honorably
and justly. Cicero had said that the art of living is wisdom, but
for Le Caron it is the search for truth. Justice for Le Caron aims to
give each of us our due, allows us to keep the faith and to receive
the benefit. For Cicero justice always adds some benefit (*De finibus*,
1.16.50). For Le Caron, temperance is pleasure that makes the
appetite obey, but for Cicero wisdom has that duty (*De finibus*,
1.14).

Deviating from Cicero, Rabelais defines pleasure as what others
call virtue if it is undertaken by reason and prudence. Unlike the
animals, humans endowed with mind do not desire naturally any
other pleasure than that which does not corrupt. Since the pleasurable is synonymous with the rational, Rabelais feels compelled to
embrace the opinion of Plato outlined in book 9 of the *Republic* in
which the three parts of the soul, the rational, the high-spirited,
and the appetitive, seek to fulfill three forms of pleasure, corresponding to each part (580d–e, 581c). Both the Le Caron text and
Plato's *Philebus* emphasize that harmony results in man when the
three parts of the soul are led and moderated by reason. In the
Philebus Plato interprets, as does Rabelais in Le Caron's dialogue,
pleasure and joy as *temperance*, of prime concern for an understanding of "Fay ce que vouldras" in the Thélème episode of *Gargantua*.

Again following classical texts, and as if to anticipate an erroneous interpretation of "Fay ce que vouldras," Rabelais warns against
esteeming all so-called pleasure as such. He gives as an example
Demosthenes's admonition against adopting every pleasure except
that born for honest things. The example of Demosthenes in Rabelais's discourse is followed immediately by the nearly exact word-
ing that appeared in *Gargantua*:

> Les hommes noblement instituez et frequentants les compagnies de
> leurs semblables ont de nature un instinct et eguillon, qui tous-
> jours les pousse et incite à faits vertueux, et retire de vice, lequel
> plusieurs appellent honneur.   (Dialogue 3, 237)

> [Men nobly taught and frequenting the company of similar people
> have by nature an instinct and spur which always pushes them and
> incites to virtuous acts and draws them from vice, which many call
> honor.]

The passage in *Gargantua*, identical in meaning, states:

FAY CE QUE VOULDRAS

parce que gens libères, bien nez, bien instruictz, conversans en
compaignies honnestes, ont par nature un instinct et aguillon, qui
tousjours les poulse à faictz vertueux et retire de vice, lequel ilz
nommoient honneur.   (chap. 57)

Rabelais then defines *honor* as that praiseworthy pleasure that is
most appropriate to wisdom.

In his *Philosophie* Le Caron had written that we know nothing
to be more natural to man than the instinct to know, engendered
by Nature into the spirit of every person (15r), an echo of the
opening of Aristotle's *Metaphysics*, and an idea that later reappears
at the head of Montaigne's *De l'expérience*.

In "Some Stoic Elements in Rabelais's Religious Thought," Michael Screech (1956) emphasizes not only the apparent Stoic influence on the description of the Thelemites, but above all, the
syncretic nature of Rabelais's Christian ethics (73–97). He contrasts in his *Evangélisme de Rabelais* (1959) the joyous optimism
of the humanist with Luther's ascetic notion of the ideal life.
Furthermore, he sees Rabelais's cult of honor that spurs the Thelemites to virtuous deeds as a form of *synderesis* described in Aqui-
nas's *Summa theologia*, (Ia, 16, 4), and in St. Bonaventure's *Commentary* on the *Sentences* of Peter Lombard: "Synderesis dicit illud
quod *stimulat* ad bonum," synderesis is that which spurs us to the
good.[5] Synderesis, then, is *habitus* which is an innate, natural gift,
an inclination toward the good that is part of free will and that
is also called virtue (Screech 1959, 37; Gilson 1924, 403, 406;
Gargantua, chap. 55).

Florence Weinberg (1972), citing Rabelais's contemporary,
Cornelius Agrippa, identifies *instinct*, a double for *aguillon*, as divine inspiration (129, 173). The *Dictionnaire étymologique latin*,
under "stinguo," defines "instinctus" as "l'aiguillon, l'instinct"
and sends us to Cicero's *De divinatione* (1.18), which identifies a
type of spontaneous divination devoid of art: "those oracles uttered
under the *impulse* of divine inspiration" (368). Weinberg notes
that for most humans more than an innate impulse is necessary to
achieve virtue (133). On the other hand, Emile Telle (1953) in
"Thélème et le Paulinisme matrimonial érasmien" perhaps over-

5. See Michael Screech, "L'Evangélisme de Rabelais," in *Etudes Rabelaisiennes* 2
(Geneva: Droz, 1959), 34–41. Etienne Gilson, in *La Philosophie de Saint Bonaventure*
(Paris: Vrin, 1924), cites *11 Sent.* 39, 2, 1, 403.

emphasizes the Erasmian opposition between marriage and monasticism inherent in Thélème (104–19).

Max Gauna (1971), in "Fruitful Fields and Blessed Spirits or Why the Thelemites Were Well Born," argues for a Stoic interpretation of *instinct* in light of Seneca's *Letters*, rather than as the synderesis of the scholastics. He points to the association of Lutheran paradox and Stoic ideas among evangelical humanists (117–19). For Gauna, Thélème "interweaves threads of Erasmian evangelism, idealized chivalry, and Stoicism" (128). He concludes with a strong note of reservation: "Selection for entry is restricted not to the nobly born, but to those choice souls alone whose good natures incline their wills instinctively to the pursuit of virtue, who have already received the best instruction modelling them to that pursuit, and who are in a real sense the elect of God during their passage on this earth" (128).[6]

For yet another Rabelaisian scholar, Mallary Masters (1969), the Thélème description symbolizes the concept of Christian *caritas* illustrated by Gargantua's emblem of the Androgyna. That emblem depicts Augustine's adaptation of Plato's conception of love and harmony in a Christian setting. Masters's Thélème includes the dialectical antitheses of earlier key episodes; it is a new order, an educational utopia in contrast with the old monastic system (22–23, 33–35).

Given, then, the variety of stances among the critics—Stoic, hedonistic, evangelical Christian, Platonic, syncretistic—we can better understand the meaning of "instinct" and "spur to virtue" for both Le Caron and Rabelais by turning to the speech of Valton at the conclusion of Rabelais's part in Dialogue 3.

To end his own speech, Rabelais cites reason as that which gives man peace and allows him to know what are the true pleasures. Rabelais, differing from Cicero, calls pleasure what some name virtue; it is pleasure that permits us to endure difficulties in hope of an honest rest. Epicurus himself had, on the other hand, insisted that pleasure was the *removal* of pain. Both Cicero and Rabelais agree, however, that the individual, endowed with understanding, only desires that pleasure which does not corrupt but

6. See also Wayne A. Rebhorn, "The Burdens and Joys of Freedom: An Interpretation of the Five Books of Rabelais," in *Etudes Rabelaisiennes* 9 (Geneva: Droz, 1971), 72–77.

upholds the order of Nature (*De finibus* 1.19.62). Reason will moderate and constitute our inner harmony.

Rabelais esteems no other pleasure than that of a wise and prudent person characterized by a joyous and agreeable temperance. To be sure, not everything that is called pleasure is to be esteemed as such, for true felicity is only that which is born for honest things, Cicero's Epicurean adjustment of Stoic doctrine (*De finibus* 1.19.62). Le Caron's text affirms that those who are nobly taught and who frequent the company of similar people have by nature an instinct that incites them to virtuous deeds of which the end is pleasure. Other pleasures are only vain shadows.

Finally, Rabelais equates the cause of pleasure with the knowledge of divine things. Its duty is to make us content according to perfect Nature and to moderate the passions according to its order and judgment so that we can enjoy a lasting pleasure. He stands strongly against Stoic apathy or nonpassion, for it does not move one to virtue. For the same reason he criticizes contemporary writers who propose to interrupt our natural tranquillity to force us to follow their amorous passions. He feels that they have wished to limit the study and thought of others, diminishing therefore the grandeur and glory of knowledge. Rabelais believes that he has won the rhetorical debate, but Valton has the last word, responding to Cotereau, L'Escorché, and Rabelais as if he had been present at their discussion.

Valton is clearly Le Caron's spokesman, drawing upon neo-Pythagorean and Platonic systems to arrive at his own conception of tranquillity within a Christian framework. He admonishes the others for not considering more closely the nature of the highest good which locates felicity not in human things but in eternal ones. On the separation of the soul from the body and the knowledge of God after death, he cites the example of Socrates in the *Phaedo*.

He reminds us that true good cannot be in this life, for the body is the tomb of the soul where we neither see nor hear perfectly. But souls live after death, enjoying true knowledge of God. Therefore we ought not to propose to attain true good in this life, but hope for it after death. This will excite us to live well.

But what is the highest good? For both Pythagoras and Plato it is God (*Protagoras* 329c, 344c; *Theatetus* 176b–c; *Republic* 2.379b, 10.613b; *Laws* 716a, c). Nothing is good by itself but by some resemblance to him. Since God is the only wise being, those who seek knowledge of him are lovers of wisdom, or philosophers (*Republic* 6.508d). Indeed, humanity's greatest good is its likeness to God (*Theatetus* 176b–c). He is the height, perfection, and Idea of all good. The end of each person is pure and true knowledge of God, yet the body prevents us from obtaining this knowledge. Thus happiness can be found only in the contentment of eternal life—when we enjoy the total contemplation of God.

Of the three considerations of the highest good—cause, form, and communication—the cause is God, the form is an idea or understanding of God, and communication is the human mind, which, grasping the nature of the highest good by true knowledge, is made participant by divine goodness and perfect wisdom. To be like God is nothing more than to imitate him, following his will in the hope of obtaining felicity. God gave us a sign of this by the excellence of the mind born to the virtues and the arts. Following Plato as he does consistently, Valton identifies the substance of the good as entirely in God.

Even friendship begins first with God who alone has wisdom; it continues with men, depending on God; and finally it exists on an animal level for nourishment and preservation of life. The highest good destined for humanity includes perfect contemplation of God, participation in truth, and enjoyment of eternal life after death. In *La Philosophie* (10v), citing book 5 of the *Republic* (Le Caron calls it *dialogue* 5), Le Caron defines the true philosopher as one given over to the contemplation and search for truth. Near the end of *Le Philosophe*, Le Caron summarizes: "La fin du philosophe n'est autre que de cognoistre ce qui appartient à la felicité et souverain bien de l'homme" [76: The end of the philosopher is none other than to know what belongs to happiness and the highest good of man]. Wisdom, then, is knowledge of first causes (Xenocrates) and incomprehensible except by the mind. Good is only the hope of the highest beatitude. Three actions, however, lead man to divine virtue or wisdom: action or moral virtue (duty in public life), contemplation of truth and love, and burning affection to enjoy such an excellent good.

We do not become God but we can transform our nature by virtuous living and will, through the grace and goodness of God, so that we participate in the perfection and purity of eternal life. Our repose, then, comes from self-knowledge. Of all the passions, we will embrace only those that are good by nature and can be called the spurs to virtue.

Here again is the phrase in the description of the "Fay ce que vouldras" of Thélème. This expression, like several others from the final pages of Valton's discourse, draws heavily from the *Stromata* of Clement of Alexandria. Compare the following passage in Clement's *Stromata* (4.22):

> The man of understanding and perspicacity is, then, a Gnostic.
> . . . But only the doing of good out of love, and for the sake of its own excellence, is to take the Gnostic's choice. . . . This [choosing the knowledge of God], then, is the perfect man's first form of doing good, when it is done not for any advantage in what pertains to him, but because he judges it right to do good; and the energy being vigorously exerted in all things, in the very act becomes good; not good in some things, and not good in others, but consisting in the *habit* of doing good, neither for glory, nor as the philosophers say, for reputation, nor from reward either from men or God; but so as to pass life after the image and likeness of the Lord.   (1872, p. 203)

The statement includes the concept of synderesis later formulated by the Scholastics, the *honestum* of the Stoics, the Platonic moral virtue of the philosopher and the guardians, and the *caritas* of Christianity. Above all, it reflects the *voluptas* of Epicurus as perceived by Lorenzo Valla, Rabelais, and Le Caron, for the Alexandrian Platonists shared with the Renaissance humanists a strong syncretism of philosophical doctrines. Literally dozens of passages in Clement reveal the community of spirit between the early Church Fathers and the humanists.

Salvatore Lilla (1971) in his book on Clement of Alexandria's philosophy, reasons, regarding *Stromata* 5, that Clement's real thought must have been that virtue is the product of the combined activity of God and humanity, the concept of synergism (66). Lilla also demonstrates that the doctrine according to which virtue is produced by the combination of Nature (physis), learning (mathesis), training or practice (askesis), and custom or habit (ethos) is Aristotelian (67).[7] Could this be yet another way of considering "gens liberes, bien nez, bien instruitz, conversans en compaignies honnestes?" The classical doctrine of prudence (phro-

7. See also Aristotle's *Politics* 1332a.38–40, and *Nicomachean Ethics* 1103a.17–19, 23–26.

nesis) is for Clement pure activity of mind that leads one to the knowledge of the intelligible realities and also directs our behavior in practical life: wisdom (Lilla 1971, 73).

The highest moral ideal for Clement, as we have seen, is becoming like God, an idea expressed also in the *Theaetetus* (176b). Clement interprets Genesis 1:26 to mean that, upon creation, the living being received a rational faculty that was a copy of the divine Logos, an image of God (*kat eikona*). Yet he spends his life reaching toward moral perfection by practicing virtue. Lilla (1971) suggests that "the first is a natural possession of everybody; the second is achieved by means of personal efforts" (108).

Clement writes in *Stromata* (4.23):

> For instruction harmonizes us, and by harmonizing makes us natural; and it is no matter whether one was made such as one is by nature, or transformed by time and education. The Lord has furnished both; that which is by creation, and that which is by creating again and renewed through the covenant. And that is preferable which is advantageous to what is superior; but what is superior to everything is the mind. So, then, what is really good is seen to be most pleasant, and by itself produces the fruit which is desired-tranquillity of soul.

Lilla (1971) demonstrates effectively that Clement's philosophy, while owing much to Plato, Aristotle, and the Stoics, also includes the Middle Platonism of Philo Judaeus, Albinus, Apuleius, and Plutarch (44).

Rabelais denies in the Le Caron text that he is a follower of Epicurus, most likely because of Epicurus's atheism. Clement, like the Middle Platonists, also condemns Epicurus for the same reason. And yet, we have seen from Valla's *De voluptate* that the humanists accepted their own version of Epicurus, an Epicurus whose "voluptas" can be interpreted in light of Christian *felicity*, "céte louable volupté" (Le Caron 1986, 237), which is none other than virtue or wisdom. Valton also identifies pleasure with "la souveraine beatitude."

Valton concludes Dialogue 3 with the thought that since this world is a shared city of which each person is a part, all must be joined in natural harmony and friendship, that is, by living under the same laws. Repose in our life is maintained by our hope in youth, and by our memory of benefits received in old age.

Having identified the highest good, tranquillity and pleasure,

Valton recognizes temperance and music as necessary for tranquillity. Temperance, as the *Cratylus* says, maintains and preserves prudence or wisdom. Music too excites pleasure in us, allowing us to recall the gracious harmony within, awakening our mind to greater things, and drawing us away from evil and troublesome thoughts.

Le Caron's innovation is particularly evident in this dialogue. First of all, borrowing from the resources of three philosophical schools—Stoic, Peripatetic, and Epicurean—Le Caron synthesizes his own system of ethics, relying for the most part on Platonic and Christian teachings. And yet, Le Caron, unlike Cicero in *De finibus*, presents his Stoic, Peripatetic, and Epicurean viewpoints not to denounce them, but to reveal complementary notions of virtue, wisdom, knowledge, and temperance. Like Valla in *De Voluptate*, he uses the pre-Christian representatives in a dialectical manner, drawing from each those characteristics that reflect consonance and harmony with Christian ethics. It is fitting, then, at the close of the dialogue, that Valton, having identified the highest good—tranquillity and pleasure—should recognize temperance and music, the Socratic and Pythagorean resolutions, as necessary for tranquillity.

Thus the central dialogue provides the pivotal thematic transition between the first two courtier-prince dialogues and the last two metaphysical sections. In Dialogues 1 and 2, guidelines for ethical behavior, laws, education, and government permit one to order a meaningful life in this world on social, political, and human levels—the concern of L'Escorché, Cotereau, and Rabelais in Dialogue 3. Valton redirects the focus to the higher level, without which man cannot realize his highest potential—affinity with the divine nature. The first half of the five dialogues is outward in focus while the second half looks within. One can attain completion, wholeness, and unity out of multiplicity through self-knowledge, the goal of the philosopher, only by experiencing the intuitive level.

Just as Cicero's and Valla's dialogues are more rhetorical than philosophical, the same may be said for Le Caron's. Instead of presenting a totally accurate development of each philosophy, Le Caron limits his topic to tranquillity which leads him to develop his own epistemological scheme. He selects from each philosophy those elements that he wishes to present as a sort of historical-philosophical background to his prime argument by Valton, that tranquillity of soul derives from a true knowledge and understanding of God and his divine will. In so doing, Le Caron retains the form of the classical dialogue while treating it in the humanist tradition that sought to reconcile rather than destroy, to emphasize similarities rather than disparities, and to envision Christian wisdom as the culmination of a long philosophical as well as religious tradition.

Dialogue 4

Another aspect of the tradition informs Dialogue 4, "Ronsard or Concerning Poetry," which features four speakers: the poets Ronsard and Jodelle and the orators Pasquier and Fauchet. Le Caron explains his choice of the four spokesmen:

> Recueillant donc en mon esprit infinis autres semblables discours je ne les ai peu mieux expliquer, qu'en une maniere de familier devis, lequel desirant embellir et decorer de toutes ses bienseances, à l'exemple des anciens qui avoient accoustumé d'enrichir leurs dialogues de telz ornemens, j'ai pensé qu'il representeroit bien sa dignité, s'il estoit discouru par les deux, qui sont au jourdhui à bon droit reputez les premiers poëtes de nostre tems, Ronsard et Jodelle, avec deux orateurs Pasquier et Fauchet, lesquelz l'excellence de leur esprit pour la bonne esperance d'eux m'a fait tousjours aimer.

> Recollecting in my mind many other similar speeches, I couldn't explain them better than by a type of casual conversation which I desired to embellish and decorate appropriately, like the ancients who were accustomed to enrich their dialogues with such ornaments, I thought that it would represent its dignity, if it were spoken by the two who are rightly judged the best poets of our time, Ronsard and Jodelle, with the two orators, Pasquier and Fauchet, whose excellence of mind has always made me esteem them.   (259)

Furthermore, he justifies his license to select his own speeches for them: "Mais si aucun d'eux s'estonne, que je la fai [128v] parler de ce que paraventure il n'a jamais ne dit ne pensé, ou est entierement contraire à son opinion: je croi, que se resouvenant de la coustume des dialogues il ne trouvera estrange, que j'aie emprunté son nom et sa personne" [259, my italics: "If any of them is surprised that I have him speak what he never said nor thought, or is contrary to his opinion, I believe that, *remembering the custom of dialogues*, he will not find it odd that I have borrowed his name and his identity"]. These two statements reveal that Le Caron has consciously chosen to imitate in his *Dialogues* what he perceives to be classical and contemporary practice in dialogic composition.

Ronsard begins as if the dialogue were taking place at the Palais-Royal in Paris. In his thirteen-page speech Ronsard outlines the four roles of poetry in antiquity: to reveal the secrets of Nature; to imitate truth; to sing of the greatness of God and of the virtues of heroes; and to inspire men by a holy furor to do honorable deeds to immortalize their names and to know their celestial origins. In fact, the beginning of political society is one of the marks of the excellence of poetry, as the myth of Orpheus and Amphion attests. Poetry compares with the paintings of the finest artists in that both express the perfection of beauty in all its graces. Ronsard likens the *Odes* of Pindar to the sayings of the divine Plato who affirms that wisdom and virtue derive neither from Nature nor from art but from divine might and will. Poetry has a divine origin since God is the author of all things, the beginning and end of all human endeavors.

Government is not absolutely perfect; only God's law is. Plato cites Pindar who says that the law is queen of all mortals and immortals. Yet Ronsard hesitates to admire too fervently the poets and philosophers of the past lest he offend those of his own age. He hopes to see his France so bountiful that the boasts of foreigners will have nothing over the accomplishments of the French; here Le Caron affirms the potential expressed in Du Bellay's *Deffence et illustration de la langue françoyse* published only seven years previously.

Poets, then, recall the greatness of universal Nature. They are prophets of the Gods and veil their writings from ordinary men through fables in order to be understood by the wisest and most learned. The greatest pleasure for the mind when it is drawn away from terrestrial concerns is to compose speeches in order to find the truth. Le Caron includes five verbs to delineate the construction of orations. By thus defining speeches, the author is at the same time justifying his own dialogues and the dialogic form in general in so far as it treats noble, worthy subjects and seeks truth. Even though the philosopher is often rejected by his own people, the poet is esteemed and honored. By extension, the composer of dialogues and the public lawyer, exemplified by Cicero himself and by Le

Caron, is so honored. The poet must not enslave himself to a subject with a verbatim description; instead, he must speak of its universality or of what could have been done, that is, of its verisimilitude and its appropriateness. Here Le Caron is already using the terms "vraisemblable" and "bienseance" that later become so essential a part of the French classical canon.

Poets depict human behavior, feelings, and worth, and philosophers, orators, and historians learn from poets to enrich their creations with the poetic illustrations designated as "fables" by Ronsard. He cites the myth of Hercules at the crossroads which symbolizes the path we must choose and the means by which we must reach it. He also points to the myth of Prometheus whose theft of celestial fire represents the seizing of the pure Idea, divine knowledge that God wished to keep hidden.

Ronsard proposes, at the end of his discourse, to leave aside antiquity because today "our France" devotes itself to the highest and most excellent creations possible in poetry. Again, recalling the hopes for the French language expressed in the *Deffence*, the spokesman, Ronsard, concludes that true felicity of the mind shines more in the grace and naturalness of the French than in the inflated pride of the Greeks, the Romans, and the Italians. He agrees (with Horace) that since noble poetry comes from wise and industrious Nature or from natural talent, one need seek nowhere else than in France many recent examples of excellent and rich creations.

Jodelle, taking up the discussion for the next ten and a half pages, agrees with Ronsard's assessment of France, but regrets that she has not honored her finest minds sufficiently. He will confine his thoughts to poetry rather than the other arts because of its divine qualities which surpass the ordinary. He attributes the high level that poetry attains to the celestial furor that raises the poet above the common herd to the temple of the Muses, site of the highest knowledge of the secrets of Nature. The inspiration of the Muses breathes into the soul a divine fire that kindles it entirely with the divine, as manifested in the songs of true poets.

Jodelle points to the words of Socrates in response to Ion the Rhapsode: only divine furor, compared to a magnet, inspires the poets to the richest and noblest creations. Jodelle feels that minds ennobled by both natural talent and art approach closest to the divine. Without divine inspiration these gifts lack value or creative force. He affirms that the good poets are those seized by the holy furor of the Muses; although others may work hard, without divine inspiration they cannot achieve significant and memorable works.

Like Ronsard, Jodelle agrees that more poets flourish in his own age than at any time in the past. Even though inspired poets may seem tormented or afflicted with a malady or madness, they receive poetic furor because of their exceptional qualities that enable them to experience the higher knowledge of divine perfection and celestial harmony. This knowledge includes numbers, measures, and harmonies that surpass the comprehension of ordinary beings. Thus the poet-magus succeeds in tempering the soul's feelings by imitating the order and concord of the heavenly spheres.

Although music of the most sublime type reflects celestial harmony, it is through poetry that we seek the higher consonance outlined by Pythagoras. Through poetry, a music born of the Muses, we can learn to moderate the passions of the human soul and to imitate the soul of the universe. Poetry was bestowed on us by the Muses for the consolation of the spirit, joining music with philosophy which become one and the same. Both have their beginning in and become one with poetry.

Jodelle ends his response with a discussion of the significance attributed to certain numbers such as three for hidden perfection, nine for the Muses and for the nine harmonies of the eight heavens and the universal soul, and seven for the seven planets divided into seven spheres and for the seven tones of the musical scale. Jodelle affirms the Neoplatonic fascination with numerology as an effort to comprehend the wonders and mysteries of the universe. As a member of the French Pléiade, he believes that the divinely inspired poet can know these mysteries and can express them in the poetic creation.

The third speaker, Pasquier the orator, wishes to know why Plato banished poets from the republic and yet honors them in other dialogues. Pasquier cites one passage in which Socrates quotes Homer before drinking poison to show that the nature of the soul is not like that of the body. Other passages from Homer illustrate the perpetual motion of the universe and the harmony of the spheres, for example, the golden chain of the sun that represents order in the cosmos, the round figure of the shield of Achilles as the universe, and Vulcan, in charge of light. Pasquier reminds us that Plato includes the poetic concepts of the justification and truth of names imposed by the gods, the exemplum of a perfect republic based on the model of divine justice, a focus upon the world of the intellect rather than that of the senses, and rejection of beauty in worldly terms for a more admirable moral beauty.

Fauchet the orator, responding to Pasquier, wishes to know which poetry merits inclusion in the well-educated republic. Because the teaching and discipline of youth is the first consideration, Fauchet could not approve of the fictions of Hesiod and Homer for children because of the violence and discord they present. Rather, he would form the well-born spirit to the love and pleasure of virtue.

If one uses fiction, one should choose examples of virtuous and memorable deeds. Fauchet believes that the Romans gave a better example than the Greeks by not mentioning the vices and calamities of princes. Thus the good poet who relates his study to the public benefit must use only true images of rectitude. Fauchet notes that in Plato poetry ranks third from the truth, for it is covered by a veil that masks truth from the harm of all lies. It follows art, a mere image of truth. Fauchet prefers, like the wise leader of the republic, the wisdom of the philosopher to the fictions of the poet. He regrets that poets include unworthy as well as meritorious examples in their works.

Jodelle agrees with Fauchet; he too has found fault in the ancients and especially in the Italians who have not treated poetry with the dignity that it merits. But he hopes that France will bring poetry to its highest perfection.

Pasquier echoes that hope and agrees with Fauchet about deceit in the fictions of the ancients. However, he condones the depiction of what is ugly and deformed in Nature, for it enables us to see what we could not look upon in real life. Such a poetic creation is called living or speaking painting, and painting is a mute poetry (this statement Le Caron borrows from Plutarch's *How Youth Should Read Poetry*). Pasquier advises us to consider not so much the subject as the appropriateness of the art that has expressed it, an enlightened plea to avoid arbitrary censorship and to focus upon the artistic process and its integrity. He justifies Homer's brutal descriptions and tales because the poet interweaves his judgment about what ought to be said or done with the speeches and actions he describes.

Pasquier asserts that even tragic poetry is useful, for it illustrates human fragility and the snares of the passions. Poetry serves two functions: it alerts us to virtuous honor and it warns us about dishonesty. He emphasizes poetry's useful purpose of depicting both moderation and high-mindedness.

Fauchet by way of reply quotes Cicero, who states that no art can imitate the subtlety of Nature. Fauchet believes like Demosthenes that those inclined toward unworthy endeavors will never be high-minded.

Ronsard summarizes the discussion, observing that art and Nature are gifts of God and necessary to the poet. But divine inspiration is a higher benefit enjoyed by only a few chosen by God, similar to the gift of prophecy. Thus poetry that is inspired by divine furor can only imitate the heavenly, the illustrious.

While Ronsard and Jodelle speak at greater length than Pasquier and Fauchet, both the poets and the orators define and defend poetry. As with Cicero and Quintilian, both the writers and the speakers in this dialogue avow a moral obligation to employ eloquence and elegance in the service of moral living and truth. Poets and orators alike participate in philosophy in so far as they adhere to and embrace wisdom. Both must serve the state with ethical conduct and observe the law. But the poet is responsible to an even higher divine law. Twenty-five years before Sir Philip Sidney's *Apology for Poetry*, Le Caron argues for the superiority of poetry to philosophy. Like Sidney, he believes in the practical function of literature of promoting virtuous action. By means of the imagination, the poet creates his speaking pictures which reveal divine principles (Evans 1977, 20–24). Le Caron's views on poetics appear to be Aristotelian-Horatian, resulting, as Marvin Herrick (1946) suggests, from a transfer of Ciceronian rhetorical theory to poetic theory (3, 106).

Le Caron clearly understands and accepts in this dialogue the Pléiade doctrines of poetic furor, the nobility of mind of the poet who strives for truth, the image of the poet-seer-prophet, the poet's role as teacher of ethics, and the belief that poetry in France will shortly not only equal but surpass the poetry of the ancients.

From the concrete level of the individual in society in the first two dialogues, from the defense and justification of the philoso-

pher-statesman of Dialogue 2, from the resolution of Christian
Platonism combined with Stoic and Epicurean notions as a path
of ethical conduct for the humanist citizen of the city-state in Dialogue 3, we ascend to a higher plane of the poet-seer in Dialogue
4. Le Caron continues the path of ascent in Dialogue 5, although
at first glance this does not appear to be the case.

Dialogue 5

"Claire, or Concerning Beauty," Dialogue 5, is according to its
subtitle, "the argument or epitome of the others." It is not clear
whether "the others" refers to the preceding four dialogues, or to
the projected dialogues that were to follow but never materialized;
given the titles of the dialogues to follow, they are most likely
"the others." Different in tone from the first four dialogues in its
opening lines, Dialogue 5 represents for its author the repose and
consolation of philosophy in the midst of the calamities of the
present age.

In an idyllic location along the banks of the Marne near Poul-
langis, his father's estate, Le Caron proposes that his friend Narcisse speak to the group of young men and women there assembled
on the topic of beauty. Narcisse, who will "speak in the ancient
manner of discourse," asserts that one judges evidence with the
senses and with the mind. For Narcisse, beauty is an attribute for
women alone; he would use a different word to express beauty in
other objects. In the heavens, beauty would be order and harmony. Men possess virtue or nobility, not beauty.

Narcisse insists on form as the true cause and origin of beauty,
and discovers this form in the physical disposition of beauty
within the body. To corporeal grace he would add elocution or
grace in speech. He equates the truth of love with the desire to
enjoy beauty. For Narcisse, beauty is the motivating force of all
deeds and undertakings, and it bends the mind as it wishes. Narcisse's glib praise of beauty recalls Panurge's praise of debtors in
the *Tiers Livre*, chapter 4. Both parody the elogy, misusing rhetoric to win their argument.

Claire rejects the excessive praise and flattering speech of Narcisse. She declares that true beauty cannot be as he has described
it, for it is more than an adornment for women. Claire also criti-

cizes other errors in his argument. Instead of describing true beauty, he depicts only its shadow. He would do well to consider the harmony of the universe which owes its order to Divine Providence and to Nature.

The same is true of man, the human creation, who is a microcosm or small world. Claire reminds Narcisse that when she says "man," she also means woman. Since we are both soul and body, we must judge beauty on more than merely the outward, bodily appearance. She agrees with Andromache that virtue rather than an attractive body delights husbands.

Narcisse continues to accept only empirical evidence while Claire points out that sensual pleasures are uncertain and short-lived. Men capable of a higher understanding love more a woman's excellence of mind that is not readily visible. Artificial methods to retain or restore exterior beauty offend Nature, for true beauty results from the prudence of well-born women that is an interior quality of grace.

Now L'Archer speaks. He, like Narcisse, comprehends beauty though the senses but notes that each person perceives beauty differently. The same, he holds, is true for love.

Another young woman, Rose, replies that the uncertainty and mutability affirmed by L'Archer would lead to irreconcilable discord and such is not the case in life. Thanks to Nature we can distinguish virtue from vice, the proper from the inappropriate. Beauty is above all excellence or perfection contingent upon intrinsic truth, an Idea in the mind. Herein lie constancy and unity.

L'Archer, seemingly unable to grasp the significance of Rose's reply, points out woman's fading beauty and flighty nature. His argument echoes the clichés of the sort of love poetry that focuses on man's ill effects from woman: madness, captivity, and misfortune due to woman's cruelty and tricks. He accuses women of feigning honor, and of desiring marriage only to seize a man's goods.

Claire now pleads for moderation, defending true love as uncorrupted and eternal. She agrees that both sexes receive beauty from God, that is, Nature. Some perceive of love as a God of friendship who maintains order and governance in the state. Others in antiquity saw love accompanied by the gods of eloquence and might. Claire advocates temperance in love as with drinking wine. Those seeking beauty on the physical level only will not advance beyond the ordinary, but those searching with the mind will consider love differently.

Without realizing it, Narcisse reinforces Claire's observations. But he rejects the spiritual level of the Idea, since he relies upon the senses. (His description of man transported by the splendor of beauty that originated in the eye may have been inspired by Ficino's *Commentary on the Symposium.*)

Claire now easily maneuvers the argument to place beauty in the domain of the soul, for the concept encompasses more than the mere object. As a point of illustration, Le Caron inserts three French *dizains* that paraphrase a passage from a Greek prose treatise from an anonymous *Life of Pythagoras*, dating most likely from the period of Proclus and Iamblichus (Taylor 1707, 61–62).

Narcisse again attempts to define beauty and love as three types: the delightful, the profitable, and the virtuous. The latter, belonging to the mind adorned with virtue, is a higher beauty. The problem arises in the other types. Those of the first two categories are "counterfeiters of beauty," and are not included in the circle of love, for they embrace vain pleasures. Since we participate in everyday life on earth, we are unable to contemplate the divine. Therefore we will temper usefulness and virtue in our love.

Continuing in Neoplatonic terms, Narcisse refers to Plato's Androgyna in maintaining that love endures for the one who has found his desired other half. The cause of love is beauty, stimulating the observer and engraving the image of the object in his heart. The great power of love moves the passions to reinforce it. Thus love is none other than a passion moved by beauty. For Narcisse, love is a tyranny resulting in a disparity between lover and beloved. Now Rose, wishing to oppose Narcisse on Claire's behalf just as Claire responded to L'Archer, designates instead Marguerite to answer.

Marguerite and Le Caron, the third speaker of each sex, close the dialogue, reconciling divergent viewpoints. Marguerite comes to the defense of Rose but chooses to speak of beauty rather than love. Instead of observing the exterior objects of the senses, she argues, we should seek the excellence within, for that is beauty. If she had more time, she claims, she would demonstrate that love like beauty cannot be found on the outside. Choosing the noble form of poetry, as did Claire, Marguerite, quoting in French a poem by a Greek poet, modifies the words of Narcisse, suggesting that the enjoyment of true beauty justifies pure and holy love. The poetry, presented in sonnet form, paraphrases a passage from the prose treatise *On Happiness* by Hippodamos, in which the conjunction of two into one, joined by pure beauty, reflects tranquillity, the triumph of reason over the passions, and a redirection toward the highest good. Once again, as he did earlier in Dialogue 5 when Claire cited three stanzas from an ancient poet, Le Caron, by switching from prose to poetry, demonstrates the power of the poetic text to persuade and to transform, in this case, by permitting the most sublime form to express the highest philosophical concepts. Not only does Marguerite have the last word for the women; her final statement, in sonnet form, elevates her position to that of poet-vates, endowing her thoughts with the gravity and prescience of divine inspiration. Le Caron may be contributing yet another commentary on the quarrel of *Le Roman de la Rose*, where both Narcisse and L'Archer appear as figures holding similar points of view. The sonnets, unlike the poetry of *Le Roman de la Rose*, grant to the woman, through the incantation of sublime verse, transformation and victory. No other argument is possible.

Le Caron, the dialogic participant, summarizes in the final pages the outcome of the debate. He credits the women with silencing the men as a result of their admirable beauty and *their eloquent speeches*. He believes that we cannot understand the nature of beauty unless we raise our mind above the shadows of the terrestrial to a higher realm. By means of a Platonic synthesis of the women's observations, he equates beauty with goodness, justice, and wisdom, and with the just individual. Beauty is in both the abstract quality or Idea, and in the particular. Unity, purity, universality, and immutability—not subject to the passions—characterize the idea of the beautiful. We must contemplate it with the mind which is governor of the soul and closer to divine nature through which we achieve knowledge of God and of ourselves. Bodies, lacking intrinsic beauty from themselves alone, are only the shadow of divine beauty.

In order to reach the enjoyment of the highest beauty, we must understand that this beauty, which is unity with God, causes and creates the universe. Earthly beauty appears only as the perfection of things as they participate in the Idea of beauty.

Le Caron resolves the discussion in the manner of the Ciceronian dialogue as outlined by C. J. R. Armstrong (1976) in "The Dialectical Road to Truth": "In Cicero's philosophical dialogues, for example, *all* speakers are clearly using dialectic, but every man's dialectic has equal rights with every other man's. . . . The decision in the matter under discussion . . . is left to someone outside the discussion itself: to you and me, the readers, to Brutus to whom the dialogue has been sent as to a judge who will adjudicate in the debate" (43).[8]

In *La Philosophie* Le Caron defined ethics as the knowledge of living well. Its end is to conduct the thoughts and actions of citizens toward the highest good. He says that he imitates Plato the most, not by the translation of his dialogues, but by borrowing his ideas on the knowledge of true wisdom.

Dialogue 5 in its ascending path to dialectical truth endows the speakers with symbolic or allegorical names. Narcisse, from the Ovidian tradition, represents *philautia* or self-love, like Panurge in Rabelais's voyage. L'Archer belongs to the continuation of the *Roman de la Rose* written by Jean de Meung, in which women are treated as physical objects of male conquest. Claire, Marguerite, and Rose, light and flower images as well as real women in Bourges and Paris, include the idea of the Rose which in the thirteenth century represented a fragile, beautiful creature, object of physical pleasure and conquest. Now, in humanist terms, the three reflect by their philosophical arguments that silence the men that not only do women possess the same intellectual capacities as men, but they often surpass them. By their insight into the true meaning of love and beauty, they manifest a clear understanding of the highest aspects of philosophy which remains for Le Caron not an abstract ideal but a principle and vision for daily life.

Along with the assertions of Rabelais in the Thélème chapters of *Gargantua* and in the dedication to the *Quart Livre*, and with the *Heptameron* of Marguerite de Navarre in her spokeswoman of Parlamente, Dialogue 5 of Le Caron, in addition to his *La Claire*, stands as one of the strongest statements for the dignity, nobility, and true equality of women with men in the French Renaissance. All three authors demonstrate the potential for women as enlight-

8. See also K. J. Wilson, *Incomplete Fictions: The Formation of English Renaissance Dialogue* (Washington, DC: The Catholic University Press, 1985), 28–32. Mustapha Bénouis, *Le Dialogue philosophique dans la littérature française du seizième siècle* (Paris: Mouton, 1976), serves as preliminary consideration of Le Caron's *Dialogues*.

ened, intelligent members of society *capable of a leadership position*. This judgment is based on a consideration of the questions of moral philosophy in the classical tradition as well as of their political and social roles within a framework of Christian ethics.

Within his five *Dialogues*, Le Caron succeeds in exploring new dimensions of the dialogic form. While at the same time discussing and refining significant considerations for the development of a personal code of conduct as well as a means of achieving personal fulfillment, Le Caron has, it seems, come to terms with his own life plan, his strategy for contributing to society. Henceforth, secure in his own vision of ethics and of the active life undertaken in Christian as well as classical terms, Le Caron will dedicate himself to upholding, preserving, and interpreting law as an active member of the Parlement of Paris for over forty years, and as a prolific compiler of Roman and French law. Not only did he publish more than thirty books, many in large folio format, but he revised and updated a number of them, some of which had more than five editions in his lifetime. His own life and works best reflect the precepts of his dialogues.

CATHY YANDELL

🎵 The Dialogic Delusion

Jacques Tahureau's *Dialogues* and
the Rhetoric of Closure

Sed non omnes qui habent citharam sunt citharoedi.

{Having a cithara does not make one a cithara player.}

—VARRO

The French sixteenth-century dialogue has received much critical acclaim for its insistence upon the process of contradiction between interlocutors and thus its exposure of multiple sides of a
particular problem. Eva Kushner (1972) asserts that "l'écrivain de
la Renaissance est presque toujours homme de dialogue. . . .
Même s'il a une idée à faire triompher il désire la passer au crible de
la contradiction" (489). In the introduction to his book on French
sixteenth-century dialogue, Mustapha Bénouis (1976) defines dialogue as "le produit d'une pensée qui se penche sur elle-même et
se dédouble ou se multiplie" (22). Another critic (Tyard 1980,
53–54) champions the suppleness of the dialogue form of the sixteenth century as distinguished from the *syggramma*. Because of
the dialogue's capacity to expose a multiplicity of ideas in a political "safe zone," the dialogic genre has been seen as well suited to
the introduction of new ideas and to the challenge of authority
(be it religious, moral, political or literary) in sixteenth-century
France. Poststructuralist readings of the dialogue, in insisting on
the indeterminacy of the text, also posit the multiplicity of mean-

ings inherent in the genre.[1] To some extent these readings are just, since regardless of the dialogue's conclusion, the reader has witnessed the play of several ideas throughout the course of the dialogue.[2] It is my intention to show here, however, that these claims for the openness of sixteenth-century dialogue are problematic, particularly in the case of Jacques Tahureau's *Dialogues* (1565). Rather than creating an open forum for the exposition and discussion of ideas in his *Dialogues*, Jacques Tahureau engages in a rhetorical enterprise of confinement or closure. Moreover, the dialogic form serves in this case not to disperse but rather to conceal the dialoguist's own authority in the text.

Several formal and logical elements contribute to what I will call the rhetoric of closure ("closure" in the sense of moral or intellectual finality rather than aesthetic unity) in Tahureau's dialogues: the tensions between dialogue and satire, the relationship between primary and secondary interlocutors, the nature of Tahureau's dialectic, and the author's ultimate adherence to intellectual authority.

Dialogue and Satire

As a genre, the dialogue's greatest strength is its ability to bring multiple voices and opinions to bear on an otherwise monologic question. Reino Virtanen (1977) examines several of the dialogue's possible functions: to attain maieutic ends in the Platonic sense (*maieutikos*, skilled in birth, as a midwife), to represent unfettered discussion (uncritical acceptance of contradictory beliefs), and to consider philosophical questions that are obscure and uncertain.[3]

1. See also Daniel Brewer, "The Philosophical Dialogue and the Forcing of Truth," *Modern Language Notes* 98 (1983): 1234–47, who argues that we must read the classical form *against itself*, being aware of "our own always unfulfilled critical desire for closure, stability, and meaning" (1246).

2. I am grateful to Eva Kushner for raising this important point in informal comments. See also Kushner, "Le Dialogue en France de 1550 à 1560," in *Le Dialogue au temps de la Renaissance*, ed. M. T. Jones-Davies (Paris: Touzot, 1984), 151–67.

3. Reino Virtanen, *Conversations on Dialogue* (Lincoln: University of Nebraska Press, 1977), 13–15. He also includes as other functions giving a fresh turn to trite but important truths, engaging in intellectual sport, and safeguarding the presentation of controversial ideas. I will address this last problem in a subsequent section on religion and belief.

Briefly examining these functions as they are present in Tahureau's *Dialogues*, we quickly find that none of them reflects entirely
this sixteenth-century dialoguist's project. The technique of Tahureau's character, the Democritic, is maieutic in the sense that
he helps to bring about the "birth" of his pupil's ideas. But the
unabashed credulity of the pupil often makes for what appears to
be an induced labor. After the Democritic has explained that societal attitudes toward courtship and dance are unreasonable, for example, the pupil (the Cosmophile) promptly concludes that *all*
societal attitudes are therefore unreasonable:

> Je recommence maintenant à cognoistre par experience que la dis-
> pute de quelque chose que ce soit fait le plus souvent eclarcir les
> choses douteuses et ambigües, et ce que la simple opinion des
> hommes se forge et pense le plus vrai, estre par raison le plus
> faus.   (Tahureau 1981, 76)

> [I am now beginning to know through experience that dispute
> about anything at all usually clarifies doubtful and ambiguous
> things and that the simple opinions men fabricate and think to be
> the truest are by reason the most false.][4]

In a larger sense, also, Platonic maieutics differ markedly from
Tahureau's. Whereas the former claims as its primary goal knowledge and understanding, the latter seeks a monolithic moral consensus (however unorthodox).

As for the possibility of unfettered discussions, given the specific pedagogical designs of the Democritic, truly egalitarian conversations never take place in Tahureau's *Dialogues*. Further, the
difficult moral questions (such as the advisability of duels, the role
of doctors and lawyers in society, and belief in God) considered by
the interlocutors are resolved definitively in favor of the Democritic's position. Of all the moral affirmations proclaimed by the
Democritic, only belief in God is challenged within the text itself,
as we shall later see upon an examination of the dialectic.

If, then, Tahureau eschews these open structures that the dialogue traditionally includes, does the challenging voice of satire
render his text more multivocal? An examination of the marriage
between dialogue and satire in Tahureau's text will reveal that, on
the contrary, satire in the *Dialogues* precludes developed discussions of the issues addressed. The Democritic's description of "mo-

---

4. Translations of all French texts are my own.

querie," the most frequently used of Tahureau's satirical techniques, illustrates the dialoguist's own notion of the satirical
genre:[5] "Moquerie, c'est le mépris *non aucunement feint ni dissimulé*
d'une chose sote et ridicule, fait avec raison et bonne grace" [199,
my italics: Mockery is contempt—*neither feigned nor dissimulated*—
for a foolish and ridiculous thing, executed with reason and good
grace]. There is nothing "feint" or "dissimulé" about the Democritic's disdainful though humorous account of men in the Petrarchan or courtly tradition who,

> aians perdu toute cognoissance de leur perfection et bon sens na
> turel, n'ont point dedaigné de s'abatardir jusques à dire qu'ils
> baisent l'umbre des souliers de leur dame, appellans leur ame
> chambriere et esclave d'icelle, voulant ainsi abaisser et aneantir
> chose si haute et tant precieuse, et ce qui ne doit estre employé qu'à
> la contemplation des choses grandes et secrets de nature, l'adonner
> jusques au service de chose si petite et tant vile comme est la
> femme, animant de tous ceux de la nature le plus pernicieux et ab
> hominable!   (30–31)

> [having lost all knowledge of their perfection and natural good
> sense, have deigned to lower themselves to the point of kissing the
> shadow of the shoes of their mistresses, calling their own souls ser
> vants and slaves of the women, thus debasing and destroying such
> a lofty and precious thing, which must be used only for the con
> templation of nature's great secrets, rendering their souls to the
> service of something so small and base as woman, the most perni
> cious and abominable living creature!]

These hyperboles presented under the guise of frankness recur
frequently in Tahureau's satire, where the Democritic's obstinacy
provides occasional moments of comic relief. Yet despite the exaggerated character of the Democritic's positions, those positions escape ridicule by their ultimate textual triumph. The Democritic's
logic, however whimsical, wins the debate, to which the Democritic's spirited reply to the Cosmophile testifies:

> C.: Comment se pourroit doncq' faire que la danse semblast bonne
>   à tant de personnes?
> D.: De la mesme sorte que les chardons semblent bons aux asnes.
>   (68)

---

5. For a very useful analysis of Tahureau's satire, see Margaret P. Sommers,
"Jacques Tahureau's Art of Satire," *French Review* 47 (1974): 744–56; see also Bénouis
1976, 105–11.

[C.: How can it be that dance seems good to so many people?
D.: In the same way that thistles seem good to donkeys.]

Similarly, the Democritic's colorful epithets for sophists, magicians, and doctors, "jappeurs aristoteliques" [93: yapping Aristotelians], "lourdaus superstitieus et philosophes renfrognés" [65: superstitious oafs and scowling philosophers], "fins fous speculatifs, chahuans timonistes du genre humain" [66: speculative fools, rowdy misanthropes], "ces gros butiers qui s'estiment sages" [135: idiots who think they're smart], illustrate the uncompromising tenor of Tahureau's critique. Once again the satirical rhetoric excludes both subtlety and attenuation.

"Satyr," says Swift, "is a sort of glass, wherein Beholders do generally discover every body's face but their own."[6] The secret of good satire is, of course, to enlist the laughers on one's side, which the Democritic accomplishes very nimbly with his student the Cosmophile, as we have seen. He does this by means of a technique frequently used by Lucian, creating a character that C. A. Mayer (1986) has called "le témoin domestique." The witness, a member of the group being satirized, becomes conscious of the misconceptions, vices, or wrongdoings of his own group, which gives the discovery far greater force than if it had been made by an outsider. In Tahureau's dialogues the Cosmophile fills this role most admirably. Representing the "mondain par excellence," he is soon disabused of his respect for courtiers, doctors, and others by the persuasive discourse of the Democritic.

While the satirical author must have a certain knowledge of the object to be mocked, she or he does not—and indeed cannot—attempt to address any given problem in all its complexity. As Matthew Hodgart (1969) asserts, "the satirist, after all . . . does not want to understand everything. He is committed to militant action" (247). The satirist seeks in fact to reduce the object of satire to a limited number of attackable characteristics, sometimes feigning incomprehension in order to denounce (as in the case of Tahureau's [Gauna 1981, 64–76] wholesale condemnation of dance) (see Hodgart 1969, 213ff).

6. Cited by Robert Elliott, *The Power of Satire: Magic, Ritual, Art* (Princeton: Princeton University Press, 1960), 266. Henri Bergson analyses this phenomenon in *Le Rire* (Paris: PUF, 1940), 135ff. See also Freud, *Le Mot d'esprit et ses rapports avec l'inconscient* (Paris: Gallimard, 1979), 168ff.

Lucian himself, preeminent practitioner of the satirical dialogue, raised doubts about the combination of dialogue and satire in an apology called "To the One Who Said 'You're a Prometheus in Words'":

> Can nothing beautiful come from the synthesis of two things of high quality, as the mixture of wine and honey is exceedingly pleasant? Yes, certainly. But I cannot maintain that this is the case with my two: I'm afraid that the beauty of each has been lost in the blending. Dialogue and comedy were not entirely friendly and compatible from the beginning. Dialogue used to sit at home by himself and indeed spend his time in the public walks with a few companions; Comedy gave herself to Dionysus and joined him in the theatre, had fun with him, jested and joked, sometimes stepping in time to the pipe.   (6.425)

Similarly, in *The Double Indictment*, Lucian's character Dialogue claims that he was formerly dignified, pondering the "gods and nature and the cycle of the universe, treading the air high up above the clouds." He accuses the Syrian of breaking his wings and putting him on the same level as the common herd, making him an equal of jest and satire and cynicism (3:147ff).

In Tahureau's dialogues the satirical and dialogic genres appear incompatible not because of differences in their level of dignity, but rather because of their conflicting structures. Whereas the dialogue tends by its very form to elaborate, to argue *in utramque partem*, to complicate, satire typically simplifies and focuses on single traits in order to produce a separation between the reader and the satirized object. If the satirist presents a character with too many sides, we might begin to see "our own Face" in one of them, and the character would cease being satirical. If spectators of Molière's *Bourgeois Gentleman* were made aware of Monsieur Jourdain's complex family history, for example (we could imagine that his mother's greatest desire was to be bourgeois; since his father had been unable to provide that status for her, becoming a gentleman was Jourdain's only hope for gaining his mother's affection), then the comedy would lose all its force. Likewise, in Tahureau, if we looked too carefully at the devotion of men who "baisent l'umbre du soulier de leur dame," we might understand something of their motives, and the derision would be mitigated if not thwarted. This is not to say, of course, that readers of satire cannot be invited to laugh at themselves (much modern satire does precisely that), but in the case of Tahureau the dialoguist clearly sets up categories of "us" (the reasonable) versus "them" (the unreasonable). He indeed attempts to assemble the laughers on his side by his satirical portraits of those in the latter category. Thus Tahureau's dialogues reveal a first principle of closure: the bipartite nature of his satire effectively prevents the full development of the voices of dialogue.

Structure of the Dialogues: Interlocutorial Imbalance

While it is true that the dialogic form allows and indeed invites conflicting points of view, it must also be acknowledged that in most French sixteenth-century dialogues a hero of sorts emerges; even if he is not a maieutic *magister*, one particular character advances more coherent, more comprehensive, and generally more copious arguments than do the others. This is true not only in the Socratic form as practiced by Pontus de Tyard in his early works and by Louis Le Caron, but also in Tahureau's purportedly Lucianic model.[7]

The Democritic, Tahureau's primary interlocutor and spokesman, establishes his own privileged position and explains his right to speak in his first statement in the *Dialogues*, thanking nature for having given him

> cette sincerité d'esprit, qui ne me laisse aucunement surmonter par une infinité de foles opinions et faits irraisonnables, qu'ils observent aujourd'huy entre eus avecques aussi grande superstition que si c'estoient les choses les plus parfaittes du monde.   (15)

> [this sincerity of spirit that keeps me from being overcome by an infinity of foolish opinions and unreasonable deeds, which are now viewed among people with as much reverence as if they were the most perfect things in the world.]

The secondary interlocutor, the Cosmophile, is a stock character who blindly follows the currents of society and its "idées re-

7. It will be recalled that in such dialogues as *The Lover of Lies, or the Doubter* and *Dialogues of the Dead*, Lucian's interlocutors speak with equal authority; no particular character triumphs over the other. The same can be said of Cicero, but there is no evidence that Tahureau imitated his work as he did Lucian's. See C. A. Mayer 1984, 30–31, 54, 139–40; Sommers 1974, 345ff.; C. Robinson, "The Reputation of Lucian in Sixteenth-Century France," *French Studies* 29 (1975): 385–97; and Bénouis 1976, 103–7.

çues," as his name implies. For a brief moment at the beginning of the dialogue, the Cosmophile questions the Democritic's motives:

> Comment? Il semble à t'ouyr parler qu'en meprisant la maniere de faire de nous autres tu approuves seulement ta façon de vivre, et ton esprit, comme si tu estois le plus grand ami de la nature, et seul engendre d'elle ayant la conoissance des choses bonnes, et que tous les autres hommes auprès de toi fussent bastardz et illegitimes en leur creation.   (16)

> [What? To hear you speak it seems that, by disdaining our way of life, you only approve of your way of life and of your thoughts, as if you were the greatest friend of nature and her only progeny possessing the knowledge of goodness, and as if all other men around you were illegitimate bastards.]

But like Socrates (and like Montaigne), the Democritic denies any intention of preaching or of placing himself in a position of superiority vis à vis the secondary interlocutor (or the reader):[8] "Je ne veux point me faire si grand, ni tant abaisser les autres que je me die estre seul entre tous les hommes qui ayt la cognoissance de ce qui est necessaire pour le contentment de son esprit" [17: I don't want to make myself appear so great, nor degrade others so much that I believe that I alone among all people know what is necessary for a contented mind].

Yet, ultimately, as the Democritic emphasizes on several occasions throughout the text, it is he who speaks with the voice of authority on the moral matters he has chosen to address. It is he who "knows best": "Te suffise que je t'ai dit une proposition vraie, et contre laquelle tu ne sçauroi dire chose qui ne tourne à ton prejudice" [92: Suffice it to say that I have put forth a true proposition, against which you won't be able to say anything that doesn't work against you]. And again: "Si tu n'as autre chose à dire, je . . . rendrai le plus foible ce que tu penses estre le plus fort de ta cause" [61: If you don't have anything else to say, I . . . will show what you think is your strongest reason to be the weakest]. The

---

8. In describing his maieutic method, Socrates reminds Theaetetus, "You forget, my friend, that I myself know nothing about such things, and claim none of them as mine, but am incapable of bearing them and am merely acting as a midwife to you, and for that reason I am uttering incantations and giving you a taste of each of the philosophical theories, until I may help to bring your own opinion to light" (*Theaetetus* 157 c–d; Loeb Classical Library, 2:59–61; all subsequent pagination will refer to this edition.

Democritic is justified in assuming the authoritative voice, he explains, because he (unlike the *demos* that he critiques), uses reason as his guiding force ("la raison m'a tant jusques à présent commandé" [59]).

Much like the secondary interlocutors in Socratic dialogues, by assuming the role of student, the Cosmophile accords the pedagogue the Democritic full license to explain step by step and in great detail ("par le menu") his moral philosophy. As the Democritic asserts, "je te voi desja prendre goust en mes paroles . . . je suis content d'y demeurer tant qu'il te plaira pour te declarer par le menu ce que tu voudras entendre de moi" [86: I see that you're already taking a liking to my words . . . I am happy to stay here as long as you like to explain in great detail what you wish to hear from me].

The Cosmophile corroborates the Democritic's high opinion of the magister's superior knowledge, as the pupil effusively praises the mentor. Just as Ion remarks that it is a joy to hear the wise words of Socrates, (*Ion* 535a), so the Cosmophile expresses his gratitude to the Democritic for having "shown him the light." This debt is articulated in terms of filial respect: "je te remercierai de bien bon coeur de quoi tu m'as dessillé les yeux . . . il ne sera jour de ma vie que je ne m'en sente autant voire plus tenu à toi qu'à cettui-là qui mesmes a esté la cause de mon principal estre" [240: I will thank you with all my heart for opening my eyes . . . there will never be a day of my life when I don't feel more attached to you than to the one who was the cause of my principal being]. But the father-son relationship implied here takes on paternalistic tones when the Democritic reproaches his pupil for not producing the acceptable response: "Vraiment j'attendoi bien quelque chose meilleure de toi" [111: I really expected something better from you].

Just as Socrates accuses Ion of changing shapes like Proteus, of twisting up and down to escape Socrates's demands (*Ion* 541e), so the Democritic accuses the Cosmophile of cutting his own throat as he argues his case: "je ne vi jamais homme . . . qui plus bravement se coupast la gorge de son couteau mesme que toi" [167: I never saw a man . . . who cut his own throat more valiantly than you]. The master criticizes the argumentation and methodology of his pupil in a considerable number of other contexts as well: "Tu ne me dis chose qui ne soit du tout contre toi . . ." [27: You

aren't saying anything that doesn't work completely against you
. . .}. "Pour un brave maistre maçon aristotelic, si as-tu tant mal
basti et fondé tes argumens que l'un est cause de la ruine de l'autre"
[71: For such a fine Aristotelian mason, you have so badly built
and founded your arguments that one causes the ruin of another].
"Si j'ai dit quelque chose en cela qui soit contre ta fantasie, remets
en la faute sus toimesme . . ." [84: If I said something you object
to, place the blame on yourself . . .]. "Il semble que tu aies quel-
quefois etudié en l'art d'argumenter, mais . . . tu le pratiques assez
mal . . ." [102: It seems that you have sometimes studied the art
of argument, but . . . you practice it rather badly . . .].

The Democritic, like the Stranger in *The Sophist* (217c–d), prefers not to engage in a true dialogue with his pupil. "The method
of dialogue," the Stranger tells Socrates, "is easier with an interlocutor who is tractable and gives no trouble; but otherwise I prefer the continuous speech by one person." Because of his malleabil-
ity, then, the Cosmophile is the ideal interlocutor for the
Democritic.

As we have seen, the relationship between the Democritic and
the Cosmophile is clearly delineated from the beginning of the
text. Even apparently superficial remarks linking discussions of
various moral questions indicate the Democritic's belief in the infallibility of his own opinions. Hegel warned that the dialogue
often takes on qualities of catechism, the answers to questions being previously prescribed.[9] Tahureau's dialogues cannot be called
catechistic in the sense that the Cosmophile does not inevitably
respond with a single, desired answer. But in the discussions between the two primary interlocutors, the Cosmophile always "converts" to the Democritic's beliefs in an ultimate gesture of closure.

Dialectic and the Triumph of Dogmatism

Dialectic, the heart of the philosophical dialogue, has acquired a
plethora of definitions and nuances over the course of the past 2500
years, as Donald Gilman shows in the opening chapter of this book.
The term comes from the Greek expression for the art of conversation, *dialektikē technē*. In its most general definition, dialectic is the

---

9. Hegel, *Lectures on the History of Philosophy*, ed. E. S. Haldane and Frances H.
Simson (London: Kegan-Paul, 1894), 2:16–17.

method of seeking and arriving at truth by reasoning, and more specifically, the method of refutation based on examining logical consequences. According to Diogenes Laertius, *De vitis philosophorum*, Aristotle recognized Zeno of Elea as its inventor (*Lives* 8, 57). Plato imagined dialectic as the discipline by which one can best discover the Truth.[10] Aristotle posited that every dialectical argument is either a syllogism or an *epagōgē*, which involves leading an opponent to a generalization by getting him to accept the truth of a series of propositions about particular cases. Aristotle coined the term *epagōgē*, defining it as "the approach to the universal from the particulars, for example if the best navigator is he who knows and so with the charioteer, then universally he who knows about each thing is best" (*Topics* 1.12). The *epagōgē* can take three different forms, as an argument from one proposition (1) to a coordinate proposition (for example, women are weak and therefore men are weak), (2) to a superordinate proposition (for example, women are weak and therefore human beings are weak), or (3) first to a superordinate proposition and then to a coordinate one (for example, women are weak and therefore human beings are weak and therefore men are weak).[11]

Dialectic as conceived by Tahureau's contemporaries is, of course, quite different from the Platonic or Aristotelian definitions of it. Agricola, in book 2 of *De inventione dialectica*, offers his own description: "Dialectic does not arrogate to itself the role of judging, does not by its own dubious resources clinch this or that dubious matter; it simply furnishes the wherewithal for such a judgment to be made by someone conversant with the subject matter."[12]

10. See *Republic* 532–33; compare Richard Robinson, *Plato's Earlier Dialectic* (Ithaca: Cornell University Press, 1941), 74ff. In Aristotle dialectic is relegated to a secondary position; for him, it is better to understand through the processes of one's own mind rather than through discussion, as he explains in *Sophistical Refutations*: "Deception occurs to a greater extent when we are investigating with others than by ourselves, for an investigation with someone else is carried on by means of words, but an investigation in one's own mind is carried on quite as much by means of the thing itself." See Aristotle, *Sophistical Refutations* (*De sophisticis elenchis*), E. S. Forster, ed., 169a37.

11. These examples are cited by Richard Robinson 1941, 35ff.

12. "Dialectices disserendi probabiliter rationem tradit, hoc est, instrumentum tantum veri falsique discernendi, cuius usu ministerioque expeditius cuncti artifices, quid veri aut falsi sit in rebus sibi propositis explorent" (Agricola, *De inventione dialectica*, ed. I. M. Phrissemius [Paris, 1534], 2:184; cited and translated by C. J. R. Armstrong, "The Dialectical Road to Truth: the Dialogue," in *Humanism and the Encyclopedia* (Edinburgh: University of Edinburgh Press, 1976), 43.

Agrippa, on the other hand, defines dialectic as the wretched discipline responsible for making the other "sciences" even more difficult to understand. He describes it as

> un art de contentions et brouillis, et qui rend les autres sciences plus tenebreuses et difficiles à comprendre: et l'appelle on science enseignant à parler par raison. O miserable genre humain, et vrayement despourveu de raison, s'il ne peut parler par raison sans l'aide de ceste discipline."[13]

> [an art of contention and disagreement, which makes the other sciences more obscure and difficult to understand: and teaching to speak with reason is called science. Oh, miserable humankind, truly lacking in reason, if it cannot speak intelligently without the help of this discipline.]

Tahureau, however, seems not to harbor any grudges against the ancient discipline, at least in some of its practical applications. Although in his *Dialogues*, unlike Plato's, no transcendent principle is revealed (except perhaps the affirmation that transcendent principles are to be rejected in favor of "natural" ones), the sixteenth-century dialoguist does retain certain rhetorical formulae and even certain aspects of formal logic from his ancient sources, as an examination of specific discussions between the Democritic and the Cosmophile will illustrate.

Three subjects of particular interest to sixteenth-century (and twentieth-century) readers lend themselves readily to an analysis of Tahureau's dialectic techniques or lack thereof: love and ladies, the role of foreign influence on French culture, and religion and belief. In the instance of the first two subjects we will find that Tahureau forces the rhetoric or the dialectic (or both) so that the text will arrive at his own moral conclusions. In the third subject, we will see that while there is a glimpse of dialogism, the text never moves to explicit openness.

Love and Ladies

In the opening pages of the *Dialogues* the Cosmophile quickly advances his thesis that "l'amour sert plus à instruire un gros et

---

13. Cornelius Agrippa, *De incertitude et vanitate scientiarum* (1530); *Declamation sur l'incertitude, vanité et abus des sciences*, trans. Louis de Mayerne-Turquet (Paris: Jean Durand, 1582), 57.

lourd cerveau que ne font toutes les autres inventions et artifices qu'ilz puissent trouver" [23: love serves more to teach a heavy and thick skull than do all other inventions and techniques that one can find]. The Democritic counters that, on the contrary, love often drives mad otherwise perfectly reasonable men, and this is entirely the fault of women, "creatures tant imparfaites qu'elles ne sont engendrées de la nature seulement que pour une necessité de la conservation humaine" [23: such imperfect creatures that they were produced by nature only for human conservation]. Using the Socratic dialectical technique *et idem non*, the Democritic sets out to show that woman is more imperfect than man.[14] The Cosmophile's replies consistently furnish further ammunition for the Democritic, as their discussion regarding women's ability to govern reveals:

> D. Premierement regarde si la femme sçauroit gouverner et entretenir une Republique . . .
> C. Pourquoi ne le feront-elles pas aussi bien que les hommes? N'en voyons-nous pas les exemples toutes evidentes des Amazones . . .
> D. . . . c'est qu'à peine les pauvres enfans masles avoient le loisir d'estre mis hors du ventre, qu'incontinent par leurs cruelles mains il[s] ne fussent privés de la vie, chose tant detestable, et contre nature, que le plus cruel des hommes auroit en grand' horreur . . .   (24–25)

> [D. First look at whether women would be capable of governing and maintaining a republic . . .
> C. Why wouldn't they do so as well as men? Don't we see the obvious examples of the Amazons?
> D. . . . the poor male infants had scarcely emerged from the womb when suddenly they were deprived of life by the women's cruel hands, such a detestable and unnatural act that even the cruelest of men would be horrified by it . . .].

In like fashion the Cosmophile proffers a number of examples in support of the equality of women, all of which are immediately

14. The Democritic's ultimate goal is to show that women are not worth courting. But first he must demonstrate that they are "imparfaittes," *not* perfect. Brief examples of three principal Socratic argumentative techniques may be useful here; taking the example of a ladle being described as a circle: (1) other recipients are just as round (*et alia*); (2) a strainer has exactly the same form (*et oppositum*); and (3) thousands of irregularities can be seen under a microscope (*et idem non*). See V. Goldschmidt, *Les Dialogues de Platon: Structure et méthode dialectique* (Paris: PUF, 1947), 37ff.

discounted by his mentor: God created men and women equal. (No. The New Testament prohibits women from publicly preaching God's word.) Such respectable characters as David and Hercules became servants to the women they loved. (Precisely. And David was punished for such a liaison by the death of his son; Hercules' strength and "grandeur de courage" were debased [26–28].) In these examples the Cosmophile furnishes straw men and women, as it were, to be knocked down by the Democritic, which the latter accomplishes in both cases with alacrity. One dialectical principle at work here is the *epagoge* to a superordinate proposition: Amazonians govern poorly, therefore women govern poorly; women are responsible for the ruin of David and Hercules, therefore women are responsible for the ruin of men.

Any attenuations of the Democritic's position serve, paradoxically, to reinforce that position. The dialectic unfolds in such a way that each time the Democritic raises an objection, that objection is used to prove the rule (as in the case of the Amazons). But each time the Cosmophile raises an objection, it is either immediately discounted (again as in his mention of the Amazons), or it is used to prove the *exception* to the rule. When the Cosmophile accuses the Democritic of blaming women simply because the mentor has not succeeded in his own amorous exploits, for example, the Democritic riposces that he did not intend to blame *all* women—only those women who exhibit "une mechanceté, cauteleuse invention, et sottise outrecuidee (vices communs en la plus grand' partie de leur sexe)" [wickedness, wily deceit, and arrogant stupidity (vices common to the majority of their sex)]. There are, the Democritic continues, a few sweet and virtuous women, but these qualities are extremely rare: "helas! tant rares en un tant petit nombre d'entre elles que la plus grand'partie des autres se peut dire pour le tout" [60: alas! so rare in such a small number of women that the majority seems to speak for the whole].

Thus for the Democritic if a few women have such redeeming qualities as goodness and sweetness, it only goes to show that most of them do not. Similarly, after the Cosmophile reminds the Democritic that since the mentor himself has recommended all that is useful or necessary and pleasant (according to an Epicurian principle that was frequently discussed at the time of Tahureau's writing),[15] he should thus be in favor of love, which is necessary for human preservation. While the Democritic first appears to condone love as "une amitié moderee," his response once again transforms the Cosmophile's objection into a proof of the exception to the rule: "Mais de quoi servent à nostre procreation une infinité de singeries, sotes harengues, passions demesurees, poignantes jalousies, foles et outrecuidees entreprises, et une infinité de tant d'autres badineries . . . ?" [61–62: But what do an infinity of gross imitations, stupid declarations, excessive passions, piercing jealousies, mad and presumptuous undertakings, and infinite other banterings do for our procreation?].

The debate over love and ladies also encompasses several related subjects, notably music and dance. For the Democritic, music is an acceptable practice insofar as it provides pleasure for the one who produces it, but it should never be undertaken in the spirit of pleasing ladies, to whom men all too easily become subservient (64). And dance should not be practiced under any circumstances, according to the Democritic. The dialectic in this passage is slightly more subtle and involves a greater variety of techniques than does the discussion cited above. The Democritic states his thesis at the outset: "Quant est de danser, les hommes ne sçauroient mieux tesmoigner leur folie et peu d'esprit qu'en approuvant une telle singerie et folie superflue" [64–65: As for dance, there is no better testimonial to men's madness and lack of wit than their approval of such an apelike, superfluous folly]. Catapulting the discussion, the Cosmophile accuses the Democritic of condemning all that is pleasurable: "Tu voudras tantost ressembler le vieil Caton Romain, qui estoit tant severe correcteur des meurs et conditions humaines qu'à peine vouloit-il jamais approuver chose qui feut plaisante et delectable" [65: Now you want to be like the old Roman Cato, who was such a severe corrector of human morals that he scarcely approved of anything pleasing and pleasurable]. This statement furnishes an ideal point of departure for the Democritic's diatribe: quite to the contrary, he affirms, I only approve that which brings pleasure, and dance does not. To advance a logical proof, the Democritic launches into a kind of *diairesis* or division, for the purposes of defining the word "plaisir":

15. On sixteenth-century notions of Epicurianism, see Trevor Peach, *Nature et raison: Etude critique des "Dialogues" de Jacques Tahureau* (Geneva: Slatkine, 1986), 42–44.

je veux bien recevoir ce qu'à bon droit et par raison se peut nommer plaisir, ce qui ne se peut aucunement prouver en la danse, entendu que nul se doit appeller plaisir si ce n'est en tant qu'il delecte et chatouille l'un de nos sens, ou que par iceux il puisse penetrer jusques à nous recreer l'esprit.   (66–67)

[I am happy to accept what can rightfully and reasonably be called pleasure, which cannot be proven in any way for dance, given that no one can call something pleasurable unless it delights and tickles one of the senses, or amuses the spirit while penetrating us through the senses.]

He then considers each of the five senses, demonstrating in every case that dance provokes no pleasure there. Dance brings no auditory pleasure because the harmony of moving feet is in no way delightful to the ears. One can find pleasure neither of taste nor of touch, and the only possible olfactory sensation is the following: "de l'odorer il n'y en a rien, s'il n'advenoit d'avanture que quelque mignon pour danser plus legierement vousist oster l'escarpin, et parfumer la compagnie de la souefve et precieuse odeur de ses pieds" [67: As for (the pleasure of) smell, there is none, unless perchance some dandy takes off his shoe to dance more nimbly, perfuming the company with the sweet and precious smell of his feet]. As for visual pleasure, there is so little color represented in dance that the eyes cannot enjoy it. The syllogism thus unfolds: if that which is pleasurable must be pleasing to the senses, and if dance is not pleasing to the senses, then dance is not pleasurable. This logic brings the Democritic to the indisputable conclusion that, bereft of all capacity to bring pleasure, dance should be discounted as an acceptable activity for any reasonable person. Here the Cosmophile could have continued the discussion in any number of interesting ways by challenging the assumptions of the Democritic. (How is it possible for one person to judge that dance brings no tactile pleasure to another? Why is the definition of visual sensation limited to the perception of color? and so on.) Instead, once again to the Democritic's advantage, the Cosmophile continues to furnish "idées reçues": "j'aime mieus suivre l'experience que toute ta philosophie, cognoissant assurement qu'il y a plaisir à bien danser, puis qu'une infinité de personnes et gens de bon esprit s'y delectent" [69: I would rather follow experience than all your philosophy, knowing assuredly that there is pleasure in dancing well, because an infinite number of good-spirited people enjoy it]. The

Democritic, now on solid terrain, returns to the central argument
he has been advancing from the beginning of the *Dialogues*: "Ne
te souvient-il plus de ce que tu m'as promis, qui est de suivre la
raison plus qu'une sote coutume?" [69: Don't you remember that
you promised me to follow reason rather than a silly custom?].

The Cosmophile does, however, dredge up one last argument
in favor of the pastime he has been attempting to defend: dance is
good physical exercise,

> chose tant recommandable de soi, profitable, et mesme tres neces-
> saire pour augmenter la force et maintenir l'homme en bonne dis-
> position, cette seule raison seroit assez suffisante pour renverser
> tout ce que tu t'es allé de si loing chercher par tes argumens et
> sillogismes, encores que je ne parle point . . . de la grace et faveur
> qu'en ce faisant il peut acquerir pour plaire à toute l'assis-
> tance.   (71)

> [so commendable and profitable, even necessary for strengthening
> the body and maintaining a good disposition, that this reason alone
> would be sufficient to overturn all that you've gone out of your way
> to show by your arguments and syllogisms, not to mention the
> grace and favor acquired by dancing to please all those in atten-
> dance.]

But once again the Cosmophile obfuscates his own thesis by providing bait for the preying Democritic, who accuses the Cosmophile of formulating poorly constructed arguments, since the criterion of pleasing others ("principalement à ces belles deesses"
[especially these beautiful goddesses]) has already been proven unworthy of pursuit. The Cosmophile's argument, though not tech-
nically constituting an *elenchus* or refutation (a subcategory of the
syllogism), does contain a similar mechanism. The *elenchus*, a practice originating in Zeno, involves the mentor's causing the interlocutor to evoke a consequence that contradicts his original thesis.
In this case the Cosmophile, in attempting to prove that dance is
good, evokes a reason that he himself has already been persuaded
to discount.

The Cosmophile, having been thoroughly convinced by the
Democritic's impeccable logic, concludes the passage by announc-
ing that he will henceforth change his ways (76). The dialoguist
clearly accords a superiority of forensic force to the Democritic in
the discussion of love and ladies, as we have seen. Though in several instances the Cosmophile raises difficult questions (for exam-

ple, "if dance is not pleasurable, why do so many people find it so?"), those questions are inevitably squelched, whether it be by a dogmatic reply that closes the debate (for example, "just as donkeys like thistles"), or by an egregious misuse of argumentation on the part of the Cosmophile that calls for immediate refutation.

Much of Tahureau's dialectic, sometimes undertaken in a Socratic vein, is in fact what Socrates himself called "rhetoric" as opposed to true dialectic—the rhetorical structures arrive at the desired conclusion, but the logic does not. In the case of the Democritic's arguments against such activities as courting ladies and dancing, the Cosmophile counters with flimsy protests, as we have seen. But upon examination we find that contradictions surface even within the Democritic's own arguments. Intending to belittle the ladies who withhold their favors from even their most devoted suitors, the Democritic proclaims:

> Mais ce dont je me fache le plus est de quoi ces pauvres sotes estiment leur honneur estre caché entre leurs cuisses, le logeant en un lieu tant sale et deshonneste, et croi que c'est la raison pour laquelle elles en font le plus souvent part à quelque gros vilain et lourdaut de valet, et plustost qu'à un honneste gentilhomme qui le meriteroit.
>
> (43–44)
>
> [But what makes me the maddest is that these poor idiots think their honor is hidden between their thighs, harboring it in such a dirty and unrespectable place. I think that's the reason they give the best part of it to some wretched clod of a servant instead of a respectable gentleman who would deserve it.]

Why, one wonders in reading this statement, would an "honneste gentilhomme" want to have anything to do with "un lieu tant sale et deshonneste," and why, more specifically, would he—rather than the "gros vilain et lourdaut de valet"—have deserved such an ignominious reward? It seems unlikely, given Tahureau's straightforward affirmation in the "Advertissement de l'autheur" that "il y a je ne sçay quoi en l'homme plus grand et plus parfait qu'en la femme" [14: there is something greater and more perfect in man than in woman], that this contradiction was intended by Tahureau to poke fun at his own exaggerated stance.[16] Thus while Tahureau successfully employs a number of dialectical techniques

---

16. Sommers, in "Jacques Tahureau's Art of Satire," notes the absence of self-satire in Tahureau's *Dialogues* (753).

in the discussions of love and ladies, the exchange is severely limited in the sense that the Democritic's argument inevitably wins, even if such a triumph necessitates jumps in logic or detours within the dialectic.

Foreign Influence on French Culture

Like Du Bellay in his *Deffence et illustration de la langue françoise* (1549), Tahureau proffers in the *Dialogues* an *apologia* for the French language in particular and for things French in general. Yet the differences between the two apologists are significant. Du Bellay champions a language that has been under attack by the learned for being "incapable de la philosophie,"[17] arguing that French, particularly with enrichment from Greek and Latin, is a promising language for both philosophy and poetry. Tahureau, on the other hand, asserts in his *Oraison au Roy* (1555) that the French language is the fairest of them all, such that even the most articulate Greeks and Romans could not triumph over "tant de douces et sçavantes pleumes qui font auiourd'huy profession ou de bien parler, ou de bien écrire en leur naturel Françoys" [6r: so many sweet and learned pens that today have a calling to speak or write in their native French] (compare *Dialogues*, 215).

The genre of *oraison* of course lends itself readily to this kind of congratulatory rhetoric. But Tahureau goes further still. It is impossible to imagine a better civilization anywhere, he claims, particularly because of the king and his "race":

> Nous sommes en un siecle tant heureux qu'il est impossible de plus, et faut croyre s'il y devoyt arriver du changement que ce seroyt bien du pire, car d'estre meilleur ne plus excellant il ne se pourroyt faire. . . . Certes Dieu fait beaucoup pour nous de nous avoir donné un Roi si curieux de la vertu . . . non seulement un Roi, mais toute une race de lui si bien née, que les gens de lettres se peuvent bien vanter d'estre maintenant au regne le plus heureux et le plus favorable pour eux qu'ilz sçauroient souhaiter.   (3r, 8r)

> [We could not live in a more fortunate century, and we have to believe that if there were a change it would be for the worse, because to be better and more excellent would be impossible. . . . Certainly God has done much for us in giving us a king who is so

---

17. Du Bellay, *La Deffence et illustration de la langue françoyse* (Paris: Abel L'Angelier, 1549), chap. 10; *Les Regrets, précédé par Les Antiquités de Rome et suivi de La Défense et illustration de la langue française*, ed. S. de Sacy (Paris: Gallimard, 1967), 220.

mindful of valor . . . not only a king, but an entire race so highly born that people of letters can boast of living now in the most fortunate and favorable reign imaginable.]

Tahureau's nationalist discourse also appears in the *Dialogues* in several contexts. He once again upholds and amplifies the causes of Du Bellay (whom he describes as "l'un certes des plus doctes et mieux ecrivans en nostre poesie françoise" [95: one of the most learned and best writers of our French poetry], but this time speaking in the voice of the Democritic, whose language is considerably more earthy:

> je veus bien soustenir qu'il ne faut point estre si profond admirateur des etrangers, que nostre langue maternelle en soit pour cette curiosité amoindrie ou deprisee, ainsi qu'elle a esté anciennement par je ne sçais quels braves silogisateurs d'argumens cornus, qui donnoient la moitié plus de gloire à quelque petit maistre ès arts croté . . . pour deus ou trois mots de latin degorgés en une dispute ambiguë, qu'ils n'ont fait aus autres, lesquels estans parfaits en nostre françois nous ont retiré tout le meilleur des obscurs etrangiers et facilement expliqué en nostre vulgaire.   (212)

[I submit that we shouldn't be such deep admirers of foreigners that our own mother tongue becomes lessened or underestimated by this interest, as it was formerly by certain fine makers of syllogistic, absurd arguments, who gave twice as much glory to some dirty little master of arts . . . if he coughed up two or three words of Latin in an ambiguous argument as they did for those who, with perfect mastery of French, extracted the best from the obscure foreigners and easily explained it in our own language.]

Thus, for Tahureau, those who praise Latin over French are narrow minded, or, as he calls them in a subsequent passage, "tous barbares ignorans" [214: all ignorant savages].

But Tahureau's linguistic chauvinism extends beyond the condemnation of Latin and Greek. He also reproaches the linguistic Italomania of his contemporaries, preceding Henri Estienne's *Deus Dialogues du nouveau françois italianizé et autrement desguizé* (1578) by at least thirteen years.[18] In the midst of a lengthy tirade (52)

18. Henri Estienne, *Deus Dialogues du nouveau langage françois italianizé et autrement desguizé* (Geneva: Philalèthe, 1578). Here I include "at least thirteen years" because Tahureau's *Dialogues* were published in 1565, ten years after his death; it is not known exactly when he wrote them, but probably shortly before his death. See *Les Dialogues non moins profitables que facétieux*, ed. Max Gauna (Geneva: Droz, 1984), xi–xiv; see also Peach 1986, 9–13.

against the language of courtiers, the Democritic enumerates such currently popular words and expressions as "folatre" [playful], "un poltron" [coward], and "il n'y manque rien" [nothing is missing]. These expressions share a "foreign," for the most part Italian, origin, and they were newly introduced into the French language at the time of Tahureau's writing, as B. H. Wind (1928) shows in *Les Mots italiens introduits en France au seizième siècle.*

Tahureau's nationalist sentiment in linguistic matters is amplified in his mockery of a good number of contemporary traits originating in other lands. The passionate, exaggerated forms of courting were all imported from Italy or Spain, according to the Democritic: "se passionner à l'italienne, soupirer à l'espagnole, fraper à la napolitaine, et prier à la mode de cour" [29: to be enraptured Italian style, to sigh like the Spaniards, to smite like the Neapolitains, to beg like courtiers].

One might argue that the "mode de cour" is French, and thus the French are at least mildly implicated in these reproaches. But in other passages it is clear that the worst aspects of "courtly" behavior, specifically insincerity and dissimulation, were prescribed by Castiglione in *Il Cortegiano* (see Peach 1986, 59–69), and thus are of Italian extraction as well.

The Democritic's treatment of Mohammed further illustrates the dialoguist's belief in the potentially nefarious nature of things foreign ("ce voleur, ce larron, ce brigant, ce pipeur" [236: that thief, robber, bandit, deceiver]). The Democritic situates Mohammed at the summit of religious dishonesty: "ce belistre et imposteur l'a bien sceu masquer de dissimulations feintes . . . [237: that warmonger and imposter was able to hide by feigned dissimulation . . .].

Unlike Montesquieu's *Lettres persanes* in which the outsider becomes a vehicle for illuminating the insiders' culture, in Tahureau's *Dialogues* the outsider is used to illustrate the insiders' own relative superiority, particularly concerning what is "reasonable" and "natural." Dishonesty and dissimulation, at least in amatory and religious matters, have their roots elsewhere.

The preceding examples, while not furnishing conclusive evidence of Tahureau's absolute xenophobia, suggest nonetheless a Manichaean tendency on his part. Throughout the dialogues he appears to establish categories of good and bad, good being all that comes from "la nature," "la raison," and the same (that is, like him: French, male, anticourtier, and so on); and bad being all that derives from artifice, unreasoned belief, and the Other. Interestingly, Tahureau's rhetorical procedure mirrors the subject of his statements about things foreign: just as the Democritic champions the virtue of sameness, so in these passages dialectic has given way to a single, unchallenged authorial voice.

Religion and Belief

Tahureau's remarks concerning religion and belief have given rise to very contradictory readings by modern scholars. Of those writing on the *Dialogues* during the past two decades, Sommers (1974) and Peach (1986, 17–18, 26ff) conclude that he is a rationalist, Bowen (1976) and Bénouis (1976, chap. 7) postulate his orthodox position, and Gauna (1984, ix,lii–liv) purposely hedges the question while strongly suggesting Tahureau's atheism. Given the ambiguity of Tahureau's text, the dialectic in the passages treating religion and gods is all the more interesting to pursue. I will argue that, in spite of the closed nature of the rhetoric itself in these passages, discussion of religious belief constitutes the only point of aperture in the *Dialogues*.

In the second dialogue the Democritic and the Cosmophile broach the subject of false gods. The Democritic tells of Numa Pompilius, legendary first king of Rome, who "created" the goddess Egeria, instituted sacrifices, and founded the order of vestal virgins, thus introducing the veneration of divinities into his too pugnacious populace (223–24). The Democritic then enumerates a long list of kings who also inculcated their subjects with religion for political purposes. But he stops short when he reaches the name "Moses":

> De dire que Moyse en ait fait autant et qu'il se soit aposté à une divinité comme les autres, c'est une chose tant mechante et detestable . . . qu'elle ne doit pas sortir hors de la bouche des fidelles en quelque sorte que ce soit, combien qu'il y en ait pour le jourd'hui d'abandonnés et perdus jusques à là qu'ils ne laissent pas de s'engoufrer en l'abisme d'une si dangereuse et damnable opinion.   (224–25)

> [To say that Moses did the same and that he aligned himself with a deity like the others, is such a wicked and detestable thing . . . that it must not come from the mouths of the faithful in any form,

given how many are so lost and abandoned today that they are not far from being swallowed up by the abyss of such a dangerous and contemptible opinion.]

The opinion that Moses too might have founded a religion for political purposes may be "mechante," "detestable," "dangereuse," and "damnable," but the Democritic makes no reference to its being "fausse." Having expressed the hope that such miscreants will be put back on track ("en la vraie voie de salut"), and ignoring the obvious comparison, the Democritic quickly and deftly changes the subject (225).

Other passages treating religion in the *Dialogues* are equally ambiguous and troublesome, particularly when Tahureau uses religiously based expletives. During the discussion of sex mentioned above (when the Democritic remarks that courtly women think they have their honor hidden between their thighs), the Democritic adds: "et voilà par le corps Dieu (j'en jure) de quoi je me scandalise le plus" [44: and I swear by God's body that this is what I'm the most scandalized about]. The Democritic later describes a warrior who begins an amorous declaration to his lady: "Par le corps Dieu, par le sang-Dieu, je renie Dieu, Madame . . ." [48: By God's body, by God's blood, I deny God, Madam . . .].

More amusing, but also more baffling, are these same expletives used in the context of affirming belief in God. As the Cosmophile remarks near the end of the *Dialogues*, "Cancre de dire qu'on ne croit pas en Dieu, si, de par le Diable, si"! [44: Idiot for saying you don't believe in God, yes, in the devil's name, yes!]. A similarly unusual combination of terms occurs in another passage where the Cosmophile recounts the story of the "bon compagnon" who was accused of not believing in the Trinity. The accused responds:

Comment! Jesus de par Dieu, penseriez-vous bien que j'entreprinse de soustenir une telle opinion. . . . O le bon Dieu! Estimeriez-vous que je me vousisse faire brusler sus cette querelle? . . . car devant que d'entrer au feu, si ce n'estoit assez d'une Trinité je confesserois plustot une Quaternité!   (234)

[What! For Jesus' sake, do you think that I would try to hold such an opinion. . . . Good God! Do you think I would want to be burned in this quarrel?. . . because before going into the fire, if it weren't enough to confess a Trinity, I'd confess a Quaternity!]

This passage, radically altered by censors in three contemporaneous editions (see Gauna 1984, 234–35, XLI), poses several interesting problems. Ironically, as a safeguard against censors, neither the Democritic (Tahureau's mouthpiece) nor the Cosmophile (who consistently adopts the Democritic's opinion) speaks these words; instead, they are spoken by a third unnamed "bon compagnon," whose reply is recounted in the third person by the Cosmophile. Yet the anecdote itself, clearly provoking not only laughter but also surprise by its audacity, can hardly be seen as anodine in its intentions. These contradictions could not have gone unnoticed by a dialoguist who takes great care to include "final words" that support the existence of God and the infallibility of the Catholic church in discussions between the Cosmophile and the Democritic. Near the end of the text the Cosmophile asserts, "Certes il est bien aisé à voir que toutes ces fauces religions (excepté la nostre) ne sont que bourdes . . ." [239: Certainly it is easy to see that all these false religions (except ours) are only lies . . .].[19] Since elsewhere in the *Dialogues* Tahureau expresses himself quite clearly, as Gauna (1984, 238n115) points out in his edition, it seems unlikely that the grammatical ambiguity of "ces fauces religions (excepté la nostre)" would escape the dialoguist's attention.

As one of the final statements of the *Dialogues*, the Democritic once again recommends adherence to God above all else in a paraphrase from the Psalms: "Heureus celui duquel l'esperance est au nom du Seigneur Dieu et qui ne s'est point arresté aus vanités et fausses reveries du monde" [239: Happy is he whose hope is in the Lord God and who has not been detained by the vanities and false dreams of the world].[20]

Because the interlocutors explicitly endorse Christian beliefs at the end of the *Dialogues*, Bénouis (1976) concludes that those are Tahureau's "last words" on the subject. But several subversive elements work against such a conclusion. First, religious belief is quite obviously undermined in Tahureau's choice of the central character's name, Democritus. While the Greek philosopher was

---

19. It should also be noted that, although Tahureau's own religious affiliations are not entirely clear, his family was largely Huguenot. After Tahureau's death, his widow, Marie Grené, married Nicolas de Bèze, half-brother of the well-known Genevan reformer; see Peach 1986, 11–12.

20. Cf. Psalms 112:1, 4:2, 39:5–7, 62:7–9, 199:37–38.

principally known in sixteenth-century France for his mockery of human folly (as opposed to Heraclitus, who wept in the face of human folly),[21] Democritus was also the inventor of the first strictly materialistic physics that excludes the intervention of the gods in any explanation of the universe. Tahureau's appropriation of this atheist's name for a character who is to serve as the mouthpiece for Christianity (despite the possibility that the atheist association might not have occurred to all contemporary readers) cannot be attributed to ironic coincidence. Second, the subversive nature of Tahureau's use of religious terminology occurs too frequently for it to be considered an occasional slip. Third, when the Democritic explains the political motives of religious founders and the dangers inherent in false religions, he makes no attempt whatsoever to analyze differences between all other founders and Moses or between all other religions and Christianity. He simply states that the others were wrong, as we saw above. Finally, Tahureau himself furnishes conclusive evidence supporting the dialoguist's wariness of censure for religious reasons. Already, in his preface to the *Poésies complètes*, he is careful to explain his use of religious terms:

> J'ay bien voulu advertir ceux qui passeroyent le temps à lire mes oeuvres de ne trouver estrange si quelquefoys à l'imitation des anciens poëtes je donne le titre de Dieu et de divin aux personnes excellentes, ce qui est fort commun en la poësie: aussi que les choses grandes et belles semblent avoyr je ne sçay quoi de la divinité.
> (223–24)
>
> [I wanted to warn those who will spend time reading my works not to find it strange if in imitating ancient poets I use the title "God" and call excellent people "divine," which is quite common in poetry. It also seems that great and beautiful things have something divine about them.]

Thus it appears that rather than making an orthodox statement of faith at the end of the *Dialogues*, Tahureau furnishes instead an appended apology that he has already subverted elsewhere in the text.

The discussions of true and false religions progress not ac-

---

21. Tahureau refers, for example, to Antonio Phileremo Fregoso's *Riso di Democrito et pianto di Heraclito* (Milan: I. A. Sciuaenzeler, 1511), on pp. 208–209 of the *Dialogues*; cf. also p. 18.

cording to dialectic, but rather as a series of repartees punctuated by polite formulae: "mais je te pris, de grace, di-moi un peu ce qu'il te semble de telle maniere de christaudins" [232: please tell me something about Christians]; "je croi que tu en dis ce qui en est . . ." [235: I believe you're right]; "certainement je cognoi que ton dire est tresbon" [239: certainly I know that your statement is good]. No idea is scrutinized since the two interlocutors are in perfect agreement. But in spite of the characters' explicit opinions unanimously endorsing the Christian faith, the *Dialogues* leave the reader considerable room for interpretation in this regard. Because of the undermining rhetoric and logic, it is in matters of religion and belief that the text escapes—however briefly— the rhetorical closure elsewhere preponderant in the *Dialogues*. Yet even the ambiguity in matters of belief is not projected in the interlocutors' explicit argumentation, as the reader would expect; instead, the contradictions play themselves out implicitly in the text.

Intellectual Authority

Tahureau clearly avows his aims in the "advertissement de l'autheur" where he begins by railing against "folles opinions" and human authority:

> je veus plustot bien dire et croire avecques un peu de gens de bon esprit, que faillir avecques un grand nombre d'ignorans, m'estant du tout appuié sur le fondement de la raison, et non point d'authorité humaine simplement forgee de quelque pauvre cerveau renversé.   (13)

> [I would rather say and believe the right things with a few rightminded people than to be wrong with a great number of ignorant people, always grounding myself in reason rather than human authority simply fabricated in some poor twisted brain.]

Ostensibly, then, one of Tahureau's principal purposes in the *Dialogues* is to refute human intellectual authority, in favor of reason, and often in favor of divine authority. I have already examined in the previous section Tahureau's treatment of religion and belief. In this section I will consider not questions of belief but rather those of religious authority as they are favorably contrasted with human authority in the *Dialogues*.

Both dialogues begin and end with the question of erroneous opinion; from the "infinité de foles opinions et faits irraisonnables" [15: an infinity of crazy opinions and unreasonable deeds] in the first sentence of the first dialogue to "les enseignemens de ces sots et superstitius amis du monde" [240: the teachings of these silly and superstitious friends of the world] in the concluding remarks of the second dialogue, incredulity provides both a structural framing and a central preoccupation of Tahureau's text. The author thus sets out to dismantle false "opinion," most of which is based upon obsequious adherence to such established ancient authorities as Plato and Aristotle and such contemporary authorities as Cornelius Agrippa and Erasmus. Tahureau further asserts that divine reason is superior to human reason. Summarizing his position on religious authority, Tahureau has the Democritic proclaim in the last few pages of the *Dialogues*:

> nous n'avons autre chose à tenir que les ecris des anciens prophetes, et le Nouveau Testament qui nous a esté presché par Jesus Christ et ses disciples, avecques les interpretations des saints docteurs en ce qui en a esté approuvé par la vraie et catholique Eglise . . . hors d'icelle, tout homme n'est autre chose que folie et vanité.   (238– 39)

> [We have nothing to hold to save the writings of the old prophets and the New Testament preached to us by Jesus Christ and his disciples, with interpretations of learned saints in what has been approved by the true Catholic church . . . outside of which man is nothing but folly and vanity.]

Thus in principle Tahureau endorses the religious authority of the Bible and Catholic theologians while challenging human authority, yet in practice he does precisely the opposite, as the following examples will reveal.

One proof of Tahureau's failure to advance the religious authority he allegedly seeks to endorse can be found in the *index nominum* of Gauna's (1984) edition of the *Dialogues*. It is at the very least curious that while there are almost fifty references to mythological or literary Greek characters, there are only eight references to biblical characters. Whereas Tahureau mentions over forty Greek and Latin literary, medical, philosophical, and scientific authorities, he refers to no more than two biblical scholars; there are twenty-some references to Greek gods and Arab prophets, while Jesus Christ is mentioned only four times.

The Bible's status as inviolable divine text is particularly problematic in Tahureau's second dialogue, where the Cosmophile cites Ovid in affirming that the Creator commanded humanity to contemplate the heavens: "A l'homme il a haute elevé les yeus / Et commandé de contempler les cieus" [164: Upward toward heaven the Creator raised man's eyes, / Enjoining him henceforth to contemplate the skies].

The Democritic then counters the Cosmophile's argument by proffering an oblique reference to a passage from Psalms stating that "Dieu s'est reservé le ciel pour sa demeure" [164: God reserved heaven for his lodging place].

In rebuttal, the Cosmophile, now alerted to the biblical preference of the Democritic, responds in kind with a specific reference to the fourth chapter of Deuteronomy, "où il est dit que Dieu a faict et creé les cors celestes pour servir à toutes gens" [165: where it is said that God created the heavenly bodies to serve all people]. In this passage the Democritic's principal cross-examination technique is to show that the Cosmophile bases his reading of the Scripture on another *human* reading of the text (namely, that of Pierre Turel, well-known contemporary astrologer) which ignores the contextual significance of the passage cited.

Thus, for the Democritic, the Cosmophile's erroneous reading can be traced to a corruption of the "vive mouëlle et substance du verbe divin" [167: living marrow and substance of the divine word]. However, the undermining of the "verbe divin" in Tahureau's text is not always accomplished by human misreading as it is in the above passage. Sometimes the dialoguist uses the Bible itself to furnish contradictions. The important debate between the Democritic and the Cosmophile about the nature of duels, for example, illustrates that the Bible can be appropriately quoted to support either side of a given conflict, which further problematizes the authority of the sacred text. Tahureau clearly intends to show that the taking of human life in duels is a savage practice, and he begins by having the Democritic attack the Cosmophile's reading of the Scripture. The Cosmophile claims, in agreement with Francis I, that in a duel God will justify "celui qui a bon droit . . . car il est tout certain, et assez congneu par les anciennes et modernes histoires, comme le bon droit a tousjours esté gardé et la victoire pareillement demeurée au juste et à l'innocent" [81: the one who is right . . . because it is certain and well known by both ancient and modern history, that right has always prevailed and victory remains with the just and the innocent]. The Democritic then cites a New Testament text demonstrating that those who preach the gospel will endure the persecution of the wicked.[22]

Rather than engaging in a debate that would address the numerous ambiguities surrounding the question of God's mercy to those who are "right" ("qui ont bon droit") in the Bible itself, Tahureau chooses to remain on the safer ground of external logic. The Cosmophile of course could have cited any number of biblical passages to support his claim that God rewards those who are good.[23] Instead, he questions the advisability of simply enduring persecution, of turning the other cheek, "etans plus laches que la petite fourmis, qui essaie mesme à se rebecquer contre les plus fors" [84: being more cowardly than the little ant who even tries to revolt against the stronger ones]. The dialogue then shifts from biblical questions to the necessity of punishment of offenders in society; the principal questions raised by the interlocutor here, not unlike the modern debate surrounding the death penalty, are justice and deterrence versus "un cruel spectacle par la mort d'un de nostre espece" [85: a cruel spectacle through the death of one of our own kind]. Since the biblical debate never concludes but merely fizzles, the question of the Bible's infallibility remains unresolved.

In what appears to be an appended apology, Tahureau renders "pen service" to the absoluteness of biblical and religious authority by stating that only God's word is inviolable against the storms of time (239). But, once again, in spite of Tahureau's quasi-fideist conclusion, neither divine knowledge nor "God's word" ultimately supersedes "reason" or philosophy. As we have seen in the preceding examples, biblical logic does not necessarily triumph over any other logic.

Given Tahureau's rejection of religious authority which he explicitly endorses, it is all the more interesting to consider his adherence to human intellectual authority, which he explicitly condemns. This adherence is confirmed not only by the dialogue form that Tahureau adopts (albeit a somewhat idiosyncratic use of the

22. Luke 21:12, though Tahureau does not cite the passage explicitly.
23. Deuteronomy 32:4; 2 Samuel 22:21; Psalms 18:25; Jeremiah 51:56; Luke 1:50, Romans 8:28; and so on.

form), but also by Tahureau's themes themselves, which come from Plato and Lucian.

If the sixteenth century enjoyed a renaissance of the dialogue form, it is largely because of the humanist revival of such classical sources as Plato, Cicero, and Lucian. Lucian was first translated into French in 1529 and Cicero in 1493.[24] Plato's work saw numerous translations and a plethora of editions,[25] especially in the forties and fifties, a period during which both dialogues and poetry inspired by Neoplatonism flourished. Tahureau's choice of form cannot have been made in a vacuum, particularly since the relationship between interlocutors and certain dialectical techniques are specifically those of Plato, as we saw above.

Even the very theme of rejecting intellectual authority (particularly false scholars) comes from classical sources. In Lucian's dialogue "The Dead Come to Life," Frankness attacks philosophers, so Plato, Aristotle, Socrates, and Pythagoras want to have him put to death. But it soon becomes apparent that Frankness is criticizing not *those* philosophers, but rather "self-styled philosophers." The dialogue concludes with Frankness and Investigation leaving to seek out all philosophers to crown or brand them ("we'll need few crowns but many brands") (3: 55–81).

Tahureau, like Lucian, couches his moral lessons in satire, creating dialogues that are intended to be at once enjoyable and morally instructive (doux/utile). The title of Filbert Bretin's French translation of Lucian in 1582 reads: *Les Oeuvres de Lucian de Samosate, non moins utiles que plaisantes*, quite comparable to Tahureau's *Dialogues, non moins profitables que facecieux*. Both authors promote an incredulous, skeptical attitude toward received ideas. Lucian thus provides the sixteenth-century dialoguist with an authoritative model for ostensibly refuting authority.

The final test of Tahureau's position on intellectual authority is the degree to which he calls upon it himself. First, the Democritic retains the position of authority throughout the *Dialogues*, as we have seen. In turn, his arguments refuting authority are taken from authorities. The arguments the Democritic advances against the art of dance, for example, are taken from Cornelius Agrippa

24. *Lucien des vrayes narrations* (Paris: Galliot du Pré, 1529); *Traité des offices de Ciceron* (Lyon, 1493).

25. Plato's individual work most frequently edited between 1542 and 1559 was the *Timaeus*, Neoplatonic sourcebook par excellence.

or Cicero via Cornelius Agrippa. Similarly, the Democritic's arguments advancing the inferiority of women—all commonplaces reminiscent of the *Querelle des femmes*—are carefully gleaned mostly from classical sources, some of which Tahureau condemns elsewhere in the same text—Diodore de Sicile, Lucretius, Ovid—and from such contemporary sources as Erasmus and Antonio Phileremo Fregoso.[26]

Tahureau's implicit adherence to intellectual authority provides evidence of his unwillingness to break away from established intellectual and moral models and thus furnishes a final example of closure in the *Dialogues*. Just as Cicero's character Crassus astutely notes that Plato is too eloquent to denigrate eloquence (*De oratore*, I, II), so the reader of Tahureau recognizes that the dialoguist calls upon intellectual authority too frequently for his rejection of it to be credible.

* * * *

A priori, the reader of Tahureau's *Dialogues* has several reasons to expect that the text will unfold according to principles of "openness." The adoption of the dialogue form, the use of dialectic, and the overt challenging of intellectual authority all suggest a heterogeneous approach. But paradoxically, as we have seen, in each case the rhetorical result is one of closure, drawing a dogmatic conclusion, be it about love, dance, or nationalism. In each case the dialoguist's own authority triumphs, despite the plurality of opinions expressed. Only the question of religious belief provides evidence of ambiguity, leaving slight fissures in an otherwise hermetically sealed vessel.

Jacques Tahureau has been seen, alternately, as a precursor of Montaigne and as a precursor of Molière. This status of "precursor," often accorded to obscure authors in the hope of bringing them out of the archives, is of course unnecessary in the case of Tahureau, who, judging from recent publications, is being read in the twentieth century whether he was anyone's precursor or not. Nonetheless, comparisons between these authors prove to be illuminating.[27] Tahureau's trenchant, exuberant satire has much in common with Molière's, and the two authors share their uncom-

26. Tahureau 64–75; Agrippa 88–91.
27. These comparisons, given the present context, are in no way intended to be comprehensive.

promising critique of dissimulation and pretense. Despite the differences in genre adopted by the playwright and the dialoguist, Tahureau's colorful epithets and lively characterizations convincingly dramatize the *Dialogues*. With Montaigne, Tahureau shares certain philosophical preoccupations (Epicurianism, skepticism, rationalism), as well as the challenging of "idées reçues." But in terms of rhetoric and form, the two authors are for the most part diametrically opposed. Whereas in Tahureau opposing views serve to indicate the veracity of a given opinion, in Montaigne opposing views serve to expose a problem in all its ambiguity. Whereas in Tahureau dialectic between interlocutors often collapses into a single voice, in Montaigne a single voice gives way to multiple expression. Ironically, the essayist's texts reveal themselves to be far more dialogic than the *Dialogues*. In the end, Tahureau's closed text suggests an engagingly open question for those pursuing the study of dialogue as a genre: if certain texts written in the form of dialogues do not contain true dialogue, and if other formal structures prove to be more dialogic, then what in fact constitutes a dialogue? Indeed, faced with the dialogue, we must concur with Varro that "non omnes qui habent citharam sunt citharoedi."[28]

28. I would like to thank Heather Dubrow and Eva Kushner for their valuable comments on this chapter.

ANN ROSALIND JONES

❦ The Muse of Indirection

Feminist Ventriloquism in the Dialogues
of Catherine des Roches

In 1579, from Poitiers, where Etienne Pasquier had been stay-
ing to carry out legal business and visiting the salon held by Madeleine des Roches and her daughter, Catherine, he wrote a letter
describing his debates with Catherine:

> C'est une Roche inexpugnable que celle que je combats par mes
> vers. Car je ne la sçaurois si bien assaillir qu'elle ne se defende trop
> mieux, d'une plume si hardie que je douteray desormais de luy es-
> crire. Non seulement elle ne veult rien devoir, mais qui plus est
> payer ses debtes avec un interest excessif, ny ne demande point de
> delay pour s'en acquiter. Je ne veis jamais esprit si prompt ny si
> rassis que le sien. C'est une dame qui ne manque point de response.
> Et neantmoins il ne sort d'elle aucun propos qui ne soit d'une sage
> fille.   (Quoted in Diller, 1936, 67)

> [She's an indestructible rock, this woman I battle against in my
> poems. No matter how skillfully I attack her, she defends herself
> better still, with a pen so bold that I hesitate to write back. Not
> only does she dislike owing me a response, she pays her debts with
> too much interest and asks for no grace period to rid herself of
> them. I've never seen a wit as quick or poised as hers. This is a lady
> who never lacks a response. Yet, even so, no word ever comes from
> her that is unworthy of a proper maiden.][1]

Pasquier's praise reveals a good deal about the social context in
which Catherine composed the seven dialogues printed in the col-

---

1. All translations, unless otherwise noted, are my own.

190

lected *Oeuvres* she published twice with her mother in 1578 and 1583. The Des Roches coterie, frequented by lawyers, scholars, and writers, was obviously a place where women as well as men held their own in conversation and literary composition. One thing Pasquier relishes is Catherine's ability to defend her own positions in their debates, her articulate stubbornness; hence his wordplay on her name. He also implies that her wit is sharp, even daring ("hardie"), by admitting that her written repartee nearly silences him for good. The speed of her responses also intrigues him: on the spot, orally or in writing, she replies immediately— and, as the language of lenders and debtors implies, often by out-doing him, paying back more than his challenges deserve. Combative, witty, quick on the uptake: Catherine is obviously a worthy opponent in the dialectics of the salon.

But at the same time Pasquier reveals his era's ambivalence regarding eloquent women. He is pleasantly surprised ("Et neant-moins") that Catherine's quick speech goes hand in hand with moral propriety: she is not a loose-lipped woman but "une sage fille."[2] Pasquier's view of Catherine des Roches shows how widespread suspicion of female talkativeness was. The assumption that quick speech and female chastity were incompatible appears throughout the conduct books and sermons of the sixteenth century, especially those addressed to daughters of the bourgeoisie such as Catherine des Roches, whose father and stepfather had both been lawyers in Poitiers.[3] A local example is Jean Bouchet's *Les Triumphes de la noble et amoureuse dame*, published in Poitiers in 1530 and often reprinted up to 1563. Bouchet quotes Proverbs in support of shamefast reticence as a crucial requirement for well brought up daughters:

> La seconde condition que doit avoir une pucelle est d'estre hon-teuse, et quant elle va entre les gens tenir sa vue basse. . . . Car, comme dit le Sage, la fornication d'une femme est cogneue à lever

2. Randle Cotgrave, in his 1611 *Dictionarie of the French and English Tounges*, translates "sage" as "honest," a word which, when applied to a woman, referred exclusively to her sexual purity.

3. For the biography of Madeleine and Catherine des Roches, see George Diller, *Les Dames des Roches: Etude sur la vie littéraire à Poitiers dans la deuxième moitié du XVIe siècle* (Paris: Droz, 1936), chap. 1. Studies of conduct-book prescriptions for daughters of the bourgeoisie include Ruth Kelso, *Doctrine for the Lady of the Renaissance* (Urbana: University of Illinois Press, 1965; rpt., 1978); Maïté Albistur and Daniel Armogathe, *Histoire du féminisme français* (Paris: des femmes, 1977), chaps. 3 and 4; and Ann

sa veue haulte, et à sa bouche en parlant incessamment. Les filles
effrontées sont voulentiers en mauvais estime du commun peuple:
Et celles qui sont honteuses et peu parlans sont estimées et aymées.

(Guillerm, Guillerm, Hordoir, and Piéjus 1983, 47)

[The second quality a maiden must have is to be shamefast, and to
go among people with her gaze cast down. . . . For, as the Prophet
says, a woman's fornication is revealed in her challenging glance
and incessantly speaking mouth. Forward girls are held in contempt by the common people, but girls who are shamefast and
modest in speech are admired and loved.]

The suspicion Bouchet attributes to the common people was
shared by humanists as well. Francesco Barbaro's Latin treatise *De
re uxoria* (On wifely duties, 1416), translated into French and re-
published frequently (1513, 1533) throughout the 1500s, typifies
humanist appropriations of classical gender ideology. Barbaro re-
cycles Aristotle, Xenophon, and Plutarch in praise of the silent
woman; concluding his discussion of women's speech, he writes,
"Women should believe that they have achieved the glory of eloquence if they will honor themselves with the outstanding ornament of silence" (Kohl et al. 1978, 206). However perverse Barbaro's paradox seems, the virtue of "silent eloquence" became a
commonplace. Bouchet, in his *Epistres morales et familieres* (Poitiers, 1545), repeats it in a rhymed version:

[Que la femme] Cherche tousjours compagnée consonne,
Et parle peu si le pris veult avoir
De femme honneste ou gist le bon sçavoir,
Car l'ornement et la riche parure
D'une femme est la silence qui dure.   (Epistre III, "Aux mariez" [22v])

[Always seek company suited to you, / And speak only rarely if you
want esteem / As a chaste woman who knows what she should; / For
the proper ornament and rich decking out / Of a woman is silence
that lasts a long time.]

It is easy to understand, then, why Madeleine des Roches em-
phatically refutes the topos in the opening to her and her daughter's first *Oeuvres*. To defend their shared project against a potentially hostile female readership, Madeleine writes in her "Epistre

Rosalind Jones, "Nets and Bridles: Early Common Conduct Books and Sixteenth-
Century Women's Lyric," in *The Ideology of Gender*, ed. Nancy Armstrong and Len
Tennenhouse (New York: Methuen, 1987).

aux Dames:" "si . . . vous m'advisez que le silence, ornement de la femme, peult couvrir les faultes de la langue et de l'entendement, je respondray qu'il peult bien empescher la honte, mais non pas accroistre l'honneur" [A2r–v: If you warn me that silence, the ornament of women, can conceal weaknesses of language and understanding, I will reply that it may prevent shame but it cannot increase honor]. Like her mother, Catherine found herself in a dilemma: although she was praised for lively speech in the semiprivate sphere of a haut-bourgeois salon, she faced a culture generally opposed to female eloquence. One way out of this dilemma, I will argue, was her choice of the dialogue as genre—a genre that not only reflected the actual conversations held in Renaissance salons and academies (as many of its historians agree),[4] but was particularly suited to win honor rather than "mauvais estime" for a woman writer.

Both Madeleine and Catherine des Roches seem to have sensed the practical advantages of representing themselves in dialogue, in the loose sense of a dramatized conversation—or perhaps, more accurately, in a duet that stressed its interlocutors' intimacy rather than their disagreement. In their *Oeuvres*, *Secondes Oeuvres*, and *Missives* (1586) they dramatize their mother-daughter bond in order to affirm the propriety of writing as women. Like Louise Labé, invoking the etiquette of chaperonage in her "Epistre" to Clémence de Bourges in 1555 ("Et pource que les femmes ne se montrent volontiers en publiq seules, je vous ay choisie pour me servir de guide" [43: and because women never willingly appear in pub-

---

4. On the relation between coterie conversation and written dialogue, see Diller (1936, chap. 3); [Louis] Clark Keating, *Studies on the Literary Salon in France, 1550–1615* (Cambridge: Harvard University Press, 1941), 65; Eva Kushner, "Réflexions sur le dialogue en France au seizième siècle," *Revue des Sciences Humaines* 48 (1972): 490; Mustapha Bénouis, *Le Dialogue philosophique dans la littérature française du seizième siècle* (Paris: Mouton, 1976), 25–39; Carol Sherman, *Diderot and the Art of Dialogue* (Geneva: Droz, 1976), 14–15, 150; David Marsh, *The Quattrocento Dialogue: Classical Tradition and Humanist Innovation* (Cambridge: Harvard University Press, 1980), chaps. 1 and 4; K. J. Wilson, *Incomplete Fictions: The Formation of English Renaissance Dialogue* (Washington, D.C.: The Catholic University of America Press, 1985), 2–4, 69–71; and Elizabeth Merrill, *The Dialogue in English Literature*, Yale Studies in English, no. 42 (New York: Holt, 1911), conclusion. For a counterargument, that theoreticians of dialogue recognized its artifice and the artifice of the social circumstances in which it occurred, see Jon R. Snyder, *Writing the Scene of Speaking: Theories of Dialogue in the Late Italian Renaissance* (Stanford: Stanford University Press, 1989).

lic alone, I've chosen you to be my guide]), Madeleine dramatizes her alliance with another woman in her "Epistre a ma fille," the first poem in their 1578 collection. The poem celebrates learning and letters for both sexes and insists that the life of the intellect is compatible with traditional feminine virtues: Madeleine praises Catherine as an affectionate and supportive daughter, exemplary in the private sphere, and predicts that she will earn immortality in the public realm through the "sainctes moeurs" [the saintly habits] she is acquiring by her devotion to the Muses.[5] Catherine returns the compliment in the "Epistre a sa mère" with which she prefaces her poems in this first collection: to follow her mother as poet and as daughter, she writes, is to follow a rare example of "vertu" (52). Later in the *Oeuvres* she dedicates her translation from Proverbs of "La femme forte descritte par Salomon" to Madeleine, claiming that the Old Testament portrait of the perfect housewife is also a portrait of her mother (147). This compliment jars slightly with Madeleine's outspoken complaints about the burdens of domesticity in her own poems, particularly her "Ode première" (see Stanton 1986, 40–45), but the contradiction reveals a strategy similar to Madeleine's: Catherine is assuring her readers that a scholarly woman poet can still exemplify traditional feminine virtues.

Similar assurances of intergenerational female loyalty link the mother's and the daughter's sections in *Les Secondes Oeuvres*: Madeleine thanks Catherine for publishing only in company with her, Catherine thanks Madeleine for giving her not only physical but intellectual life. Yet however such exchanges link the Des Roches' family tie to their fame as writers, they also mark both women as extraordinary. So does their editors' insistence on the title pages of all their books that the Dames des Roches, "mere et fille," are authors of the poems that follow. Although there were two of them, each protecting the other against the disapproval aimed at a single, exceptional woman in their century, they were even more spectacular as a pair than they would have been singly. Their contemporaries and recent critics have been fascinated, precisely, by

5. For an English translation of the "Epistre," see Anne Larsen, "The French Humanist Scholars: Les Dames des Roches," in *Women Writers of the Renaissance and Reformation*, ed. Katharina Wilson (Athens: University of Georgia Press, 1987), 244–45.

their relationship to each other.[6] So it may well have been for the sake of downplaying her claim to fame as a spotlit performer, as a nonpareille, that Catherine adopted dialogue form throughout her career. To speak through invented characters rather than directly in her own voice, particularly through allegorical or masculine figures, was to keep a safe distance from the self-celebration of the mother-daughter exchanges. Like her compatriot Louise Labé in her *Débat de Folie et d'Amour* (1555), Catherine ventriloquizes her own position through invented characters, using them to demonstrate her wit and logic without claiming either outright. Obviously she did not share the opinion of her male contemporaries that feminine virtue lay in silence, but theirs was a powerful point of view. To circumvent it, she adopted the oblique author-speaker identifications as well as the cultural prestige of dialogic discourse. She composed allegorical debates in a comic medieval mode; she adopted the role of conduct-book writer in an exemplary exchange between an ideal Neoplatonic couple; and, in her most ambitious and engaged use of the genre, she worked out an extended Platonic dialogue in defense of women's education.

Five Easy Pieces: The Allegorical Debates

Catherine's first dialogues are built on medieval models, the *débat* and *invective* elaborated by the Grands Rhétoriqueurs, from which she takes the convention of allegorical figures whose discussion clarifies their fixed properties (Zumthor 1972, 1978). Amusing, diverse, these texts seem like practice pieces, experiments with comic characterization, yet certain traits in all five reappear in Catherine's later defense of learning for women. The first dialogue pits the flighty, self-confident figure Jeunesse against the sober Vieillesse. Neither character changes the other; rather, they demonstrate their own fixed natures through an exchange of chal-

6. Diller cites a number of traveling humanists who remark on the des Roches as a pair (1936, chap. 2); see also Keating (1941, chap. 3). For modern comments on the mother-daughter bond, see Tilde Sankovitch, "The Dames des Roches: The Female Muse," chap. 2 in *French Women Writers and the Book* (Syracuse: Syracuse University Press, 1988), and Anne Larsen, "Catherine des Roches, 'Epistre a sa mère' (1579)", *Allegorica* 7 (1982): 58–64, and "Legitimizing the Daughter's Writing: Catherine des Roches' Proverbial Good Wife," *Sixteenth Century Journal* 21, no. 4 (1990): 559–74.

lenges. Catherine works out the mimetic aspect of dialogue here, adjusting opinion to character—what Torquato Tasso in his *Discorso dell'arte del dialogo* (1585) called "sentenza e costume," the two essential aspects of "imitazione" that align the writer of dialogue with the poet (32). Jeunesse trips onto Catherine's stage with a gay song, bragging about her power to help lovers in various kinds of difficulty, and concluding with a deprecating remark about age as the enemy to such ingenuity:

> Si un amant depourveu de sagesse
> Est dedaigné d'une sage maistresse,
> Je luy appren dix mille inventions,
> Pour parvenir à ses intentions.
> Mais ceux qui sont ja captifs de viellesse,
> L'on ne sçauroit animer leur foiblesse:
> Mesme l'amour y sentiroit glacer
> Son feu ardant, et ses flesches casser.   (54)

> [If a lover who lacks good sense / Is rejected by a wise mistress, / I teach him ten thousand devices / Through which to arrive at his goal. / But those who are captives of age / No one can rejuvenate their frailty; / Among them, Love himself would feel / His torch freeze and his arrows break.]

Vieillesse responds with a grumpy, down-to-earth prose explanation of her exasperation: "Vraiement jusques icy je m'estois contraincte d'endurer patiemment toutes ces petites vanitez, mais puis que c'est à moy qu'elle en veut, je luy demanderay pourquoy" [54: All right, so far I've forced myself to put up patiently with all this nonsense, but since I'm the one she's attacking now, I'll certainly ask her why]. What follows tends more toward rapid-fire insult than reasoned debate; to Jeunesse's "O vieille hideuse!" [55: you hideous old bag!] Vieillesse responds "O jeune sotte!" [55: you young idiot]. Each speaker simply claims greater power and prestige than the other.

Vieillesse, however, argues for at least a logical reconciliation. As principles of change, she says, "ne sçavez vous pas bien que nous sommes creatures d'un mesme Createur, qui nous a faict venir au monde toutes deux pour mesme fin?" [58: Don't you know that we were both made by the same Creator, who brought us both into the world for the same purpose?]. Catherine resolves the contest by stepping outside prose dialogue to write a long rhymed prayer for Vieillesse, in which she insists, as one half of the death-regeneration cycle, that she has a positive function: the grace and beauty that she steals from the young "je rends à la nature affin qu'elle reface / Et maintiene le monde en son ordre ancien" [61: I return to nature, so that she can re-create / and preserve the world in its original form]. Jeunesse, in contrast, is given a thoroughly flighty song in which, throughout three six-line stanzas, she cannot decide whether to tell her secrets to the "Dames" who need them (62–63). Catherine's judgment of the two figures is implicit in the sheer silliness of the second poem. She also plays with the conventions of allegorical dialogue itself by literalizing its treatment of abstractions as characters. When, for example, Vieillesse threatens to beat Jeunesse with a stick, Jeunesse retorts that she cannot reach her: "Je ne vous crain pas beaucoup, sçachant bien qu'un moyen age vous empesche d'aprocher de moy, pource qu'il est tousjours opposé entre nous deux, comme le printemps et l'automne entre l'hyver et l'esté" [36: I'm not afraid of you, because I know perfectly well that middle age keeps you apart from me by always standing between us, as spring and fall stand between winter and summer]. The depth of the dialogue lies in Vieillesse's demonstration of the interconnectedness of life and death: "Pour mille fois mourir et mille fois renaistre, / Rien pourtant ne se perd, toute chose a son estre" [61: Through dying a thousand times and being reborn a thousand, / Nothing is ever lost, every thing keeps its being]. But the wit of the dialogue goes into Catherine's characterization of Jeunesse as a kind of Erasmian Folly figure, chattering, speedy, and emptyheaded—a comic heroine shown, by dramatic means, to be sorely in need of Vieillesse's balancing seriousness.

The second dialogue, between "Vertu" and "Fortune," similarly sets two female types against each other. Fortune brags of the heroes she has brought low and raised up (the tyrant Dionysius versus the king Agatocles, Aegeus versus Arion); Vertu counters that Fortune has no power over noble and reasonable minds. Again, literalizing the symbolic trappings of the allegorical figures by turning them into topics for discussion, Catherine has each character mock the other's emblematic appearance: Fortune's ball, Vertu's pillar. But the dialogue is suddenly grounded in historic reality. After Vertu points out that her pillar resembles an altar, both speakers agree that actual altars have been shamefully destroyed in "le pays de Poitou," that is, throughout the province where the

Des Roches lived, in which Protestant forces led by Gaspard de Coligny in 1563 sacked cities, including Poitiers, and attacked churches. Even Fortune condemns the iconoclasts as hypocrites and thieves, and, in character, she offers to raise them higher still so that their fall will be steeper. Vertu responds in alarm:

> Non, je vous supplie, ne les haussez point d'avantage, vous avez trop faict pour eux, aussi bien ne vous en sçavent ils point de gré; mais aidez moy dornesavant à deffendre Poëtiers, je ne seray pas envers vous ingrate de ce plaisir.   (67)

> [No, no, I beg you, don't raise them any higher, you've already done enough for them, although they are not at all grateful to you for it; from now on, help me instead to defend Poitiers, I will not be ungrateful to you for such a favor.]

Catherine then turns Fortune, like Vertu, into a mouthpiece for her own civic loyalty and staunch Catholicism: Fortune agrees to help the Protestants no longer, and the dialogue ends with a rhymed prayer from each interlocutor, with Vertu begging God to protect "noz Citoyens" from the enemy, and Fortune acknowledging her subordination to God and repeating Vertu's plea: "vueillez mettre à repos / Nostre pauvre Poëtiers" [70: Please bring peace to our poor Poitiers]. To end, Fortune tells Vertu that she has been so won over by "la douceur de voz propos" that she wants to follow her from now on, "sçachant bien qu'il vaut mieux estre guidee par un clair-voyant que de conduire un grand nombre d'aveugles" [because I know it's better to be guided by one clear-sighted person than to lead a crowd of the blind].

Here, then, the reasonable woman's rhetoric brings about a reconciliation between the opponents. Moreover, by emphasizing the necessity for cooperation in an immediate political crisis and by celebrating the power of eloquence over even a famously irrational force, Catherine moves beyond the assumptions built into allegorical debate. The topical framing of the dialogue moves it beyond a rehearsal of eternal abstractions into representation of a specific, politically motivated response to an urgent contemporary problem: Fortune changes her nature in order to protect the city. And the combination of logic and flattery through which Vertu persuades her to follow a wiser path will also be central to Catherine's later dialogues.

Political considerations and reconciliation also structure the third dialogue, played out among three parts of the body: La Main, Le Pié[d] and La Bouche. The anatomical debate arises from the rivalry between La Main, who believes her delicacy and nimbleness entitles her to greater honor, and Le Pié, who insists that his practical endurance is worth more to their master, the Body. A new element in this dialogue is the gender difference between its first interlocutors, a difference that Catherine underlines in an early exchange between the hand as textile-working, feminine stay-at-home and the foot as outgoing masculine acquirer of goods. What is sketched out here is a conventional marriage, but an unhappy one, amusingly dramatized in the colloquial language of a couple's quarrel:

> La M.: Ha mignon, que tu parles bien à ton aise, cependant que je travaille tous les jours à filer la layne ou la soye, dont tu est vestu, ou bien à descouper les escarpins, dans lesquels tu fays les caprioles devant les Dames.
> Le P.: Comment ne me reprocherois-tu mes faultes, si tu les pouvois connoistre, quand mesme tu me reproches ce que je fay de bien? Or dy moy s'il te plaist, qui t'apporteroit la laine, la soye, et l'or si je ne te l'allois querir?   (74–75)

> [Hand: Ha, sweetheart—how easy you have it, while I work every day at spinning the wool and silk you dress in, or cutting out the slippers you caper about in for the ladies.
> Foot: How surely would you blame me for my faults, if you knew what they were, since you even reproach me for what I do right? But tell me, please, who would bring you wool, silk, and gold if I didn't go to fetch it?]

The bickering continues, entertainingly but without resolution, until La Bouche breaks in to assert order from above: "Et qu'est cecy, qu'est cecy, quel mesnage faictes vous, canaille que vous estes? . . . sus sus, que chacun de vous se range en sa place accoutumée et me dittes qui a commencé ce desordre" [77: What's this, what's all this? What kind of household is this, you worthless riffraff? . . . Calm down, calm down; each of you take your usual seat and tell me who started this uproar].

The Mouth puts an end to the corporeal civil war by invoking a political simile. She compares the Body to a city—not, more conventionally, to a kingdom. This is an understandable variation on the traditional metaphor, given the des Roches' status as *bourgeoises* rather than courtiers: "nous desirons vivre en paix sçachant bien que

les querelles des citoyens causent la ruine d'une ville: aussi les de-
bats qui pourroient advenir entre nous causeroient la perte de nostre
maistre" [78–79: We want to live in peace, for we know that citizens' quarrels can bring about the ruin of a city; in the same way,
disagreements between us could destroy our master]. Here, then,
an axiom of urban social order reconciles the two parts of the greater
whole. More importantly, however, the mouth appeals to the sur-
vival instinct of the disputants, explaining that their well-being
depends on their mutual cooperation and recognition that they are
"d'une mesme condition," that is, that they depend equally on a
well-ordered body. Unlike the preceding dialogues, this one is resolved by a superior figure, the first time that a single interlocutor
is so clearly the truth-bearer.[7] Literalizing her allegory again, Catherine makes a good deal of the physical position of each organ: the
higher the better, so the Mouth takes precedence over both the
Hand and the Foot. Yet the winning speaker wins through persuasion, as well: La Bouche, clearly Catherine's mouthpiece in both
attitude and verbal style, has rhetoric as well as "natural" authority
at her command. As usual, the interlocutors who concede are defeated less by rigorous logic than by appeals to their self-interest, a
technique Catherine will use again in her later feminist dialogues.

The fourth dialogue, between Povrete and Faim, dramatizes the
commonplace that poverty and hunger go together, but Catherine
also gives the pair a concrete historical location: both characters
admit that they have been haunting the peasants of Poitou since
the Protestants' attack and will soon rejoin each other there (86).
The joke is that Catherine represents them as disliking each other
as much as they are both disliked by human beings. Povrete tries
vainly to avoid the parasitical Faim, who she satirically predicts
will be welcome only at the table of rich misers; Faim complains
that great lords, treasury officials, political counselors, lawyers,
and merchants have no place for her. No reconciliation occurs;
there seems to be no possibility of change or improvement. In
spite of its comic linking of two figures who would prefer to be
apart, the dialogue presents a bleak and static world and comes to
a gloomy conclusion.

7. The entry of the third, authoritative speaker suggests that this dialogue may
be modeled on the medieval *disputatio*, a training dialogue used in the *trivium*
(Sherman 1976, 20) or on the *tenson*, in which a judge finally resolves the question
under debate (Merrill 1911, 126).

The satire of estates continues into the fifth dialogue. This one, however, ends with a major change. Beauté, fighting off the importunities of Amour (especially insistent, she says, among poets, rich men, and courtiers), tells her mother, Physis, "la fille aisnee du Createur tout puissant" [the eldest daughter of the all-powerful Creator] that she has decided to take refuge with Athene: "je m'en iray chez Pallas . . . ; ainsi je me sauveray de la tyrannie d'Amour par les livres, par les ouvrages, et par les yeux de la Meduse" [91: I am going to take refuge with Pallas; that way I will escape love's tyranny through books, needlework, and the eyes of Medusa]. Amour, fearing imprisonment, decides not to pursue Beauté, whose final words close the dialogue: "je m'en iray [me] rendre en mon temple de franchise" [I go to live in my temple of freedom]. This is the most dramatic of the dialogues, in the sense that Beauté's action rather than any character's argumentation resolves the issue. Moreover, her action produces a synthesis of normally opposed terms: Beauty takes refuge in Minervan chastity, heroine and goddess unite while retaining their defining characteristics. Catherine's allusion to Medusa, the Gorgon whose head figured on Athene's shield and who could petrify men gazing on her, allies Beauté with the warrior goddess's fierce protectiveness of virginity. This demonstration that opposites can coexist—that erotic human femininity can be effectively protected by divine celibacy, and that Beauty can both read and sew under Athene's protection—is crucial to Catherine's argument in her "Dialogue de Placide et Severe."

Fatherly Fictions: "Le Dialogue de Placide et Severe"

In this dialogue, published in *Les Secondes Oeuvres* (1583), Catherine abandons allegorical figures for human characters: two fathers of families, Severe and Placide. But she carries the sharp repartee of the earlier dialogues through into this one, along with the contemporary urgency of their references to Poitiers and their strategies of lucid argument and appeal to self-interest. The topic of the dialogue, the proper education for a daughter, had been debated throughout the sixteenth century and would continue to be discussed throughout the seventeenth. Indeed, the issue was raised as early as Leonardo Bruni's 1405 *De studiis et litteris*, in which he advised Baptista di Montefeltro, a young countess, that to a woman "neither the intricacies of debate nor the oratorical artifices of action and delivery are of the least practical use. Rhetoric in all its forms—public discussion, forensic argument, logical fencing, and the like—lies absolutely outside the province of woman" (Woodward 1963, 126). Christine de Pizan and Anne de Beaujeu, both writing for women of the aristocracy, took a different position, recognizing that queens and wives of great lords needed to be able to assess arguments and produce their own when they presided over hearings as representatives of their husbands. But theirs was a minority opinion, even among humanists. Juan Luis Vives, for example, in his widely circulated *De officio mariti* (1529, published in a French translation in Paris in 1542), warned against learned and talkative women: "Let not thy wife be overmuch eloquent, nor full of her short and quick arguments, nor have the knowledge of all histories, nor understand many things, which are written. She pleaseth not me that giveth herself to poetry, and observing the art and manner of the old eloquence, doth desire to speak facundiously" (Watson 1912, 207). This view prevailed as late as 1598, when Agrippa d'Aubigné wrote to his daughters that he saw no use in their studying logic. "Such knowledge," he tells them, "is almost always useless to Demoiselles of your middling rank." He adds that "too much mental training makes [a girl's] heart haughty" and can produce contempt for housework and for a less learned husband (Réaume 1: 449–50). For many men, female learning was seen not as a desirable accomplishment but as a catalyst for marital dissension.

In the context of such ideological assumptions, Catherine des Roches's self-presentation as an educated and eloquent woman must be recognized as nonconformist, an accomplishment she would recognize as a potential source of tension and criticism. Precisely to the extent that she confronted a culture saturated with suspicion of the kind of woman her mother had trained her to be, she needed skill in argument to oppose detractors of such women. She found in dialogue a way to counter such criticism before it could occur: cross-gendered ventriloquism, the adoption of a masculine mask as defense against mistrust of the eloquent woman. In the dialogue in which she defends the value and virtue of educated women, she takes on the voice and persona of a man: Placide, the eminently reasonable paterfamilias whose daughter Pasithée puts his profeminist educational theory into action. Through Placide,

Catherine systematically counters objections being made to women's learning in her time. The "Dialogue de Placide et Severe" sets into dramatic form the fourth element of a Ciceronian oration, the *reprehensio* or *refutatio*,[8] in which the speaker exposes and responds to his opponent's position. In addition, through the character of Severe, the antieducation father, Catherine carries out an ad hominem attack on the enemies of women's learning. Constructing Severe from a mass of mutually contradictory experiences and prejudices, she exploits the dramatic and satiric dimensions of dialogue[9]—its mimetic aspect, as Tasso labeled it—to reinforce her position. And by setting up both characters as urban neighbors, she justifies the familiar, colloquial language of a text obviously intended to convince men of her own social class to offer an education like her own to their daughters. In all three ways, then, Catherine's particular circumstances led her to compose a dialogue that corresponded to Tasso's ideal for the genre. In his *Discorso dell'arte del dialogo* (1585), he remarks that the best dialogues are structured around "a false opinion to be refuted"; that in imitating men's "opinions and habits of action" vividly, as poets do, they include villainous as well as exemplary characters; and that a simple, direct style is best suited to representing "the conduct of the disputation itself" (Lord and Trafton 1982, 33–37).

Catherine opens the dialogue by assigning Placide the reigning perspective: he sees Severe coming and gives him a friendly greeting. In contrast to Placide's narrative and social control of the situation, Catherine brings Severe onstage "ayant la face merveilleusement refrognée" [35b: with an amazingly scowling face], as his neighbor remarks. Severe launches into a lamentation on the miseries of family life: "j'ay une Femme rioteuse, fascheuse, dédaigneuse; j'ay une Fille éventée, affetée, éfrontée" [I have a wife who is disorderly, bad-tempered, scornful; I have a daughter who is flighty, affected, and defiant]. But, as Placide's gentle interrogation reveals, the fault is Severe's own. He has forbidden both his

8. For an interesting argument that the representation of the opponent changing his mind is the most convincing aspect of dialogue as a form, see Jean-Claude Carron, "The Persuasive Seduction: Dialogue in Sixteenth-Century France," in *Contending Kingdoms: Historical, Psychological, and Feminist Approaches to the Literature of Sixteenth-Century England and France*, ed. Marie-Rose Logan and Peter Rudnitsky (Detroit: Wayne State University Press, 1991).

9. Lucianic and Erasmian humor is discussed as a dialogue strategy in Bénouis (1976, 50–54) and in Marsh (1980, 26–40).

wife and his daughter to read or study because he shares the misogynist assumption of his era (which he attributes to "un renommé Philosophe," probably Aristotle) that women lack any reasoning powers. Catherine immediately sets his evidence against his argument by having him complain that his daughter Iris, the beneficiary of such noneducation, is trivial and unsteady: "Jamais je n'ay vu si grande trotieré: elle voudroit voir en un jour l'un et l'autre my-ciel, comme les grües" [36a–b: I've never seen such a gadabout; she'd like to see both hemispheres in a day, as cranes do]. The counterexample is Placide's daughter, Pasithée, whom he describes rather mysteriously in response to Severe's question about where she is: "En sa chambre . . . avec des ames sans cor[p]s, et des corps sans ames, faisant marcher les premiers dans un chariot ailé, donnant aux autres espritz et mouvements" [in her room, with bodiless souls and soulless bodies, setting the first moving in a winged chariot and giving spirit and motion to the others]. Severe misreads these circumlocutions in a way that confirms his predisposition to expect the worst from women: "Il semble que vous veuilliez representer quelque Medée!" [You seem to be describing some Medea!]. To which Placide responds that, on the contrary, he means that his daughter is revivifying Seneca and Plutarch by reading them and animating lutes and viols by playing them. The metaphorical ingenuity of Placide's turn of phrase here does as much to establish his credibility as what he says. Catherine aligns manner and matter of speech in Severe too, but with opposite effect. He asks bluntly whether it is not indecent to permit girls to read such writers: "ne craignés vous point de les profaner, laissant passer leurs noms seulement par la bouche d'une Fille?" [Aren't you afraid of profaning them simply by letting a girl's mouth speak their names?]. In the first page of the dialogue, then, Catherine establishes an eloquent, enlightened character for Placide and a harried, suspicious one for Severe.

In what follows she shifts from mimesis to dialectic, systematically assigning antiwoman commonplaces to Severe in order to refute them through the voice of Placide. Many of Placide's arguments may seem conservative to a twentieth-century reader; certainly, it is clear that Catherine des Roches is not demanding new careers for women. Rather, her goal is to persuade her readers that a learned woman will also be a good woman according to conventional standards: an obedient daughter, a chaste wife, a responsible mother. What Anne Larsen (1987) calls the Des Roches' "propitiatory feminism" (239) finds an appropriate form in Placide's refutation of Severe's errors; the dialogue is devoted to correcting false ideas about means—how to produce a good woman—rather than used to construct a new definition of ends, that is, to revise what a good woman might be. In Tasso's terms, it is a civil rather than a speculative argument, a debate on practical morality rather than an open-ended exploration of unforeseen possibilities. Yet the possibility of a sustained classical education at home, encouraged in wives as well as daughters, was a new one for most women of Catherine's class. Accordingly, she draws on all the rhetorical ammunition available to sixteenth-century humanists in order to make her case.

One of her most frequent logical strategies is to break down Severe's assumptions about cause and effect. When, for example, he says that giving women permission to read whatever they like is the same as giving them "licence de faire tout ce qu'elles veulent" [permission to do anything they like], Placide undercuts his assumption that such freedom will lead to moral anarchy: "etant guidées par les bonnes let[t]res, elle ne voudront rien faire qui ne soit raisonnable" [37a: but if they are guided by good writing, they won't want to do anything unreasonable]. Similarly, when Severe argues that a woman who has become learned will think too highly of herself to be an obedient wife, Placide counters that the study of philosophy strengthens a woman's spirit so that she is able to behave exactly as her husband wants her to (38b). When Severe admits the darker suspicion that a clever woman will cuckold her husband, Placide assures him at length that educated women value honor more than other women do, and have less time for the "pensées oisives" that lead to "volontés lascives" [41: idle thoughts, lustful desires]. He concludes his counterargument with a personification: books are better teachers than men because more objective and more persuasive. He uses this conceit as the basis for a completely positive portrait of the results of women's education:

> Apres avoir veu ce que les livres enseignent sans courroux et sans flaterie (car ils sont maistres qui monstrent franchement), elles tâchent de faire leur devoir envers leurs espoux, leurs menages, leurs

familles, leurs parens, se maintenant humbles, modestes, et offici-
euses envers tout ce qui leur appartient. Elles n'ont pas loisir de
recevoir une affection impudique.   (41b)

[After reading what books teach without anger or flattery (for they
are teachers who explain frankly), they make every effort to fulfill
their duties to their husbands, their households, their families,
their parents, remaining humble, modest, and obedient toward all
their responsibilities. And they have no time to develop any un-
chaste affection.]

Placide clinches his point by forcing Severe to concede that his
own experience proves the reverse of his argument: his uneducated
wife has none of the virtues he thinks are threatened by education.
Severe concedes, "je suis aux liens d'une sotte, qui me gourmande
incessament" [41a: I'm entrapped by a foolish woman, who tor-
ments me constantly], and he eventually promises to send his
daughter Iris to talk to Placide's Pasithée the next day.

Another of Catherine's dialectical strategies is to break down
the oppositions that rigidify Severe's thought. When he says, for
example, that a learned woman is a monster, a freak of nature, he
exposes his assumption that the ignorance he sees in women results from their essential irrationality: women are "beastly" by nature, while men are on the side of culture. But Placide transvalues
the term "monstre" to defend exceptional women by arguing that
what is common is not necessarily what is best: "Les monstres ne
sont pas tousjours tesmoins de l'erreur de Nature, mail ilz
demonstrent combien sa puissance est grande" [35a–b: Monsters
are not always proof of a fault in nature; rather, they demonstrate
how great her power is]. Similarly, when Severe opposes proper
housework to improper reading, he invokes an opposition between
the distaff and the book that appeared everywhere in the conservative gender theory of his day. [10] Catherine confronts this opposition
in a nervously propitiatory way in her sonnet "A ma quenoille" by
assuring her distaff that she will never abandon it, asserting her
domestic virtue in order to justify her use of the pen as well. [11]

10. Vives (1529), Barbaro (1513), and Bouchet (1530) all invoke the *"quenoille"/
livre* opposition. See, for a discussion of the *topos*, Ann Rosalind Jones, *The Currency
of Eros: Women's Love Lyric in Europe, 1540–1620* (Bloomington: Indiana University
Press, 1990), chap. 1.
11. For French and English versions of "A ma quenoille," see Domna Stanton,
*The Defiant Muse: French Feminist Poems from the Middle Ages to the Present: A Bi-Lingual
Anthology* (New York: Feminist Press, 1986), 70–71. Critical commentary on the

Here, however, in the voice of Placide, she confronts the antithesis directly and dissolves it by invoking Pallas Athene as the goddess of weaving and wisdom both. When Severe remarks threateningly that if he were to find his wife reading, "je luy ferois sçavoir que sa main doit toucher la quenoille, non pas le livre" [37b–38a: I'd let her know that her hand should reach for the distaff, not a book], Placide responds, "L'un de ces exercices aide l'autre. Pallas les avoit tous deux" [Each of these activities assists the other. Pallas practiced them both]. This exchange typifies Catherine's technique of collapsing traditional antitheses. Through the person of Severe she calls sexed hierarchies of value into view so that she can interrogate their grammar: their linking of the normative to the masculine, their dissociation of knowledge and feminine virtue as mutually exclusive.

Another opposition that Catherine uses Severe to expose and to break down has to do with the use of exempla in debates over women's roles. As a minimally educated man himself, Severe is at first unimpressed by Placide's naming of Greek and Roman women who disprove his axioms. For example, when Placide tries to refute his claim that "les Femmes qui excedent la Commune aiment peu leurs maris" [exceptional women dislike their husbands] by mentioning the counterexamples of the Roman Emponina and Arria (from Plutarch's *Moralia*, a source for many of Catherine's classical heroines), Severe responds sharply, "Il seroit difficile d'en trouver de telles maintenant" [40a: It would be hard to find such women nowadays]. To oppose ancient virtue to modern vice is to launch a potentially disabling attack on the humanist technique of adducing ancient examples in support of contemporary opinions. But when Severe opposes the heroines of antiquity to the women of his own time, Placide has two responses, both of which call traditional views into question. To the first objection, he answers that if educated women loyal to their husbands are rarely seen today, it is precisely because such classical examples have been concealed from wives by antieducation husbands: "Ouy, pour-ce que defandant les livres, vous derobez à leurs yeux ces ex-

---

sonnet varies widely: see Jane Marcus, "Still Practice, A/Wrested Alphabet: Toward a Feminist Aesthetic," *Tulsa Studies in Women's Literature* 3 (1984): 79–97; Larsen (1987, 239); Sankovitch (1988, 52–53); Ann Rosalind Jones, "Surprising Fame: Renaissance Gender Ideologies and Women's Lyric," in *The Poetics of Gender*, ed. Nancy Miller (New York: Columbia University Press, 1986), 84–87.

emples, qui les pourroient émouvoir a sentir pour vous cet[t]e extreme affection" [40a: Yes, because by forbidding books to them,
you keep from their sight examples that could inspire them to feel
equally deep affection for you]. Later in the dialogue, when Placide explains that he often gives his daughter examples of famous
and virtuous women, Severe assumes that he draws them from the
past; trying out a little classical learning of his own, he suggests,
"Comme ces Sibilles qui se faisoyent renommer au tans [temps]
passé" [43a: Like those Sibyls, who became so famous in past
time]. Placide's counterresponse puts him firmly on the side of
modern women: "Mais commes les sages sçavantes, qui se font renommer de nostre tans" [No, like the good learned women who
are famous in our time]. He goes on to list seven contemporary
women writers: four Italians (Laura Terracina, the commentator
on *Orlando furioso*; the humanist historian Cassandra Fidele; the
poet Olimpia Morata; and Hippolita Taurella, Castiglione's wife),
a Spanish woman (Luisa Sigea, Latin tutor at the Portuguese court
and author of the poem *Sintra*), and two Frenchwomen (Clémence
Isaure of Toulouse and Diane de Morel, the youngest of the three
daughters of Jean Morel, leader of a Parisian salon throughout the
1580s) (Larsen 1987, 242 n23). To support her modern pedagogical liberalism, Catherine deploys modern examples of women's accomplishments. She uses Severe to push Placide's argument into
the sixteenth century.

Catherine also uses practical knowledge of contemporary social
fact to appeal to men's self-interest. Placide responds to another
traditional opposition—the public sphere as men's territory, the
home as women's—when Severe raises it to reject the idea that
women should study the same professional subjects as men do.
When Severe asks sarcastically, "Aprendront elles la Theologie,
pour se presanter en chaire, faire un Sermon devant le peuple,
aquerir des Benefices?" [Will they learn theology, so they can take
to the pulpit, preach to the congregation, and obtain church positions?], Placide responds by insisting on the private benefits a husband will gain from a wife who reads "la parole Divine": it will
teach her how to obey her husband and she will train her children
to do the same. He argues further that women should have some
knowledge of law; according to French custom, he points out,
they can leave a third of their possessions to their husbands in their
wills (38b). Is it not an advantage to a man to have a wife aware

of this possibility? And he concludes that a housewife's practical knowledge of medicine can only help her family and her friends. Rather than defend theoretical knowledge for women on a theoretical basis—equality of intellect between the sexes or an ideal of equal access to learning—Catherine stresses the immediate profit a practically educated woman can bring her father and husband. Like La Bouche convincing La Main and Le Pié that their best interests lie in mutual cooperation, Placide invites Severe to consider the concrete gains men can expect from wives learned in the ways of the world.

Considering the irritable, down-to-earth character Catherine constructs for Severe, in fact, it would be dramatically implausible to represent him capable of imagining loftier freedoms for women. To some extent, her design for Placide's opponent prevents her from proposing radical arguments for women's education—from recommending it for the sake of their pleasure and emancipation, for example, rather than for the advantages it entails for men. Linda Woodbridge (1984), in a study of early English uses of the judicial oration, based on Quintilian's hypothetical examples of courtroom charges and defenses, points out that defenses of women in this rhetorical mode were always contained by the attacks they answered; to refute old arguments is still to be caught up in them (38). Catherine must defend the "femme sçavante" against negative representations of her as grotesquely vain, domestically disorderly, a threat to marital hierarchy. Dialogue as refutation prevents her from innovatory fantasy, from the much bolder and more idealistic possibilities she imagines for women in such poems as "Une Mascarade des Amazones" or "L'Agnodice," the story of a Greek woman whose medical expertise saves her sisters and reconciles men to women's intellectual and professional power (see Stanton 1986; Larsen 1987).

But if the logical framework of Catherine's dialogue limits what she can say, its dramatic dimension reinforces her refutation of Severe in other ways. Through humor, in a spectrum that ranges from irony to slapstick, she discredits the antiwoman man's *logos* by means of his *ethos*.[12] His overweening sense of masculine superi-

---

12. For the use of these categories from Aristotelian rhetoric as a basis for reading Renaissance texts, *logos* meaning argument and *ethos* the character of the speaker, see William J. Kennedy, *Rhetorical Norms in Renaissance Literature* (New Haven: Yale University Press, 1978), chap. 1.

ority, for example, is undercut from the first page of the dialogue
by his status as henpecked husband and inept father, and Placide's
mild remark that their opinions of women vary as much as their
wives suggests that Severe has chosen the woman he deserves. The
claim that men are rich in the reason that women lack sounds absurd in the mouth of this particularly unprepossessing member of
the "first" sex: "comme si l'imbecillité de ces petites Bestioles de-
voit estre comparée à la grande suffisance qui journellement se
connaist en nous" [37a: as though the stupidity of these little
beasts could be compared to the fullness of intellect that we men
demonstrate every day]. Catherine also reveals Severe's lack of
awareness of the futility of his domestic tyranny in his description
of life with an ignorant wife: "Ho, ce n'est qu'une grosse beste,
qui ne sçait pas honorer son mari, ni ordonner son menage, ce que
je veus qu'elle aprenne seulement, et non pas a frequenter les livres. Il ne luy faut autre Docteur que ma voix" [37b: Ha! she is
nothing but a brute animal, who does not know enough to honor
her husband or run her household, and that is all I want her to
learn, not how to spend time with books. The only professor she
needs is my voice]. Catherine discredits Severe's misogyny further
by having him quote a satiric poem he has found woven into a
tapestry another of his neighbors has hung in front of his fireplace.
The poem, which accuses learned women of pride, discon-
tentment, and envy, concludes with advice that Severe has evidently followed in his own life: "Fuiez donc la Femme sçavante, /
Recherchez plutost l'ignorante" [Leave the learned woman behind, / Seek one with nothing in her mind]. But this counsel is
sharply called into question by Placide, who asks Severe whether
he has garnered the rest of his ideas from "les enfumées authoritez
des devants de cheminées" [39a: the smoky experts of chimney
curtains]. Here, in fact, Catherine mobilizes class snobbery to discredit Severe. The amused contempt in Placide's remark about the
chimney curtain identifies his opponent as an undiscriminating,
lowbrow reader, lacking the education that would lead him to
more trustworthy texts.

Like Plato, whom Tasso admired for his use of metaphor, Catherine also uses poetic language to strengthen her arguments. Normally, her style is direct and familiar, but in one remarkable exception, she composes an elaborate meteorological simile in praise

of the learned woman as devoted wife—perhaps because the opposite idea, that education would disrupt marital hierarchy, was so widespread. Placide compares unlettered women to wispy clouds that melt in the face of the sun, a figure to whom the husband in a family was frequently compared in Renaissance marriage manuals.[13] To the unsubstantial moral character of such women he contrasts the solid conscience of the woman who has read ethics:

> Les Femmes simples et de foible entendement ressemblent ces rares nuées, qui craignant de fondre vont fuïant l'Astre journalier, ou s'il passe au travers d'elles, il n'y reste aucune trace de ses raions, mais comme la nue espaisse reçoit la clarté du Soleil, redoublant plusieurs fois en elle cet[t]e belle face, qui la rend illustre: Ainsi la Femme prudente aiant rendu son Esprit fort par les discourses de la Philosophie morale, reçoit humblement tel image que luy veut donner son Mari, de qui le bien-aimé pourrait paroist toujours en ses pensées, en ses paroles, et en toutes ses actions.   (38a–b)

[Untrained women of weak understanding are like those thin clouds, which, for fear of melting away, flee the day's star, or, if it shines through them, retain no trace of its rays; but as a dense cloud absorbs the light of the sun and then reflects outward and multiplies the beautiful face that illuminates her, so a wise woman, having strengthened her spirit with discussions of moral philosophy, humbly receives whatever image her husband wants to give her, and his beloved portrait constantly appears in her thoughts, words, and deeds.]

The imagery of evanescent versus resplendent clouds works aesthetically rather than logically to reinforce the point Catherine wants Placide to score here, a point that she may have sensed needed support from poetic language. Historically, few learned wives were available as demonstration objects to men like Severe; the vividness of the double metaphor strengthens where the scarcity of empirical evidence might weaken Placide's claim.

As in her earlier dialogues, Catherine uses poetry to punctuate her dialectics. She writes short verses and songs to characterize her performers and to further—or undercut—their arguments. An early exchange between Severe and Placide adapts the sticho-

---

13. For the husband as sun to the wife's moon, see, for example, Vives's *Institution d'une femme chrestienne*, in *Le Miroir des femmes 1: Moralistes et polémistes au XVIe siècle*, ed. Luce Guillerm, J. P. Guillerm, Laurence Hordoir, and Marie-Françoise Piéjus (Lille: Presses Universitaires, 1983), 76.

mythia of tragedy: in a rhymed couplet the two speakers state opposed views. When Severe quotes the old saw "Car toutes [femmes] sont des hommes Adversaires" [For all women are enemies to men], Placide promptly answers him with a parallel but prowoman line: "Mais toutes sont aux Hommes necessaires" [36a: But to men they are most necessary]. At greater length, Catherine offers the misogynist quatrains of the chimney poem only after discrediting it by means of Severe's description of its source and the judgmental name she assigns its owner [*Achariste*, "he who lacks grace"]. A countersong, which Placide tells Severe his daughter, Pasithée, has composed, answers both Severe's attack on educated women and the humanist commonplace that women's greatest ornament is silence. By placing the song in the mouth of Pasithée's father, displacing it one step away from its fictional female author and two steps away from herself, Catherine appropriates masculine authority for her own discourse. The ditty begins:

> Je pense bien que le Silence
> Est l'ombre du vrai ornement,
> Comme la discrete Eloquence
> Lumiere de l'entendement.

> [I do believe that silence / Is a shadow to true ornament, / As considered eloquence / Is the light to true understanding.]

The song repeats Placide's dissolution of traditional antitheses in his example of Pallas as weaver and friend of the Muses both:

> Les Dames qui veulent bien vivre
> Desireuses d'aprendre et voir,
> Hantent les vertus et le livre,
> Mariant les meurs au sçavoir.

> [Ladies who want to live well, / Desiring to learn and understand, / Stay close both to virtue and books, / Uniting their actions and knowledge.]

"Mariant" here as metaphor suggests that Catherine is attempting subliminally to reassure her male readers that brains and wifely devotion need not cancel each other out. In the same vein, she goes on to name ancient Roman examples of wifely loyalty and motherly wisdom: Portia, Brutus's unfailingly supportive wife, and Cornelia, who educated her sons in philosophy and inspired them to political duty. But the poem closes with a lighthearted invocation of contemporary justice, the wish that the man opposed to education be entrapped by "quelque sotte Maitresse":

Qu'en tout ce que vous pourrez faire,
Soit pour servir, prier, crier,
Jamais vous ne puissiez luy plaire,
Ny de ses mains vous delier.   (41a)

[May everything that you can do, / Serving her, pleading, or wailing, / Never make you agreeable to her, / Or free you from her hands.]

This fate, Severe ruefully admits, has in fact been granted him. The poem's direct apostrophe to the man who shares "le commun erreur" exposes the ad hominem maneuver throughout Catherine's treatment of Severe, but it does so in an indirect and playful way that furthers her case against him.

In the "Dialogue de Placide et Severe," then, Catherine uses a variety of logical and literary techniques to refute attacks on women's education. She represents a process of reasoning through which mistaken assumptions about cause and effect and sexual oppositions are defeated; she legitimates the progressive side of the argument through the urbane literacy of Placide, whose eloquence exposes Severe as a confused thinker and a boorish speaker; and she draws on the rhetorical force of metaphor and uses short lyrics to vary the tone of the debate. Placide's eventual triumph, evidenced in Severe's decision to send Iris to Pasithée as a model, comes as no surprise. Madeleine des Roches's daughter uses the reasoning, the dramatic imitation, and the oratorical embellishment recommended by Tasso to produce a thoroughly artful text. Moreover, as Mustapha Bénouis (1976) remarks about other dialogues written in this period, the dialogue itself demonstrates its major premise:[14] it shows an educated woman writing a morally sound and

14. Bénouis (1976, 82) makes the point that a dialogue can demonstrate its own premises in a comment on Jacques Peletier du Mans's *Dialogue de l'ortografe et prononciation françoese*. On the Dames des Roches, however, he is several times in error. For example, he argues that Catherine's dialogues are merely "un exercice, un jeu de société" (33), misreading the "Dialogue de Placide et Severe" as merely a neutral record of the opposing opinions that circulated in the Poitiers salon. Bénouis also confuses the names of the female characters in "Le Dialogue d'Iris et Pasithée": Iris is not the learned woman (283) but the foolish daughter, and Pasithée, contrary to his statement, does in fact demonstrate grace in verbal action.

engagingly modest work in which learning and virtue are married. Catherine's oblique presentation of her point of view, wrapped in the fictional protection of Placide as fatherly authority, is a more cautious strategy than, for example, the outright denunciation of Charlotte de Brachart's later (1604) *Harengue . . . qui s'adrese aux hommes qui veuillent deffendre la science aux femmes* (Kelso 1965, 63–4). Catherine's adoption of dialogue as a form allows her to disguise herself as a woman writer who has a polemical intent. Nonetheless, she uses the form to defeat enemies of women's education by speaking through and for fathers as the powerholders in sixteenth-century families. The dramatis personae convention of dialogue allows her to attribute rational thought to an ideal father and to expose the illogical bias of the antipedagogue, discrediting him as would-be wielder of the Nom/Non du Père.

Sweet-Talking Lovers:
Charite and Sincero, Pasithée and Iris

If the "Dialogue de Placide et Severe" sets out a theory for women's education, the "Dialogue d'Iris et Pasithée" puts theory into practice. The plot of the dialogue is that Iris, visiting Pasithée for the first time, is so impressed by her thoughtful yet entertaining speech that she resolves to return as often as she can. But Iris, as her name suggests, is so unsubstantial and changeable that she offers no real resistance to Pasithée. If, as K. J. Wilson (1985) remarks, "dialectic relates men to one another as minds" (17), the form presents problems in this case because Iris hardly has a mind. Lacking two serious interlocutors, the text is not so much a dialogue as a didactic encounter between empty-headed student and judicious master, a demonstration of how eloquence, gently applied, can impress even a frivolous illiterate like Severe's daughter. Catherine represents Pasithée as a model teacher, stimulating Iris's curiosity, appealing to her self-interest, and charming her with compliments and poems.

But the regendering of the didactic dialogue produces some interesting tensions. In classical and medieval dialogues the master in teaching dialogues was usually a man—not surprisingly, since the teaching profession was a male preserve. The same was true in Renaissance adaptations of the mode. Women appear in Italian dialogues—Bembo's *Gli Asolani* (1505), Tullia d'Aragona's *Dell'infinità di amore* (1547)—but they are learners rather than leaders in the discussion. In France the pattern was the same. In Jacques Tahureau's *Dialogues* (1565), for example, two men speak: "Le Cosmophile" asks for enlightenment from "Le Democritic." In Pontus de Tyard's *Solitaire premier* (1552), Pasithée has some talents and ideas of her own—she is musical, and she knows enough to ask questions about the Greek muses—but she is, in the main, instructed by the male Solitaire. So Catherine's Pasithée has a name rich not only in ancient but in contemporary associations. In book 14 of the *Iliad*, she is named as one of the Graces; and the name probably also echoes the salon pseudonym of Catherine de Retz, who led a Paris salon in the 1570s and joined the Académie du Palais in 1576 (Vaganay 1935; Bénouis 1976, 35, 182–4), as well as alluding to Tyard's text. What is important is that Catherine's Pasithée has a new role, as leader rather than disciple.

This role was not new in Catherine's work, however. In her earlier "Dialogue de Sincero et de Charite," the last of those published in 1578, she applied her own salon nickname—also, in the *Iliad*, the term for the Graces in general (Diller 1936, 59–60)—to the character of an articulate Neoplatonic heroine. As Catherine's preface to her section of the first *Oeuvres* suggests, she sets up both characters as ideals, models for the perfect couple. She writes to her mother in terms that suggest her familiarity with such exemplary dialogues as Cicero's *De oratore* and Castiglione's *Il Cortegiano*:

> J'escry ce que j'ay pensé et non pas ce que j'ay veu en Syncero, lequel je ne connoy que par imagination. Mais comme il est adveneu à quelques grands personnages de representer un Roy parfaict, un parfaict orateur, un parfaict courtisan, ainsi ai-je voulu former un parfaict amoureux.   (53)
>
> [I write what I have thought and not what I have seen in Sincero, whom I know only through my imagination. But just as it has happened that some great writers have represented a perfect king, a perfect orator, a perfect courtier, so I have tried to fashion a perfect lover.]

Through the exchange Sincero initiates with Charite, Catherine transcribes a step-by-step enactment of courtly recommendations about repartee on the subject of love: the man pursues, training himself in eloquence; the woman resists, but in a witty way that neither discourages him nor discredits her.[15]

The entire exchange between Sincero and Charite reveals how clearly Catherine understands and can manipulate the conventions of Neoplatonism as an erotic code: she represents a man and a woman speaking, but as the woman author she controls all the terms of the discourse. Sincero opens with a Neoplatonic creation myth: he tells Charite that she was formed by the Idea of Beauty in cooperation with the Fates and Nature, so that the gods in heaven protest her descent to earth. He concludes his narrative by claiming that he has enclosed her divine image in his breast: "voila, Madame, comment par la faveur de vostre beauté je voisine les Cieux" [96: this is how, my lady, through the power of your beauty I approach the heavens]. Charite responds with a mocking remark that pinpoints the quasi-philosophical pretension endemic to masculine Neoplatonism at the same time that it allows Sincero to continue the ritual: "Je croy plustot que par la faveur de voz propos vous portez mon nom au Ciel (Syncero) et que vous l'en reportez quand bon vous semble" [96: I think, rather, that through the power of your words you take my name up to heaven, Sincero, and bring it back down when it suits you]. But once Charite has explained that she is aware of the roles men and women play in this game, she gives Sincero permission to go on: "Or pource que vous desirez d'estre estimé amoureux et poëte, vous pouvez feindre sans en estre repris, et moy qui ne pratique ny avec la Poësie, ny avec Amour, je puis seurement ouyr sans adjouter beaucoup de foy à voz parolles" [96: But since you want to be recognized both as a lover and a poet, you may feign without being reproached for it, and I, who have nothing to do either with poetry or love, can surely listen to you without putting much faith in your words]. Thus Charite not only enacts but also spells out the proper role for a woman in amorous conversation. She goes on to teach Sincero, in gently controlling remarks as the dialogue ends and in a series of sonnets (responses to his), how "un honneste amant" should behave. In the last of her early dialogues, then, Catherine adopts the role of a teacher/mentor to seduce yet contain

15. For a discussion of such recommendations in conduct books by Agostino Nifo and Stefano Guazzo as well as Castiglione, see Jones (1987, 43–48; 1990, chaps. 1 and 2).

her student. Charite's canny handling of her less skilled and less self-conscious interlocutor proves that Neoplatonic training enables a woman to script a love that combines eloquence with chastity—a synthesis urged several times in the "Dialogue de Placide et Severe."

But the male/female roles of the Neoplatonic dialogue fit into literary convention more smoothly than does Pasithée's role as a female tutor. Catherine can hardly set up Pasithée as Diotima to Iris's Socrates; the student is not of such promising mettle. Instead, Pasithée appeals to the wandering daughter's self-interest, amuses her with compliments, and demonstrates that woman-to-woman conversation provides greater pleasures than exchanges between ignorant women and men. Close examination of the "Dialogue d'Iris et Pasithée" reveals that it is a darker and more complex text than at first it seems. Its humor at the expense of foolish women approaches cruelty, and its view of heterosexual courtship, especially the men who practice it, is thoroughly skeptical. Moreover, when Catherine des Roches shifts from dialectic to a satiric comedy of contemporary manners, she reveals her contempt for the "normal" women and men produced by the gender ideology of her culture. Simultaneously, Pasithée's position as Iris's mentor sets her up as a seducer in ways that subtly destabilize the patriarchal values supported in the "Dialogue de Placide et Severe."

The character of Iris certainly confirms what Severe says of her in the first dialogue. Besides being a conceited gadabout, she is functionally illiterate: at several points she asks Pasithée to read her the love poems men have addressed to her. Such a request allows Pasithée to take over male voices as she recites male-authored poems. But Catherine also uses her heroine to discredit Iris by interrogating her in ways that reveal her laughable ignorance. When Iris tries to describe the one book she has read, which turns out to be an almanac her father brought home, she can recall neither its title nor its author, and she confesses that a headache soon made her stop reading even this simple text. The only detail she remembers about a book she saw Eole, one of her lovers, holding is that it was handsomely gilded; she cannot answer Pasithée's questions about its title, topic, date of publication, or whether it was written in verse or prose. When Pasithée reads or sings poems to Iris, her only criterion for judging them is whether she can dance to them. In a typically merciless comic exchange toward

the end of the dialogue, Catherine has Iris protest, in response to
Pasithée's suggestion that reading might teach her to speak better, that she speaks well enough. But she cannot find the word to
explain that the lament that Pasithée has just sung for her,
"Nymphes hôtesses de ces boix," lacks lively rhythm. Pasithée
must supply the simple monosyllable for her:

> Pasi.: [After singing the song] Et bien Iris qu'en dites vous? est
> elle aisée a dancer?
> Iris.: Nenny pas beaucoup Pasithée, il m'est advis qu'elle est trop,
> la, je ne sçay comment: Elle n'est pas assez.
> Pasi.: Voulez vous dire qu'elle n'est pas assez gaie?
> Iris.: Ouy, ouy, c'est cela mesme.   (51b–52a)

> [Pasithée: Well, Iris, what do you think of it? Is it easy to dance to?
> Iris: No, not really, Pasithée; I think it's too—too—well, I don't
> know what. It's not—not enough.
> P.: Do you mean it's not gay enough?
> I.: Yes, yes, that's it exactly.]

Iris's naiveté and childish speech are absurd, and Catherine obviously relishes dramatizing her limitations. Through satiric reversal, the illiterate character provides strong evidence for the argument that an educated daughter will be a credit to her parents.

Yet the woman writer is not entirely unsympathetic to the ignorant girl's plight. The dialogue makes it clear that however dim
Iris's understanding may be, her ignorance causes her to suffer in
ways that are not her fault. Her father forbids her to entertain herself by visiting neighbors but will not allow her to read at home;
her mother forbids her to write, claiming that she herself has never
felt the lack of it; her brother tells them all that musical instruments are a waste of money. Thus Iris is bored at home and avid
for love as her only distraction. She has pursued six men, it turns
out, with minimal success: Nirée reproaches her for her change-
ability; Chrysobole has been rejected by Severe for demanding too
high a dowry; Achryse's poverty has driven her away from him;
the lightweight Eole waits for her outside Pasithée's house because
he is afraid of learned women; the rich foreigner Felix has engaged
her in a conversation that she found enticing, but she does not
understand a word of his language; and Eucrite, Pasithée remarks,
is unlikely to return Iris's interest until she has developed some
discretion. The symbolic names Catherine assigns these male characters suggest that they may not be much of a loss: the seagod

Nereus may have been wise but he was also changeable, Richcoin and Moneyless are disabled by their finances, the Windbag and the Lucky Man have nothing solid to offer, and Iris's ignorance is an obstacle to the wise judge, Eucrite, whom she loses. Pasithée's strongest argument is that only an educated and accomplished woman will find a love worthy of her. Yet the cast of characters assembled around Iris suggests that in this world, such a belief may be idealistic. Pasithée, judging from the beauty of her language and her genuine concern, is the best lover Iris is likely to have.

In this pedagogical dialogue Pasithée's strategy with Iris is not to move too fast, to adapt her arguments in favor of learning to the very low level at which she finds her pupil—a level of amorous preoccupation as well as verbal simplicity. She begins by suggesting that change and variety are good things, a philosophical position that she illustrates with an immediately accessible case in point: female beauty needs diversity of hue, including golden hair, a white forehead, a dark brow, and green, black, or sky-blue eyes (44b). She confirms the illustration with a short poem composed by one "Philide," in which he compares each of his lady's features to a flower: lily-white forehead, iris-blue eyes, rose-red lips. As she recites the poem to Iris, Pasithée speaks from the position of the male poet, and her flattering last word belongs to the same kind of discourse, although in this case the lover's compliment is spoken by a woman: "Il me semble, Iris, que vostre beauté se voit represantée par ces vers" [45b: I think, Iris, that your beauty is represented in these lines]. To the extent that Pasithée occupies the authoritative role toward Iris, and to the extent that the younger woman will judge her speeches for the pleasure they provide more than for their profundity or logical finesse (given her character, how else could she assess them?), Pasithée directs a male-authored rhetoric of seduction toward her young charge.

Such rhetoric also positions Pasithée as a rival to Iris's other suitors. Later in the dialogue she has the wit to counter Nirée's critical comparison of Iris to the rainbow (both are changeable, bent, and falsely beautiful) with a far more complimentary conceit: as a symbol of "honnête Amour," Iris is like the divine rainbow that signaled peace to men after the Flood; as the rainbow bends to fit the heavens, she turns her soul into a circle of self-contemplation; as the rainbow looks into the sun, she looks to-

ward Reason. Although Pasithée suggests at several points that
Iris will win better suitors once she has educated herself, she has
sharp words for the men who court her, especially Eole, and for
other men who share their errors. When Iris explains that he refuses to come into the house to fetch her because he is afraid of
learned women, Pasithée exclaims, "Ha ha, vraiment je l'en dis-
pence, luy et tout autre qui le ressemble. Je ne pense point que les
lettres soient en vain aprises par les filles, puis qu'elles donnent la
chasse a telz gallans" [53b: Ha, ha, truly I can do without him,
him and others like him. Girls certainly don't study literature in
vain if doing so chases gallants like these away]. Obviously, such
a statement has sources in Catherine des Roches's life as an intellectual woman who never married.[16] In the literary dialogue Pasithée's sharp observation about Iris's amorous followers encourages
her readers to share her contempt for men who seek out women
they can count on to be their intellectual inferiors.

Pasithée also criticizes Iris's suitors as writers. After she recites
Nirée's rhymed complaint, for example, in which he claims that
time has dimmed Iris's beauties, she deflates poet and poem both:
"Mais pourquoy dit-il cela, Iris? Vous ne fûtes jamais plus belle
que vous étes" [48b: But why does he say that, Iris? You were
never lovelier than you are now]. Similarly, after reading Eole's
chanson in praise of Iris, she appropriates his compliments in a neat
bit of one-upmanship by remarking, "La Chanson est agréable
pource que vous en étes le sujet: Mais ce n'est pas l'invention
d'Eole. Car aiant veu ce qu'il dit, en vostre visage, il l'a seulement
transcrit" [53: The song is pleasant because you're its subject. But
Eole didn't make it up. Having seen what he describes in your
face, he simply copied it out]. Predictably, the dialogue ends on
a note of verbal triumph for Pasithée. Although Iris is rushing off
to join Eole, she asks for permission to return to the woman's
"ecole": "Mon Dieu que vous dites bien Pasithée! . . . Je prends
tous les plaisirs du monde a discourir aveques vous" [53b: My
Lord, how well you speak, Pasithée! I feel every delight in the
world when I discuss things with you]. In the contest over Iris's

16. Etienne Pasquier, among Catherine's contemporaries, criticized her for failing
to marry, and George Diller, writing in the 1930s, judged her attachment to her
mother and her celibacy as symptoms of psychic abnormality. For a different view,
that Catherine's refusal to marry was essential to her autonomy and career as a writer,
see Larsen (1990) and Jones (1990, 75–76).

admittedly short-lived attention, Pasithée defeats her male rivals through flattery as erotic as theirs, but more effective because she has the last word. However carefully Placide argues that educated wit need not challenge a woman's loyalty to family and sexual arrangements in the world as they stand, Catherine's wit consistently targets men.

Indeed, one subversive implication of the "Dialogue d'Iris et Pasithée" is that women are better off without men. Pasithée assures Iris that dedicating herself to the Muses will bring her an inner serenity that can free her from the anxieties of love, and she remarks that it might not be so terrible to live without it if a wise and appreciative lover does not materialize: "Sinon vivez sans amour, et vous proposez les malheurs qui viennent pour aimer" [50a: If not, live without love, and consider the misfortunes that love brings]. At this point the *institutrice* is no longer lecturing Severe's daughter on the duties of the proper wife-to-be but preaching a quiet form of resistance: life among the Muses is calmer, richer, more gratifying than marriage to a less-than-perfect man—and almost all the men the dialogue shows us are imperfect. Linking women as characters and readers, Catherine des Roches gives her proeducation argument a more radical dimension than it can have when she articulates it through male characters speaking to each other. The daughter/daughter dialogue displaces men as patriarchal authorities and as love objects. It also suggests, if only fleetingly, that women's speech to women can transcend, in intelligence and affection, the amorous effusions of men.

This difference between the two texts raises a further question, about a dramatic possibility that is significantly absent from both of Catherine's dialogues on education: an exchange between a mother and daughter. Why, given the obviously intense emotional and didactic rapport between Madeleine and Catherine des Roches, does the daughter not represent a mother as an authority on women's education? Fathers, not mothers, frame both dialogues; Iris, after all, visits Pasithée on her father's orders. One reason for the absence of maternal authority is that both of the genres Catherine uses, the dialogue and the advice book, were generally written by men for men: fathers to fathers, fathers to sons. By following this pattern, Catherine may seem to succumb to paternal authority. Yet in the "Dialogue de Placide et Severe" she rewrites historical fathers into a progressive present tense. She constructs the narrative each man tells, she positions him against an opponent, she judges him and invites her reader to do the same. The daughter is not rejecting paternal power, but she is enlisting it in a new cause. It may be too that dialogue's generic requirement for logical combat, for rhetorical winners and losers, unsuited it for the collaborative bond dramatized in both collections of the Dames des Roches's *Oeuvres*. This daughter had no argument with her mother.

But Catherine des Roches did have a battle to fight with the world at large, in defense of women's learning and the autonomy she saw as its reward. For this campaign, she appropriated the combative mode, manipulated its rules of argument and its benefits of characterization, and tilted its masculine traditions toward her own interests. Her dialogues represent a canny adaptation of the genre. To construct a defeatable bad father and to ventriloquize a good one may have been the most effective strategies she could adopt in a century still dominated by fathers. When Pasithée speaks through Placide, for herself and her sisters, a new message is heard.

PAULA SOMMERS

✒ Agrippa d'Aubigné and the Literary Dialogue

Between 1611 and 1630 Agrippa d'Aubigné composed three
dialogues, *Le Caducée ou l'ange de paix, Mathurine et Du Perron,* and
Les Avantures du Baron de Faeneste. His interest in the genre per-
sisted for almost twenty years, yet only the preface to *Faeneste* offers any hint of theoretical orientation:

> Un esprit, lassé de discours graves et tragiques, s'est voulu recreer
> à la description de ce siecle, en ramassant quelques bourdes vrayes.
> Et pource que la plus generale difference des buts et complexions
> des hommes est que les uns pointent leurs desirs et desseins aux
> apparences, et les autres aux effects, l'Autheur a commencé ces Dia-
> logues par un Baron de Gascongne, Baron en l'air, qui a pour Seig-
> neurie *Faeneste,* signifiant en Grec *paroistre*; cetui-là jeune eventé,
> demi courtisan, demi soldat; et d'autre part un vieil Gentil-homme
> nommé *Enay,* qui en mesme langue signifie *estre* homme consommé
> aux lettres, aux experiences de la Cour et de la guerre; cettui-ci un
> faux Poictevin, qui prend occasion de la rencontre de Faeneste pour
> s'en donner du plaisir, et mesme en faire part à quelque voisin qui
> pour lors estoit chez lui.   (671)

[A writer, tired of grave and tragic discourse, decided to amuse
himself by describing these times and collecting a few true but
comic tales. Because the most common difference in the goals and
motives of men is that some direct their desires and intentions toward appearance and others toward reality, the author began these
dialogues with a baron from Gascogny, an imaginary baron, who
has for his domain *Faeneste,* which means *appearance* in Greek. Confronting this young blunderer, half-courtier and half-soldier, is an
old gentleman named *Enay,* which in the same language means *being,* a man accomplished in letters, in experience of the court, and
in war. The latter is a wily Poitevin who profits from the meeting

223

with Faeneste by amusing himself and sharing his pleasure with a neighbor who happened to be visiting.][1]

From this brief statement one may deduce that, at least with regard to *Faeneste*, d'Aubigné considers the dialogue a vehicle for the conflict of ideas that are embodied in clearly defined characters. Since the philosophical opposition between being and appearance is set in a comic framework, the reader may anticipate the influence of Platonic humor or an imitation of Lucian, who boasts of his conflation of philosophical dialogue and comic theater and whose interlocutors at times display the *eiron-alazon* interplay d'Aubigné establishes for Enay and Faeneste.[2] Finally, since the Baron is a "demi courtisan" and Enay "un homme consommé . . . aux experiences de la Cour," *Faeneste* recalls the anticourtier dialogues of Henri Estienne and Jacques Tahureau.

Lucian, Estienne, and Tahureau, however, gave their works titles that clearly fall within the dialogue tradition—*De Parasito, Deus Dialogues du langage françois italianizé, Dialogues*—but d'Aubigné's title suggests a parallel with the emerging comic novel. The word *avantures* implies the existence of plot and narrative and sets up an immediate conflict with concepts of dialogue developed by Renaissance theorists in their efforts to expand and clarify Aristotelian principles. As Jon Snyder (1989) convincingly demonstrates in his recent review of dialogue theory in the late Italian Renaissance, theoreticians, however they chose to deal with the inherent conflicts between rhetoric and dialectic, or humor and philosophy, generally described dialogue as a vehicle that presented ideas rather than fictionalized accounts of action.[3] Torquato Tasso (*Discorso dell'arte del dialogo*, Venice, 1586) echoes Carolus Sigonius (*De dialogo liber*, Venice, 1561) in emphasizing the dialectical essence of dialogue:

1. All quotations from the *Caducée* are taken from the Réaume and de Caussade edition of d'Aubigné's *Oeuvres complètes* (Paris: A. Lemerre, 1873–92). The source of quotations from *La Confession du sieur de Sancy* and *Les Avantures du baron de Faeneste* is Henri Weber's edition of d'Aubigné's *Oeuvres* (Paris: Gallimard, 1969). All translations in this chapter are mine unless otherwise indicated.

2. Lucian boasts of his combination of philosophical dialogue and comic theater in two dialogues, *Prometheus es in verbis tuis* and *Bis Accusatis*. For a discussion of his influence in France, see C. A. Mayer, *Lucien de Samosate et la Renaissance française* (Geneva: Slatkine, 1984).

3. Jon Snyder, *Writing the Scene of Speaking: Theories of Dialogue in the Late Italian Renaissance* (Stanford, CA: Stanford University Press, 1989).

Abbiam, dunque, che 'l dialogo sia imitazione di ragionamento,
fatto in prosa per giovamento degli uomini civili e speculativi, per
la qual cagione egli non ha bisogno di scena o di palco; e che due
sian le specie: l'un nel soggetto, della quale sono i problemi che
risguardano l'elezione e la fuga; l'altra speculativa, la qual prende
per subietto quistione, ch'appertiene a la verità e la scienza; e nel-
l'una e nell'altra non imita solamente la disputa, ma il costume
de coloro che disputano, con elocuzioni in alcune parti piene di
ornamento, in altre di purità, come par che si convenga a la materia.   (345–46)

[Let us say, therefore, that the dialogue is an imitation of reasoning
written in prose for the benefit of civil and speculative men, and
for this purpose it requires no stage or platform; and there are two
kinds of dialogue: one deals with problems that concern choice or
rejection; the other is speculative and has for its subject that which
pertains to truth or knowledge; and in both the writer will imitate
not only the discussion, but the customs of those who participate
in the discussion, with elocution at times richly ornamented, at
times simple, as is suitable to the subject matter.]

The elimination of any intent to stage or dramatize the dialogue
serves to distinguish it from theater, an important distinction,
since Tasso notes earlier in his treatise that the literary dialogue
may resemble a tragedy in the actions it describes just as it may
recall some aspects of farce or comedy.[4] As a form of mimesis, the
dialogue has as its object, not the actions of men that are suitable
to theater, but the actions of the mind.

Faeneste is a problematic text precisely because the relationship
between action and reasoning challenges the conventions of dialogue. It combines a rudimentary plot that depicts the Baron's
adventures at court and on the battlefield with a satiric dialogue
opposing the values of appearance and reality. As the text progresses the dialogical component tends to serve less as a vehicle for
ideological opposition and more as a support for interpolated *contes*
and anecdotes. Given the structural complexity of the text and the
tendency for the concept represented by the title to deconstruct

4. Modern theorists—C. J. R. Armstrong (1976), John W. Cosentini (1952),
Herbert E. Read (1926, 141–42), and Frederick M. Keener (1973, 15–17) agree
with Tasso's emphasis on dialogue as an imitation of reasoning. For a consideration
of Aristotelian theories and the formation of Renaissance dialogue K. J. Wilson's
Incomplete Fictions (Washington, D. C.: Catholic University of America Press, 1985),
1–17, is helpful. Eva Kushner's (1972, 1977, 1978, 1981, 1982, 1984, 1986)
articles explore the concept of generic dialogue in sixteenth-century France.

the dialogical emphasis of the preface, it is not surprising that a number of modern scholars have disagreed about the generic identity of *Faeneste*. For some it is a pamphlet, for others a Menippean satire, for still others a novel.[5] Theoretical principles derived from the preface provide an imperfect understanding of d'Aubigné's praxis in writing *Faeneste*. Their value is even more questionable when applied to his other dialogues. The *Caducée* makes it clear that d'Aubigné did not always view the genre as a vehicle for recreation and "bourdes vrayes." *Mathurine* anticipates the satiric thrust of *Faeneste*, yet lacks the philosophical breadth and range of the longer work. Only a close reading of all the dialogues can reveal the constants, and the evolution, of d'Aubigné's concept of dialogue.

Le Caducée ou l'ange de paix

The *Caducée* was written in the late summer of 1612 in response to political tensions that developed during the meeting of the Protestant Assembly at Saumur in 1611.[6] The purpose of this assembly was to nominate representatives who would serve as intermediaries between the Reformed church and the Crown, but some members of the assembly, concerned for the welfare of their church in the years following the assassination of Henri IV and suspicious of the new government of Marie de' Medici, attempted to address broader political issues. They sought to increase the number of *places de sûreté* accorded to the Protestant community and demanded the restoration of some provisions that had been

5. Those emphasizing affinities with the novel include: Keith Cameron, *Agrippa d'Aubigné* (Boston: G. K. Hall, 1973), 82–103; Henri Weber, "Structure et langage dans *Les Avantures du Baron de Faeneste*. De Jean Lemaire à Jean Giraudoux," in *Mélanges d'histoire et de critique littéraire offerts à Pierre Jourda*, ed. E. Bouvier (Paris: Nizet, 1970), 111–30; Weber, *Oeuvres*, xli–xlvi. In "Agrippa d'Aubigné conteur" (*La Nouvelle française à la Renaissance*, ed. L. Sozzi [Geneva: Slatkine, 1981]), Jacques Bailbé discusses d'Aubigné's abilities as a *conteur*, but appears to accept *Faeneste* as a burlesque novel (653–69). For Gabriel Pérouse it is a manifestation of *discours bigarré*; see his *Nouvelles françaises du XVIe siècle: Images de la vie du temps* (Geneva: Droz, 1977), 467.

6. Most scholars now accept Pierre Villey's (1922) theory that the work was composed in 1612. For additional discussion, consult Armand Garnier, *Agrippa d'Aubigné et le parti protestant* (Paris: Fischbacher, 1928), 3:1–26, and Ian MacDonald, "Three Pamphlets by d'Aubigné. Manuscripts and Dates of Composition," *French Studies* 14 (1960): 38–51.

deleted from the Edict of Nantes as originally proposed. Because the Assembly was divided between these militants and a more moderate group eager to make concessions to the Crown, Marie de' Medici was not obliged to grant the Reformed church any new privileges.

D'Aubigné, who had been among the militants at Saumur, was alarmed by the political factionalism that developed there and the way in which that factionalism enabled the queen and her ministers to manipulate the assembly in their own interest. The *Caducée ou l'ange de paix* is his attempt to reconcile the moderate or promonarchist faction of his church with members of his own group. The conciliatory purpose of the dialogue is conveyed by the title, which also suggests that the author has, in typical Renaissance fashion, based his text on a conflation of Christian and classical values. The author's Christian purpose is foregrounded by the narrator who as witness, judge, and participant in the discussions has a powerful role in shaping the reader's response to the *Caducée*.

The narrator is a Reformed church minister who assumes, at some personal risk, the task of reconciling members of his church:

> Je n'atends icy pour ma recompense que le salaire des bons et justes arbitres, qui est la hayne des deux costez. Car nous sommes, et les uns et les autres, si plains de nostre droit imaginaire qu'il n'y a plus de logis pour la veritable equitté. Je veux donc fascher et les uns et les autres pour aider aux deus, sans autres recompenses que de faire paix moy-mesme à ma conscience, laquele me piquant de mon devoir et de ma profession, depuis quelque mois m'a tiré du lit avant l'aube du jour, pour courir à la visitation des divisez.   (74)

> [I expect for my reward only the salary of good and just arbiters, which is the hatred of both sides. We are, on one side and the other, so full of our supposed rights that there is no longer any room for justice. I intend therefore to anger both parties in order to help them both, without any other reward than bringing peace to my own conscience, which, reminding me insistently of my duty and my profession, has for some months drawn me out of bed before daybreak in order to hasten my visitation of the divided parties.]

In his efforts to promote reconciliation the narrator visits a distinguished representative of each faction: the moderates (*Prudents*) and the militants (*Fermes*). The author takes great care to maintain the dignity of each spokesman, but the order of the speakers and the length and quality of the introductory passages reveal d'Aubigné's authorial bias. The Prudent speaks first and thus loses the opportunity to refute his adversary. The reader learns in a concise introduction that he is an important nobleman who attended the assembly at Saumur and subsequent assemblies (74). The Ferme merits an eleven-line introduction that identifies him as a gentleman from Saintonge, whose experience at Protestant assemblies includes those held at Châtellrault, Vendôme, and Saumur. More important, we are told that he has nothing to gain from a war that is likely to "troubler ses grandes et exquises commoditez, les plaisirs de ses exelans jardinages" [78: disturb his great and exquisite possessions, the pleasures of his fine gardens]. The gentleman from Saintonge is, as a number of scholars have noted, d'Aubigné himself. The importance, if not the location of his estates, and the description of his service to the Reformed church are sufficient to identify him and to endow him with greater authority than the Prudent. With this introduction, however, the impartiality of the narrator is compromised. Since the Prudent has accused the Fermes of warmongering, the minister's insistence on the peaceful intentions of the gentleman from Saintonge engages him on the side of the Ferme. The alert reader will not be surprised when the narrator endorses the Ferme's point of view.

In the first segment of the *Caducée* (73–88) d'Aubigné's narrator introduces the opposing parties, but it is not correct at this point to speak of a dialogue. Since the minister travels from one estate or château to the other, the protagonists never encounter one another and the text resembles a rather formal debate whose participants are separated by distance and by time. The narrator records and judges the "position papers" of the two factions. Essentially, the Prudent sees his colleagues as the party of peace and loyalty to Louis XIII. He denies that their patriotism is tantamount to betrayal of their religious cause or that they have been bought and paid for by agents of the queen. The Ferme maintains that the best way to achieve security for the Reformed church is through the cultivation of military and political strength. Past events, he argues, demonstrate that peace is achieved not through concession or accommodation, but through *mutua formidine*. The minister endorses the second point of view, although he remains critical of the vehemence with which it is expressed (88–89).

The first part of the *Caducée*, then, is a debate rather than a dialogue. It is characterized by emphasis on order, on courtesy, and on the diplomacy of the minister as he tries to reduce tensions and moderate the offensive rhetoric of the various factions. The reader of the *Caducée*, guided by the wise and "disinterested" minister, also learns that the Prudent, although he may not be guilty of some of the more scandalous charges made against his colleagues, is wrong and that the Fermes are right. Since these important issues are resolved before the dialogue sequence in the *Caducée* even begins, what is the function that d'Aubigné assigns to dialogue? Is it merely a dramatic means of expanding upon material already presented? Does the failure to use it as the exclusive vehicle for his ideas indicate that dialogue, as d'Aubigné perceives it at this time, is too fluid or too unstable to trust with the delicate task of persuading the reader?

A brief outline of the *Caducée* shows that the dialogue exchange is the heart of the text. The debate shades into an episode of reported conversation between the Ferme and his cousin, a second Prudent who arrives at the château in time for dinner (88–90). This conversation then yields to a climactic dialogue between adversaries whose antipathy was revealed in the course of the minister's pastoral visits (90–106). There is no doubt that the arguments expressed by the Ferme and the Prudent in their confrontational dialogue provide more information about the factionalism within the Reformed church. Indeed, the amount of political minutiae makes the text all but inaccessible to a modern reader without sufficient historical background. Since the dialogue is ultimately a *dialogue des sourds* [dialogue of the deaf], however, it also provides a demonstration of the dangerous intractability of the two groups and serves the concluding arguments of the narrator as he pleads for unity within the church. Rather than merely detailing the differences between the contending groups, d'Aubigné's dialogue dramatizes their conflict and the need for immediate reconciliation.

While *Faeneste* is a problematic text, the *Caducée* fits neatly within the categories described by Torquato Tasso (1586). It is an *imitazione di ragionamento* in prose and deals with problems that concern *l'elezione e la fuga* (345). The Ferme's estate, which provides the setting for the *Caducée*, recalls the *locus amoenus* of classical tradition, but it contributes to the overall concern with the destructive effects of the schism following the Assembly of Saumur because d'Aubigné's text negates the euphoric values traditionally associated with the conventional garden and banquet. The banquet here is characterized by political tension. The Prudent pursues a personal agenda and the narrator notes that "[il] ne marchoit pas sans desseing" [88: his behavior was not disinterested].

The Ferme is reluctant to express himself openly at table: "Je cognu bien aux responces à teles choses et à la modestie de mon hoste . . . qu'il ne metoit pas en avant toutes ses pensées pour plusieurs respectz" [90: I knew from his answers to such things and from my host's modesty . . . that he was not expressing himself freely for various reasons]. The country estate thus shelters a divided family and the banquet table becomes a place for constrained and manipulative discourse rather than truthful encounter.

At the suggestion of the narrator, who is now known as Le Modeste, the cousins retire to a private room for a more open conversation. Le Modeste proposes an objective discussion of the reasons for the current schism: "C'est au nom de Dieu, auquel vous servez l'un et l'autre, par sa bonté que je vous conjure que nos propos soyent sans fiel, ayans la paix pour but, la verité pour guide, et l'humilité pour moien" [90: It is in the name of God whom you both serve, and by his kindness that I beg you that our discussion be without bitterness, having peace as its goal, truth as its guide, and humility as its means]. He also continues to serve as witness and judge of the dialogue, intervening in the discussion on those occasions when the cousins have reached an impasse. This will occur twice because neither the Ferme nor the Prudent achieves the intellectual detachment he recommends.

Differences in tone of speech and moral character distinguish the Ferme and the Prudent from the first lines of the dialogue. Here, as in the debate sequence, it is the Prudent who speaks first. He responds to the Modeste's appeal for an explanation of the schism, but scarcely provides a disinterested perspective: "C'est que nos Fermes ont voulu faire gloire d'obeissance et nous d'humilité" [90: Our Fermes insisted on taking pride in obedience while we took pride in humility].

There is something imprudent in the rush to present his case and more than a trace of pride in his absolute conviction of righteousness. The rashness of his initial statement emerges even more clearly when the Ferme responds. He begins with a "conte plaisant." Poor Geordy is compelled to jump into a pile of chairs and tables in order to amuse a sadistic master. When he protests, the master reminds him of the loss of glory that will result from failure to obey. The Ferme then accuses the Prudents of similarly enjoying the anguish of their opponents and of taunting them as well with accusations of pride, sedition, and disobedience. The Ferme's use of humor reveals a degree of intellectual detachment that is beyond the Prudent who, not surprisingly, soon finds himself on the defensive. Here, as throughout the dialogue, moreover, the Ferme disconcerts the Prudent by turning his own words against him. Thus when the Prudent declares: "Nous croyons qu'il fault rendre à Caezar ce qui apartient à Caezar, que Dieu maudit ce qui se fait sans justice" [90: We believe that one should render unto Ceasar that which is Caesar's, that God curses that which is done without justice], the Ferme responds, "Qu'avez vous veu depuis, vous et le Grand que vous aleguiez, pour vouloir que le droit de Caezar estouffe celuy de Dieu?" [91: What have you seen since, you and the great nobleman that you mentioned, so that you want Caesar's right to prevail over God's?]. With this question the Ferme reveals the steel will and shrewd intelligence behind his initial good humor. He also wrests the initiative from his impetuous cousin.

While d'Aubigné took care to respect the dignity of both speakers in the debate sequence, the Prudent emerges as a much less sympathetic figure in the course of the dialogue sequence. The prudence for which he is named is revealed as signifying worldly wisdom, not the cardinal virtue. Although embarrassed by the queen's replies to the *cahiers* forwarded by the assembly, he is unable to join the Fermes because of commitments made to certain *grands Seigneurs*. He regards the oaths he took as a member of the assembly at Saumur with a flexibility of conscience that suggests a strong Jesuit influence. Finally, it is difficult for him to defend himself and the members of his party from accusations of corruption. Whenever the Ferme raises this issue, he reaches for his sword:

Il n'y a plus moien de suporter vos piques, car outre ce que je jure devant Dieu et ses Anges, je n'ay receu un seul denier à Saumur. Le premier qui me voudra imputer ce que vous dittes, je porte une espee pour luy faire avoüer le contraire.   (98)

[I can no longer bear your cutting remarks because, beyond what I
swear before God and his angels, I didn't receive a single penny at
Saumur. And as to the first fellow who wants to charge me with
what you said, I carry a sword that will make him change his mind.]

This threat of violence illustrates the deep rift between the two
cousins, who are engaged in a tenuous and fragile dialogue, but it
also reveals the possible civil war that threatens members of d'Aubigné's divided church. It dramatizes the moral weakness that opposes the Prudent and the Ferme to the narrator, who urges them
to place the honor of God above the family honor so dear to the
nobility, and it serves as a transitional passage because it is followed by a marked change in the rhythm of the dialogue.

Prior to the passage cited above d'Aubigné's interlocutors participate evenly in the discussion. They exchange replies that are of
short-to-moderate length, with the exception of a lengthy tirade
spoken by the Ferme. The rapidity of the exchange enhances the
dramatic tension of the dialogue and permits effective use of repetition, parallelism, and wordplay. It creates the impression that
the Prudent is being given a fair opportunity to voice the opinions
of his faction. Soon after the reference to swordplay, however, the
rhythm of the dialogue accelerates until the interlocutors confront
one another in a bitter stichomythic sequence:

Le Ferme: Faut-il pour estre bon serviteur violer sa foy?
Le Prudent: Le Prince peut dispenser de la foy.
Le Ferme: Ouy, de la foi qu'il a receu, mais non de cele que Dieu
   a stipulé.
Le Prudent: Il n'y a point de serment sans quelque condition.
Le Ferme: Le serment non conditionel est violé quand on le condi-
   tionne apres.   (103)

[Le Ferme: Must one violate a promise in order to be a loyal
   servant?
Le Prudent: The Prince can dispense you from what you've sworn
   to do.
Le Ferme: Yes, for what's been sworn to him, but not from that
   which God has stipulated.
Le Prudent: There is no oath without some condition.
Le Ferme: A nonconditional oath is broken when you establish conditions afterward.]

Montaigne's "Art de Conferer" places "apresté" and "esgratinures"
in the service of truth but supposes that the interlocutors will al-

ways be ready to recognize the legitimacy of their opponent's arguments. D'Aubigné's characters lack this fundamental integrity. As Le Modeste notes, "Chescun de vous veult avoir la gloire de la dispute" [106: Each one of you wants to claim the glory of (winning) the dispute].

Recognizing the futility of further discussion, the minister takes leave of the cousins. The final pages of the *Caducée* return to the first-person narrative that characterized the opening sequences. The narrator describes a brief interview with the duke of Rohan and then gives his reactions to news from the Synod at Privas that has endorsed the position of the Fermes. Now that official steps have been taken to resolve the schism, the Modeste argues that recent quarrels prove the Reformed church's divine mission: "Ce n'est pas parmi les chardons que l'esprit malin seme son yvoire, mais dans le froment du Seigneur" [108: It is not among thistles that the evil one sows his rye, but in the wheat fields of the Lord]. He concludes the *Caducée* with a prayer for unity and hopes that the bitter quarrel between Fermes and Prudents can be forgotten while a revitalized Huguenot community dedicates itself to fulfilling the divine will.

The *Caducée* consists of a narrative introduction and debate, a dramatic dialogue, and a narrative conclusion. The introduction presents the disinterested, patriarchal minister and announces his intention to pacify the divided church, while the debate expresses the main points of opposition between Fermes and Prudents and gives preference to the former. The dialogue repeats and amplifies the discussion of contested issues and gives more support to the Fermes, but its primary function is to dramatize the danger and the seriousness of the schism. A vehicle for contrast and opposition, it provides no resolution to political or theological tensions. The failure of individuals to resolve the dispute themselves points to the need for obedience to established institutional authority. Only the Synod at Privas can heal the wounds caused during the Assembly at Saumur.

Mathurine et Du Perron

In the *Caducée* dialogue is a dramatic encounter between two opposing voices in the presence of a moderator. With the exception of the dramatic format, the preponderance of two speakers, and the tendency toward theatricality (the threatened swordplay), d'Aubigné's other dialogues will differ radically from this conciliatory text. *Mathurine* and *Faeneste* are devoted to ridicule rather than reconciliation. Dialogue satire thrived in the highly charged intellectual climate of the Reformation era and benefited from the revival of interest in Lucian, who inspired well-known humanists such as More, Erasmus, and Rabelais. Also important for d'Aubigné as a Protestant writer, Théodore de Bèze and Pierre Viret had composed satiric dialogues, with Bèze writing in Latin and Viret in French.[7] Like Lucian, whose cynicism they deplored, but whose works they read, Bèze and Viret combined dialogue with techniques of farce and comedy, the natural allies of satire. In his dialogue *Cyclops sive Sophista* (1561) Bèze transforms the scholarly German Heshus into an ass and has him beaten for stupidity. In the *Epistola magistri Benedicti Passavantii* (1553) he combines a reported dialogue between Passavant and some Genevan Protestants with Rabelaisian mockery of Pierre Lizet's physical appearance: "Vos ergo loquimini de Domino Nuper-Praesidente, certe ecce bonum numerum. Quomodo valet Dominus nasus ejus? Est-ne semper vestitus de cramesino?" [11: You've been speaking of my lord the former president. Certainly, there's a character! How is my lord his nose? Is it still dressed in crimson?].

While the writings of Lucian, Bèze, and Viret may have encouraged d'Aubigné's interest in satiric dialogue and influenced his techniques of ridicule, they do not anticipate the complex exploitation of theatricality that will govern both the form and content of *Mathurine*. However much Bèze and Viret borrow from farce or comedy, their dialogues retain some connection with the tradition of philosophical discourse. They present the reader with as many as four characters who embody different points of view and, if there is an *eiron* figure like Tobie in Viret's *Le Monde à l'empire* or Hilaire in his *Disputations chrétiennes*, there is also a *raisonneur*, appropriately named Théophile, standing by to give serious scriptural commentary. In *Mathurine* d'Aubigné restricts the dialogue to two interlocutors, eliminating any character who might resemble Le Modeste. In a sense, such a character is not necessary

7. In *La Satire en France ou la littérature militante au XVIe siècle* (Paris: Hachette, 1866) Charles F. Lenient provides background on Reformation satire. Robert D. Linder, although he focuses on political ideas, offers recent biographical and bibliographical data on Viret; see his *The Political Ideas of Pierre Viret* (Geneva: Droz, 1964).

because the ironic context in which *Mathurine* appears makes it clear that the reader is dealing with a *monde à l'envers*.

Composed between 1597 and 1616, *Mathurine* forms the first chapter in book 2 of *La Confession de Sancy*.[8] It is linked to the *Confession* by theme and technique. Nicolas Harlay de Sancy, a Protestant who had converted to Catholicism after the Saint Bartholomew Massacre and again in 1597, is the target of d'Aubigné's satire and a symbol of all those Protestant-to-Catholic converts whom he regarded as betrayers of his church, from Henri de Navarre to lesser figures like Jean de Sponde. As the fictional Sancy informs the reader, *Mathurine* too deals with conversions: "C'est une honneste conference entre les conferences que ce siecle a conferees; et vous verrez par là combien la bonne mesnagere Saincte Eglise Romaine employe de gens à ramener le monde à la grande voye" [623: This is a fine conference among the conferences that this century has conferred; and you will see thereby how that good manager Holy Roman Church uses people to bring everyone back to the true path]. The *convertisseurs* who participate in the dialogue are Mathurine, a court fool portrayed by d'Aubigné as an officious and bawdy prostitute, and Jean Davy Du Perron, brother of the famous cardinal who converted Henri de Navarre. Unlike the characters in the *Caducée*, they are not divided by any ideological conflict. The subject of the quarrel between them—who really converted Baron Sainte-Marie du Mont—is inspired by personal and sexual rivalry.

Since a man and a woman are competing in *Mathurine*, d'Aubigné's dialogue recalls the male-female competition often depicted in farce where the domineering wife humiliates her husband. This Omphale archetype, to borrow a concept from Jung, is often reversed in the concluding scenes of the farces and masculine authority is restored.[9] As a satirist, d'Aubigné will not reestablish

---

8. The *terminus a quo* for *Sancy* is 1597, but it is likely that *Mathurine* was written later. References to *Faeneste* in *Mathurine* suggest that d'Aubigné had written or at least edited the two works at approximately the same time.

9. Northrup Frye notes the prevalence of the Omphale archetype in satire in his *Anatomy of Criticism* (Princeton: Princeton University Press, 1957): "The figure of the low-norm *eiron* is irony's substitute for the hero, and when he is removed from satire we can see more clearly that one of the central themes of the *mythos* is the disappearance of the heroic. This is the main reason for the predominance in fictional satire of what may be called the Omphale archetype, the man bullied or dominated by women, which has been prominent in satire all through its history, and embraces a vast area of contemporary humor, both popular and sophisticated" (228–29).

the authority of Du Perron. The Omphale archetype, moreover, provides a convenient means of introducing into the dialogue familiar themes from Protestant polemical literature, for example, the identification of the Roman Catholic church with the great Whore of Babylon and, as Henri Estienne expresses it in the *Apologie pour Hérodote* (1566), "la lubricité et paillardise des gens d'Eglise" (book 2, chap. 1).

Mathurine and Du Perron meet by chance at the residence of Madame de Montluc where Mathurine has just been speaking with Bertrand de Vignolles (a convert to Catholicism in 1604). The importance of the Omphale archetype, the nature of the setting, the pace and tone of the dialogue are all apparent in the expository sequence:

> Mathurine sortoit de faire une leçon à Vignolles chez Madame de Montluc: Du Perron alloit faire la sienne, qui changea de couleur à la vue de Mathurine, passa la main sur son front chauve, puis commença. Perron. Et a vous belle dame: on m'a dit que vous vous vantez par tout que vous avez converti Sainte Marie du Mont. Mathur. Et qui seroit ce donc, mon bel amy: Perron. Par ma foy il y auroit bien de l'apparence, vous estes une belle theologienne. Mathur. Ouy, comme s'il falloit convertir les gens par la troulogie. C'estoit du vieux temps quand on faisoit à la pareille.   (623)

> [Mathurine was just leaving after having given a lesson to Vignolles at Madame de Montluc's. Du Perron was going in to give his but, changing color at the sight of Mathurine and passing his hand across his bald pate, he began as follows. Perron: "Well, lady, they tell me that you are bragging everywhere that you converted Sainte Marie du Mont." Mathurine: "And who else would have done it then, my fine friend?" Perron: "By my word, it would indeed be likely! You're a fine theologian!" Mathur: "Yes, as though it were necessary to convert people by holeology (reference to Mathurine's role as prostitute). That's the way they did it in the old days."]

The grotesque rivalry of prelate and prostitute is emphasized by the initial parallelism of *faire une leçon* with regard to Mathurine and *faire la sienne* with respect to Du Perron and by the subsequent opposition of *théologie* and *troulogie*. Du Perron claims for himself the domain of theology and the values or privileges that are associated with it: intellect, spirit, power. Mathurine recognizes, yet resists, her identification with *troulogie* and the related themes of carnality, matter, and feminine subordination. Her "strategy" throughout the dialogue will be to reverse these roles, claiming for herself the privileges of theology and linking Du Perron with the realm of illicit sexuality. His gesture and change in color in this opening sequence reveal a degree of irritability that contrasts with Mathurine's calm, and this emotional disequilibrium betrays the presence of the Omphale archetype. Mathurine will, in fact, be the dominant character of the dialogue. She is both a victim of d'Aubigné's ridicule and a vehicle for his satire of Du Perron.

In the *Caducée* d'Aubigné's brief acknowledgment of the Ferme's estate recalled the villa that provided a traditional setting for many classical and humanist dialogues. In the *Mathurine* he relies exclusively on the use of proper names to evoke the atmosphere of the court. Since proper names are constantly being introduced, the setting is defined with greater detail as the dialogue progresses and the court, rather than the machinations of Du Perron and Mathurine, ultimately becomes the principal topic of conversation. Dialogue and setting thus fuse in a way that anticipates the complex interplay of setting and dialogue in *Faeneste*.

The dialogue in *Mathurine* possesses the nervous energy of farce, with the characters addressing one another in brief exchanges of five to ten lines. Enhancing the already rapid rhythm of the dialogue are the emotional volatility of the interlocutors and the constantly changing tone of the conversation. The initial hostility regarding the conversion of Saint Marie du Mont yields to an angry exchange of invective and culminates when Mathurine threatens Du Perron with her club "Flamberge". Du Perron is able to calm her and recognizes her contributions as a fellow *convertisseur*. They then gossip amicably about the court and share with one another arguments guaranteed to refute their Protestant adversaries and win converts for the Roman church.

In the first phase of the dialogue (623–26) as the interlocutors each support their claims to have converted Sainte-Marie, d'Aubigné draws upon the extensive repertory of sixteenth-century anticourtier satire.[10] Tahureau, whose dialogues went through more than twenty editions between 1564 and 1585, had already created a detailed portrait of the Italianizing courtier. Estienne's *Deus Dialogues du langage françois italianizé* (1578) catalogued his

---

10. Pauline Smith studies this phenomenon in *The Anti-Courtier Trend in Sixteenth-Century French Literature* (Geneva: Droz, 1966).

linguistic mannerisms and attacked the lack of moral and civil values they revealed. In *Mathurine* d'Aubigné renews this familiar material by relating it to the contemporary court and, more important, by integrating it into a dramatic dialogue that is quite distinct from the works of Tahureau or Estienne.

Tahureau and Estienne set their portraits of the courtier in dialogues that feature a traditional master-student interaction. The wise character (Celtophile for Estienne, the Democritic for Tahureau) defines the French point of view and warns his interlocutor of the dangers inherent in courtly fashions. In *Mathurine* two foolish characters endorse the most superficial of courtly behaviors and link these behaviors with religious conversion so that the vices of the conventional anticourtier are perceived as a moral preparation for Catholicism. Each of d'Aubigné's interlocutors, moreover, has a specific method of indoctrination. Mathurine gives the Baron personal instruction at night. Du Perron emphasizes reading and serious study during his daytime visits. Both characters strive to provide Sainte-Marie with the appropriate language. Given his claim to the world of intellect and power, Du Perron logically offers a religious and political vocabulary:

> Il estoit tout brutal et barbare, je luy ay appris à parler des Peres sans les avoir leus; des Conciles de mesmes, et luy ai fait part, non seulement de la *Matheologie*, mais à parler de l'Estat, à admirer ce grand corps d'Espagne, à reigler tout au Conseil de Rome, et m'a falu montrer jusques aux termes: au lieu de dire le Pape, je lui ay appris à dire Sa Saincteté; au lieu du Roy, sa Majesté.   (624)

> [He was quite brutish and uncivilized and I taught him how to discuss the Church Fathers, without having read them, and the Church Councils in the same way. I not only shared the *Matheology* with him, I taught him to speak of state affairs, to admire the great nation of Spain, to decide everything according to the advice of Rome, and I even had to provide him with specific words: instead of saying "pope", I taught him to say "His Holiness"; instead of "king", "His Majesty."]

These language lessons have several levels. In religious matters, the Baron blindly repeats the authoritative teaching of the clergy, which he accepts without ever consulting the Fathers or, for that matter, Scripture. With regard to politics, he is being trained to look beyond France and to identify matters of state with Catholic Spain. Finally, he is being taught a new and exaggerated reverence for authority. The simple titles that had long satisfied the French aristocracy are deemed insufficient and fashion now dictates a more pretentious language ("Sainteté," "Majesté") which is itself a sign of Spanish influence.

Mathurine specializes in fashionable exclamations—"oh, oh, oh, il y a de l'excez, c'est pour en mourir"—and in the semiology of fashion and gesture: "Je luy appris à tourner les talons en dedans, à cheminer en oye, et de pareille gravité, à escrimer des deux bras, à s'emmonceler le ventre, à reculer la teste, à la dodeliner de bonne grace" [624–25: I taught him to turn his heels inward, to walk like a goose and with similar gravity, to gesture with both arms, to thrust out his belly, pull his head back, and nod it gracefully]. Her instructions seem less sinister, although the exaggerated posturing of the courtier indicated here is sufficiently ridiculous.

In their indoctrination of Sainte-Marie, Mathurine and Du Perron supply the Baron with lines, gestures, and costumes that will guarantee his success in the theater of the court. As the dialogue continues the *theatrum mundi* topos that is implied by their actions will gradually reach the surface of the text. Stronger emphasis on both the formal and thematic theatricality of *Mathurine* occurs almost immediately as the interlocutors, unable to decide the issue of who converted the Baron, nearly come to blows:

> Perron: Ho, vertu bieu, je te feray taire, maraude.
> Mathur: Aux mains, coquin! Voila Flamberge qui en fera raison;
>   ne te joue pas à moi.   (626)

> [Perron: Ho, by God, I'll silence you, scoundrel.
> Mathur: Defend yourself, rogue! Flamberge here will deal with
>   you; don't toy with me.]

Du Perron responds to Mathurine's threats in this farcical passage with the first explicit reference to theater: "Mais ne faisons point icy la comedie, ne reprochons point nos ordures, et te contente que c'est moy qui ay converti Saincte Marie" [627: But let's not play a comedy, let's stop reproaching each other with our dirty deeds and agree that I am the one who converted Saincte Marie].

In the immediate context and from the character's point of view, the phrase "ne faisons point icy la comedie" represents rejection of undignified feminine violence, but the reader accustomed to the ironic structure of the dialogue will recognize that Mathurine and Du Perron are "en train de faire la comédie." They are actors in search of an audience that will validate their performance as *convertisseurs*. Their whole view of life, moreover, values appearance over essence, form over substance.

D'Aubigné's interlocutors are quick to perceive and comment upon the theatrical aspects of life at court. The *theatrum mundi* topos enters the conversation as they discuss the King's love of theater and suggest that professional actors are unnecessary because the court has become a living version of the *commedia dell'arte*. *Mathurine* thus progresses from implicit to explicit theatricality, from the performance-oriented behavior of Mathurine and Du Perron through the indoctrination of Sainte-Marie to the description of the court as *commedia dell'arte*. As the dialogue continues, d'Aubigné focuses with increasing intensity on the place and the price of illusion in the courtly milieu. Mathurine and Du Perron cultivate dramatic techniques that must be mastered by the successful courtier, and they pass their knowledge of deceptive discourse, gesture, and fashion on to others, but they are ultimately the victims of their own illusions. Like the fools in Lucian's dialogues and the characters in the *Satyre Menipée* (1594), they see only half-truths and, as the following argument from Mathurine indicates, they subvert what they would defend:

> Mathur. Vous dites, Messieurs les Huguenots, que ceus qui aujourd'huy tiennent les grands rangs en l'Eglise de Rome sont brigands et voleurs, qui pillent le bien des pauvres: or il est dit: Ma maison est maison d'oraison, mais il en ont fait une caverne de brigands, ores donc puis que nos gens d'Eglise sont brigands, nostre Eglise . . . est par necessité maison d'oraison.   (628)

> [You claim, you Huguenots, that those who hold high positions in the Roman church today are thieves and robbers who steal from the poor, but is it written: "My house is a house of prayer and you have made it a den of thieves." Since our clergy are thieves, our church is, by necessity, a house of prayer.]

Mathurine's "argument" here marks a shift away from the discussion of external, political corruption (theatre of the court) and a return to the theme of religious conversion that characterized the beginning of the dialogue. Once again Mathurine appears as the dominant figure. It is she who now explains Scripture for the benefit of Du Perron. His role, as the dialogue concludes, is to pose the obvious question: "Tu m'as appelé maquereau, je t'ay appelé paillarde, qui t'es encore plus honorable. Qui croiroit que tels gens sont propres à retirer de l'heresie, et à sauver les ames qui sont en danger?" [630: You have called me a pimp; I have called you a whore, which is even more honorable for you. Who would believe that such people are qualified to rescue others from heresy and save souls that are in danger?]. Displaying her familiarity with Scripture, Mathurine answers by identifying herself as a modern Rahab, but the comparison does not serve her well since she saves Sainte-Marie *from* and not *for* the Israelites (Huguenots).

Les Avantures du Baron de Faeneste

In *Mathurine* and the *Caducée* d'Aubigné has produced dialogues that are remarkably different from one another. The *Caducée* with its deep tone of religious commitment and its point by point discussion of issues dividing the Fermes and the Prudents has little in common with the Lucianic *Mathurine* except for the dramatic confrontation between clearly drawn protagonists. D'Aubigné's major work, *Les Avantures du Baron de Faeneste*, incorporates some technical aspects of both these "pamphlet" dialogues. As in the *Caducée*, where the thinly disguised Ferme was a mask for d'Aubigné, he again portrays himself as one of the interlocutors. The authorial character, Enay, is once again associated with a country estate and with wisdom. So flexible is the structure of *Faeneste*, moreover, that Enay at times addresses the reader directly, assuming the narrative and moderating function of Le Modeste. *Faeneste* and *Mathurine* are linked by the satire of *convertisseurs*, Catholicism, and the Italianizing courtier as well as by a Lucianic format and the incorporation of setting into the dialogue. As the longest work, however, *Faeneste* also represents the amplification, if not the *dépassement*, of techniques and themes explored in the shorter dialogues.

Books 1 and 2 of the *Avantures du Baron de Faeneste*, inspired in part by the Battle of Aunis which pitted the forces of the duke of Epernon against those of La Rochelle, were published in 1617.[11] The third book with a revised version of the preceding books ap-

---

11. As Weber (1969) observes in his edition of d'Aubigné's *Oeuvres* (1347), the title of the 1617 edition of *Faeneste* suggests the possibility of an earlier edition, but none has been found.

peared in 1619. Book 4 was included in the 1630 edition of *Fae-neste*.[12] The bibliographical data show that d'Aubigné maintained his interest in the Baron and his exploits for more than twelve years, a period of time sufficient for him to resolve or succumb to the tensions between novel and dialogue so aptly reflected in the preface. In 1617 the dialogical aspect of the work is paramount. This is not merely a matter of title—the word *Dialogues* appears in the preface and again preceding the first chapter—but of literary structure. The opening exchanges of *Faeneste* demonstrate d'Aubigné's intention to exploit the dialectical potential of dialogue in order to refine the appearance-reality contrast presented in the prefatory passages:

> Faeneste. Bon yor, lou mien. —Enay. Et à vous, Monsieur. —F. Dou benez-vous ensi? —E. Je ne vien pas de loin; je me pourmene autour de ce clos. —F. Comment Diavle, clos, il y a un quart d'ure que je suis emvarracé le long de ces murailles, et bous ne le nommez pas un parc.   (675)

> [Faeneste: Good day, sir. —Enay: And to you, sir. —F: Where do you come from?—E: I don't come from a great distance, I am walking around this field. —F: What the devil, field! I've been enclosed by these walls for a quarter of an hour, and you don't call it a park?]

These few lines of exposition, written in the brief rhythmic patterns characteristic of d'Aubigné's dialogues, reveal a series of carefully articulated oppositions. The Baron's Gasconized speech contrasts with Enay's more literary French. Faeneste's confusion and disorientation distinguish him from the solid and confident Enay, and, finally, there is the crucial difference between *clos* and *parc*. The appearance-reality topos generates a series of contrasts and d'Aubigné's characters each represent a range of values.[13] Faeneste is the comic Gascon adventurer, but he is also the lost soul who cannot "read" signs around him whether they are topographical or linguistic. In spite of his "countrified" accent, he is an incarnation of present courtly values. Enay, in appearance the

12. Book 4 was condemned by the authorities in Geneva. Garnier (1930) discusses the affair in his article on relations between d'Aubigné and the leaders of Geneva.

13. Ian Morrisson (1973) offers a useful discussion of the appearance-reality theme; see "'Paraître' and 'Etre': Thoughts on d'Aubigné's *Avantures du baron de Faeneste*," *Modern Language Review* 68 (1973): 762–70. Other interpretations of *Faeneste* are provided by Celce-Murcia (1978), Jouanna (1979), Rocheblave (1910), Plattard (1975), and Weber (1970).

country gentleman, shows no linguistic trace of his Poitevin background, and it becomes increasingly clear that he too is a courtier, although a courtier of times past. Enay is a good reader of signs, both verbal and physical, but he lacks the Baron's transparency. The "faux Poictevin" sends veiled or concealed messages. The simple clothing he wears masks his identity as owner of the estate. The blade hidden in his cane screens a readiness to defend himself in case of attack. The modest vocabulary—*clos*, not *parc*, *étable* not *écurie*, *petite maison* not *château*—understates the value of his possessions. Characteristically, he responds to the Baron's repeated attempts to engage in political gossip with discreet refusal: "Mais, s'il vous plaist, passons le temps ailleurs qu'à ceux à qui nous devons obeissance" [261: But, if you please, let's spend our time in some other way than in criticizing those whom we must obey]. The Baron is a Catholic and Enay a Protestant, but their dialogue shows none of the hostility that d'Aubigné exploited in *Mathurine* or the *Caducée*. As a *convertisseur* Faeneste lacks the aggressive zeal of Mathurine and Du Perron:

> Pour moi ye deffendrai tout . . . et vous convertirai, si bous en abez la boulontai. Contentez bous que ma priere parest pour priere, comme l'*Ave Maria*. —E. Je voi bien à ce que vous dites que ceux que vous convertissez le veulent desjà estre.   (699)

> [As far as I am concerned, I'll defend everything . . . and I'll convert you if you are willing. Just be content that my prayer appears to be a prayer, like the *Ave Maria*. —E. I see what you mean when you say that those you convert have already decided to be converted.]

In creating this antithetical couple d'Aubigné may have been influenced, as Henri Weber (*Oeuvres*, xli) has noted, by the antithetical heroes of Cervantes and Rabelais, but the preface to *Faeneste* also suggests the influence of dialogue satire. The Baron does not represent an assistant or *adjuvant* as Sancho does for Don Quixote, or the possessor of valuable wisdom as Panurge does for Pantagruel. Faeneste is, rather, a comic figure whose conversation Enay cultivates in order to amuse himself (271). By listening to the Baron and drawing him out, as Socrates does Gorgias or Tychiades does Simon in Lucian's *De parasito*, Enay performs the function of the traditional *eiron*. The function of listener to and ironic commentator on the Baron's discourse is, moreover, supplemented by another role that often appears in the literary dialogue. As master or teacher, Enay strives to enlighten Faeneste. In books 1 and 2 he occasionally corrects the Baron's perception of *être* and *paraître*. In Book I correction occurs with regard to the *raffinés d'honneur*, those brilliant duelists so admired by Faeneste (690), but who no longer "appear" because they chanced to meet a better swordsman. In book 2 Enay draws the Baron's attention to the trickery behind a number of contemporary "miracles" (707). He also describes how certain enchantments were produced and warns Faeneste to be more discriminating in his pursuit of honor.

The questions Enay asks of Faeneste fall into two general categories. In his role as *eiron* he requests specific information—the meaning of terms like "raffinés d'honneur" (689) for example, or details about courtly fashion (687). The Baron replies with definitions or facts that become the focus of further dialogue. Enay also asks the Baron for information about himself. The answer may provide a short description of one of Faeneste's multitudinous "querelles" and a resumption of dialogue or assume the form of a long, uninterrupted biographical narrative. The Baron provides, in effect, detailed stories of his past life. He describes his voyage to Paris, his arrival at court, his entry into the service of the duke of Guise, his invitation to serve the king extended by a mysterious "rousseau" whom he thought he had befriended, and his role in four wars: Savoy, Juliers, Bois Dauphin, and Aunis. Supplementing this chronological action are episodic narratives of the Baron's many duels, his love affairs, his encounters with magicians, and his adventures as a student at Poitiers or the College de Guyenne.

The interlocutor in a dialogue may have a past that is known to the reader. Cicero's historical figures have authority and interest precisely because of their past achievements. Socrates has a wife who nags him and a friendship with Alcibiades, but these details filter into the dialogue as background information while attention is focused on an appropriately philosophical subject. In d'Aubigné's text Faeneste does *express* ideas, but he is also required to *live* them on the battlefield, at court, and in the provinces. It is this duality that enriches and distinguishes him from the interlocutor in a more conventional dialogue, providing some evidence for those who see *Faeneste* as a novel or protonovel. In effect, all that is required in the way of dramatic action for dialogue is that which

suffices to introduce the interlocutors into a given setting and mo-
tivate the conversation that will supply the crucial clash of ideas.
The chance encounter of Faeneste and Enay, the invitation extended to the former to visit the latter's château, the arrival of
the Baron's valets, dinner and after-dinner conversation—all these
features of d'Aubigné's text support and facilitate the dialogue exchange. It is the ample description of the Baron's life that creates
generic tension. Other disruptive elements include the third-person view of the Baron provided by his valets and the introduction
of *contes* and *histoires intercalées*.

In books 1 and 2, nevertheless, d'Aubigné controls the disruptive or novelistic aspects of his text with techniques that reinforce
the conflict of ideas essential to *Faeneste* as a satiric dialogue. However detailed and diverting the Baron's adventures may be, they
conform to a single pattern that draws attention to his role as em-
bodiment of *paraître*. Typically, Faeneste, who is incapable of
making the transition from appearance to reality, is duped and
defeated, and his defeat is marked by physical humiliation—the
punishment often meted out to the fool in farce and satire. In one
such episode he asks a necromancer to summon the devil and when
Satan or Beelzebub appears (in reality a figure disguised and
mounted on stilts), he flees in terror, falling into a ditch that contains the bodies of plague victims. In another the lady he serenades
rewards his efforts by emptying the contents of a chamber pot on
the Baron and his musicians. The stories that Cherbonnière,
Faeneste's aging yet impudent valet, tells Enay about the Baron
present him in his perennial role as victim of appearances. Even
the game-playing sequences that seem to interrupt the course of
the dialogue can be read as symbolical scenes that allow Enay to
comment upon the current lack of political morality:

> E. Quel meslange d'affaires en la teste de ce pauvre Baron! Le voila
> pris, et son Cherbonniere qui le garde. Vien ça, Carmagnolle: vois-
> tu pas comment ton compagnon frappe ton maistre par le derriere,
> au lieu de le garder: c'est ainsi que quelques uns on gardé l'Estat.
> Ne craint-il pas qu'il s'en apperçoive? —Carmagnolle. Par ma foi,
> Monsieur, nous avons le plus drole de maistre. . . . Quand vous
> estes tous deux ensemble, il y en a un plus fin que l'autre: le voila
> delivré.   (707)

[What a muddle of business in the head of the poor Baron! Now
he's caught and Cherbonnière is protecting him. Come here, Car-

magnolle: don't you see how your companion is striking your master from behind instead of protecting him? This is the way some
people have defended the state. Isn't he afraid he'll find out what's
happening? —Carmagnolle: By my word, sir, we have the most
amusing master. . . . When you're with him, one always out-
smarts the other; now, he's free.]

Governed by a single narrative pattern, the Baron's adventures
are also marked by explicit references to the *être-paraître* pattern,
references that recall for the reader the dialectical center of the dialogue:

Le profit de vostre histoire est sur ce mot: *Où est l'honneur?* C'est une
resolution qui mene les gens . . . au gibet et à l'echaffaut. . . .
Seulement vous veux-je faire souvenir que *l'Estre* et le *Parestre*
tomberent d'accord en vostre accident.   (723)

[The lesson of your story depends upon the phrase: Where is honor?
Pursuing it leads people . . . to the gibet and the scaffold. . . .
Only I must remind you that Being and Reality coincided in your
mishap.]

A review of the contents of books 1 and 2 shows too that the
narration of Faeneste's exploits is dispersed throughout the text in
a regular pattern that frames the Baron's exploits with chapters
devoted to issue-oriented dialogue. This pattern tends to work
against the "novelization" of the text and assert the dialogical
structure. The opening scenes of book 1 establish and multiply
the thematic conflicts between Enay and his guests: court versus
country, Gascon versus non-Gascon, present versus past, folly versus wisdom. The two succeeding chapters present Faeneste's account of the trip to Paris and initial experiences at court. In chapter 5 d'Aubigné resumes the dialogue as Faeneste questions Enay's
use of a *galerie* for a *grenier*. In the following chapters the Baron
relates incidents in his career as soldier and lover. These narratives
yield to a lengthy dialogue with Enay on the subject of dueling. In
chapters 11 and 12 Faeneste, frustrated in his attempts to discuss
religion, resorts to storytelling, a talent that he has cultivated because it is a "mouien de parestre en grand compenio" [693: a way
of appeasing in a large group]. The tales he trades with Enay concern the Dognon (d'Aubigné's fortress) and the comic enterprises
of Captain Lignoux, subjects in keeping with Faeneste's pose as a
military hero. The storytelling episode is brief and preserves, in

Faeneste's naïve enthusiasm and Enay's sophisticated raillery, the fundamental differences between the interlocutors. The concluding pages of book 1 return to the rapid dialogue exchange that characterized the beginning of the text. Faeneste's loquacity continues to contrast with Enay's reserve, his ostentation with the latter's practical simplicity, and the conversation ends with yet another statement of the appearance-reality conflict:

> F. D'aillurs nous autres pratiquons tellement l'aunur en toutes chauses, que nous ne faisons rien parestre qui ne soit fort abantajus. —E. Vous austres . . . donnez vos pensées au paroistre, et nous à l'estre seulement.   (695–96)
>
> [We cultivate honor in everything so much that we don't allow anything to appear unless it's very advantageous. —E. You . . . give your thoughts to appearance, and we give ours only to being.]

Book 2 reveals a similar alternation of dialogue with comic adventures and a parallel progression from controversial issues (this time in the domain of religion) to *contes*, with a reaffirmation of the *être-paraître* theme in the last chapter. In the initial pages contrasts are strongly drawn between the Baron, who requires visible manifestations of divine power and displays a casual attitude toward religious language—"Nostre Theolougie n'a que faire de la grammaire" [698: Our theology has nothing to do with grammar]—and the sober Enay who seeks more spiritual values and expects his prayers, like his scriptural readings, to make sense. These serious matters are interrupted by sequences devoted to game playing, but the conversation then turns back to the Baron's pursuit of love and magic. Enay initiates a tale-telling sequence in chapter 13, promising a *conte de village* and referring to the example of Boccaccio as he relates a story of four *curés* and their mistresses. Given the religious satire in book 2, Enay's tale can scarcely be considered a digression. Faeneste's *contes* are linked to his role as braggart or *miles gloriosus* and to the theme of honor as a manifestation of appearance.

In the final chapter d'Aubigné revives the linguistic opposition between Faeneste (flambeaux) and Enay (chandeliers). He also provides yet another discussion of the appearance-reality conflict. Here, in fact, Enay drops his role as fictional interlocutor and speaks directly for the author:

Enay. Nous avons au commencement protesté de bourdes vrayes et nous n'avons rien dit en tout nostre discours qui ne soit arrivé, seulement avons nous attribué à un mesme ce qui appartient à plusieurs. Le profit de tout nostre discours est qu'il y a six choses desquelles il est dangereux de prendre le Parestre pour l'Estre: le gain, la volupté, l'amitié, l'honneur, le service du Roi ou de la Patrie, et la Religion.   (726)

[We spoke at the beginning (of the book) of telling amusing stories that were true and we have not included anything here that didn't happen, although we have attributed to one individual what happened to several. The lesson in our text is that there are six things in which it is dangerous to take Appearance for Reality: gain or profit, pleasure, friendship, honor, the service of king or country, and religion.]

The structure of book 2 thus parallels the structure of book 1. The regular alternation of dialogue and comic or satiric tale telling emphasizes the conflict between the interlocutors and serves to reinforce the dialogical character of the text, but d'Aubigné's concluding paragraph suggests that his work may evolve in a different direction. He returns to the theme of "bourdes vrayes" from the preface and balances it with the further discussion of the *être-paraître* topos, yet he avoids the word *dialogue*, now favoring *discours*. Combined with the longer and more abundant *contes* in book 2, this slight shift in emphasis suggests that d'Aubigné may be less inclined to adhere to the conflict between his interlocutors and more disposed to follow the example set by works like the *Contes et discours d'Eutrapel* (1585) or the *Printemps* (1572) of his fellow Poitevin Jacques Yver. Such works use dialogue, but make no pretense of adhering to generic conventions an Aristotelian reader like Tasso would recognize. In effect, the characters that d'Aubigné has designed, the pattern of interaction between them, and even the setting tend to encourage movement away from generic dialogue toward a less formal collection of *propos* or *discours*. Faeneste and Enay are not intellectual equals and cannot explore the conflicts between them by means of deeply philosophical discussion. Their conversation is motivated by differences in dress or manner or by the Baron's astonished reaction to Enay's estate. Once these areas have been explored, they tend to communicate as host and guest, more often than not, seated at the table. As Faeneste observes, the situation encourages the exchange of amusing anecdotes or stories.

The movement toward a loosely structured combination of tales and *discours* or *propos* anticipated in the concluding pages of book 2 occurs in book 3. The opening discussion takes place between Enay and Cherbonnière early in the morning before Faeneste has risen. The initial topic of conversation is the contrast between Faeneste's physical appearance and lack of personal hygiene, but Cherbonnière continues with other bits of information that describe how the Baron maintains himself and three servants in spite of a chronic lack of funds. To the degree that this discussion completes the portrayal of Faeneste, providing details that he would himself conceal, there is continuity with the first two books. Enay and Cherbonnière, however, are soon trading stories that deal with a variety of subjects and, when Faeneste arrives on the scene in chapter 8, he too joins the tale telling and proposes to explore a subject that touches him personally:

> Dès mon enfance j'ay esté tousjours resolut, et pour cela fouetté en diavle. Monsur, en commençant lou desyunai, ye bous en bux dire trois ou quatre qui levent la paille, pour monstrer qu'un galant homme doit prendre parti, et estre ferme en ses resolutions.
> (740)

> [Even as a child I was always very resolute and, for that reason, given a devil of a thrashing. Monsieur, as we begin our meal, I would like to tell you three or four really good ones to show how a gallant gentleman must make up his mind and be firm in his resolutions.]

While the Baron describes his nonduels, Enay and Cherbonnière contribute tales that are more difficult to categorize. Many of them are linked by the theme of trickery that continues the *paraître* topos because of the necessary manipulation of appearances.[14] There is no close connection, however, with the satiric focus of books 1 and 2. D'Aubigné adopts a tolerant attitude toward human craftiness in most of the stories related by Enay. The Conte de Manle, for example, is a simple *greffier* whose pretended nobility allows him to win a wealthy wife (759–61). When the ruse is

14. Morrisson (1973, 768) argues that the continuing emphasis on appearances helps unify the work.

discovered, the bride's father is content that his son-in-law, although not rich, is "un habile homme." Pautrot attends the fair at Niort where he quarrels with and then sleeps with the woman whose room at the inn had somehow been assigned to him. Lawyer Chesne-verd buys a tract of land from his client, only to discover that he has been sold the village cemetery.

Most of the *contes* in book 3 are, to borrow a term from Enay, *contes de village* that provide a strong contrast with the courtly subject matter in books 1 and 2. The change in milieu, the comic perspective, and the variety of the tales lighten the tone of book 3 and relieve the tension created by the constant opposition of *être* and *paraître* in the preceding books. Lighthearted imitation of Rabelais and Cervantes also adds a new dimension to d'Aubigné's text. As Jacques Bailbé (1959) and others have noted, d'Aubigné is a disciple of Rabelais throughout *Faeneste*, displaying a similar penchant for wordplay and lists.[15] In book 3, however, he explicitly invites comparison of his tales with those of Rabelais. Having heard the tale of La Roche-Boisseau and the *sergents*, Enay makes reference to Rabelais's tale of Basché and the *chicanous* (734). When he subsequently tells the story of Baumier, he notes that the mule who causes the death of his protagonist is finally found "au mesme lieu où fut amassé frere Jean Tappe-couë . . . comme escrit Maistre François, autheur excellent" [738: at the very place where they picked up brother Jean Tappe-couë . . . as Master François, that excellent author, writes]. Even the narrative of Faeneste's adventures bears the mark of Rabelais, for the reported account of the Baron's escape from the Turks recalls Panurge's story of a fanciful escape in *Pantagruel*. Like Panurge, moreover, the Baron has a prophetic dream. D'Aubigné's inclusion of an enigma in chapter 16 of book 3 is yet another area in which he shares the comic propensities of R⌐belais.

Lighthearted imitation of Cervantes involves no reference to any specific episodes from the Spanish novel. Instead d'Aubigné is content to evoke and then transform the general mission that Don Quixote assumes. Enay summarizes for Faeneste a yet-to-be-completed work entitled *Le Rabilleur* or *Aesculape* whose hero "comme Don Guichot voyagea pour remettre la Chevalrie errante" [764:

---

15. Nearly all scholarly critics have noted this influence. Among them are Bailbé (1981), Béné (1981), De Guer (1941), and Weber (1970).

traveled like Don Quixote in order to reestablish knight errantry].
D'Aubigné's burlesque protagonist, however, has none of Quixote's high ideals and reads no chivalric novels. His idea of reform
is limited to securing the respect due him from lesser members of
the nobility, and in attempting to accomplish this selfish task he
wreaks nearly as much havoc among those he visits as the more
idealistic Don Quixote at those inns that are unfortunate enough
to receive him. As book 3 concludes even Faeneste is able to recognize the protagonist of *Aesculape* as a broad symbol of the inept
reformers Enay wishes to condemn: "J'entens vien: bous boulez
dire que nous abons force medecins de l'Estat aussi propres à cela
comme un crucifix à jouër d'un estiflet" [771: I understand very
well. You mean that we have many doctors for the State who are
as good for that as a crucifix is to serve as a whistle].

In contrast with books 1 and 2, this conclusion offers no further
consideration of the appearance-reality opposition. Since the conflict between Faeneste and Enay is less prominent in book 3 and
with it the dialogical or dialectical aspect of the text, the conclusion is appropriate and serves as a further sign of the structural and
generic tensions that characterize *Faeneste*. Book 3 is, ultimately,
an inversion of the first two books. The inversion is made manifest
in the importance given Enay and the smaller role assigned to
Faeneste, in the increased number of *contes* and the diminished role
of dialogue, in the emphasis on country rather than court, and,
finally, in the prevalence of humor rather than satire.

This is not to say that issue-oriented dialogue and satire play no
role in book 3. The story of *Le Rabilleur* draws attention to a major
theme, the decline of the state under Concini. Because this theme
returns to the courtly subject matter with its inherent opposition
between appearance and reality, d'Aubigné's few chapters of political satire continue the dialogue pattern that characterized the preceding books. D'Aubigné has Enay resume his habits of interrogation, asking Faeneste to define a new term: "coyons de mille
livres." The Baron again plays the role of courtly informant. The
interlocutors assume their familiar functions, but the tone of the
satire has grown much darker. Political passages in book 3 evoke
an atmosphere of danger and intimidation. Even the Baron, confronted with the repressive political administration of Concini and
his party, realizes that those who dare to speak out will suffer:

"Bous ne bouiez par les rues de Paris que poutances plantées pour cus qui ozent oubrir la vouche contre Monsur ou Madame" [762: In the streets of Paris you see nothing but gallows set up for those who dare to speak out against Monsieur ou Madame]. Enay continues to praise the comparative freedom of the rural aristocracy, but he himself has felt the disapproval of the court, particularly through the hostility of those linked with the so-called Comte de Lorme, an adventurer trying to mount a maritime expedition that would bring great wealth to France. Enay also comments on the presence of spies sent out by the court to ascertain the loyalty of country gentlemen like himself. There may be fewer *poutances* away from Paris, but the times call for discretion, and it will take someone more competent than the hero of *Le Rabilleur* to solve political problems.

Book 4 does not continue the pattern of inversion that characterizes book 3. The first few chapters revive the loquacious, inept, but engaging Faeneste who appeared in books 1 and 2. The Baron reports his experiences in three military encounters—Valteline, Saint-Pierre, and Ponts-de-Cé—to Enay and his friend the Sieur de Beaujeu. In the dialogue that ensues, a dialogue very similar to the rapid give-and-take of books 1 and 2, d'Aubigné renews the *être-paraître* theme and the contrasts it generates. Faeneste designates as *bataille* what is a *rencontre* for Enay. A "belle armée" in the Baron's eccentric vocabulary is one whose soldiers are fashionably dressed and whose infantrymen, adorned with boots and spurs, aspire to the high rank of "aide-enseigne." Beaujeu's function in these early chapters is to sharpen the contrast between the army of his time, characterized by discipline and efficiency, and the disorderly bands described by Faeneste. Through Enay d'Aubigné returns to the explicit play upon appearance and reality that was typical of the first two books. With regard to the Baron's escape from the debacle of Ponts-de-Cé, he remarks: "Vous fistes fort bien, et cette fois là, vous aimastes mieux l'estre que le parestre, et peut-estre estes vous encor aujourd'hui pour n'avoir pas paru" [774: You managed very well and that time you preferred being to appearing, and perhaps you are still here today for not having appeared]. As he did in books 1 and 2, d'Aubigné also includes in the dialogue details that continue the story of Faeneste. The Baron's arms show an open window with the motto "Entrez comme lou vent." He claims that he can prove the nobility of his family by means of biblical texts and admits, although reluctantly, that he was once a Protestant.

Book 4 is, however, more than a reprise of techniques embodied in the first two books of *Faeneste*. There is a substantial amount of tale telling. Beaujeu interrupts the discussion of glory in order to relate a *conte de village* entitled "la glori Bernat." Religious satire (chapters 8–13) takes the form of an exchange of anecdotes as well as parody. D'Aubigné also introduces descriptive passages reminiscent of the *Satyre Menipée*. The detailed satiric images of the tapestries that decorate the meeting room of the Estates General in that book may have influenced the tapestries that appear in the concluding chapters of book 4, although these triumphs of the vices are also a burlesque counterpart to Petrarch's *Trionfi*. Structurally, book 4 is a combination of tale telling and dialogue and, while the proportion of one to the other is much more even than in book 3, it is clear that d'Aubigné has chosen not to maintain the carefully balanced dialogical emphasis of books 1 and 2.

In composing *Faeneste* d'Aubigné is no more committed to the rigors of generic dialogue or to constancy of form than is Rabelais in his stories of Pantagruel and Gargantua. It is not surprising, then, that scholars interested in the evolution of literary genres have not developed any consensus. Gabriel Pérouse (1977) associates *Faeneste* with the late sixteenth-century *discours bigarré*:

> Idées politiques et religieuses, actualité militaire, propos de vie quotidienne, tout est melé et "bigarré." La confusion de l'ensemble est encore accrue par la surabondance de noms propres, notamment quand il est traité des phases de la guerre. . . . Et la plus grande animation du dialogue ne suffit pas à changer vraiment les choses.   (467)

> [Political and religious ideas, military news, comments on daily life, everything is muddled and confused. The confusion of the whole is enhanced, moreover, by the oversupply of proper names, especially when it is a question of various phases of the war. . . . And even the great energy of the dialogue doesn't really change things.]

Henri Weber (1969), while he acknowledges the thematic unity of *Faeneste*, uses a musical comparison in order to convey the complex harmonies of d'Aubigné's text:

Dès le second livre, toute progression est abandonnée, les récits de Faeneste et les bons contes d'Enay s'entrelacent au hasard des associations d'idées. Cependant cet entrelacement, même avec l'alternance et le retour de principaux thèmes . . . constitue une sorte de composition musicale analogue au groupement et à la réapparition des images dans *Les Tragiques*.   (xlv)

[Beginning with the second book, all progression is abandoned and the narratives of Faeneste and the tales of Enay interlace with one another according to associations of ideas. Nevertheless, this interlace pattern, even with the alternance and return of the principal themes . . . constitutes a sort of musical composition analogous to the grouping and reappearance of images in *Les Tragiques*.]

As these critical assessments show, we have come a long way from the dialectically based dialogue described by Tasso and Sigonius and the reasoned arguments of the *Caducée*.

Conclusion

Between 1611 and 1630 d'Aubigné experiments with the expressive potential of dialogue and it is possible to identify a number of constants that form a personal aesthetic if not a detailed concept of the genre. In all these texts, from the *Caducée* to *Faeneste*, he establishes a binary structure. No more than two voices are represented at the same time, although there may be as many as three interlocutors. Generally, the third speaker duplicates the functions of another interlocutor, thereby reinforcing the authoritative voice in the dialogue. Rohan supports the Modeste and Beaujeu doubles or echoes Enay. This reinforcing of the authoritative speaker reflects the essentially polemical or monological character of d'Aubigné's dialogues. With the exception of *Mathurine*, where the depiction of the *monde à l'envers* refers to an authoritative view that is "outside" the text in the values of author and intended reader, the conversations that he depicts do not engage characters who are moral or intellectual equals. There is always a sharp division between wisdom and folly, and the wise character, often subtly identified with d'Aubigné himself, ably assists the garrulous fool to reveal his ineptitude. The Prudent is treated with some respect, but he is a rash and impetuous individual who values his own interest more than that of the Reformed church, and finds himself constantly on the defensive. Faeneste's discourse ironically strips away the facade of appearances he tries to create. The verses he carries about thinking that they support his cause do exactly the opposite and the duels that should demonstrate his courage display cowardice and self-deception. Finally, his preference for *mots honoravles* shows the ease with which he separates *verba* from *res*.

While the polemical aspects of the dialogue establish who is right and who is wrong, d'Aubigné never allows his interlocutors to resolve all the conflicts that are raised in the course of their conversation. The Modeste fails in his attempt to reconcile the Ferme and the Prudent, and their quarrel is ultimately resolved by the deus ex machina decision of the Assembly at Privas. Mathurine and Du Perron settle their personal differences, but this does not affect the broader conflict between Protestantism and Catholicism. Faeneste and Enay, as their names indicate, represent irreconcilable differences. The unending conflict between them is developed in the dialogue and set in a metaphysical context by the triumphal processions that close book 4. Here it is apparent that Faeneste's principles are those of the damned while Enay stands with the elect:

> Or ca, Monsieur le Baron, voys voyez la diversité de ces tableaus; de quelle bande aimeriez vous mieux estre?—F. Cap Sant Arnaud! J'aimerois vien mieux parestre dans le triomphe et dans la felicitai.— E. Et moy y estre veritablement.   (830)

> [Now, Monsieur le Baron, you see the diversity of these tableaux; in which group would you prefer to be?—F: By Saint Arnaud! I'd much prefer to appear in triumph and felicity.—E: And I to be there truly].

As a satirist and a Calvinist, d'Aubigné depicts the enduring struggle between good and evil, or what Alvin Kernan (1965) describes in *The Plot of Satire* as the inevitable opposition between the "primal energy of dullness and the powers which oppose its progress" (18).

D'Aubigné's dialogues are also consistently dramatic. Even though Le Modeste reports what he has heard, d'Aubigné minimizes indirect discourse and arranges for his interlocutors to address one another directly. In *Mathurine* and *Faeneste* the dramatic format is combined with formal and thematic interest in theater. While there may be an underlying philosophical issue, dialogue in these texts is motivated by personal grievances or by objects in the environment and accompanied by bits of stage "business." Mathurine threatens Du Perron with her club, and we are allowed to "see" Faeneste's gestures as he speaks or walks:

> Ye met lou coude sur tavle, l'oureille dans la paume, ye me ride lou front, you vranle la teste quatre vonnes fois, et puch addressant ma parole au haut vout. . . .   (693)

> Pour bous dire, ye ne marche pas en bourgeois ni en recoulé; ye bai un peu de grabitai, trainant une yamve à la cadence de la teste, comme font tous les galands hommes.   (716)

> [I put my elbow on the table, lean my ear on my palm, wrinkle my forehead, shake my head a good four times and then, speaking out loud . . .

> To speak frankly, I don't walk like a bourgeois or a humble religious; I move with a bit of gravity, drawing one leg along in cadence with my head, like all the other galant gentlemen.]

For the Baron as for Mathurine, moreover, life itself is theater and it is incumbent upon the individual to conform to the established roles of courtier or *convertisseur*.

To say that d'Aubigné's dialogues are characterized by dramatic format and polemical techniques or that they deal with enduring moral conflict is to recognize some formal consistency, but it is not possible to understand his concept of the genre without taking into consideration the development that occurs as he progresses from the *Caducée* to satire, and from short single issue texts to the larger and more universal *Faeneste*. The transition shows that his attitude toward dialogue was flexible and that he did not adhere rigorously to any particular classical or contemporary model. It also indicates that he skillfully adapted his dialogues to specific occasions and intentions. The *Caducée*, which addresses a delicate politico-religious issue, displays the most conservative format. As a meditation on the relationships between appearance and reality set in a comico-satiric mode, *Faeneste* exhibits a more complicated structure. The complexity is evident in d'Aubigné's initial references to *dialogues*, *avantures*, and *bourdes vrays*. While they suggest the incorporation of narrative elements, *bourdes* are not in themselves inimical to generic dialogue. Humor is, after all, a component of Platonic dialogue and a major topic of discussion in the *Cortegiano*. *Avantures* poses more difficulties because they imply not only narration, but the kind of action that is normally excluded from generic dialogue. *Faeneste* is thus poised on the frontier between ideas in action and embodied action. On the one hand, the Baron's numerous adventures evoke the comic novel. On the other hand, the symbolic function of the interlocutors— Faeneste (Appearançe) and Enay (Being) constantly reminds the reader of the connection between *avantures* or *contes* and the ideological orientation of the text. Still, there is singularly little in the way of Tasso's *ragionamenti* in *Faeneste* and, as we have seen, there are times in books 3 and 4 when the Baron is not present or the tension between the interlocutors dissipates and the reader witnesses scenes of good-natured storytelling. On these occasions d'Aubigné slips from dialogue to dialogism and from dialogue as genre to dialogue as a supporting structure for narrative. This movement is facilitated by the lack of any consistent theory or praxis among French writers of dialogue, and consequently the absence of any strongly determined horizon of expectations on the part of the reader. French dialogists with a philosophical orientation—Guy de Brués, Pontus de Tyard, Louis Le Caron—created their own versions of Platonic or Ciceronian models.[16] Des Périers cultivated a strict imitation of Lucian in the *Cymbalum mundi*, while Rabelais provided innovative, farcicophilosophical dialogues in the *Tiers Livre*. Polemists and storytellers contributed a variety of dialogical forms that combined argumentation, social observation, comedy, and *contes*.

Reflecting this generic diversity, *Faeneste* draws upon the sixteenth-century satiric dialogue, the *conteur* tradition, and the emerging novel. Indeed, novelization as Bakhtin (1981) describes it, is a convenient way of accounting for the transformations of dialogical function that occur in the later books of *Faeneste*: "In the process of becoming the dominant genre, the novel sparks the renovation of all other genres, it infects them with its spirit of process and inconclusiveness. It draws them ineluctably into its orbit precisely because this orbit coincides with the basic direction of the development of literature as a whole" (7). Given the variety of d'Aubigné's dialogues—variety that is both a sign of apprecia-

16. Mustapha Bénouis (1976) reviews the French philosophical dialogue in the sixteenth century. Kushner includes in her articles (see note 4) some discussion of poetic and polemical works as well.

tion for the rich potential of the genre and a desire to go beyond the limits it imposes—this transformation is not surprising. In each of his dialogues d'Aubigné engages in subtle flirtation with a related genre, with narrative and debate for the *Caducée*, farce for *Mathurine*, novel and *conte* for *Faeneste*. In the latter he succeeds gradually in working through the constraints, in liberating dialogue from itself.

EVA KUSHNER

❦ Epilogue

The Dialogue of Dialogues

Research is a dynamic process in which many minds may be
engaged simultaneously, for different reasons and from different
viewpoints, until a convergence occurs and results coalesce. This
book is the result of the research of several individuals who happen
to have agreed that it is time to reexamine the situation of the
dialogue in sixteenth-century French literature. It fully accepts
the mood of epistemological questioning that currently characterizes literary studies, which means that its authors are fully conscious of the instability of all definitions and all traditional historical categories. Their methods are inductive. They are also aware
that a study of the dialogue cannot be devoid of subjective invest-
ment. One can, of course, try simply to echo the concepts of the
sixteenth-century writers themselves; but one soon realizes that
these concepts require interpretation, not only because texts from
the distant past always require interpretation, but because the
massive use of the dialogue by Renaissance writers did not and
could not always be fully aware of its collective *episteme*. By and
large, they were impressed by the capacity of the dialogue to imitate, in both senses current then: imitating classical texts of similar form, and imitating actual life situations. They were less consistently conscious of seizing upon what strikes us most in the
dialogue today: its potential for imagining, confronting, and addressing the Other. Yet it is that dimension that accounts for the
continued importance of the study of the Renaissance dialogue,
inasmuch as the very concept of the Renaissance in Western society implies both an expansion and a fragmentation of man's vision

of the world. It should be observed, however, that here such a renewal is hypothesized, not affirmed. It would indeed be most attractive to be able to consider the Renaissance as the age (or at least *an* age) of dialogue in which the "colloque continu des humanistes" served in practice (as it might serve now toward our historical understanding of it) as model for the discussion of divergence. But for that hypothesis to be viable two conditions would have to be fulfilled: first, that dialogue as a discursive form consistently coincide with unrestrained discussion; and second, that such discussion occur by means of the dialogue form in the Renaissance era significantly more, and in a significantly different way, than in the previous and perhaps even in the following era.

Did dialogue permit unrestrained discussion? Or is it the case that we, in the twentieth century, simply tend to credit it with that capacity, and link it with a certain image of the Renaissance mentality? The answer should come from research, rather than from a priori views of the matter. Let us only say at the outset that in our collective view a transformation did occur in the nature of the dialogue, a transformation that bears witness to a change in mentality; but that in order to evaluate that change we must carefully trace the horizon of possibilities open to the sixteenth-century writer and reader. In other words, with our contemporary preconceptions about dialogue, it is all too easy to overstate the case, and at the same time to understate the importance of the degree of change that did occur. For the linguist, dialogue is an everyday occurrence consisting of an exchange of utterances. To delve into the linguistic research on dialogue (and monologue, its obverse) is to realize its linkage with the nature of language itself, with the production and communication of meaning, with the conditions of validity for statements. This realization, in turn, introduces a fruitful but dizzying complexity into what appears as a simple matter: namely, that what is known as the "literary" dialogue has everyday dialogue as its referent. In other words, the relationship between the literary dialogue and its everyday referent is far from simply being one of embellished, artful, organized rendition of a past conversation. Any single utterance is (or is not) already dialogic by dint of recognizing the Other who is about or might be about to receive it. What dialogue does is to formalize the pattern of reciprocal response. Herein lies the commonality of "literary" dialogue and "mere" dialogue: transmission is problematic, so much so in fact that it is what spurs on and on the dialogue. By the same token, then, we are dealing with three rather than two valences of the concept of dialogue, that is, not only with the everyday or historical occurrence and its textual rendition, but also with the unuttered and unwritten "dialogue" of consciences that transpires as a hope in German existentialisms and as a reality in Bakhtin.

It might be a temptation to project this latter concept onto a history of the Renaissance dialogue, in an attempt to show that the prolonged period of forced agreement on matters of faith and life that prevailed in the Middle Ages succumbs to an explosion of individualisms (Luther's famous pronouncement as he faced the Diet of Worms could serve as the foundational cry of this movement); and that the Renaissance dialogue ushers in an era of clarified communication among individuals who no longer share a unitary vision, and who therefore grasp with nostalgia and passion at any opportunity to demonstrate kinships among one another's visions. Indeed, the Renaissance abounds in opportunities to recognize, and attempt to imagine, other possible worlds.

But do we know to what extent it was possible for the individual self, the fashioning of whom has received much attention in recent years, to opt decisively, or even hesitatingly, for an alternative vision? The history of the Renaissance dialogue holds part of the answer to this question; for this reason, our inquiry cannot limit itself to establishing what did and did not belong to dialogue as a literary kind, or to what was or was not appropriate to it. It has to do with a certain representation of the process of searching for truth and of validating it. The corpus of texts entirely written in dialogue form in France and other European countries is a vast one and certainly warrants independent inquiry, not on the basis of any unbending conviction about genre limits, but on the basis of theoretical and practical consistency. There is no reason, however, not to examine texts of which dialogue is a part rather than the whole, such as Marguerite de Navarre's *Heptaméron*, where it frames the narratives. The relevant link among all the texts we are studying is that a problem, a situation, an aspect of knowledge is examined there by two or more actors using direct discourse. There are other ways in which such adventures of ideas can be reported. Rabelais's *Third Book*, in which Panurge goes on a truth quest about his marriage, includes interventions by numerous characters, representing professions, institutions, and beliefs, all embedded in the novel in the form of indirect discourse, to convey the plurality of possible answers. In the *Apologie de Raymond Sebond* Montaigne confronts philosophical voices among themselves to show how one affirmation challenges another; the essay form requires that the interaction of voices be internalized and woven together in retrospect, while the dialogue form endows each voice with a fictional existence and allows the reader to follow the entire course of the argument.

This minimal fictionality, which divides the expression of argument among two or more characters rather than reports it in a more didactic (or differently didactic) manner, had great attraction for Renaissance writers. It created a theater of ideas through which to communicate with the reader, and undoubtedly to act upon the reader, with maximum immediacy: it combined, or so it was thought, efficiency of communication with the elegance of an art form. Undoubtedly, the fact that this form had been widely practiced in classical antiquity is a major reason for its popularity in the Renaissance. Three main traditions flow from the ancients: that of Plato, Cicero, and Lucian of Samosata. The distinction between the first two models is a crucial one for our inquiry. It has not always been made clearly, since both Platonic and Ciceronian dialogue function in a mode of "semantic concord," according to Lubomir Dolezel's (1977) expression. In Plato's own dialogues, especially the Socratic ones, and regardless of the number of speakers, one voice dominates and gradually overcomes objections until harmony is attained. The maieutic method acts as foil for the reality of monological discourse in that Socrates claims to elicit ideas that were dormant in the mind of the inquirer, but the concept of innate ideas itself guides the discourse toward its conclusion. The semantic concord reached in Platonic dialogues tends to be one in which a dominant voice obtains the final agreement. This does not mean that other voices are not heard—indeed, often other voices are given substantial hearing— yet access to speech is unequal. Pontus de Tyard's first two dialogues, *Le Solitaire premier* (1552) and *Le Solitaire second* (1555), are very representative of that kind of semantic concord. In both the Solitaire, Tyard's fictional persona, is the dispenser of wisdom and acts as teacher and guide to Pasithée, on matters of poetics in the first dialogue and of music in the second. The presence of an important female character is the exception, rather than the rule, among the midcentury philosophical dialogues in France. In this connection Tyard follows Leo Hebraeus's *Dialoghi d'amore* (1551), where both Philo and Sophia are inner voices discussing love, with the female voice embodying a female, that is, more intuitive and desire-oriented principle. Tyard's Pasithée conforms to the principle of mimesis, so highly prized by the Renaissance dialogue writers: she resembles, indeed she is, the mysterious lady extolled in the poems of the *Erreurs amoureuses*, contemporaneous with the Solitaires. She exhibits the cultural interests, and the humanistic knowledge, of certain elite women of her time. Nevertheless, in the two conversations with the Solitaire she plays the role of learner; her access to speech in the discussion is limited in consequence, although it is active in that her questions constitute turning points, and the episodes in which she attracts attention to the melancholy personality of the Solitaire, or to herself as seeker of knowledge but friend only in the purest sense, serve as interludes among the long expository passages. It is precisely those long expository passages uttered by the mentor that generally characterize the didactic dialogues following the Platonic model.

In comparison, the more "Ciceronian" dialogues, similarly characterized by semantic concord, offer their various actors a much fairer share of access to speech. Rather than the triumph of one voice over the other, the goal of the Ciceronian dialogue is that the problem be argued with fairness on all sides; the Ciceronian dialogue purports to "in utramque partem disserere." In Pasquier's *Monophile* (1554), one of the many dialogues dealing with the nature of love, two extreme viewpoints, that of Monophile who believes in a lifelong, single-minded, spiritual and physical commitment to one mate, and that of Philopole who defends a multiplicity of experiences and relationships, both sides are given the opportunity to expose their views, argument by argument, in an organized manner.

Any typology of the Renaissance dialogue that may be established will be lacking in some respects, and our distinction between the "Platonic" and the "Ciceronian" model is equally vulnerable. The more so since, as K. J. Wilson (1985) reminds us in his *Incomplete Fictions*, Cicero's model is after all a rhetorical modification of Plato's. Suffice it to say that both tendencies are amply represented in the French dialogue of the sixteenth century. But

what is of major interest to the collaborators of this volume is not
the typology itself (which at any rate must also take into account
a third type of dialogue, that represented in classical antiquity by
Lucian of Samosata) but the underlying tension between the closed
and the open, the "monological" and the "dialogical." It is our
view that the rhetorical evolution of the Renaissance dialogue, for
reasons deeply embedded in the evolution of mentalities, is toward
the breaking up or at least the nuancing of the static, the monolithic, the closed. The reader will realize that I am attempting
here to avoid any simplistic evolution-oriented statement, especially one that would oppose a "Medieval" to a "Renaissance"
worldview sharply distinct from each other and demonstrating a
forward march toward the intellectual emancipation of humanity.
What is exactly the case, however, is that the body of texts we are
examining, and which consists of samples of a far larger corpus,
shows how, in fits and starts, inquiry fictitiously involving a self
and another (or others) embodies the process of internalizing alternative visions. The point is not to ascribe chronological starting
points and final ends, but to show that the process is occurring.

Within the doxographic literature of humanism, and more generally that of the early modern era, the dialogue can, therefore, be
designated as a body of texts whose special function it is (although
a text or group of texts may also have multiple other functions)
to help along organized discussion by representing it mimetically
while also internalizing its thought processes. The "Platonic" and
the "Ciceronian" model form, together, a spectrum within which
classes of texts can be differentiated according to the mode of argumentation that occurs in them, and especially the manner in
which the final consensus is obtained.

In this perspective, Donald Gilman's contribution to this volume blazes a new path in two complementary ways. First, he has
brought together the theoretical literature of the Renaissance itself
about the Renaissance dialogue. Previous attempts to do this have
tended to paraphrase the Renaissance theorists who wrote specifically about the dialogue (Tasso, Speroni, Sigonius, Erasmus and so
on) or to infer from the major poetics of classical antiquity, mostly
reading between their lines, what the dialogue ought to be and
do. In broad terms, to follow Donald Gilman's exploration is to
discover that not only has he combined these concerns, but that,
second, he has also helped us to understand the choices that lay

before the writers and readers of dialogues; and the fact that these choices related to the expansion of what we might call the emphymematic field within rhetoric. What are the fields, and topics, where didactic persuasion continues to obtain? And those where there may actually be an alternative (or several alternatives) to be debated? One of Gilman's major contributions is to lead us chronologically through the theories of dialogue in a way that shows the consideration of (other) possibles to be increasingly the case. I would go as far as saying that it is the pursuit of this development that lends unity to Gilman's chapter, and more generally to our common inquiry. For the dialogue corpus itself is most diverse both in subject matter and in technique. Its apparent unity stems from the distribution of direct discourse among various characters, a fragile unity as soon as one considers the immense difference between dialogues that are catechistic and those that are truly philosophical, especially those that take the form of banquets, or again those that amount to dramatic sketches. Yet the division between Platonic and Ciceronian dialogues cuts across and goes beyond this diversity, and so does the parallel distinction, which Gilman follows from Diogenes Laertius on, between the type of inquiry that aims at "training the mind," and the peirastic one that serves controversy and debate, and tends to undo the original proposition. This division follows that made by Aristotle in the *Sophistical Refutations*, between eristic and peirastic debates, those that seek to demonstrate the irrefutable and those that speculate and inquire. We are indebted to Gilman's sequential account of the way in which sixteenth-century theory of dialogue becomes more and more fond of the spirit of inquiry characteristic of the latter. But it was necessary first of all to point out that beyond matters of genre definition and genre typology (whether in classical antiquity, in the Renaissance, or today) the question arises of the epistemological function for which the dialogue served as introduction, or perhaps as foil. More and more, certainty eludes sixteenth-century thinkers, until it is seen with Montaigne that it is unattainable except perhaps by reaccepting tradition, or by consensus.

Hence the importance of a form that lays stress upon itself as a communicative form in the very process of creating that which is being communicated. Of course, any genre was and still is replete with communicative codes and signs; in the case of the dialogue, however, this stress on the process of communication demands, in order to produce its maximum effect, a minimal degree of fictionality; often, the only diegesis is in the progression of the argument. What the Renaissance theorists emphasized—Sigonius especially—is that despite these constraints the dialogue is alive and well inasmuch as its specific poetics is admitted, in the same way as aesthetic constraints were actually thought to benefit the sonnet, or the tragedy. Imitation of life (in this case lively though usually orderly discussion), decorum (in this case, often, characters reflecting, or refracting, the ideas they defend), verisimilitude, *enargeia*—such are some of the main elements that the major classical poetics have transmitted to the dialogue because they were already present in the dialogues of classical antiquity.

Our distinction between a Platonic and a Ciceronian model, and Gilman's distinction, derived from an in-depth analysis of the Renaissance theories of dialogue, between the purely expository, or dialectical, and the argument-examining dialogue, refer far more to the structure of the process of argumentation than to its poetic quality: Plato's own dialogues are, in that sense, deceptively dramatic. The more lively and persuasive the process of contradiction, the more resounding the final victory of what we know to be the auctorial voice. In other words, the appearance of liveliness, of naturalness, of sociability is a powerful rhetorical weapon that can be present in any type of dialogue. What may appear as an examination of argument sometimes barely disguises a "match-winning" situation and a relentlessly didactic attitude.

This remains true when dialogue approximates drama, as is the case in the Lucianic model, characterized by semantic discord and by a conflict of words and worlds. Cathy Yandell, in her essay on Tahureau, shows that contradiction, provocation, and sarcasm announce closure and a different kind of didacticism so that in the case of Tahureau at least, it cannot be said that the satirical approach clears the air, destroys preconceptions, and allows a new, prejudice-free start. On the contrary: in Tahureau's *Dialogues* access to speech is doubly unequal, since the Democritic's interventions far outweigh, in length and fierceness of attack, the arguments of the Cosmophile, who ultimately becomes a witness to the veracity of his attacker's utterances. But does that mean that satire and dialogue are indeed incompatible? In asking this question we should remember that what is at stake is not the tracing of genre limits—the kind of question that literary historians often ask in retrospect, while the production of works thrives on the transgression of limits—but the coexistence of different modes within a work. In his discussion of the origins of the dialogue Bakhtin (1981) posits the ultimate unity of the Platonic tradition, in the widest sense, and the Menippean. Obviously, his criteria are not those of sixteenth-century poetics, or of twentieth-century genre theory in a narrow sense, since this claim is made in the context of establishing the dialogicity of the novel: the characters in the novel must be freed of the subjectivity of the author so as to develop into other personalities whom the author can truly confront (this phase of Bakhtin's thought has been likened to the resistance Sartre opposes to Mauriac's authoritarian treatment of his own characters). Bakhtin considers that the Menippean tradition does give a voice to that which is uneasily, imperfectly, or never voiced in that it reverses (by carnivalization) the demands of authority. In that case, it is the dominated voice that is fictionally made to be heard. This means, then, that satire can assist dialogicity, and even that it itself assumes the format of dialogue, when a radically Other voice is thus made manifest.

Yandell sketches out an opposition between the general aspirations of the sixteenth-century dialogue and what Tahureau actually does: she rightly points out that in Tahureau's *Dialogues* the voice of the Democritic is privileged both formally and philosophically, on one issue after another. Satire is a heavy weapon. However, the "dialogicity" of the dialogue also operates intertextually. That is, the two voices within Tahureau's text echo and systematize others among which Tahureau makes a radical choice, a choice by which many of the most favored "prises de position" of humanist writers are turned around. For example, the Democritic's attitude toward women clearly contradicts that of Pontus de Tyard in his poetry, in the preface to the *Solitaire premier*, and in the latter text as well as the *Solitaire second*: in both dialogues there is a learned woman protagonist, although her voice could not exactly be described as dominant. Or again, the manner in which the Democritic ridicules dancing evidently jars with the tradition of *Il Cortegiano* and for that matter with the practice of contemporary courts.

In other words, satire as practiced by Tahureau does exactly what Yandell says it does; yet the wise reader would be able to detect the reason for the Democritic's shockingly easy victory in each argument, namely, that it is a reversal of the situation that dominates in the real world of the courts, close to the royal power and to the nobility. In that sense, we could say that Bakhtin's claim (1963, 151–69) concerning the final oneness of the Platonic and the Menippean example is not uprooted here, but, on the contrary, accomplished. The semantic discord that the satirical model carries with it unseats the establishment, prestige, values that have remained traditional, or new ones that are in fashion. Laughter, if satire can be allied with humorous and comical elements, can be cathartic. In Tahureau's text we are seeing something of the obverse side of philosophical, Platonically oriented dialogues. Although Tahureau's text was published in 1565, his death occurred in 1555. This means that the latest possible date for the composition of the *Dialogues* was the latter date and that they were therefore contemporaneous with several philosophical dialogues expressing, generally speaking, worldviews much closer to that of the Cosmophile than of the Democritic: Tyard's two *Solitaire* (1552 and 1555), Pasquier's *Monophile* (1554), more specialized than Tahureau's dialogues in the subject of love but on that subject opposing a realistic and an idealistic stance, as does Tahureau, Le Caron's *Dialogues* (1556), and those of Guy de Brués (1557). Tyard published four more dialogues after Tahureau's death (*Discours du tems, de l'an et de ses parties*, 1556; *Le Premier Curieux* and *Le Second Curieux*, 1557; and *Mantice*, 1558). Chronologically, in this dialogue of dialogues as I have called it elsewhere, the context of Tahureau's text can be narrowed down to Tyard's *Solitaires* and to Pasquier's *Monophile*. But that is precisely the grouping that would call for the integration of Tahureau's *Dialogues* within itself, not as an imperfect example of what the philosophical dialogue ought to be, but as a perfect example of what it ought not to be. In other words, we are dealing with the antidialogue of the group. In this perspective, Yandell's analysis of the closed character of the argumentation staged by Tahureau helps us to understand how easily the sheer dialogue form can become a tool for uncompromising and reductive reasoning parading as dialogue because of the distribution of speech among actors.

Whether, under these conditions, such a satirical dialogue belongs to our corpus is a matter of criteria. I would opt for an affirmative answer because it completes the grouping by showing it as what in all likelihood the author intended it to be: the antidote, just as anti-Petrarchism was the antidote of Petrarchism at the time (and on the subject of women, it is indeed made part of the scene). Nobody, except perhaps Bakhtin for the reason explained above, would regard the Menippean features of such a text as part of an integrative philosophical tradition; but it may be admitted that a genre generates its antiexamples. Apart from matters of classification, the important thing is that the satirical use of a genre is a form of reflection upon it.

In Tahureau's text this interpretation would also point to consistency between the rhetorical closure prevailing on all topics except religion, and the absence of a final pronouncement on the Christian religion, which is in turn upheld and ridiculed in several passages. In Lucian's dialogue nothing evades the sharp eye and pen of the satirist, let alone the gods, to the apparent ridiculing of whom the whole set is devoted. The ambiguous nature of the religious discussion in Tahureau's text, which is adroitly shown by Yandell, is in no way inconsistent with the satirical praxis of dialogue writers inspired by Lucian.

Here we might think, by way of comparison, of Bonaventure des Périers's *Cymbalum mundi* (1537), characterized by the multiplicity and variety of entities entering upon the stage, and enlivening the scene in such a way that remarks are made, but no conclusions drawn: its bite comes from expressing the scandalous, the uncanny, the laughable, the contradictory. When that is done, no systematic refutation is needed. The Lucian model not only permits, but encourages, rapid shifts in focus. Argumentation is disrupted. The reader is kept alert by the nonlinearity of it all. It cannot be denied that the end result appears to be, if we consider for example the *Dialogues of the Gods*, a scathing satire of the inhabitants of Olympus. Or could it be that the satire is aimed at the common representation of the deity? The lack of consensus, in recent decades, regarding the interpretation of Bonaventure des Périers's *Cymbalum mundi* amounts to a demonstration of the indecision that the Lucianic model makes possible in the mind of readers. Is the *Cymbalum* a profoundly anti-Christian text, according to Lucien Febvre's (1942) hypothesis? It could be, if Mercury represents Jesus Christ, and more especially if Bonaventure discovered and believed Celsus by means of his reading of Origen's *Contra Celsum*. But again, one could easily go along with Peter Nurse's (1967) hypothesis, according to which what is indicted in the *Cymbalum* is human weakness, in a spirit of evangelism, with Greek mythology playing an expressive rather than a theological part in the dialogues. Analysis has shown that their deep structure bears witness to the latter interpretation; but the very necessity to search for such latent meanings demonstrates that there is no simple way to determine the nature of the dominant, let alone the auctorial, voice in this work; and that therefore satirical dialogue, in this case also, does not stifle the examination of alternatives, even if it has to bury it beneath the surface.

The *Dialogues* of Le Caron, analyzed by Joan Buhlmann, are at the very center of what we have termed the dialogue of dialogues occurring among French writers of the middle of the sixteenth century. In comparison with Pontus de Tyard, whose dialogues have attracted much scholarly attention, not the least because of the effectively academic role attributed to them by such historians as Frances Yates (1947) and Robert J. Sealy (1981), Le Caron is a less often studied figure. Why he only completed one of the four projected volumes of dialogues announced in the first volume is a matter of conjecture. Competition was keen; one way of being competitive was to withdraw from fields already occupied by others in order to devote oneself to a field more one's own. It could also be true that Le Caron, who was no more than twenty years old when he wrote the *Dialogues*, subsequently decided to concentrate on law, his life's work.

At any rate, the volume of dialogues Le Caron did write embodies, from a thematic viewpoint, his response to some of the principal problems posed by Greek philosophy, as did his earlier works, *La Claire* and *La Philosophie*; all three works privilege the active and social in relation to the contemplative and theoretical. Life's main goal is wisdom; it is in the name of wisdom that Le Caron will focus on social roles: that of the philosopher, that of the king, that of the king's counselor, that of the orator, and that of the poet. The values debated in the *Dialogues* converge toward bringing the acquisition, organization, and application of knowledge to bear upon the well-being of the human community. Buhlmann shows the two innovative—and interrelated—aspects of Le Caron's *Dialogues* in relation to our inquiry. Philosophically, Le Caron does not choose among the ancient philosophers; not even between Plato and Aristotle, though the very manner in which he conducts his own inquiry, drawing on both philosophers, contributes to the history of the harmonization of their two systems in the Renaissance.

In this respect, each of his five dialogues brings its own resolution to its specific problem; and it does so by using the dialogue form in its own way in comparison with the other four dialogues. Every dialogue is a somewhat different experiment, situating itself differently between the two extremes of undisguised persuasion and open discussion allowing for alternatives. While examining the question whether in each dialogue the form of the argument fits the resulting philosophical stance, Le Caron's "laboratory" can also be viewed in conjunction with that of Pontus de Tyard, especially as regards the formal progression between dialogues in their respective cases.

Buhlmann is able to show that there is indeed a pattern in the thematic disposition of the five dialogues: the first two are "courtier-prince" oriented; together they pose the questions arising from the situation of the thinker in the practical, indeed the political, world in which his wisdom and knowledge must be lived. Dialogue 3 occupies a pivotal position not only from a simply numerical point of view but, demonstrably, because in it the voice of Valton, both auctorial and Platonic, reorients and "internalizes" the discussion, which turns to the most fundamental principles underlying the wise conduct defined in Dialogues 1 and 2: the metaphysical bases of human communication in the form of poetry and rhetoric; and the nature, and ontological interrelationships, of beauty.

It would be a gross oversimplification to assert that Le Caron's itinerary from dialogue to dialogue goes from "Plato" to "Aristotle"; nor are we entitled, with respect to the formal aspects of the successive dialogues, to assert that there is a progression from the "Platonic" to the "Ciceronian" model. Le Caron is a Christian humanist who carefully sifts among the writings of the classical authors passages, viewpoints, and attitudes that have endured sufficiently to be of service in the contemporary context. The dialogue setting helps him to probe each thought, not as an absolute to be accepted or rejected, but as an element relative to a given speaker within the whole. It is as if the Platonic worldview were being tested throughout, in relation to the attention accorded to

Aristotle in philosophical circles. This is true of all five dialogues, but carried out in each of them in different manners, according to the task at hand and the consequent grouping of speakers.

Undeniably, in Dialogues 1 and 2, the social ethics of Aristotle and the civic emphasis for which social and political humanism found so much sustenance in Cicero combine to focus the discussion upon the wise conciliation of thought and action. In Dialogue 1 the conversation occurs between two actors, Le Caron and Philarète; in terms of access to speech Le Caron has the lion's share in presenting the prince, his rights and duties—especially with respect to violence, and the nature and sources of his wisdom, including of course philosophy. His discourses are lengthy, and purely expository; Philarète's role consists in asking the right questions at the right time. His interventions, however, imply that questions can and should be asked about royal authority, its foundations but also its limitations. Similarly, in Pontus de Tyard's first dialogue, the *Solitaire premier*, Pasithée's part is predominantly that of a questioner although at times she is allowed to express her own concerns as a disciple of the Solitaire and as a woman who, while not sharing his passion, worries about his well-being. This element of mimesis does little, however, to mitigate the expository nature of the dialogue: the auctorial voice is that of the male teacher, and although—intertextually with respect to Tyard's poetry and the Petrarchan tradition in general—this male teacher suggests in a number of ways that his female disciple's will dominates over his own, there is little evidence of comparable access to speech, argumentation, and authority. In Tyard's second dialogue, the *Solitaire second*, the teaching situation is even more pronounced, and the dialogue more expository: the Solitaire presents Pasithée with digests of several musicological treatises and some of Tyard's own interpretations of classical musicology. The disciple participates in making measurements and calculations, however; and a third participant arrives, Le Curieux, whose presence, even more than Pasithée's activity, announces the advent of more pluralistic thinking in the subsequent dialogues, embodied in more visibly balanced exchanges of views.

As to Le Caron's second dialogue, *Le Courtisan II, ou de la vraie sagesse, et des louanges de la philosophie*, it is more complex in form than the first dialogue: it features an animated exchange between Le Caron and the Courtier, by way of introduction, concerning the source and nature of royal authority within the state; after which, in the presence of Philarète, each of them pronounces a discourse on the relationship between wisdom and philosophy, still in the context of the state. The Courtier argues, in broad terms, that Philosophy is not indispensable to government, that the art of discourse is a means to a political end, and that the authority vested in the sovereign comes from the people and can therefore only be maintained by frequenting assiduously "la vie humaine," which is "le vrai théâtre" (52r). Le Caron, when his turn comes, argues that wisdom and wise government are based on reason, and therefore on the cultivation of philosophy which transcends the human scene. The two speeches interact only by dint of their diametrical opposition; but that, in itself, has fulfilled at least one of the necessary conditions of true discussion: that both sides be heard. The last speaker, namely Le Caron's persona, not only has the last word (just before the return to the convivial situation of a meal) but is allowed an encomiastic peroration in praise of philosophy. And yet a better balance has been achieved than in the first dialogue, which was blatantly monological. The comparison of the first two dialogues already shows, then, that Buhlmann is right when she says that Le Caron is experimenting with the dialogic form.

This becomes even more obvious with the "mise en abyme" of the third dialogue, with Valton recounting to Le Caron a conversation, which he witnessed, between Cotereau, L'Escorché, and Rabelais, who represent the Stoic, the Epicurean, and the Peripatetic stance, respectively, on the subject of tranquillity of the mind. The framing dialogue constitutes an introduction, even longer than that of the second dialogue; its subject, human nature, sets the stage for the framed dialogue, which is more specific. In the latter, attitudes are not static: Rabelais, for one, propounds a doctrine of pleasure so grounded in the life of the intellect that it virtually merges with the Peripatetic position. In other words, the characters' statements no longer merely assert: they now take into account the statements of previous speakers. There are timid signs of discussion, including promises to think of what the other speaker said, requests for further explanation, and, on the part of Rabelais, a forestalling of his interlocutors' expectation that his stance would be unconditionally Epicurean.

One can observe, from dialogue to dialogue, a progression from the social to the metaphysical (in this respect, as Buhlmann suggests, Dialogue 3 provides a transition); it is perhaps not a mere coincidence that each dialogue also manifests more interaction among the speakers so that, as Buhlmann points out, the final result takes the form of Le Caron's own humanistic synthesis, on the subject of spiritual tranquillity, of the three philosophical viewpoints formally represented.

In Dialogue 4 we find a configuration foreshadowing that which prevails throughout the *Dialogues* of Guy de Brués (1557), namely, four speakers, whose names are familiar to the readership, and who represent two points of view. Although, actantially and logically, each pair of speakers could be reduced to one voice, the mimetic effect is multiplied and diversified by the fourfold distribution of roles. In Le Caron's Dialogue 4 the conversation centers upon the nature of poetry. It might be said that both sets of speakers rely on complementary aspects of Plato's thought: Ronsard and Jodelle insist on the visionary and prophetic role of the poet and the ability of poetry to capture and represent the truth about the universe, while Pasquier and Fauchet, as "orators," see poetry as depicting human nature, with all the moral risks this entails. All four speakers contribute to the defense of poetry; they do so by extending to this subject the dichotomy between the metaphysical and the concrete level of inquiry (and the corresponding one between the realm of the ideal and that of the practical) that underpin all five dialogues, as well as Le Caron's previous works.

Dialogue 5 further diversifies speakers among themselves while also bringing the conversation to bear upon ultimate values: the subject is beauty, which leads to goodness. Three of the six speakers are women and it is one of them, Claire, who defends beauty as a spiritual quality that is grasped by the understanding and the source of which is in God, against Narcisse who sees it as a quality of the physical person, perceived by the senses. Although—as in the previous dialogue—the disquisition refers to a problem set by Plato, the handling of the discussion is seen by Buhlmann as Ciceronian in that both sides of the argument are adequately heard. Obviously Claire and Narcisse represent two extremes with respect to the concept of beauty as well as that of love. Thus, even if the rhythm of responses is not as active as that which prevails in Pasquier's *Monophile* (1554), which is entirely devoted to these questions, there is an interaction of views. I would venture to say that even the conclusion drawn by Le Caron under his own name, with all the advantages thus given the auctorial voice, reflects the contribution made by the other voices, and thus aids dialogicity, in insisting that physical beauty embodies beauty itself; in all nature, ideas are present: "rien n'est vraiment en nature, que par la participation de l'idée" (175v). Claire's opponents are not entirely wrong; they simply have not yet seen the true grounds of their passion for beauty.

As we have attempted to show, Tahureau's *Dialogues* make ironical use of the dialogue form, by showing how dialogue can be a front for incurable disagreement; and that demonstration confirms the deep intertextual link between his and Le Caron's *Dialogues*, in which disagreement is made to crystallize as a spectrum of possible attitudes, and Tyard's first two dialogues, in which the gender distinction as well as the hierarchical relationship between the two intellects leads to differentiation but stops short of disagreement. All these texts, which together with Pasquier's *Monophile* form a major part of the "dialogue of dialogues" of the midcentury, could be said to concentrate on being dialogues, that is, dramatized discussions in the sense inherited from the major classical models. Our next three sets of texts, corresponding to three other chapters of our book, enlarge not only the definition and the poetics of dialogue, but the scope of the inquiry into the nature of sixteenth-century dialogicity.

Chronologically, Marguerite de Navarre's works, analyzed by Colette Winn, precede the "dialogue of dialogues," which in some ways could be considered as a philosophical accompaniment of the poetic movement around Ronsard. The works of Catherine des Roches, studied by Ann Rosalind Jones, and those of Agrippa d'Aubigné, examined by Paula Sommers, belong to the end of the sixteenth and the beginning of the seventeenth centuries, respectively. All three groupings can be said to depart from the classical models in the situations and characters as well as the imaginary worlds they create.

It is Colette Winn's view that Marguerite de Navarre practices a "dialectic of reconciliation" of which dialogue is the preferred instrument. The queen's works in various genres all contribute to her multifaceted story of spiritual growth. Her dramas are colloquia among characters embodying various moral or religious stances; her poems, such as the *Navire*, and her dialogues, such as the *Dialogue en forme de vision nocturne*, stage debates between her own persona and a departed soul (representing, of course, debates within herself). As for her narrative work *L'Heptaméron*, its structure is such that the dialogues are far more than the framing device they are often reported to be: they involve the novellas in the debate. As Winn shows, the truth-seeking vocation of the Renaissance dialogue gradually supersedes the entertainment value of the medieval forms of debate; but in their very opposition they become inseparable, as conversation, in addition to its basic entertainment function, tends to become a philosophical tool precisely when it reaches formal perfection.

Winn's scheme is somewhat evolutionary, in that it sees Marguerite's use of the dialogue as intermediate between the medieval use of the genre and that which flowers in Renaissance humanism, with its orderly battles of ideas. And indeed, it is true that the *Dialogue en forme de vision nocturne* and the *Navire* borrow from the *disputatio* and *conflictus* tradition. But in doing so they serve a highly personal vision which, as it stages the confrontation between the earthbound and the spiritual, also seeks to transcend their dichotomy, be it by silencing reason. Although the debate seems to be between two irreducible options, of which one—in both cases the spiritual one defended by the dear departed—is clearly superior to the other, neither option totally monopolizes Marguerite's vision. Rather than to be the ultimate division of reality, Platonic dualism serves that vision as a metaphor. Here, as across the rest of the generic spectrum, we are witnessing the unfolding of Marguerite's inner drama, moment by moment.

This is not being written by way of pleading for a unique case which would then elude the imprint of chronology. Yes, Marguerite's dialogues and her dialoguelike works precede the wave of expository, didactic, and argumentative dialogues of the midcentury that were discussed above. Yes, her works reflect specific personal situations (as do those of her greatest feminine predecessor, Christine de Pisan) rather than abstract truth seeking and truth validating. This is not, however, because she is unaware of the classical models or not yet ready to adopt them, but because in her vision theories are projected back into life. In this respect, the animated world of the *Heptaméron* diversifies the two major voices of the *Dialogue* and of the *Navire*, without losing sight of their opposition. The cast of characters satisfies the aesthetic need for psychological diversity, but does not betray the author's basic commitment to expressing the dichotomy between physical and spiritual love.

For this reason, in my view, the *Heptaméron*, far from being isolated from the midcentury texts as their nonphilosophical prefiguration, is not only part of the set, but may well be its intertext. There is a striking kinship between, on the one hand, Marguerite's Hircan and Pasquier's Cosmophile and, on the other, between her Dagoucin and his Philopole. Furthermore, Dagoucin's view of life and love bears an indisputable resemblance to that of the Solitaire, Pontus de Tyard's literary persona from 1549 to 1555. All these relationships could be described in greater detail. Our purpose here is merely to point out that the work of Marguerite de Navarre, as well as its relationship to the history of the dialogue in France, are not a separate chapter but part and parcel of the "dialogue of dialogues" of the midcentury, playing in it a role of their own.

Winn shows, in relation to the works she examines, the manner in which Marguerite's text often attracts attention to itself as dialogue. In the first place, she reverses the balance between dialogue and novella so as to privilege the former; both elements possess fictionality, the difference being that fictionality seems coincident with narrative but has to be both created and *shown* to have been created when it comes to dialogue. What Winn helps us discover is that the world of characters Marguerite has constructed in the dialogues has a theatricality of its own, despite its occasional imperfections and the artificial character for which the modern reader may fault it. What is more important is that, linked to and by dialogues, the novellas themselves are drawn into dialogue so that the reader must relate their multiple, often contradictory messages to one another and finally to the central quest.

If polyphony is the quality of a fictional world in which voices are not reduced to one another, then the *Heptaméron* does possess that quality; all the more so since the exchange of arguments has been neither sequential nor systematic and since no ultimate philosophical conclusion is reached at the end (the nonclosure of the *Heptaméron* does not relate to its unfinished state alone).

The reader is presented with a number of choices all along the way, and it is in this sense that Marguerite's handling of the dialogue is Ciceronian.

It would be a mistake, however, to credit Ciceronian reliance on reason with this result entirely; it is at least partly due to what Winn characterizes as the theatricality of the *Heptaméron*, which precludes heavy systematicity. After all, from a formal point of view, Marguerite can look back on the *Decameron* and the *Cortegiano* for lighthearted yet masterfully oriented conversation models. In the *Heptaméron*, however, this formal choice is, in my view, the consequence of an ontologically based choice of openness. The dialogues of the *Heptaméron* are acting out the encounter between Platonism and evangelical Christianity—not argument by argument but person to person and situation to situation, in best *opera aperta* fashion.

Both Oysille and Parlamente are acutely sensitive to the reality and character traits of each particular person. The Christianity of these two women is not a philosophical clone of Platonism nor is it its abstract opponent; at this point in the history of the humanistic dialogue, it constitutes a new fact. It is because the love of a personal God so radically transcends the victory of reason that the *Heptaméron* factors in the silencing of reason, as did the *Cymbalum mundi*. Reconciliation must be of hearts, as well as of minds. Opposition is far more than contradiction: it involves anger and power-play.

This is precisely why Winn's analyses of personal valences and relationships in the *Navire*, and their transformations, are so revealing. The dialectic between transcendence and the sleeping soul, even when personified by the soul of the king and that of Marguerite, still has the simplistic ring of the *conflictus*. It is only when the complex web of latent relationships (lover/beloved, master/disciple, king/subject) is brought to light that we begin to understand the illusory nature of that simplicity. The spiritual male voice is quite violent in its drive to pacify the bereaved soul; it makes use of physical images and emotions to characterize and impose its spirituality. True, the author is manipulating both voices, including that of the dominant Other, and so it could be said that she espouses the violent and impatient drive to subdue the flesh, the casting of herself as woman into the more earthy role, the illogicality of describing spiritual union in terms of physical love, and even the ultimate inability of spirit to assume its dominant role, as realities to which she responds. Ultimately, the soul's journey toward God is bound to the history of its struggles with its own resistance to spirituality, and with the souls of others. In using dialogue as metaphor of this struggle, Marguerite rejoins the tradition of Saint Augustine's *Soliloquy* and Petrarch's *Secretum*.

Indeed, her approach to the dialogue is consistently an exploratory one, using form as an instrument for probing the adequacy of the word to communicate reality. Hence Winn's conclusion about the *Heptaméron*: there is nothing negligent or formally imperfect about the complicated network of dialogues and novellas responding to one another, and characters responding to one another through them. The gaps, inconsistencies, and loopholes may well be strategies to capture those that occur in humanistic communication itself. If men and women were rational, would dialogue be necessary? At any rate, our humanists continuously oscillate between appeal to reason and the extreme difficulty of following it.

When Catherine des Roches on the one hand, and Agrippa d'Aubigné on the other, arrive on the scene, that kind of humanism no longer constitutes the basis of dialogue; differences have become the order of the day, and dialogue tends to concentrate on specificities rather than to attempt reconciliations. Ann Rosalind Jones's work on Catherine des Roches breaks new ground by showing the radical change that occurred in the voice of women. Marguerite de Navarre, as well as Louise Labé in her *Débat de folie et d'amour* (1555), though they certainly speak on behalf of women in analyzing the love relationship, and attract attention in multiple ways to the situation and sufferings of women, do not make social change their prime or direct aim. Human nature, with its aspirations and its bouts of folly, is their object; men and women embody it in a way the complementarity of which is broadly seen by both authors in Neoplatonic terms. Neither of them is caught up in the superiority/ inferiority controversies. I would go as far as saying that what interests them is the nature of love rather than that of women as opposed to men.

Another difference with women dialogue writers of the previous generation also pertains to the history of the French dialogue in general: in the salons of the latter part of the century—of which Madeleine and Catherine des Roches's was one of the most famous—conversation centered upon social and moral questions of a more concrete nature than had been the case in the humanistic dialogue. They are interested in manners and mores, as will be the moralists of the seventeenth century. Should we state that women had a more decisive voice in the salon conversations because the salons were theirs? That is certainly a possibility to be kept in mind, but not to be divorced from the general evolution of mentalities toward deeper analysis of gender roles.

And toward empowerment of women as writers too. Catherine's courage in steeling herself against criticism by men and by middle-class society may be partly due to the profound solidarity that existed between her and her mother. But that alone could not explain the authority she assumes. According to Ann Rosalind Jones, the choice of the dialogue form enables Catherine to speak indirectly, "through invented characters." But her readers knew that it is the author of a dialogue who orchestrates it. Furthermore, Jones's classification of Catherine's dialogues shows a high degree of literary awareness on the part of the latter, and a profound knowledge of the traditions and conventions attached to dialogue writing. So much so in fact that the sequence of dialogue forms that Catherine chooses, and the manner in which she adopts but redirects them, demonstrates on her part the implicit will to write a new, symptomatic chapter in the history of the dialogue, and through it, to make at least a dent in the history of manners. In analyzing the five allegorical dialogues, Jones shows the feminization, and thereby the transformation, of some of the most traditional dichotomies surviving from medieval debates.

The *Dialogue de Placide et Severe* affords Catherine the opportunity of creating two male characters who will discuss women's education on her behalf indirectly, by discussing one another's positions; Severe's antieducation position is refuted by Placide and further reduced to the absurd by the lamentable performance of his wife and daughter. The unfolding of the argumentation matters as much as the final defeat of Severe, if not more so. It allows Catherine to let Severe expose all his unfounded prejudices against women, as well as the ill effects they are bound to have, given his unfavorable view of women. By the same token, through Placide's refutations, Catherine is able to turn each unfavorable possibility into a favorable one, and even to put forward exempla of educated contemporary women as opposed to those of mythology and of the Bible. In order to change Severe's stance ever so slightly, Placide has to adapt his arguments to him to some extent: for example, he points to all the advantages a man can draw from his wife's knowledge of the Bible, the law, and so on. This is also Catherine's means of coming to terms with her own fate as an educated woman: there is no easy way to claim her right to her own life-style in the abstract, for its own sake. Therefore, she will emphasize its advantages for men, and for society. Let us note the profound dialogicity of this procedure. Through Placide, Catherine is responding to the Severes of her acquaintance not only by reasserting her preferences but by taking measure of their needs, and their progress along the way.

Here, we rejoin our thoughts about Tahureau's satirical approach: semantic discord may be a complicated way to achieve mutual understanding, but a more fruitful one in the end than false harmony. Jones reminds us that both Severe and Placide are fathers discussing their daughters' education and futures; but we must note that any prospect of consensus is fractured beyond repair by Placide's outlook and behavior. The reader must realize that certain daughters are infinitely more perceptive than certain fathers. Catherine has sacrificed the false security of the father image.

The next dialogue to be discussed stages two female characters, Iris and Pasithée, daughters of Severe and Placide respectively; they will provide concrete examples of their divergent kinds of education so that the reader can assess them. The gender reversal to which Jones attracts our attention consists not only in the exclusive feminine grouping of the dialogue but also in the fact that the teaching role is attributed to Pasithée, a woman. Increasingly, women had been appearing in humanistic dialogues (for example, in Bembo's *Gli Asolani* [1505], as well as in Ridolfi's *Aretefila* [1565], and several of the dialogues discussed in this book), but they had not occupied an intellectually dominant position. Here Pasithée is not a mechanical dispenser of wisdom but a concerned and proactive instructor capable of leadership. Her very name signals a transformation, drawing attention to the fact that her namesake in Tyard's *Solitaires*, though brilliant, beautiful, and artistic, was very much a disciple and a follower vis-à-vis the Solitaire, her teacher. In teaching Iris poetic language that will enrich her conversation with her suitors, Pasithée is led to using male-authored expressions and to playfully assuming male roles in the discussion. Thus Catherine sees through the conventional language of courtship used by males; and having mastered it, she is also aware of the corresponding attitudes, and consequently able to respond to them adequately in her own life. Ultimately, although the adaptability and usefulness of the educated woman in partnership with a man was stressed throughout, it is clear that there is another option Pasithée can present to Iris, which is to become an educated and independent woman; also, she teaches her that friendship among women can be an emotionally satisfying relationship. Once again, in the case of Catherine des Roches, the dialogue is much more than a way for the author to build an argument successfully; it is an articulated response to realities within and around herself, which her male sources could not altogether have supplied.

Therefore, we have here one of the cases in which the Renaissance dialogue is at its most dialogical inasmuch as it sustains the self in the process of systematically confronting the Other (here, the male reality stripped of its stylistic devices and consequent interpersonal powers).

The case of Agrippa d'Aubigné is both major and problematic in that the dialogue, for him, appears to be a tool for ascertaining, rather than arguing for change of stance, or for consensus. D'Aubigné's poetic and historical works bespeak a vision nourished by the Bible and the classics but also by his difference and his grave solitude, as a Protestant thinker, among his contemporaries. In contrast to his practice in these genres, one of the most striking features of his dialogues is that they are humorous and light-spirited. D'Aubigné avails himself abundantly (as did Erasmus) of the cathartic function of laughter in all three dialogues studied by Paula Sommers. Clearly, he also favors adversarial rather than consensual patterns of discussion, and apparently nonsequential exchanges of words. His approach to dialogue is to provoke and stimulate. Here, we reach the limits of the usefulness of our initial distinction between the uses of "semantic concord" and "semantic discord." If semantic discord destroys so as to give free access to the unfamiliar, the unexpected, the radically Other, then for the ultimate purpose of dialogue it may be no less legitimate, perhaps more legitimate, than semantic concord. A good example of this is provided by the "dialogue de sourds" between the Ferme and the Prudent in the *Caducée*; there is no possible conclusion to this exchange of misunderstandings other than, as Sommers points out, that it demonstrates the need for reconciliation.

Mathurine et Du Perron, as well as *Les Avantures du baron de Faeneste*, factor in strong doses of theatrical fictionality. As in the case of the *Heptaméron*, this complicates the genre issue from the point of view of Renaissance thinkers, but rather completes it from our point of view, not only because we have come to understand the inherent creativeness of genre transgression, but because this helps to establish that more specifically fictional elements, and elements of argumentation proper, can very successfully combine their impact in the game of persuasion. All the more if, as in the case of the Baron, the game is aristocratically self-sustaining by the sheer pleasure it brings to its otherwise stern author. And sharing the laughter will lead to sharing the vision, and the corrective therein.

In the course of this discussion, many positive judgments were uttered about the various contributions to this book. They were not meant to be uncritical, but it was more important that they be integrative in the sense that each text had, potentially, something to say that would call forth the others. Rather than to find in this book an artificial unifying motive which would have been the desire to write a complete book about the dialogue in Renaissance France, the reader discovers in-depth analyses of significant and interrelated examples. Donald Gilman's contribution stands out as one that would have graced a work on the dialogue of any country of Europe in the Renaissance period, or better yet, a comparative work, for which he has paved the way.

WORKS CITED

Agricola, Rodolphus. *De inventione dialectica*. Edited by Joannes Mattheus Phrissemius. Paris, 1534.

Agrippa, Cornelius. *De incertitude et vanitate scientiarum* (1530). Translated as *Declamation sur l'incertitude, vanité et abus des sciences* by Louis de Mayerne-Turquet. Paris: Jean Durand, 1582.

Albistur, Maïté, and Daniel Armogathe. *Histoire du féminisme français*. 2 vols. Paris: Edition des femmes, 1977.

Almeida-Ribeiro, Cristina. "*Les Avantures du baron de Faeneste* ou l'univers baroque sous un regard satirique." *Ariane* 2 (1983): 29–41.

Ammonius. *In Praedicamenta Aristotelis commentarii*. Edited by Bartholomaeus Syvanius. Paris: Jean de Roigny, 1554.

Andrieu, Jean. *Le Dialogue antique: Structure et présentation*. Paris: Les Belles Lettres, 1954.

Aneau, Barthélémy. *Imagination poétique*. Lyons, 1552.

Aristotle. *Poetics*. Translated and edited by W. Hamilton Fyfe. 1927. Reprint. Cambridge: Harvard University Press, Loeb Classical Library, 1965.

———. *Posterior Analytics*. Translated and edited by E. S. Forster. Cambridge: Harvard University Press, Loeb Classical Library, 1960.

———. *Prior Analytics*. Translated and edited by Hugh Tredennich. 1938. Reprint. Cambridge: Harvard University Press, Loeb Classical Library, 1962.

———. *Rhetoric*. Translated by J. H. Freese. 1926. Reprint. Cambridge: Harvard University Press, Loeb Classical Library, 1947.

———. *Sophistical Refutations*. Translated and edited by E. S. Forster. 1955. Reprint. Cambridge: Harvard University Press, Loeb Classical Library, 1965.

———. *Topics*. Translated and edited by E. S. Forster. Cambridge: Harvard University Press, Loeb Classical Library, 1960.

———. "*Nicomachean Ethics*" and "*Politics*." Vol. 2, *The Complete Works of Aristotle*. Bollingen Series, no. 71. Edited by Jonathan Barnes. Princeton: Princeton University Press, 1984.

Armstrong, C. J. R. "The Dialectical Road to Truth: The Dialogue." In *French Renaissance Studies 1540–70: Humanism and the Encyclopedia*, edited by Peter Sharratt, 36–69. Edinburgh, Scotland: Edinburgh University Press, 1976.

Athenaeus. *The Deipnosophists*. 7 vols. 1937. Reprint. Translated and edited by Charles Burton Gurlick. Cambridge: Harvard University Press, Loeb Classical Library, 1950.

Aubigné, Théodore Agrippa d'. *Oeuvres complètes de Théodore Agrippa d'Aubigné*. 6 vols. Edited by Eugène Réaume and F. de Caussade. Paris: A. Lemerre, 1873–92.

———. *Oeuvres*. Edited by Henri Weber. Paris: Gallimard, 1969.

Austin, J. L. "A Plea for Excuses." 1956–57. Reprint. In *Philosophical Papers*, edited by J. O. Urmson and G. J. Warnack. 3d ed. Oxford: Oxford University Press, 1979. 175–204.

Bailbé, Jacques. "Agrippa d'Aubigné conteur." In *La Nouvelle française à la Renaissance*, edited by L. Sozzi, 653–69. Geneva: Slatkine, 1981.

———. "Quelques aspects du burlesque dans *les Avantures du baron de Faeneste*." In *Mélanges d'histoire littéraire offerts à Raymond Lebègue*, 135–45. Paris: Nizet, 1969.

———. "Rabelais et d'Aubigné." *Bibliothèque d'Humanisme et Renaissance* 21 (1959): 380–419.

Baker, M. J. "Didacticism and the *Heptameron*: The Misinterpretation of the Tenth Tale as an Exemplum." *French Review* 45, no. 3 (1971): 84–90.

Bakhtin, Mikhail M. *La Poétique de Dostoïevski*. Paris: Editions du Seuil, 1963.

———. *The Dialogic Imagination. Four Essays by M. M. Bahktin*. Texas Slavic Studies, no. 1. Translated by Caryl Emerson and Michael Holquist. Edited by Michael Holquist. Austin: University of Texas Press, 1981.

Baldassarri, Guido. "Il discorso tassiano-Dell'arte del dialogo.'" *Rassegna della letteratura italiana* 75 (1971): 92–134.

Barbaro, Francesco. *De re uxoria*. Paris: 1513, 1533. Translated as "On Wifely Duties" by Benjamin G. Kohl. In *The Earthly Republic: Italian Humanists on Government and Society*, edited by Benjamin G. Kohl and Ronald Witt, with Elizabeth B. Welles. Philadelphia: University of Pennsylvania Press, 1978.

Baridon, Silvio F. *Inventaire de la Bibliothèque de Pontus de Tyard*. Geneva: Droz, 1950.

Baumgartner, Frederic J. *Henry II King of France 1547–1559*. Durham, NC: Duke University Press, 1988.

Beaujeu, Anne de. *Les Enseignements d'Anne de France à sa fille Susanne de Bourbon* (written ca. 1505). Edited by A. M. Chazaud. Moulins: C. Des Rosiers, 1878.

Béné, Charles. "Agrippa d'Aubigné, émule de Rabelais?" In *La Nouvelle française à la Renaissance*, edited by L. Sozzi, 671–82. Geneva: Slatkine, 1981.

Bénouis, Mustapha. *Le Dialogue philosophique dans la littérature française du seizième siècle*. Paris: Mouton, 1976.

Bergson, Henri. *Le Rire*. Paris: Presses Universitaires de France, 1940.

Bèze, Théodore de. *Le Passavant*. Paris: Liseux, 1875.

Boethius. *Consolation of Philosophy*. Translated by Richard Green. Indianapolis, IN: Bobbs-Merrill, 1962.

Bouchet, Jean. *Epistres morales et familieres du Traverseur*. Poitiers, 1545.

———. *Les Triumphes de la noble et amoureuse dame et l'art de honnestement aymer*. Poitiers, 1530. In *Le Miroir des femmes, vol 1, Moralistes et polémistes au XVIe siècle*, edited by Luce Guillerm, J. P. Guillerm, Laurence Hordoir, and Marie-Françoise Piéjus, 45–50. Lille, France: Presses Universitaires, 1983.

Bourciez, Edouard. *Les Moeurs polies et la littérature sous Henri II*. Paris: Hachette, 1886.

Bowen, Barbara C. *The Age of Bluff: Paradox and Ambiguity in Rabelais and Montaigne*. Illinois Studies in Language and Literature, no. 62. Urbana: University of Illinois Press, 1972.

———. "Jacques Tahureau Revisited." *French Studies* 30 (1976): 19–27.

Bray, Bernard. "Le Dialogue comme forme littéraire au XVIIᵉ siècle." *Cahiers de l'Association Internationale des Etudes Françaises* 24 (1972): 9–29.

Bréal, Michel, and Anatole Bailly. *Dictionnaire étymologique latin*. Paris, 1886.

Breen, Quintus. "Giovanni Pico della Mirandola on the Conflict of Philosophy and Rhetoric." *Journal of the History of Ideas* 13 (1952a): 384–412.

———. "Melanchthon's Reply to G. Pico della Mirandola." *Journal of the History of Ideas* 13 (1952b): 413–26.

———. "John Calvin and the Rhetorical Tradition." *Church History* 26 (1957): 3–21.

Brewer, Daniel. "The Philosophical Dialogue and the Forcing of Truth." *Modern Language Notes* 98 (1983): 1234–47.

Brink, Charles Oscar. *Horace on Poetry*. Vol. 2: *"Ars Poetica."* Cambridge: Cambridge University Press, 1963–71.

Brués, Guy de. *The Dialogues of Guy de Brués: A Critical Edition*. Edited by Panos P. Morphos. Baltimore: Johns Hopkins University Press, 1953.

Bruni, Leonardo. *Ad Petrum Histrum dialogi*. In *Prosatori latini del Quattrocento*, edited by Eugenio Garin, 44–97. Milan, Italy: R. Ricciardi, 1952.

———. *De studiis et litteris*. Translated as "Concerning the Study of Literature: A Letter Addressed to the Illustrious Lady, Baptista Malatesta." In *Vittorino da Feltre and Other Humanist Educators*, translated and edited by William Harrison Woodward. 1897. Reprint. New York: Columbia University Teachers' College, 1963. 123–33.

Budé, Guillaume. *De L'Institution du Prince*. In *Le Prince dans la France des XVIe et XVIIe siècles*, edited by Claude Bontems, Léon-Pierre Raybaud, and Jean-Pierre Brancourt, 77–139. Paris: Presses Universitaires de France, 1965.

Busson, Henri. *Le Rationalisme dans la littérature française de la Renaissance (1533–1601)*. 1957. Reprint, Paris: Vrin, 1971.

Cambridge History of Renaissance Philosophy, edited by Charles B. Schmitt, Quentin Skinner, and Eckhard Kessler. Cambridge: Cambridge University Press, 1988.

Cameron, Keith. *Agrippa d'Aubigné*. Boston: Twayne, 1973.

Carron, Jean-Claude. "The Persuasive Seduction: Dialogue in Sixteenth-Century France." In *Contending Kingdoms: Historical, Psychological, and Feminist Approaches to the Literature of Sixteenth-Century England and France*, edited by Marie-Rose Logan and Peter Rudnitsky, 90–108. Detroit: Wayne State University Press, 1991.

Castelvetro, Lodovico. *On the Art of Poetry*. Translated and edited by Andrew Bongiorno. Binghamton, NY: Medieval and Renaissance Texts and Studies, 1984.

Castiglione, Baldassare. *The Book of the Courtier*. Translated by Charles S. Single-ton. New York: Doubleday, 1959.

Cazauran, Nicole. *L'Heptaméron de Marguerite de Navarre*. Paris: CDU and SEDES, 1976.

Celce-Murcia, Daniel. "Faeneste ou la réalisation à l'envers du héros." *Papers in Seventeenth-Century Literature* 9 (1978): 84–98.

Chambers, Ross. *Story and Situation-Narrative Seduction and the Power of Fiction*. Theory and History of Literature, no. 12. Minneapolis: University of Min-nesota Press, 1984.

Chastel, André. "L'Humanisme italien." *Bibliothèque d'Humanisme et Renaissance* 16 (1954): 374–85, especially "L'Épître et le discours," 381–85.

Cicero. *Academica*. Translated and edited by H. Rackham. 1933. Reprint. Cam-bridge: Harvard University Press, Loeb Classical Library, 1967.

———. *Brutus*. Translated and edited by G. L. Hendrickson. 1939. Reprint. Cambridge: Harvard University Press, Loeb Classical Library, 1962.

———. *De divinatione*. Translated by William Armistead Falconer. 1923. Re-print. Cambridge: Harvard University Press, Loeb Classical Library, 1964.

———. *De fato*. 2 vols. Translated and edited by H. Rackham. 1942. Reprint. Cambridge: Harvard University Press, Loeb Classical Library, 1960.

———. *De finibus bonorum et malorum*. Translated and edited by H. Rackham. 1914. Reprint. Cambridge: Harvard University Press, Loeb Classical Li-brary, 1967.

———. *De inventione*. Translated and edited by H. M. Hubbell. 1949. Reprint. Cambridge: Harvard University Press, Loeb Classical Library, 1960.

———. *De officiis*. Translated and edited by Walter Miller. New York: Mac-millan, 1913.

———. *De oratore*. 2 vols. Translated by E. W. Sutton and H. Rackham. 1942. Reprint. Cambridge: Harvard University Press, Loeb Classical Li-brary, 1960.

———. *De partitione oratoria*. Translated and edited by H. Rackham. 1942. Reprint. Cambridge: Harvard University Press, Loeb Classical Library, 1960.

———. *Letters to Atticus*. 3 vols. Translated and edited by E. O. Winstedt. 1912. Reprint. Cambridge: Harvard University Press, Loeb Classical Li-brary, 1962.

———. *Orator*. Translated and edited by H. M. Hubbell. 1939. Reprint. Cambridge: Harvard University Press, Loeb Classical Library, 1962.

———. *Tusculan Disputations*. Translated and edited by J. E. King. 1927. Re-print. Cambridge: Harvard University Press, Loeb Classical Library, 1950.

Clement of Alexandria. *The Writings of Clement of Alexandria*. 2 vols. Translated by William Wilson. Edinburgh, Scotland: Clark, 1872.

Colie, Rosalie. *The Resources of Kind: Genre-Theory in the Renaissance*. Berkeley and Los Angeles: University of California Press, 1973.

Cosentini, John W. *Fontenelle's Art of Dialogue*. New York: King's Crown Press, 1952.

Cottrell, Robert. *The Grammar of Silence. A Reading of Marguerite de Navarre's Poetry*. Washington, DC: The Catholic University of America Press, 1986.

Coulet, Henri. *Le Roman jusqu'à la Révolution*. Paris: Librairie A. Colin, 1967.

Cummins, John G. "Methods and Conventions in the Fifteenth-Century Poetic Debate." *Hispanic Review* 31 (1963): 307–23.

Dällenbach, Lucien. *Le Récit spéculaire—Essai sur la mise en abyme*. Paris: Seuil, 1977.

Daniello, Bernardino. *La Poetica*. 1536. Reprint. Munich: Wilhelm Fink, 1968.

De Guer, Charles Guerlin. "La Langue et le style d'Agrippa d'Aubigné: Étudiés dans *Les Avantures du baron de Faeneste*." *Français Moderne* 9 (1941): 241–72.

Derrida, Jacques. *Dissemination*. Translated by Barbara Johnson. Chicago: University of Chicago Press, 1981.

Des Périers, Bonaventure. *Cymbalum mundi*. Edited by Peter M. Nurse, 1958. Reprint with a new preface. Manchester, England: Manchester University Press, 1967.

Des Roches, Madeleine and Catherine. *Les Oeuvres des Mes-dames des Roches de Poëtiers, mere et fille*. Paris: Abel L'Angelier, 1578.

———. *Les Secondes Oeuvres de Mes-dames des Roches de Poetiers mere et fille*. Poitiers, France: Nicolas Courtoys, 1583.

Diller, George. *Les Dames des Roches: Étude sur la vie littéraire à Poitiers dans la deuxième moitié du XVIe siècle*. Paris: Droz, 1936.

Diogenes Laertius. *De vitis philosophorum* (1570). *Lives of the Eminent Philosophers*. 2 vols. Translated and edited by R. D. Hicks. 1925. Reprint. Cambridge: Harvard University Press, Loeb Classical Library, 1966.

Dolezel, Lubomir. "A Pragmatic Typology of Dialogue." In *Papers in Slavic Philology*, no. 1, edited by Benjamin A. Stolz, 62–68. Ann Arbor: University of Michigan Press, 1977.

Du Bellay. *La Deffence et Illustration de la langue françoyse*. Paris: Abel L'Angelier, 1549.

———. *La Deffence et Illustration de la langue françoyse*. Société de Textes Français Modernes. Edited by Henri Chamard. Paris: Nizet, 1970.

———. *Les Regrets, précédé par les Antiquités de Rome et suivi de la Défense et illustration de la langue française*. Edited by S. de Sacy. Paris: Gallimard, 1967.

Dubrow, Heather. *Genre*. New York: Methuen, 1982.

Eden, Kathy. *Poetic and Legal Fiction in the Aristotelian Tradition*. Princeton: Princeton University Press, 1986.

Elliott, Robert. *The Power of Satire: Magic, Ritual, Art*. Princeton: Princeton University Press, 1960.

Erasmus, Desiderius. *Ciceronianus*. Vol. 28, *The Collected Works of Erasmus*, edited by A. H. T. Levi. Toronto: Toronto University Press, 1986.

———. *Colloquies*. Translated by Craig R. Thompson. Chicago: University of Chicago Press, 1965.

———. *De copia*. Translated and annotated by Betty I. Knott. Vol. 24, *The Collected Works of Erasmus*. 2d ed. Edited by Craig R. Thompson. Toronto: University of Toronto Press, 1978.

———. *The Education of a Christian Prince*. Translated by Lester K. Born. New York: Columbia University Press, 1936.

Estienne, Henri. *Apologie pour Hérodote.* Paris: Lemerre, 1879.

————. *Deus Dialogues du nouveau langage françois italianizé et autrement desguizé.* Geneva: Philalèthe, 1578.

————. *Deus Dialogues du nouveau langage françois italianizé et autrement desguizé.* Paris: Lemerre, 1885.

Evans, Maurice. Introduction to *The Countess of Pembroke's Arcadia*, by Philip Sidney. New York: Penguin, 1977.

Febvre, Lucien. *Origène et Des Périers; ou l'énigme du "Cymbalum mundi."* Paris: Droz, 1942.

Ferguson, Margaret W. *Trials of Desire: Renaissance Defenses of Poetry.* New Haven: Yale University Press, 1983.

Fowler, Alastair. *Kinds of Literature: An Introduction to the Theory of Genres and Modes.* Cambridge: Harvard University Press, 1982.

Fregoso, Antonio Phileremo. *Riso di Democrito e pianto di Heraclito.* Milan, Italy: I. A. Sciuaenzeler, 1511.

Freud, Sigmund. *Le Mot d'esprit et ses rapports avec l'inconscient.* Paris: Gallimard, 1979.

Frye, Northrup. *The Anatomy of Criticism: Four Essays.* Princeton: Princeton University Press, 1957.

Garnier, Armand. *Agrippa d'Aubigné et le parti protestant.* 3 vols. Paris: Fischbacher, 1928.

————. "Les Rapports entre d'Aubigné et la seigneurie de Genève." *Revue du Seizième Siècle* 17 (1930): 112–22.

Gauna, Max. "Fruitful Fields and Blessed Spirits, or Why the Thelemites Were Well Born." In *Etudes Rabelaisiennes*, no. 9. Geneva: Droz, 1971.

————, ed. *Les Dialogues non moins profitables que facetieux* (1565). Textes Littéraires Français 291. Geneva: Droz, 1981.

Gilman, Donald. "The Reconstruction of a Genre: Carolus Sigonius and the Theorization of Renaissance Dialogue." In *Acta Torontonensis: Proceedings of the Sixth Triennial Conference on Neo-Latin Studies*, edited by A. L. Dalzell, Charles Fantazzi, and R. Schoeck, 345–55. Binghamton, NY: Medieval and Renaissance Texts and Studies, 1991.

Gilmore, Myron. *The World of Humanism, 1453–1517.* New York: Harper Torchbook, 1962.

Gilson, Etienne. *La Philosophie de Saint Bonaventure.* Paris: Vrin, 1924.

Gohin, Ferdinand. *De Lud. Charondae, 1534–1613: Vita et Versibus.* Thesis University of Paris, 1902.

Goldschmidt, Victor. *Les Dialogues de Platon: Structure et méthode dialectique.* Paris: Presses Universitaires de France, 1947.

Gray, Hanna H. "Renaissance Humanism: The Pursuit of Eloquence." *Journal of the History of Ideas* 24, no. 4 (1963): 497–514.

Grimal, Pierre. "Caractères généraux du dialogue romain: De Lucilius à Cicéron." *L'Information littéraire* 7 (1955): 192–98.

Grube, G. M. A. *The Greeks and Roman Critics.* Toronto: University of Toronto Press, 1965.

Guillén, Claudio. *Literature as System: Essays toward the Theory of Literary History.* Princeton: Princeton University Press, 1971.

Guillerm, Luce, J. P. Guillerm, Laurence Hordoir, and Marie-Françoise Piéjus, eds. *Le Miroir des femmes, vol 1, Moralistes et polémistes au XVIe siècle.* Lille, France: Presses Universitaires, 1983.

Hall, Kathleen M. *Pontus de Tyard and his "Discours philosophiques."* Oxford Modern Languages and Literature Monographs. London: Oxford University Press, 1963.

Hall, Vernon. *Renaissance Literary Criticism: A Study of Its Social Content.* New York: Columbia University Press, 1945.

Hathaway, Baxter. *The Age of Criticism: The Late Renaissance in Italy.* Ithaca: Cornell University Press, 1962.

Hebraeus, Leo (Leone Ebreo). *"Dialogue d'amour" as Translated by Pontus de Tyard.* University of North Carolina Studies in Comparative Literature. Edited by T. Anthony Perry. Chapel Hill: University of North Carolina Press, 1974.

Hegel, Georg Wilhelm F. *Lectures on the History of Philosophy.* Translated by E. S. Haldane and Frances H. Simson. London: Kegan-Paul, 1894.

Heller, Henri. "Marguerite de Navarre and the Reformers of Meaux." *Bibliothèque d'Humanisme et Renaissance* 33 (1971): 271–310.

Heninger, S. K., Jr. *Sidney and Spenser: The Poet as Maker.* University Park: Pennsylvania State University Press, 1989.

Herrick, Marvin T. *The Fusion of Horatian and Aristotelian Literary Criticism, 1531–1555.* Urbana: University of Illinois Press, 1946.

Hirsch, Eric Donald. *Validity in Interpretation.* New Haven: Yale University Press, 1967.

Hirzel, Rudolf. *Der Dialog, ein literarhistorischer Versuch.* 2 vols. 1895. Reprint. Hildesheim, Germany: Georg Olms, 1963.

Hispanus, Petrus (Peter of Spain). *The Summae Logicales of Peter of Spain.* Translated and edited by Joseph P. M. Mullally. Notre Dame, IN.: University of Notre Dame Press, 1945.

Hodgart, Matthew. *Satire.* New York: McGraw Hill, World University Library, 1969.

Horace. *Satires, Epistles, Ars poetica.* Translated and edited by H. Rushton Fairclough. 1926. Reprint. Cambridge: Harvard University Press, Loeb Classical Library, 1966.

Howell, Wilbur S. *Logic and Rhetoric in England, 1500–1700.* Princeton: Princeton University Press, 1956.

———. *Poetics, Rhetoric, and Logic: Studies in the Basic Disciplines of Criticism.* Ithaca: Cornell University Press, 1975.

Jardine, Lisa. *Francis Bacon: Discovery and the Art of Discourse.* New York: Cambridge University Press, 1974.

Jeanroy, Alfred. *Les Origines de la poésie lyrique en France au moyen âge; études de littérature française et comparée.* Paris: Champion, 1904.

———. *La Poésie lyrique des troubadours.* Toulouse, France: E. Privat, 1934.

Jones, Ann Rosalind. "Surprising Fame: Renaissance Gender Ideologies and Women's Lyric." In *The Poetics of Gender*, edited by Nancy Miller, 74–95. New York: Columbia University Press, 1986.

———. "Nets and Bridles: Early Modern Conduct Books and Sixteenth-Century Women's Lyric." In *The Ideology of Conduct*, edited by Nancy Armstrong and Len Tennenhouse, 39–73. New York: Methuen, 1987.

———. *The Currency of Eros: Women's Love Lyric in Europe, 1540–1620*. Bloomington: Indiana University Press, 1990.

Jouanna, Arlette. "Une Analyse de la maladie sociale du paraître: *Les Avantures du baron de Faeneste d'Agrippa d'Aubigné*." *Réforme, Humanisme et Renaissance* 5 (1979): 34–39.

Jourda, Pierre. *Marguerite d'Angoulême, Duchesse d'Alençon, Reine de Navarre (1492–1549): Etude biographique et littéraire*. 2 vols. Paris: Champion, 1930.

Kaiser, Walter J. *Praisers of Folly: Erasmus, Rabelais, Shakespeare*. Cambridge: Harvard University Press, 1963.

Keating, [Louis] Clark. *Studies on the Literary Salon in France, 1550–1615*. Cambridge: Harvard University Press, 1941.

Keener, Frederick M. *English Dialogues of the Dead. A Critical History, an Anthology, and a Checklist*. New York: Columbia University Press, 1973.

Kelley, Donald R. "Louis Le Caron Philosophe." In *Philosophy and Humanism: Essays in Honor of Paul Oskar Kristeller*, edited by Edward P. Mahoney, 30–49. New York: Columbia University Press, 1976.

Kennedy, William J. *Rhetorical Norms in Renaissance Literature*. New Haven: Yale University Press, 1978.

Kernan, Alvin B. *The Plot of Satire*. New Haven: Yale University Press, 1965.

Kohl, Benjamin G., and Ronald Witt, eds., with Elizabeth B. Welles. *The Earthly Republic: Italian Humanists on Government and Society*. Philadelphia: University of Pennsylvania Press, 1978.

Krailsheimer, A. J. *Three Sixteenth-Century Conteurs*. New York: Oxford University Press, 1966.

Kückelhahn, Louis, *Johannes Sturm, Strassburg's erster Schulrector*. Leipzig: J. F. Hartknock, 1912.

Kushner, Eva. "Réflexions sur le dialogue en France au seizième siècle." *Revue des Sciences Humaines* 148 (1972): 485–501.

———. "The Dialogue of the French Renaissance: Work of Art or Instrument of Inquiry?" *Zagadnienia Rodzajow Literackich* 20 (1977): 23–35.

———. "Le Dialogue en France au XVIe siècle: Quelques critères génologiques." *Canadian Review of Comparative Literature* (1978): 142–53.

———. "Le Dialogue de 1580 à 1630: Articulations et fonctions." In *L'Automne de la Renaissance 1580–1630*, XXIIe Colloque International d'Etudes Humanistes, edited by Jean Lafond and André Stegmann, 149–61. Paris: Vrin, 1981.

———. "Le Rôle structurel du *locus amoenus* dans les dialogues de la Renaissance." *Cahiers de l'Association Internationale des Etudes Françaises* 34 (1982): 39–57.

———. "Le Dialogue en France de 1550 à 1560." In *Le Dialogue au temps de la Renaissance*. Publications du Centre de Recherches sur la Renaissance. Edited by M.-T. Jones-Davies, 151–69. Paris: Touzot, 1984.

———. "Structure et dialogue dans le *Cymbalum mundi* de Bonaventure des Périers." In *Crossroads and Perspectives: French Literature of the Renaissance, Stud-*

ies in Honor of Victor E. Graham. Travaux d'Humanisme et Renaissance, no. 211. Edited by Catherine M. Grisé and C. D. E. Tolton, 181–89. Geneva: Droz, 1986.

Labé, Louise. *Oeuvres complètes*. Edited by François Rigolot. Paris: Flammarion, 1986.

Laborderie, Jean. *Le Dialogue platonicien de la maturité*. Paris: Les Belles Lettres, 1978.

Lacoue-Labarte, Ph., and J.-L. Nancy. "Le Dialogue des genres." *Poétique* 21 (1975): 148–95.

Lajarte, Philippe de. "L'*Heptaméron* et la naissance du récit moderne: Essai de lecture épistemologique d'un discours narratif." *Littérature* 17 (1975): 31–42.

———. "Le prologue de l'*Heptaméron* et le processus de production de l'oeuvre." In *La Nouvelle française à la Renaissance*, edited by Lionello Sozzi, 397–423. Paris: Droz, 1981.

Langfors, Arthur, ed. *Recueil général des jeux-partis français*. Paris: Champion, 1926.

Larsen, Anne. "Catherine des Roches' 'Epistre a sa mère' (1579)." *Allegorica* 7 (1982): 58–64.

———. "The French Humanist Scholars: Les Dames des Roches." In *Women Writers of the Renaissance and Reformation*, edited by Katharina Wilson, 232–59. Athens: University of Georgia Press, 1987.

———. "Legitimizing the Daughter's Writing: Catherine des Roches' Proverbial Good Wife." *Sixteenth Century Journal* 21, no. 4 (1990): 559–74.

Le Caron, Louis. *La Claire ou de la prudence de droit, dialogue premier*. Paris: Guillaume Cavellat, 1554.

———. *La Philosophie*. Paris: Guillaume Le Noir, 1555.

———. *Dialogues*. Paris, 1556.

———. *Dialogues*. Textes littéraires français, no. 337. Edited by Joan A. Buhlmann and Donald Gilman. Geneva: Droz, 1986.

Leff, Gordon. *Paris and Oxford Universities in the Thirteenth and Fourteenth Centuries: An Institutional and Intellectual History*. New York: Wiley, 1968.

Le Guern, Michel. "Sur le genre du dialogue." In *L'Automne de la Renaissance, 1580–1630*. XXIIe Colloque International d'Etudes Humanistes, edited by Jean Lafond and André Stegmann, 141–48. Paris: Vrin, 1981.

Lenient, Charles Félix. *La Satire en France ou la littérature militante au XVIe siècle*. 2 vols. Paris: Hachette, 1866.

Lerer, Seth. *Boethius and Dialogue: Literary Method in "The Consolation of Philosophy."* Princeton: Princeton University Press, 1985.

Lilla, Salvatore. *The Philosophy of Clement of Alexandria*. Oxford: Oxford University Press, 1971.

Linder, Robert Dean. *The Political Ideas of Pierre Viret*. Travaux d'Humanisme et Renaissance, no. 64. Geneva: Droz, 1964.

Lloyd, William Daly, ed. *Altercatio Hadriani Augusti et Epicteti philosophi*. Illinois Studies in Language and Literature, no. 24. Urbana: University of Illinois Press, 1939.

Longinus. *On the Sublime*. Translated and edited by W. Hamilton Fyfe. 1927.

Reprint. Cambridge: Harvard University Press, Loeb Classical Library, 1965.

Lord, Carnes, and Tain A. Trafton, trans. *Tasso's Dialogues: A Selection, with the Discourse on the Art of the Dialogue*. Berkeley and Los Angeles: University of California Press, 1982.

Losse, Deborah N. "The Representation of Discourse in the Renaissance *Nouvelle*: Bonaventure Des Périers and Marguerite de Navarre." *Poetics Today* 3 (1985): 585–95.

Lucian. "How to Write History." In vol. 8 of *The Works of Lucian*. Translated and edited by K. Kilburn. 8 vols. 1921. Reprint. Cambridge: Harvard University Press, Loeb Classical Library, 1959.

Lucien de Samosate. *Les Oeuvres*. Paris: Abel L'Angelier, 1582.

Lyons, John D. *Exemplum—The Rhetoric of Example in Early Modern France and Italy*. Princeton: Princeton University Press, 1989.

MacDonald, Ian. "Three Pamphlets by d'Aubigné. Manuscripts and Dates of Composition." *French Studies* 14 (1960): 38–51.

McClelland, John. "Dialogue et rhétorique à la Renaissance." In *Le Dialogue*, edited by Pierre R. Léon and Paul Perron, 157–64. Ottawa, Canada: Didier, 1985.

McFarlane, I. D., ed. Introduction to *The Entry of Henri II into Paris 16 June 1549*. Binghamton, NY: CMERS, 1982.

McGuaig, William. *Carlo Sigonio: The Changing World of the Late Italian Renaissance*. Princeton: Princeton University Press, 1989.

McKeon, Richard. "Literary Criticism and the Concept of Imitation in Antiquity." In *Critics and Criticism, Ancient and Modern*, edited by R. S. Crane, 147–75. Chicago: University of Chicago Press, 1952.

McNally, J. R. "*Dux Illa Directrixque Artium*: Rudolph Agricola's Dialectical System." *Quarterly Journal of Speech* 52, no. 4 (1966): 337–47.

———. "Rudolph Agricola's *De inventione dialectica libri tres*: A Translation of Selected Chapters." *Speech Monographs* 34, no. 4 (1967): 393–422.

———. "*Rector et Dux Populi*: Italian Humanists and the Relationship between Rhetoric and Logic." *Modern Philology* 67, no. 2 (1969): 168–76.

Man, Paul de. "Dialogue and Dialogism." *Poetics Today* 4, no. 1 (1983): 99–107.

Marcus, Jane. "Still Practice, A/Wrested Alphabet: Toward a Feminist Aesthetic." *Tulsa Studies in Women's Literature* 3, nos. 1–2 (1984): 79–97.

Marichal, Robert, ed. *La Navire*, by Marguerite de Navarre. Paris: Champion, 1956.

Marsh, David. *The Quattrocento Dialogue: Classical Tradition and Humanist Innovation*. Harvard Studies in Comparative Literature. Cambridge: Harvard University Press, 1980.

Martineau, Christine, and Christian Grouselle. "La source première et directe du *Dialogue en forme de vision nocturne*: la lettre de Guillaume Briçonnet à Marguerite de Navarre, du 15 septembre 1524. Publication et commentaire." *Bibliothèque d'Humanisme et Renaissance* 32 (1970): 559–77.

Masters, G. Mallary. *Rabelaisian Dialectic and the Platonic-Hermetic Tradition*. Albany: State University of New York Press, 1969.

Mayer, Claude A. *Lucien de Samosate et la Renaissance française*. Geneva: Slatkine, 1984.

Melanchthon, Philip. *De elementis rhetoricis*. In *Corpus Reformatorum*, edited by Carolus Gottlieb Bretschneider. Leipzig: M. Heinsius nachfolger, 1834.

———. "Respons. ad Picum Mirand." In *Corpus Reformatorum*, edited by Carolus Gottlieb Bretschneider. Leipzig: M. Heinsius nachfolger, 1834–1860. Vol. 9:687–703. Translated as "Melanchthon's Reply to G. Pico della Mirandola" by Quirinus Breen. *Journal of the History of Ideas* 13 (1952): 413–26.

Menner, Robert J., ed. *The Poetical Dialogues of Solomon and Saturn*. New York: Modern Language Association, 1941.

Merrill, Elizabeth. *The Dialogue in English Literature*. Yale Studies in English, no. 42. New York: Holt, 1911.

Michel, Alain. *Rhétorique et philosophie chez Cicéron: Essai sur les fondements philosophiques de l'art de persuader*. Paris: Presses Universitaires de France, 1960.

Milin, Gaël. "Coeur/contenance/regard: du geste à l'analyse psychologique dans l'*Heptaméron* de Marguerite de Navarre." In *Mélanges de langue et littérature françaises du Moyen Age et de la Renaissance offerts à Monsieur Charles Foulon*, vol. 1: 259–65. Rennes, France: Institut de français, Université de Haute Bretagne, 1980.

Minturno, Antonio Sebastiano. *De poeta*. 1559. Reprint. Munich: Wilhelm Fink, 1970.

Mitterand, Henri. "Dialogue et littérarité romanesque." In *Le Dialogue*. Pierre R. Léon and Paul Perron, eds., 141–54. Ottawa, Canada: Didier, 1985.

Montaigne, Michel de. *Oeuvres complètes*. 3 vols. Edited by Albert Thibaudet and Maurice Rat. Paris: Gallimard, 1962.

Morrisson, Ian. "'Paraître' and 'Etre': Thoughts on d'Aubigné's *Avantures du baron de Faeneste*." *Modern Language Review* 68 (1973): 762–70.

Navarre, Marguerite de. *La Navire*. Edited by Robert Marichal. Paris: Champion, 1956.

———. *L'Heptaméron*. Edited by Michel François. Paris: Garnier, 1967.

———. *The Heptameron*. Translated with an introduction by P. A. Chilton. Aylesbury, England: Hazell Watson and Viney, 1984.

———. *Théâtre profane*. Edited by V.-L. Saulnier. Paris: Minard; Geneva: Droz, 1978.

Neidhart, D. *Das "cymbalum mundi" des Bonaventure Des Périers: Forschungslage und Deutung*. Geneva: Droz; Paris: Minard, 1959.

Nurse, Peter H., ed. *Bonaventure des Périers, Cymbalum mundi*. Texte établi et présenté par Peter H. Nurse, 1958. Reprint, with a new preface. Manchester, England: Manchester University Press, 1967.

Ong, Walter J. *Ramus, Method, and the Decay of Dialogue: From the Art of Discourse to the Art of Reason*. Cambridge: Harvard University Press, 1958.

Pallavicino, Pietro Sforza. *Considerazioni sopra l'arte dello stile e del dialogo*. Rome: per gli eredi del Corbelletti, 1646.

Peach, Trevor. *Nature et raison: Étude critique des "Dialogues" de Jacques Tahureau*. Geneva: Slatkine, 1986.

———, ed. Jacques Tahureau's *Poésies complètes*. Geneva: Droz, 1984.

Pérouse, Gabriel A. *Nouvelles françaises du XVIe siècle: Images de la vie du temps*. Travaux d'Humanisme et Renaissance 154. Geneva: Droz, 1977.

Pindar. *Odes*. Translated and edited by Sir John Sandys. Cambridge: Harvard University Press, Loeb Classical Library, 1961.

Pinvert, Lucien. "Louis Le Caron, dit Charondas (1536–1613)." *Revue de la Renaissance* 1 (1901): 1–9, 69–76, 181–88.

Pisan, Christine de. *Le Livre des trois vertus*. Translated by Sarah Lawson as *The Treasure of the City of Ladies, or The Book of the Three Virtues*. London: Penguin, 1985.

Plato. *The Dialogues*. 5 vols. 3d ed. Translated by B. Jowett. London: Oxford University Press, 1924.

———. *The Collected Dialogues of Plato*. Bollingen Series, no. 71. Translated by Lane Cooper et al. Edited by Edith Hamilton and Huntington Cairns. Princeton: Princeton University Press, 1961.

Plattard, Jean. *Agrippa d'Aubigné: Une Figure de premier plan dans nos lettres de la Renaissance*. Paris: Vrin, 1975.

Plutarch. *Platonic Questions*. Translated and edited by Howard Cherniss. In *Moralia*, vol. 13, part 1. Cambridge: Harvard University Press, Loeb Classical Library, 1976.

———. *Table-Talk*. Translated and edited by Paul A. Clement. In *Moralia*, vol. 8. Cambridge: Harvard University Press, Loeb Classical Library, 1969.

Poggioli, Renato. "Poetics and Metrics." In *Comparative Literature*: Proceedings of the I.C.L.A. Congress in Chapel Hill, NC. 2 vols. Edited by W. F. Friederich. Chapel Hill, NC: 1959. 1:192–204.

Proclus. *Commentaire sur la République*. 3 vols. Translated and edited by A. J. Festugière. Paris: Vrin, 1970.

Quintilian. *Institutio oratoria*. 4 vols. Translated and edited by H. E. Butler. 1922. Reprint. Cambridge: Harvard University Press, Loeb Classical Library, 1963.

Rabelais, François. *Oeuvres complètes*. 2 vols. Edited by P. Jourda. Paris: Garnier, 1962.

Raffaele, Girardi. "'Elegans Imitatio et erudita': Sigonio e la teoria del dialogo." *Giornale storico della letteratura italiana* 103 (1986): 321–54.

Rainolde, Richard. *The Foundacion of Rhetorike*. 1563. Reprint, with introduction by Francis R. Johnson. New York: Scholars' Facsimiles and Reprints, 1945.

Read, Herbert E. *Reason and Romanticism. Essays in Literary Criticism*. London: Faber and Gwyer, 1926.

Réaume, Eugène, and F. de Caussade, eds. *Théodore Agrippa d'Aubigné. Oeuvres complètes de Théodore Agrippa d'Aubigné*. 6 vols. Paris: A. Lemerre, 1873–92.

Rebhorn, Wayne A. "The Burdens and Joys of Freedom: An Interpretation of the Five Books of Rabelais." In *Etudes Rabelaisiennes*, no. 9, 71–90. Geneva: Droz, 1971.

Rice, Eugene F. *The Renaissance Idea of Wisdom*. Cambridge: Harvard University Press, 1958.

Robinson, C. "The Reputation of Lucian in Sixteenth-Century France." *French Studies* 29 (1975): 385–97.

Robinson, Forrest G. *The Shape of Things Known: Sidney's "Apology" in Its Philosophical Tradition.* Cambridge: Harvard University Press, 1972.

Robinson, Richard. *Plato's Earlier Dialectic.* Ithaca: Cornell University Press, 1941.

Rocheblave, Samuel. *Agrippa d'Aubigné.* Paris: Hachette, 1910.

Ruch, Michel. *Le Préambule dans les oeuvres philosophiques de Cicéron: Essai sur la genèse et l'art du dialogue.* Publications de la Faculté de l'Université de Strasbourg, Fascicule 136. Paris and Strasbourg: Les Belles Lettres, 1958.

Rudenstine, Neil L. *Sidney's Poetic Development.* Cambridge: Harvard University Press, 1967.

Sadoleto, Jacopo. *A Translation of "De pueris recte instituendis."* Translated by Ernest Trafford Campagnac and Kenneth Forbes. Oxford: Oxford University Press, 1916.

———. *L'Attaque et défense de la philosophie.* Translated by P. Charpenne. Paris, 1864.

Saim, Mirela. "La Parole médiévale en dialogue: Les jeux-partis." *Littérature* 6 (1991): 127–38.

Sankovitch, Tilde. "The Dames des Roches: The Female Muse." Chap. 2, *French Women Writers and the Book.* Syracuse, NY: Syracuse University Press, 1976.

Saulnier, V.-L. "Le sens du *Cymbalum mundi* de Bonaventure Des Périers." *Bibliothèque d'Humanisme et Renaissance* 13 (1951a): 43–69.

———. "La Pensée de Bonaventure Des Périers dans le *Cymbalum mundi.*" *Bibliothèque d'Humanisme et Renaissance* 13 (1951b): 137–71.

———. ed. Marguerite de Navarre. *Théâtre profane.* Geneva: Droz, 1978.

Saussure, Ferdinand de. *Cours de linguistique générale.* Lausanne: Payot, 1916.

Scaliger, Julius Caesar. *Poetices libri septem.* Lyon: Antonius Vincentius, 1561. Reprint, with introduction by August Buck. Stuttgart: Friedrich Fromman Verlag, 1964.

Schmidt, Charles. *La Vie et les travaux de Jean Sturm.* Strasbourg, France: C. F. Schmidt, 1855.

Schmitt, Charles B., Quentin Skinner, and Eckhard Kessler with Jill Kraye, eds. *The Cambridge History of Renaissance Philosophy.* Cambridge: Cambridge University Press, 1988.

Screech, M. A. "Some Stoic Elements in Rabelais's Religious Thought: The Will-Destiny-Active Virtue." In *Etudes Rabelaisiennes,* no. 1, 73–97. Geneva: Droz, 1956.

———. *L'Evangélisme de Rabelais: Aspects de la satire religieuse au XVIe siècle.* In *Etudes Rabelaisiennes,* no. 2. Geneva: Droz, 1959.

———. "The Meaning of the Title *Cymbalum mundi.*" *Bibliothèque d'Humanisme et Renaissance* 31 (1969): 343–45.

Sealy, Robert J. *The Palace Academy of Henri III.* Travaux d'Humanisme et Renaissance 184. Geneva: Droz, 1981.

Seigel, Jerrold E. *Rhetoric and Philosophy in Renaissance Humanism: The Union of*

Eloquence and Wisdom, Petrarch to Valla. Princeton: Princeton University Press, 1968.

Seneca. *Epistles*. 3 vols. Translated and edited by Richard M. Gummerre. 1917. Reprint. Cambridge: Harvard University Press, Loeb Classical Library, 1967.

Sherman, Carol. *Diderot and the Art of Dialogue*. Geneva: Droz, 1976.

Sidney, Sir Philip. *An Apology for Poetry*. Edited by Geoffrey Shepherd. Manchester, England: Manchester University Press, 1973.

Sigonius, Carolus. *De dialogo liber*. Edited by Johannes Jessenius. Leipzig, Germany: Henry Osthausus, 1596.

Simplicius. *In Praedicamenta Aristotelis commentaria*. Venice: Hieronymus Scotus, 1588.

Smith, Pauline M. *The Anti-Courtier Trend in Sixteenth-Century French Literature*. Geneva: Droz, 1966.

Snyder, Jon. *Writing the Scene of Speaking: Theories of Dialogue in the Late Italian Renaissance*. Stanford: Stanford University Press, 1989.

Sohm, W. *Die Schule Johann und die Kirche Strasburgs*. Munich: R. Oldenbourg, 1912.

Sommers, Paula. "Jacques Tahureau's Art of Satire." *French Review* 47 (1974): 744–56.

———. "The *Miroir* and Its Reflections: Marguerite de Navarre's Biblical Feminism." *Tulsa Studies in Women's Literature* 5 (1986): 29–39.

———. *Celestial Ladders: Readings in Marguerite de Navarre's Poetry of Spiritual Ascent*. Geneva: Droz, 1989.

Sozzi, Lionello, ed. *La Nouvelle française à la Renaissance*. Geneva: Slatkine, 1981.

Spingarn, Joel. *History of Literary Criticism in the Renaissance*. 1899. Reprint. New York: Harcourt, Brace, and World, 1963.

Stanton, Domna. *The Defiant Muse: French Feminist Poems from the Middle Ages to the Present: A Bi-lingual Anthology*. New York: Feminist Press, 1986.

Stegmann, André. "Un Thème majeur du second humanisme français (1540–1570): L'Orateur et le citoyen. De la réalité vécue." In *French Renaissance Studies (1540–70): Humanism and the Encyclopedia*, edited by Peter Sharratt. Edinburgh, Scotland: Edinburgh University Press, 1976.

Stone, Donald. "From Tales to Truths: Essays on French Fiction in the Sixteenth Century." *Analecta Romanica* 34 (1973): 21–29.

Sturm, Johann. *Partitionum dialecticarum libri IIII*. Lyon, France: Jean Tornaesius, 1561.

Tahureau, Jacques. *Oraison de Jacques Tahureau au Roy: De la grandeur de son regne et de l'excellence de la langue françoyse*. Paris: La veufve Maurice de la Porte, 1555.

———. *Les Dialogues non moins profitables que facétieux* (1565). Textes Littéraires Francais 291. Edited by Max Gauna. Geneva: Droz, 1981.

———. *Poésies complètes*. Edited by Trevor Peach. Geneva: Droz, 1984.

Tasso, Torquato. "Discorsi dell'arte poetica e in particolare sopra il poema eroico." In vol. 22, *Prose*, edited by Ettore Mazzali, 347–410. La Letteratura italiana. Storia e testi. Milan and Naples, Italy: Riccardo Ricciardi, 1959.

————. "Discorsi del poema eroico." In vol. 22, *Prose*, edited by Ettore Mazzali, 487–729. La Letteratura italiana. Storia e testi. Milan and Naples, Italy: Riccardo Ricciardi, 1959.

————. "Discourses on the Heroic Poem." Translated by Allan H. Gilbert. In *Literary Criticism: Plato to Dryden*, edited by Allan H. Gilbert. Detroit: Wayne State University Press, 1962.

————. *Tasso's Dialogues: A Selection, with the Discourse on the Art of the Dialogue.* Translated by Carnes Lord and Tain A. Trafton. Berkeley and Los Angeles: University of California Press, 1982.

Taylor, Thomas, comp. *Iamblichus. "De vita Pythagorica."* Amsterdam, 1707.

Telle, Emile V. "Thélème et le Paulinisme matrimonial érasmien: Le Sens de l'énigme en prophétie." In *François Rabelais: Ouvrage publié pour le quatrième centenaire de sa mort: 1553–1953*, 104–19. Geneva: Droz, 1953.

Tetel, Marcel. *Marguerite de Navarre's "Heptameron": Themes, Language, and Structure.* Durham, NC: Duke University Press, 1973.

Todorov, Tzvetan. *Grammaire du Décaméron.* Paris: Mouton, 1969.

Trousdale, Marion. *Shakespeare and the Rhetoricians.* Chapel Hill: University of North Carolina Press, 1982.

Tyard, Pontus de. *L'Univers.* Edited by John C. Lapp. Ithaca: Cornell University Press, 1950a.

————. *Solitaire premier.* Edited by Silvio F. Baridon. Geneva: Droz, 1950b.

————. *Solitaire second.* Edited by Cathy Yandell. Geneva: Droz, 1980.

————. *Mantice.* Edited by Sylvaine Bokdam. Geneva: Droz, 1990.

Vaganay, Hugues. "Quatre noms propres dans la littérature: Délie, Ophélie, Philothée, Pasithée." *Revue de littérature comparée* 15 (1935): 278–88.

Valla, Lorenzo. *Dialecticae disputationes.* In *Opera omnia*, edited by Eugenio Garin, 1: 643–761. 2 vols. Turin, Italy: Bottega d'Erasmo, 1962.

Vasoli, C. "Dialettica e retorica in Rodolfo Agricola." *Academia Toscana di scienza e lettere* 20 (1957): 305–55.

Vickers, Brian. *Francis Bacon and Renaissance Prose.* Cambridge: Cambridge University Press, 1968.

Villey, Pierre. "A Propos du *Caducée* d'Agrippa d'Aubigné." In *Mélanges offerts par ses amis et ses élèves à Gustave Lanson*, 154–61. Paris: Hachette, 1922.

Virtanen, Reino. *Conversations on Dialogue.* Lincoln: University of Nebraska Press, 1977.

Vives, Juan Luis. *De officio mariti.* Translated as "On Duties of Husbands" by Thomas Paynell in *Vives and the Renascence Education of Women*, edited by Foster Watson, 204–10. New York: Longmans, Green and Co., 1972.

————. *Livre de l'institution de la femme chrestienne* and *L'Office du mary.* In *Le Miroir des Femmes.* Vol. 1, *Moralistes et polémistes au XVIᵉ siècle.* Lille, France: Presses Universitaires, 1983.

Wallerand, G. *Les Oeuvres de Siger de Courtrai.* Louvain, Belgium: Institut Supérieur de Philosophie de l'Université, 1913.

Watson, Foster, ed. *Vives and the Renascence Education of Women.* New York: Longmans, 1912.

Weber, Henri. "Structure et langage dans *les Avantures du Baron de Faeneste.* De Jean Lemaire de Belges à Jean Giraudoux." In *Mélanges d'histoire et de cri-*

tique littéraire offerts à Pierre Jourda, edited by E. Bouvier, 111–30. Paris: Nizet, 1970.

———, ed. Théodore Agrippa d'Aubigné. *Oeuvres*. Paris: Gallimard, 1969.

Weinberg, Bernard. "Scaliger versus Aristotle on Poetics." *Modern Philology* 39 (1942): 337–60.

———. "Translations and Commentaries on Longinus, *On the Sublime*, to 1600: Bibligraphy." *Modern Philology* 47 (1950): 145–51.

———. *A History of Literary Criticism in the Italian Renaissance*. 2 vols. Chicago: University of Chicago Press, 1961.

Weinberg, Florence M. *The Wine and the Will: Rabelais's Bacchic Christianity*. Detroit: Wayne State University Press, 1972.

Wells-Romer, Jane B. "Folly in the *Heptaméron* of Marguerite de Navarre." *Bibliothèque d'Humanisme et Renaissance* 46, no. 1 (1984): 71–82.

Wilson, K. J. "The Continuity of Post-Classical Dialogue." *Cithara* 21 (1981): 23–44.

———. *Incomplete Fictions. The Formation of the English Renaissance Dialogue*. Washington, DC: The Catholic University of America Press, 1985.

Winandy, André. "Piety and Humanistic Symbolism in the Works of Marguerite de Navarre." *Yale French Studies* 47 (1972): 145–69.

Wind, B. H. *Les Mots italiens introduits en français au seizième siècle*. Deventer, The Netherlands: Kluwer, 1928.

Winn, Colette H. "Le clin d'oeil de l'onomaturge: Les nouvelles VIII, XI et XXXVII de *L'Heptaméron*." *Romance Notes* 26, no. 2 (1986): 149–54.

———. *L'Esthétique du jeu dans l'Heptaméron de Marguerite de Navarre*. Paris: Vrin; Montreal: Institut d'Etudes Médiévales, Université de Montréal, 1993.

Woodbridge, Linda. *Women and the English Renaissance: Literature and the Nature of Womankind, 1540–1620*. Urbana: University of Illinois Press, 1984.

Woodward, William Harrison. *Studies in Education during the Age of the Renaissance, 1400–1600*. Cambridge: Cambridge University Press, 1906.

———, ed. *Vittorino da Feltre and Other Humanist Educators*. New York: Columbia University Teachers' College, 1963.

Xenophon. *Cyropaedia*. 2 vols. Translated and edited by Walter Miller. 1914. Reprint. Cambridge: Harvard University Press, Loeb Classical Library, 1960.

Yates, Frances. *The French Academies of the Sixteenth Century*. London: Warburg Institute, University of London, 1947.

Zumthor, Paul. "Dialogue et spectacle." In *Essai de poétique médiévale*. Paris: Seuil, 1972.

———. "Allégorie et allégorèse." In *Le Masque et la lumière*. Paris: Seuil, 1978.

INDEX NOMINUM

INDEX RERUM

The Dialogue in Early Modern France: Art and Argument was composed in 11/12.5 Gara-
mond #3 with Monotype Dante display by World Composition Services, Inc., Sterling,
Virginia; printed and bound by BookCrafters, Inc., Chelsea, Michigan; and designed by
Kachergis Book Design, Pittsboro, North Carolina.

DUE